The Complete Daily Curriculum for Early Childhood

Additional books written by Pam Schiller

Creating Readers: Over 1000 Games, Activities, Tongue Twisters, Fingerplays, Songs, and Stories to Get Children Excited About Reading

The Complete Resource Book: An Early Childhood Curriculum, with Kay Hastings

The Complete Book of Rhymes, Songs, Poems, Fingerplays & Chants, with Jackie Silberg

Start Smart

The Practical Guide to Quality Child Care, with Patricia Carter Dyke

The Values Book, with Tamera Bryant

Count on Math, with Lynne Peterson Brown

Where Is Thumbkin?, with Thomas Moore

Instant Curriculum, with Joan Rosanno

Additional books written by Pat Phipps

Multiple Intelligencies in the Early Childhood Classroom

A Handbook for Applying Brain Reasearch to the Early Childhood Classroom

The Developing Brain: A Guidebook for Communicating with Parents

The Complete Daily Curriculum

FOR EARLY CHILDHOOD

Over 1200 Easy Activities to Support Multiple Intelligences and Learning Styles

Pam Schiller and Pat Phipps

Illustrations: Richele Bartkowiak and Deborah Wright

gryphon house
Beltsville, MD

Dedication

To Howard Gardner who is bold enough and bright enough to think outside the box. Thank you for providing a framework that honors, respects, nurtures, and supports the unique qualities and contributions of every child and every adult—past, present, and future.

—Pam Schiller and Pat Phipps

Published by Gryphon House, Inc., 10726 Tucker Street, Beltsville, MD 20705 or
P.O. Box 207, Beltsville, MD 20704-0207.
(800) 638-0928, (301) 595-9500, (301) 595-0051 (Fax)

Visit us on the web at www.gryphonhouse.com

Library of Congress Cataloging-in-Publication Data

Schiller, Pamela Byrne.
The daily curriculum for early childhood : over 1,200 easy activities
to support multiple intelligences and learning styles / Pam Schiller,
Pat Phipps ; illustrations, Richele Bartkowiak and Deborah Wright.
p. cm.
Includes bibliographical references and index.
ISBN 0-87659-228-0
1. Early childhood education--Activity programs. 2. Multiple
intelligences. I. Phipps, Pat. II. Title.
LB1139.35.A37 S35 2002
372.21--dc21
2002004660

Bulk purchase

Gryphon House books are available for special premiums and sales promotions as well as for fund-raising use. Special editions or book excerpts also can be created to specification. For details, contact the Director of Sales at the address above.

Disclaimer

Gryphon House Inc. and the authors cannot be held responsible for damage, mishap, or injury incurred during the use of or because of activities in this book. Appropriate and reasonable caution and adult supervision of children involved in activities and corresponding to the age and capability of each child involved, is recommended at all times. Do not leave children unattended at any time. Observe safety and caution at all times.

Table of Contents

INDEXES 549

Introduction

As Ms. Ramirez, a new parent in the community interested in finding a school to enroll her child in, passed Ms. Carter's prekindergarten classroom, she paused to look in. This classroom was very different from what she had expected. Instead of seeing children sitting in neat rows listening attentively to their teacher, she saw children happily engaged in a variety of activities, working in pairs or small groups all over the room. How could all this playing be productive, she thought? She could not resist going inside to ask Ms. Carter to explain what was happening.

Ms. Carter welcomed the opportunity not only to explain what was happening, but also to take Ms. Ramirez on a tour of the classroom so she could see firsthand what the children were learning. Ms. Carter told Ms. Ramirez that the children were engaged in a thematic unit of study on zoo animals. She went on to explain that she used a multiple intelligences (MI) approach to her curriculum, which is a way of providing activities and experiences that address all of the ways that children are "smart." These different intelligences include spatial, interpersonal, naturalist, logical-mathematical, bodily-kinesthetic, musical, linguistic, and intrapersonal.

"What do you mean, Ms. Carter?" asked Ms. Ramirez.

"Children learn in a number of different ways, and I want to make sure I offer them the opportunity to learn in the ways in which each of them learns best," Ms. Carter explained. As they walked around the classroom, Ms. Ramirez saw children—

- in the Art Center cooperatively using yellow construction paper, oval sponges, and brown tempera paint to create giraffe skin patterns by sponging the brown paint onto the yellow paper in a design of their choice (spatial, interpersonal);
- in the Science/Discovery Center sorting plastic zoo and farm animals according to where the animals live (naturalist, logical-mathematical);
- in the Math Center playing a game called Feed the Seal. Each seal had a different number on its back and the children were counting out the number of fish crackers to match the number on each seal and placing the crackers in each seal's mouth (logical-mathematical);

- in the Dramatic Play Center dancing, singing, clapping, and following the leader's movements in a game of Monkey See, Monkey Do (bodily-kinesthetic, musical, interpersonal);
- in the Language Center making signs to label zoo cages (e.g., Aviary, Reptiles, Monkeys, Aquarium, Lions, etc.) in the Block Center (linguistic);
- in the Language Center dictating stories to a parent volunteer, then illustrating them for the class book on favorite animals (linguistic, spatial, intrapersonal).

Developing a comprehensive and inclusive early childhood curriculum is a challenging task. The children who will engage in the curriculum activities represent a myriad of individual differences. They often come from a range of ages and ability levels. They possess different learning style preferences and intelligences. Add to this the need to make sure that curriculum covers all the developmental domains (physical, social-emotional, and cognitive), includes all subject areas (science, social studies, language, math, and so on) and that it sparks the interests of the children, and you can see the early childhood teacher has his or her hands full.

In many ways a teacher's preparation of curriculum is comparable to a symphony conductor's preparation of a musical score. Both teacher and conductor have many parts to coordinate. For the conductor it is the many different sounds of the musical instruments that he or she must bring into harmony. For the teacher it is the many individual differences of children that he or she must bring into accord. As the teacher and conductor facilitate the performances of their respective students and musicians they must continue to stay alert to many elements. When the performance appears virtually effortless to outsiders, you know you are witnessing the results of comprehensive preparation.

The Complete Daily Curriculum for Early Childhood is designed to help the teacher weave the many elements of a comprehensive curriculum together. Lessons and activities—

- include suggestions that encompass all **learning style preferences,**
- offer learning center suggestions to enhance each of the eight **multiple intelligences** (high ability levels),
- encompass all aspects of the **developmental domains**,

- cover all **subject areas,** and
- are thematically based to appeal to the **interests of the children.**

Let's look briefly at these curriculum ingredients and the role each plays in a quality early childhood program.

Learning Styles

When you try to learn something new, you may prefer to learn by listening to someone talk to you about the information. Others prefer to read about a concept to learn it; and still others need to see a demonstration of the concept. Learning Style Theory proposes that different people learn in different ways and that it is good to know your own preferred learning style.

Most of us have a particular preference as to how we channel information to our brain. Some of us are auditory. This means that it is easiest for us to pay attention to information that is presented to us orally. Others are visual, which means that we learn best when we are allowed to actually look at what is being presented to us. Still others are kinesthetic. This means that we pay attention best when we are allowed to explore "hands on" the information we are trying to learn. In a few cases, individuals are equally balanced, which means they use each learning style to the same degree when attempting to learn.

Think about the last time you wrote a check at the grocery store. When the checker gave you the total did you just write the check? Did you look at the register for verification? Did you take the receipt in hand before writing the check? Your response to these questions might give you some insight as to your own learning preference.

Let's look at an example from the early childhood classroom. When a teacher reads a story, she speaks, which benefits the auditory learner. She shows the illustrations as she reads, which assists the visual learner. The kinesthetic learner is involved if allowed to actually hold the book (or a copy of the book) or help turn the pages as it is read. If teachers use all three approaches to learning when they are providing information to children, it is more likely that they will use the channel that is their preference and attend to what is being presented.

The lessons in *The Complete Daily Curriculum for Early Childhood* include activities that appeal to each of the learning styles.

Multiple Intelligences

The concept of multiple intelligences is the newest consideration teachers might take into account when planning for individual differences. The Theory of Multiple Intelligences comes from the work of Howard Gardner and was first published in 1983 in his book, *Frames of Mind*.

Until Gardner proposed the existence of seven, and now eight, ways of demonstrating one's high ability levels, popular belief held that intelligence was measured by the score obtained when taking an intelligence test, primarily the Stanford Binet. The problem with intelligence tests was that they measured only an individual's linguistic and mathematical skills. Gardner argued that there were other ways an individual could be smart. For example, musicians demonstrate a high ability to perceive, discriminate, transform, and express musical forms. Actors, dancers, and athletes demonstrate an expertise in using their whole body to express ideas and feelings. Craftspersons and sculptors show facility in using their hands to produce or transform things.

Gardner not only expanded the identification of the number of ways an individual can be intelligent, but also the definition of intelligence. He suggests that intelligence has more to do with the capacity for solving problems and fashioning products in a context-rich and naturalistic setting than it does with performing isolated tasks on a test.

Gardner believes that intelligence does not just exhibit itself in the score on a test. As a matter of fact, he used a stringent system of eight criteria through which all potential skills, talents, and mental capacities have to pass before they are determined to be true human intelligences. Thus far, only eight ways of being smart have passed the test to be recognized as intelligences.

Gardner also believes that everyone possesses all eight intelligences in varying magnitudes. Some intelligences are stronger than others, and the profile of intelligences varies from person to person. Each of the intelligences can improve with practice and will continue to be enhanced over a lifetime.

The eight intelligences and their defining characteristics are described as follows:

Intelligence	Description
Linguistic (Word Smart)	The capacity to use words effectively, whether orally (e.g., as a storyteller, orator, or politician) or in writing (e.g., as a poet, playwright, editor, or journalist). Most teaching today is geared to the expectation that children absorb information by listening, reading, speaking, and writing.
Logical-Mathematical (Number Smart)	The capacity to use numbers effectively (e.g., as a mathematician, tax accountant, or statistician) and to reason well (e.g., as a scientist, computer programmer, or logician). This intelligence also follows traditional teaching practices, using number facts and scientific principles, as well as observation and experimentation. Children who are logic smart respond well to "what if" questions.
Spatial (Picture Smart)	The ability to perceive the visual-spatial world accurately (e.g., as a hunter, scout, or guide) and to perform transformations upon those perceptions (e.g., as an interior decorator, architect, artist, or inventor). This intelligence involves sensitivity to color, line, shape, form, space, and the relationships that exist between these elements. It includes the capacity to visualize and graphically represent visual or spatial ideas.
Bodily-Kinesthetic (Body Smart)	The ability to use one's whole body to skillfully express ideas and feelings (e.g., as an actor, an athlete, or a dancer) and facility in using one's hands to produce or transform things (e.g., as a craftsperson, sculptor, mechanic, or surgeon). This intelligence is related to physical movement and the knowledge/wisdom of the body, including the brain's motor cortex, which controls bodily motion.
Musical (Music Smart)	The capacity to perceive (e.g., as a music aficionado), discriminate (e.g., as a music critic), transform (e.g., as a composer), and express (e.g., as a performer) musical forms. The musical learner also has the ability to pick up sounds and remember melodies. This intelligence is based upon the recognition of tonal patterns, including various environmental sounds, and also sensitivity to rhythm and beats.

Intelligence	Description
Naturalist (Nature Smart)	The ability to discriminate among living things (e.g., as a botanist, biologist, veterinarian, or forest ranger) as well as sensitivity to other features of the natural world (e.g., as a meteorologist, geologist, or archaeologist). The adeptness to recognize and classify cultural artifacts such as cars or sneakers may also depend upon the naturalist intelligence.
Interpersonal (People Smart)	The ability to perceive and make distinctions in the moods, intentions, motivations, and feelings of other people (e.g., as a teacher, politician, actor, or philanthropist). The ability to process information both verbally and nonverbally through interpretation of all forms of dance, hand gestures, body movements, and music (e.g., as a dancer, mime, actor, or musician). This intelligence operates primarily through person-to-person relationships and communication.
Intrapersonal (Self Smart)	The ability to act adaptively on the basis of that knowledge. This intelligence includes having an accurate picture of oneself--strengths and limitations; awareness of inner moods, intentions, motivations, temperaments, and desires; and the capacity for self-discipline, self-understanding, and self-esteem (e.g., as a theologian, psychologist, psychiatrist, or a philosopher). This intelligence is very private and uses other intelligences for self-expression.

Howard Gardner's Theory of Multiple Intelligences is now widely accepted in most educational settings. In the past decade it has become a core criteria in curriculum development. There is nothing magical about planning curriculum activities that address each of the multiple intelligences. The activities are typical experiences that are usually offered on a regular basis in a developmentally appropriate environment.

Learning centers provide a perfect format for helping teachers plan and implement activities that will appeal to the full range of intelligences. They allow children to engage in active, hands-on, concrete experiences, and ongoing interaction with appropriate materials, equipment, and people in the learning environment. Children have the opportunity to approach learning through one of their high ability levels, as well as the opportunity to practice using other ability levels. Learning centers enhance all the ways in which children are intelligent. *The Complete Daily Curriculum for Early Childhood* offers suggestions for learning centers each day that support all eight intelligences.

Developmental Domains

Whole-child instruction supports the concept that young children are developing in several areas or domains simultaneously and that each of these areas of development is equally important to the child. Not only are the developmental domains equally important, but they are also interwoven. It has been said that the social-emotional well being of the child fuels the intellect. Early brain development research states that social-emotional development and cognitive development walk hand in hand. A child cannot learn when his or her emotional and social well-being are threatened.

Children's growth is divided into four developmental domains. Cognitive growth centers on the mind and how the mind works as children develop and learn. Physical growth has to do with development of the body and its parts. Social growth centers on the development of skills for interacting with others and emotional growth refers to the development of self-esteem and self-control. Lessons in *The Complete Daily Curriculum for Early Childhood* support all four areas of growth each day.

Subject Areas

Preschool children are learning math, science, social studies, reading (language), music, and art—the same subjects as older children in elementary school. For example, when children are building with blocks they are learning math concepts, such as counting—knowing the number of blocks needed for their structure—and geometry—learning the names of the shapes of the blocks and the results of putting two or more blocks together. They are learning science as they explore gravity and balance. They are learning social skills and language skills as they cooperate and communicate with one another in a joint effort to build towers, castles, and forts. Skills and concepts are being learned and taught simultaneously. A master teacher is fully aware of what is being learned and how it is being taught during routine classroom activities.

The Complete Daily Curriculum for Early Childhood offers daily activities that promote this kind of integration.

The Interests of the Child

Research indicates that all of us, including children, are more likely to learn when the information being taught is of interest to us (Sousa, 1995). Following the interests of children helps them connect what they know to new information being taught and also helps them put new information into a meaningful context.

Using this Book

The Complete Daily Curriculum for Early Childhood is designed to help teachers create a comprehensive curriculum that is tailored to meet the individual differences of children. Each concept or skill is introduced during a Morning Circle activity and then reinforced in learning centers that utilize activities that appeal to each of the eight ways of being smart and learning style preferences. A variety of subject/curriculum areas and each of the developmental domains are addressed in each day's lessons.

Because getting children focused is so critical to learning, every Morning Circle includes a suggestion for grabbing children's attention. Closing Circle (Reflections on the Day) offers suggestions for helping children reflect on their experiences of the day. Each lesson includes several Story Circle suggestions and Music and Movement activity ideas. Each thematic group of lessons includes suggestions for assessing children's understanding of the skills and concepts presented in those lessons by using strategies that appeal to the eight ways of demonstrating high ability levels (multiple intelligences).

Lessons in this book are flexible. You can use them with scheduled units or themes or to address children's interests as they arise. Lessons can last one day, one week, or as long as the children are interested.

You will notice that some activities are repeated within different themes. Repetition is an important part of learning. It strengthens children's understanding of patterns and often helps clarify information for them. Repetition of skills is critical to mastery. When children practice what they have learned by repeating an activity, they enlarge their understanding of that skill. Think about riding a bicycle. Every time you ride you become better at balancing. New experiences provide expanded knowledge. Your muscles become stronger from repeated use. Your awareness of bicycle etiquette expands. And most important, your self-confidence increases, allowing you to try more difficult tasks.

You will also notice that some stories are retold using different formats. Children love to hear a story over and over again. Rereading familiar stories coincides with the way children learn. The repetition improves their vocabulary, sequencing, and memory skills. Research shows that children often ask as many and sometimes the same questions after a dozen readings as they do after the first reading. This is because they are learning language in increments—not all at once. Each reading brings a little more meaning to the story.

The Appendix includes songs, fingerplays, chants and rhymes, stories, recipes, games and dances, directions for making games, and patterns for games, puppets, and flannel board stories. A sample letter to parents describing the concept of multiple intelligences and ways to determine their child's high ability levels is also provided.

The lesson themes are familiar ones found in most early childhood classrooms. This means that *The Complete Daily Curriculum for Early Childhood* will fit right in with your established curriculum. What a wonderful way to view children! What a celebration of human potential! What an ideal way to build community!

References

Gardner, H. 1983. *Frames of mind: The theory of multiple intelligences.* New York: Basic Books.

Phipps, P. 1997. *Multiple intelligences in the early childhood classroom.* Columbus, OH: SRA.

Schiller, P. 1999. *Start smart! Building brain power in the early years.* Beltsville, MD: Gryphon House, Inc.

Schiller, P. 1996. *Practices in the early childhood classroom.* Columbus, OH: SRA.

Sousa, David 1995. *How the brain learns.* Reston, Virginia: NASSP.

All About Me

(Self-Concept)

My Body

Morning Circle

1. Sing "My Hand on Myself" (Appendix p. 296).
2. Discuss the parts of the body and what each part can do. Encourage children to show you the parts as you discuss them. Occasionally, ask children to imagine how things would be different if they didn't have that particular part of their bodies (e.g., eyes, hands, ears, and so on).
3. Have children face a partner and play a game of "Copycat" or "Monkey See, Monkey Do" (Appendix p. 364).
4. Tell the children that today's activities will be about body parts.

Story Circle

Everybody Has a Body by Robert Rockwell, Robert Williams, and Elizabeth Sherwood

From Head to Toe by Eric Carle (Illustrator)

The Human Body by Sylvaine Perols and Gallimard Jeunesse

Music and Movement

Play Punchinello (Appendix p. 366), the Hokey Pokey (Appendix p. 361), or Simon Says (Appendix p. 368).

Sing "If You're Happy and You Know It" (Appendix p. 290).

Act out "I Can, You Can!" (Appendix p. 319).

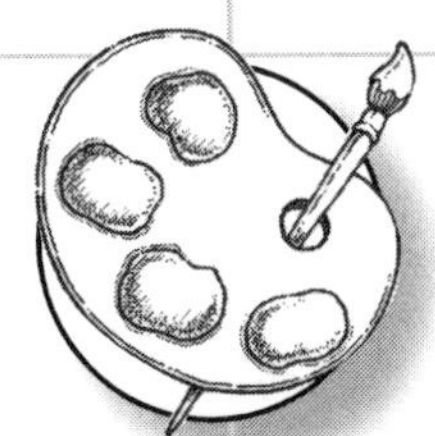

Art (Spatial, Intrapersonal, Bodily-Kinesthetic)

Lay a piece of butcher paper on the floor. It should be a few inches longer than the child. Instruct the child to lie down on the paper and strike a pose. Track around the perimeter of the child's body using a pen or marker. Invite children to color in their features and clothing.

Discovery (Musical, Interpersonal)

Challenge children to think of noises they can make with their body parts such as stomping their feet, clapping their hands, and clicking their tongue.

Dramatic Play (Spatial, Intrapersonal)

Provide a mirror and face paint (Appendix p. 375). Encourage children to paint a design on their face. This activity will require your help. While you are assisting children, talk with them about the different parts of their face, including cheeks, chin, forehead, eyes, eyebrows, and nose.

Gross Motor (Bodily-Kinesthetic, Interpersonal)

Play "Twister" or, using a tumbling mat, provide a space for children to try out a few tumbling tricks including forward rolls and Back-to-Back lifts (Appendix. p. 357).

Language (Naturalist, Linguistic)

Provide Dress Me Dolls (Appendix p. 522-525). Encourage children to dress the dolls. Talk with them about which clothes cover which parts of their body.

Math (Logical-Mathematical)

Provide small, colored rubber bands. Challenge children to use them to make patterns on their fingers. (Supervise closely at all times!)

Learning Centers

Closing Circle (Reflections on the Day)

Ask the children:

1. What have you learned about your body today?
2. What are some of the sounds your body can make?
3. Who can name the parts of your face?
4. How are our bodies different from animals' bodies? How are our bodies the same as animals' bodies?

My Fingers and Hands

Morning Circle

1. Ask each child to show you something they can do with their hands such as clap, snap their fingers, scratch their head, or pat their tummy.
2. Encourage the children to think of all the things for which they use their hands. Make a list of the children's ideas on chart paper.
3. Teach the children to say, "yes," "no," "thank you," and "please" in sign language (Appendix p. 537). Encourage them to use these signs during the day.
4. Challenge the children to think about what it might be like if they did not have hands. Stimulate thinking by suggesting they imagine they are a fish or a dog.
5. Tell the children that today's activities will be about things they do with their fingers and hands. Encourage the children to pay close attention to all they ways they use their hands today.

Story Circle

Clap Hands by Helen Oxenbury
Hand, Hand, Fingers, Thumb by Al Perkins
Here Are My Hands by Bill Martin, Jr.
My Father's Hands by Joanne Ryder
My Hands by Aliki
Touch by Sue Hurwitz

Music and Movement

Teach children a partner clapping game to "Miss Mary Mack" (Appendix p. 323) or "Pease Porridge Hot" (Appendix p. 365)

Sing "Where Is Thumbkin?" (Appendix p. 307) or "Open, Shut Them" (Appendix p. 298)

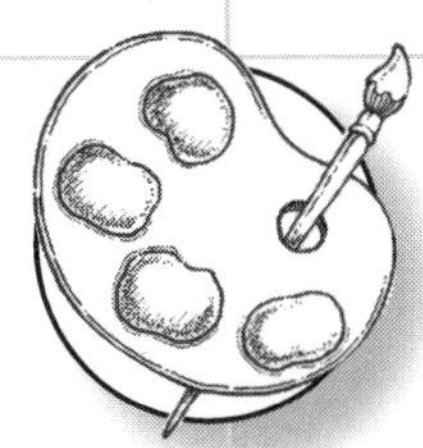

Art (Spatial, Intrapersonal)

Provide Tactile Fingerpaint (Appendix p. 378) and encourage children to create a painting.

Discovery (Naturalist)

Invite children to look at their hands through a magnifying glass. Provide a stamp pad and encourage the children to make fingerprints to examine with their magnifying glasses. Do any two prints look exactly the same?

Fine Motor (Bodily-Kinesthetic, Spatial)

Teach children how to Finger Crochet (Appendix p. 388). Encourage children to make necklaces, bracelets, or belts with their yarn.

Language (Linguistic)

Provide blank paper folded into a book and stapled. Also provide tactile pieces of fabric and wallpaper coverings. Challenge children to make a "Tactile Book." Teach children how to "finger spell" their names (Appendix p. 528).

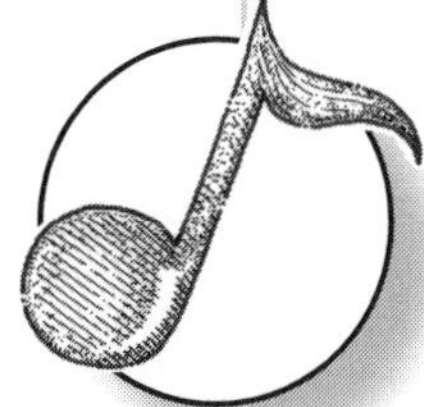

Music (Musical, Intrapersonal, Logical-Mathematical)

Encourage children to create clapping and snapping patterns with their hands.

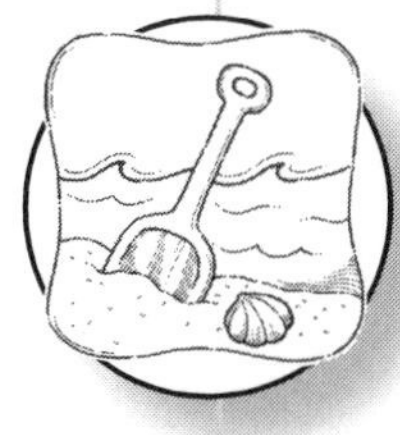

Sand and Water (Linguistic)

Fill the sand and water table with tactile items for the children to explore. Ask children to describe the items that they are touching.

Closing Circle (Reflections on the Day)

Ask the children:

1. In what ways have you used your hands today?
2. Can someone show me how to spell your name using your fingers?
3. What have you found out about your fingerprints?

My Legs and Feet

Morning Circle

1. Meet the children at the door and invite them to hop, skip, or jump to the Morning Circle area.
2. Invite the children to brainstorm a list of the things for which they use their feet and legs.
3. Tell the children that today's activities will be about how many ways they use their legs and feet. Remind them to pay close attention to their legs and feet today.

Story Circle

Dance, Tanya by Patricia Lee Gauch
The Foot Book by Dr. Seuss
Funny Feet by Leatie Weiss
Hello Toes! Hello Feet! by Ann Whitford Paul
Hop Jump by Ellen Stoll Walsh
How Many Feet in the Bed? by Diane Johnston Hamm
Lili at Ballet by Rachel Isadora
My Feet by Aliki

Music and Movement

Invite children to dance creatively to classical music or to march to marching music.

Move to the "Hokey Pokey" (Appendix p. 361), "It's a Very Simple Dance to Do" (Appendix p. 362), "The Grand Old Duke of York" (Appendix p. 288), or "Head, Shoulders, Knees, and Toes" (Appendix p. 290).

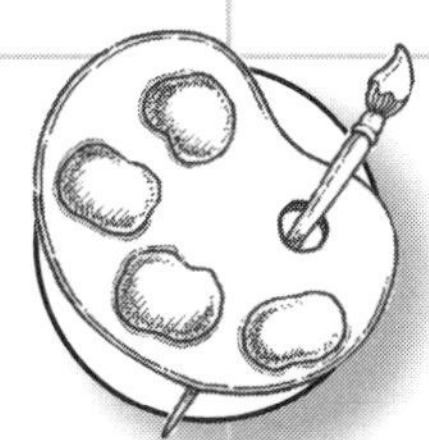

Art (Spatial, Intrapersonal, Bodily-Kinesthetic)

Invite the children to make Footprint Designs (Appendix p. 389). Challenge them to make creative foot designs along the path of paper. For example, they might walk in a circle or on their toes.

Discovery (Naturalist, Logical-Mathematical)

Provide a set of footprints made from Animal Footprint Patterns (Appendix p. 499). Encourage the children to match the prints or play a game of concentration.

Fine Motor (Bodily-Kinesthetic)

Provide small objects such as spools, beads, straws, and other items for the children to pick up with their toes.

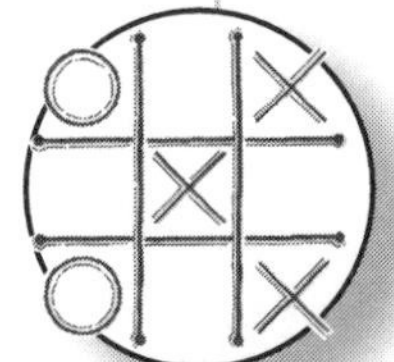

Games (Bodily-Kinesthetic, Interpersonal)

Encourage the children to find a partner. Have them stand side by side. Tie the partners' inside legs together and encourage them to try to walk. (Supervise closely at all times!)

Gross Motor (Bodily-Kinesthetic)

Place a piece of masking tape on the floor to create a start line. Encourage the children to jump from the line as far as they can. Explain that this is called broad jumping. (Supervise closely at all times!)

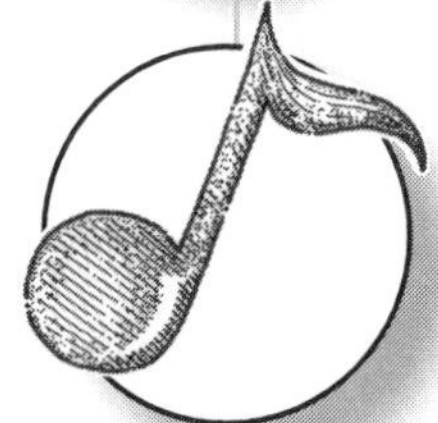

Music (Musical, Intrapersonal, Bodily-Kinesthetic)

Provide music. Invite the children to make up a dance or create a dance step. Give the children the rhythm band instruments. Which instruments can they play with their feet?

Closing Circle (Reflections on the Day)

Ask the children:

1. What was your favorite activity today? Why?
2. What did you learn about your legs and feet?
3. Is it difficult to pick things up with your toes? Why?
4. How are your toes like your fingers? How are they different?

My Ears

Morning Circle

1. Hide a music box or musical toy in the classroom. Meet the children at the door as they arrive at school and challenge them to use their ears to find the source of the music. Hold Morning Circle in the spot where the toy is found.
2. Recite "My Ears" (Appendix p. 323) with the children.
3. Encourage the children to think of all the ways they use their ears. Ask them what would they think it would be like if they did not have ears.
4. Discuss the care of the ears. How do we clean our ears? What happens if we listen to music that is too loud?
5. Tell the children that today's activities will be about ways they use their ears.

Story Circle

Bunny's Noisy Book by Margaret Wise Brown
The Ear Book by Al Perkins
The Five Senses: Hearing by Maria Rius
Here's Ears by Shirley Greenway
How Jackrabbit Got His Very Long Ears by Heather Irbinskas
Listen to the Rain by Bill Martin, Jr. and John Archambault
Mr. Brown Can Moo! Can You? by Dr. Seuss
Polar Bear, Polar Bear, What Do You Hear? by Bill Martin, Jr.
Robby Visits the Doctor by Martine Davison
Why Mosquitoes Buzz in People's Ears by Verna Aardema

Music and Movement

Take a listening walk. On a clipboard, list the sounds children hear.

Play Musical Hide and Seek (Appendix p. 365).

Sing "Do Your Ears Hang Low?" (Appendix p. 285).

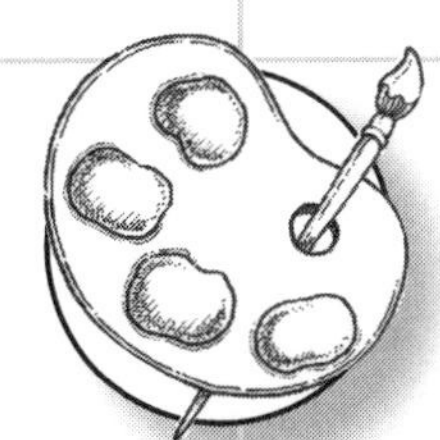

Art (Spatial, Intrapersonal, Musical)

Encourage the children to color to music of varying tempos.

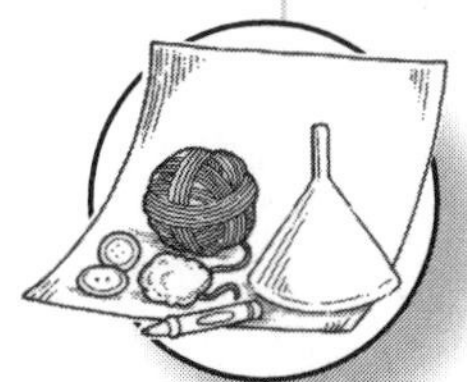

Discovery (Musical, Logical-Mathematical)

Provide music- or sound-making toys for children to explore, including music boxes, jack-in-the boxes, and tops. If you have access to a "Simon Game," place it in the center and encourage children to play it.

Fine Motor (Naturalist, Interpersonal)

Invite the children to look through magazines for things that make sounds. Challenge them to cut the pictures out of the magazines and sort them into things that make loud sounds and things that make soft sounds.

Gross Motor (Bodily-Kinesthetic)

Place a service bell on the floor and provide beanbags for the children to toss at the bell.

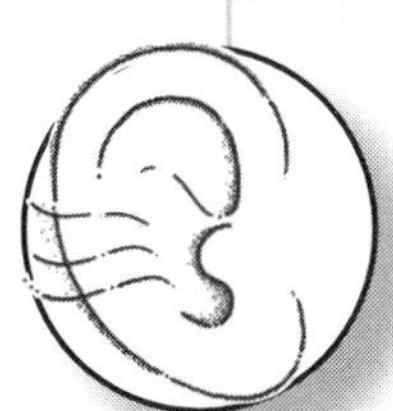

Listening (Linguistic)

Provide a story on tape for the children to listen to. You may want to use a tape that was recorded by a special person at school or by one of the children's family members.

Math (Logical-Mathematical, Musical)

Prepare five Music Makers (Appendix p. 395). Encourage the children to arrange the Music Makers in order from the one that makes the softest sound to the one that makes the loudest sound.

Closing Circle (Reflections on the Day)

Ask the children:

1. What have you learned about sounds today?
2. What is the best thing you heard with your ears? Why?

My Eyes

Morning Circle

1. Teach the children "Eye Rhymes" (Appendix p. 315). Note the different eye colors of the children.
2. Have the children cover their eyes. Describe an object, such as a book or a doll that you have pre-selected and are holding behind your back. Are the children able to guess what the object is without looking at it?

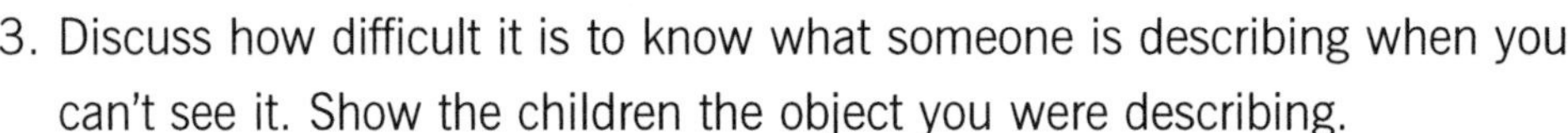

3. Discuss how difficult it is to know what someone is describing when you can't see it. Show the children the object you were describing.
4. Ask the children what would be one of their favorite things to look at. Does anyone mention a loved one's face?
5. Discuss the care of the eyes? How do we wash them? What happens if we look at bright lights or the sun? How do sunglasses help our eyes? Why is it important to have proper lighting when we read?
6. Ask the children to pay attention to things for which they use their eyes.

Story Circle

The Boy with Square Eyes by Juliet Snape
The Eye Book by Dr. Seuss
The Eye Book by Theodore Lesieg
Eyes by Ruth Thomson
The Five Senses: Sight by Maria Rius
Look at Your Eyes by Paul Showers
Look! Look! Look! by Tana Hoban
Sight by Sue Hurwitz

Music and Movement

Sing and move to "Eye Winker" (Appendix p. 309), "Here Are My Eyes" (Appendix p. 311), or "Little Red Apple" (Appendix p. 322).

ART (SPATIAL)

Encourage the children to draw or paint faces or something they can see with their eyes.

DISCOVERY (NATURALIST)

Provide a variety of eye equipment for children to explore such as sunglasses, binoculars, and magnifying glasses. Talk with them about the use of each item.

DRAMATIC PLAY (INTRAPERSONAL, INTERPERSONAL, MUSICAL, LINGUISTIC)

Provide paper plates, tongue depressors, eyes, noses, and mouths cut from felt, and yellow, brown, black, and red yarn. Help the children make "Me Puppets" with these materials and paper plates. After the puppets are made, encourage the children to put on a puppet show.

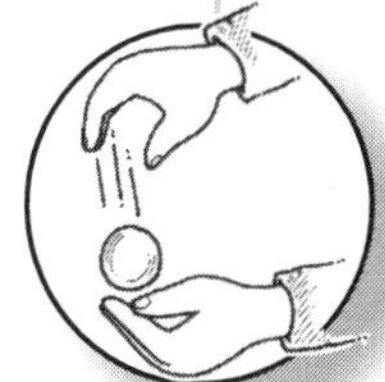

FINE MOTOR (SPATIAL)

Provide wiggle eyes and playdough (Appendix p. 377). Encourage the children to make playdough faces.

GROSS MOTOR (BODILY-KINESTHETIC)

Give the children wiggle eyes and a shallow bowl. Challenge them to toss the eyes into the bowl.

MATH (LOGICAL-MATHEMATICAL)

Make an Eye Graph (Appendix p. 387) for children to use to record their eye color. Encourage the children to predict which color of eyes most of the children will have. Invite children to look in a mirror, determine their eye color, and then place a post-it note under the eye color that matches their eye color.

Closing Circle (Reflections on the Day)

Ask the children:

1. Looking at the graph we made of eye colors, which color eyes do most of the children have?
2. How did you use your eyes today?

My Nose

Morning Circle

1. Sing "Little Skunk's Hole" (Appendix p. 293). What did the skunk do?
2. Encourage the children to brainstorm a list of good smells. Write their list on chart paper or a chalkboard.
3. Discuss the care of the nose. How do we blow our nose? How do we clean our nose?
4. Tell the children that today's activities will be about noses and smelling things. Suggest to the children that they pay attention to what their noses smell today.

Story Circle

Arthur's Nose by Marc Brown
The Biggest Nose by Kathy Caple
The Fairy with the Long Nose by Claude Boujon
The Five Senses: Smell by Maria Rius
The Holes in Your Nose by Genichiro Yagyu
The Nose Book by Al Perkins
Smell by Sue Hurwitz

Music and Movement

Act out "Let's Pretend to Bake a Cake" (Appendix p. 337). Be sure to pretend to smell each ingredient.

Go on a nature walk and collect items to make a potpourri. (Check for allergies)

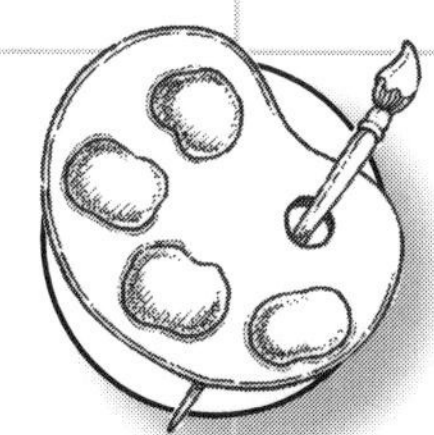

ART (SPATIAL)

Mix Scratch and Sniff Paint (Appendix p. 377) and invite the children to paint a picture. When the picture dries let them scratch the paint to release the scent.

DISCOVERY (NATURALIST)

Make a set of six Aroma Canisters (Appendix p. 381). Encourage the children to match the scents that smell the same.

DRAMATIC PLAY (INTERPERSONAL, SPATIAL)

Make vanilla-scented playdough (Appendix p. 377). Give the children cookie cutters and a cookie sheet. Encourage them to make pretend cookies.

GROSS MOTOR (MUSICAL, BODILY-KINESTHETIC)

Place a piece of masking tape on the floor to create a start line and a second piece of tape about 6" from the first to create a finish line. Encourage the children to roll a ball using only their nose from the start line to the finish line. Challenge them to sing a song while they roll the ball.

LANGUAGE (LINGUISTIC)

Invite the children to use scented markers to copy the list of smells that were brainstormed in Morning Circle or to write their names. Can they identify the smell of each marker?

MATH (LOGICAL-MATHEMATICAL, LINGUISTIC)

Invite the children to prepare Apple Cider (Appendix p. 371). Call attention to the aroma of the cider as it brews.

Closing Circle (Reflections on the Day)

Ask the children:

1. What aromas and smells did you notice today?
2. Which did you like best? Can you describe that aroma or smell?
3. Which activity did you enjoy most today? Why?

My Mouth

Morning Circle

1. Sing "Old MacDonald Had a Farm" (Appendix p. 298) with the children. Encourage the children to sing facing a partner and to watch their partner's mouth when they say "E-I-E-I-O." What do they notice about their partner's mouth?
2. Discuss the many ways we use our mouths. Serve a simple snack such as fish-shaped cheese crackers. Sing a song. You may want to sing "Chew, Chew, Chew Your Food" (Appendix p. 285). (Check for allergies)
3. Point out the parts of the mouth (lips, tongue, teeth).
4. Say a couple of tongue twisters such as "She Sells Seashells" or "Peter Piper" (Appendix p. 328) with the children. Explain that our tongues help us make many different sounds; however, when those sounds are similar but not exactly the same, our tongues have a difficult time with the words.
5. Discuss the care of the mouth. How do we brush our teeth? How often do we brush our teeth? Sing "This Is the Way We Clean Our Teeth" (Appendix p. 303) or "Clean, Clean, Clean Your Teeth" (Appendix p. 285).
6. Tell the children that today's activities will be about mouths.

Story Circle

Daddy Makes the Best Spaghetti by Anna Grossnickle Hines
Dr. Desoto by William Steig
The Five Senses: Taste by Maria Rius
Mouths by Jill Bailey
Peanut Butter and Jelly: A Rhyme Play by Nadine Bernard Westcott
Taste by Sue Hurwitz and Franklin Watts

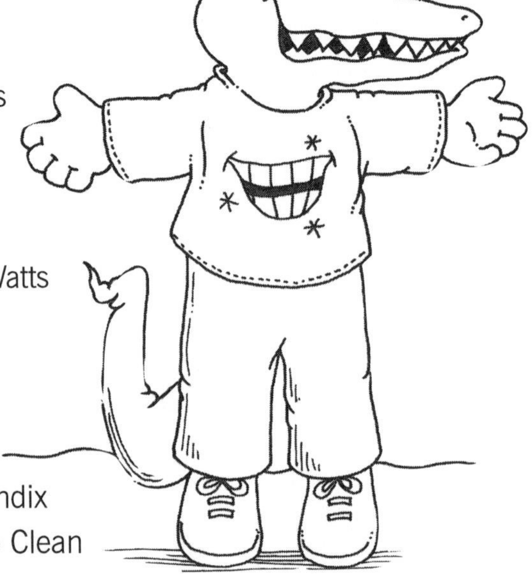

Music and Movement

Sing and move to "Peanut Butter" (Appendix p. 299), "I Have Something in My Pocket" (Appendix p. 290), or "This Is the Way We Clean Our Teeth" (Appendix p. 303).

Art (Spatial)

Provide straws, paper, and tempera paint for the children to create straw blowing designs. Ask them where they think the air that goes through the straw comes from. Remind children to blow *out* through the straw only. (Supervise closely at all times!)

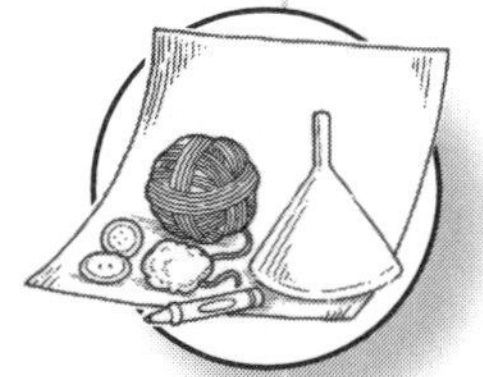

Discovery (Logical-Mathematical)

Invite the children to make Homemade Toothpaste (Appendix p. 373). Show them how to use their fingers for a toothbrush and let them brush their teeth. (Supervise closely at all times!)

Gross Motor (Bodily-Kinesthetic)

Cut a big smiling mouth out of the side of a large box. Paint on some big red lips. Provide beanbags and challenge the children to toss the beanbags into the mouth.

Language (Linguistic, Intrapersonal)

Encourage the children to dictate a recipe for their favorite food to include in a classroom recipe book. Be sure to ask why the food is their favorite and include that information with the recipe.

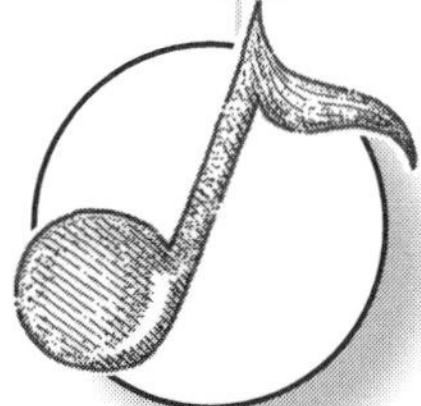

Music (Musical)

Give the children empty ½-liter bottles to blow into. Show them how adding a small amount of water alters the sound. Is anyone able to create a tune?

Snack (Linguistic, Interpersonal)

Encourage the children to follow a rebus pattern for making themselves a peanut butter and jelly sandwich (Appendix p. 495). (Check for allergies)

Closing Circle (Reflections on the Day)

Ask the children:

1. What have you learned about your mouth today?
2. What do you think we should do with our recipe book? Should we give it as a gift to our families? Would you like to share it with another class?
3. Who can describe how we make a peanut butter and jelly sandwich?

My Family

Morning Circle

1. In advance, ask the children to bring in a picture of their families or at least of one member of their family and a separate picture of themselves. Photocopy the photos so that the originals aren't damaged.
2. Encourage the children to show their pictures and tell their friends something about their family.
3. Work as a group to come up with a broad definition of family that is acceptable to and will include everyone. For example, your definition might be "a group of people who live together and support each other." Help the children understand that there are many different styles of families.
4. Teach the children "I'm a Family Helper" (Appendix p. 321) or "Family Fun" (Appendix p. 316).
5. Tell the children that today's activities will be about families.

Story Circle

All Kinds of Families by Norma Simon
Amazing Grace by Mary Hoffman
Big Sister and Little Sister by Charlotte Zolotow
By the Dawn's Early Light by Karen Ackerman
"Goldilocks and the Three Bears" flannel board story (Appendix p. 335)
Into The Napping House by Audrey Wood
Like Jake and Me by Mavis Jukes
Mama, Do You Love Me? by Barbara M. Joosse
Mufaro's Beautiful Daughters: An African Tale by John Steptoe
My Mom Travels a Lot by Caroline Bauer
Not Yet, Yvette by Helen Ketteman
Peter's Chair by Ezra Jack Keats
Relatives Came by Cynthia Rylant

Music and Movement

Play "The Farmer in the Dell" (Appendix p. 359). Change characters to reflect different configurations of families.

Re-enact the "The Great Big Turnip" (Appendix p. 336). Change characters to reflect a family.

Sing and move to "Ten in the Bed" (Appendix p. 302).

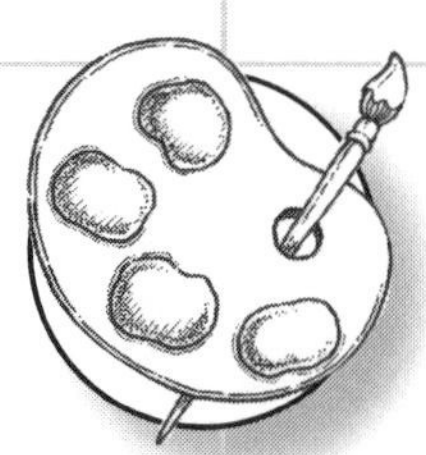

ART (Spatial, Linguistic, Intrapersonal)

Encourage the children to draw a family portrait. Encourage them to say something about their family that can be written on the bottom or back of their picture.

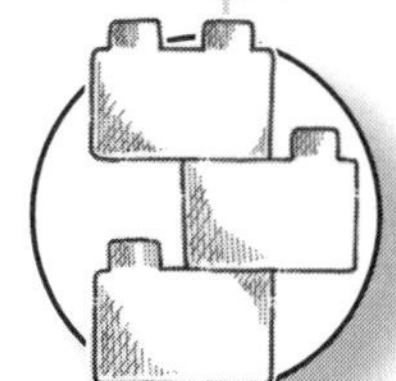

Block (Spatial, Interpersonal, Logical-Mathematical)

Challenge the children to use the blocks to build a home for their family. How many bedrooms do they need? Where will the family eat dinner? Where will the bathrooms be?

DRAMATIC PLAY (Interpersonal, Naturalist, Logical-Mathematical)

Provide materials for the children to set the table for their family. Ask them thinking questions. How many places do they need? What goes in each place?

LANGUAGE (Interpersonal, Linguistic)

Provide the flannel board story of "Goldilocks and the Three Bears" (Appendix p. 335). Encourage the children to retell the story on the flannel board.

LIBRARY (Linguistic)

Fill the library with books about families.

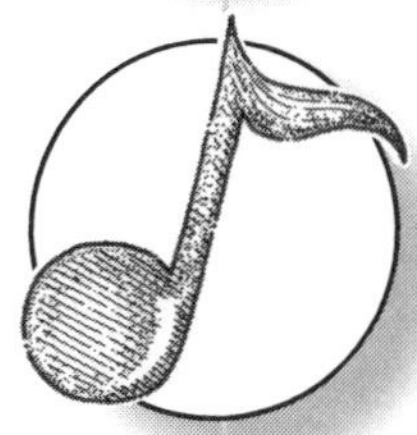

Music (Musical, Bodily-Kinesthetic)

Record "The Three Bear's Rap" (Appendix p. 305) and let the children listen to it. Encourage the children to move like Papa Bear, to move like Mama Bear, and to move like Baby Bear.

Closing Circle (Reflections on the Day)

Ask the children:

1. What have you learned about families today?
2. In what ways can families help each other?

My Friends

Morning Circle

1. Sing "The More We Get Together" (Appendix p. 295) with the children.
2. Ask children what friends are. Discuss old friends and new friends. Sing "Make New Friends" (Appendix p. 294).
3. Tell the children that today they are going to do everything with a friend. Encourage children to choose a friend, a "buddy." If you have an odd number of children make one group of three buddies.

Story Circle

The Adventures of the Rainbow Fish by Marcus Pfister
Amos and Boris by William Steig
Anna Banana and Me by Lenore Blegvad
Best Friends by Steven Kellogg
Chester's Way by Kevin Henkes
Friends by Margaret K. McElderry
Frog and Toad Are Friends by Arnold Lobel
Frog and Toad Together by Arnold Lobel
Horace and Morris But Mostly Dolores by James Howe
"The Lion and the Mouse" (Appendix p. 338)
"Mr. Wiggle and Mr. Waggle" (Appendix p. 341)
"Smart Cookie's Best Friend, Greta Graham" (Appendix p. 343)
We Are Best Friends by Aliki
Will I Have a Friend? by Miriam Cohen

Music and Movement

Encourage friends to lock elbows and to march to high-stepping march music for a Friendship March.

Play "Cooperative Musical Chairs" (Appendix p. 357).

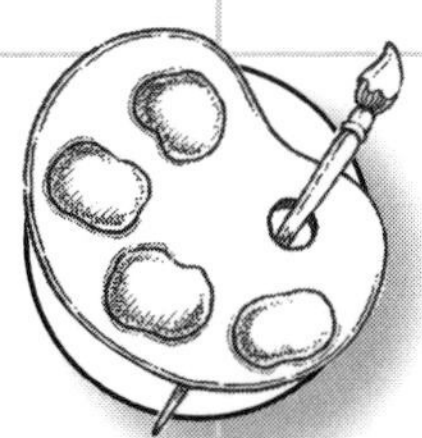

Art (Spatial, Interpersonal, Linguistic)

Encourage buddies to draw a picture of something they like about each other.

Gross Motor (Bodily-Kinesthetic, Interpersonal)

Encourage the children to try cooperative games like the Back-to-Back Lift (Appendix p. 357) or the Tug of Peace (Appendix p. 368).

Language (Linguistic, Intrapersonal)

Encourage buddies to draw a picture of what it means to be a friend. This activity will probably require questions and prompts from the teacher.

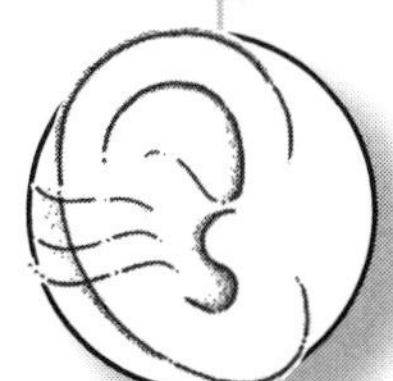

Listening (Musical, Interpersonal)

Encourage buddies to listen to music together.

Math (Logical-Mathematical, Naturalist)

Provide two photocopied photos of each child in the classroom (use the photos from the previous My Family activities on page 34) and encourage the children to match the photos to each other or to match the photos to the family pictures that each child brought to school yesterday. Then have the children pair the photos according to the buddy assignments for today.

Snack (Interpersonal)

Provide juice and cookies. Invite buddies to have "Tea for Two."

Learning Centers

Closing Circle (Reflections on the Day)

Ask the children:

1. What is your day like when you have a friend with you all the time?
2. Is there anything that was difficult to do with a friend?

Things I Like to Do

Morning Circle

1. Bring something to Morning Circle that represents something you like to do (e.g. a blanket you have crocheted, a photograph you have taken, a picture you painted, a book you enjoyed, and so on).
2. Tell the children what it is that you like to do and why. Explain that the things we like to do are important for us to include in our lives.
3. Encourage the children to talk about things they like to do. Make a list of the things they say and then use the list to make up new verses to the song "These Are the Things I Like to Do" (Appendix p. 303). For example, the lines might be "this is the way I ride my bike, this is the way I paint a picture, this is the way I read a book," and so on.
4. Tell the children that today's activities will be about things they like to do.

Story Circle

Dance, Tanya by Patricia Lee Gauch
A Day at the Beach by Mircea Vasiliu
I Can Build a House by Shigeo Watanabe
I Like Books by Anthony Browne
I Like to Play by Marilyn J. Shearer
I Want to Whistle by Anne Alexander
Let's Play House by Lois Lenski
Owl Moon by Jane Yolen
Playing Right Field by Willy Welch
The Snowy Day by Ezra Jack Keats
A Time for Singing by Ron Hirschi

Music and Movement

Play Tummy Ticklers (Appendix p. 369).
Provide bubbles (Appendix p. 375) during outdoor play.
Sing "Take Me Out to the Ball Game" (Appendix p. 302).

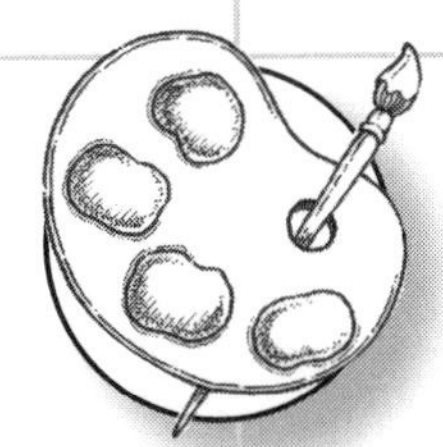

ART (SPATIAL)

Encourage the children to choose their favorite paint and paint a picture of their choice. You might suggest that they paint a picture of something they like to do.

DISCOVERY (INTRAPERSONAL)

Give the children the "Things I Like to Do" Activity Cards and Pyramid (Appendix p. 539 and 532). Encourage them to place the picture cards on the pyramid with their favorite activity on the top and the other cards arranged from top to bottom by the degree to which they enjoy the activity.

DRAMATIC PLAY (SPATIAL, INTERPERSONAL)

Provide dress-up clothes and accessories and encourage the children to dress as they like. Be sure to include a mirror.

LIBRARY (LINGUISTIC, INTRAPERSONAL)

Encourage the children to pick their favorite book and read it.

MATH (LOGICAL-MATHEMATICAL, INTRAPERSONAL)

Use the activity cards from "Things I Like to Do" Pyramid (See Discovery, above) or make up your own. Encourage the children to sort the cards into two categories: "things I like to do" and "things I don't like to do." After they have sorted the cards, invite them to sort each category again into "things I like to do some of the time," "... most of the time," "things I don't like to do ever," and "things I don't like to do sometimes."

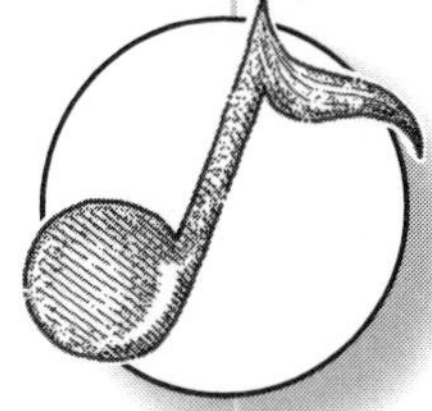

MUSIC (MUSICAL, BODILY-KINESTHETIC)

Provide music and invite the children to make up a song or a dance about something they like to do.

Closing Circle (Reflections on the Day)

Ask the children:

1. What is your favorite thing you did today? Why?
2. What have you learned today about the things you like to do?

Assessment for "All About Me"

Intellectual Strength	Assessment
Linguistic/Spatial	Invite the children to draw a self-portrait. Have them tell you about their portrait and encourage them to label their body parts.
Musical Bodily-Kinesthetic	Invite the children to sing "My Hand on My Head" (Appendix p. 296) or to chant "Head, Shoulders, Baby" (Appendix p. 318). Encourage the children to point to the body parts as they are named.
Logical-Mathematical	Have the children count their body parts. How many ears do they have? How many feet? Toes? Fingers? And so forth.
Interpersonal	Have children choose a partner and then compare the sizes of their hands, feet, legs, and arms.
Intrapersonal	Encourage the children to show how they would use different parts of their bodies to communicate emotions and feelings. For example, they might clap their hands to show happiness, jump up and down to show excitement, or rub their eyes to show exhaustion.
Naturalist	Encourage the children to classify their body parts by their function. For example, they might classify parts that help us move, parts that help us pick things up, and/or parts that help us express feelings.

Books Used in "All About Me"

A Day at the Beach by Mircea Vasiliu
A Time for Singing by Ron Hirschi
The Adventures of the Rainbow Fish by Marcus Pfister
All Kinds of Families by Norma Simon
Amazing Grace by Mary Hoffman
Amos and Boris by William Steig
Anna Banana and Me by Lenore Blegvad
Arthur's Nose by Marc Brown
Best Friends by Steven Kellogg
Big Sister and Little Sister by Charlotte Zolotow
The Biggest Nose by Kathy Caple
The Boy with Square Eyes by Juliet Snape
Bunny's Noisy Book by Margaret Wise Brown
By The Dawn's Early Light by Karen Ackerman
Chester's Way by Kevin Henkes
Clap Hands by Helen Oxenbury
Daddy Makes the Best Spaghetti by Anna Grossnickle Hines
Dance, Tanya by Patricia Lee Gauch
Dr. Desoto by William Steig
The Ear Book by Al Perkins
Everybody Has a Body by Robert Rockwell, Robert Williams, and Elizabeth Sherwood
The Eye Book by Dr. Seuss
The Eye Book by Theodore Lesieg
Eyes by Ruth Thomson
The Fairy With the Long Nose by Claude Boujon
The Five Senses: Hearing by Maria Rius
The Five Senses: Sight by Maria Rius
The Five Senses: Smell by Maria Rius
The Five Senses: Taste by Maria Rius
The Foot Book by Dr. Seuss
Friends by Margaret K. McElderry
Frog and Toad Are Friends by Arnold Lobel
Frog and Toad Together by Arnold Lobel
From Head to Toe by Eric Carle (Illustrator)
Funny Feet by Leatie Weiss

Hand, Hand, Fingers, Thumb by Al Perkins
Hello Toes! Hello Feet! by Ann Whitford Paul
Here Are My Hands by Bill Martin, Jr.
Here's Ears by Shirley Greenway
The Holes in Your Nose by Genichiro Yagyu
Hop Jump by Ellen Stoll Walsh
Horace and Morris But Mostly Dolores by James Howe
How Jackrabbit Got His Very Long Ears by Heather Irbinskas
How Many Feet in the Bed? by Diane Johnston Hamm
The Human Body by Sylvaine Perols and Gallimard Jeunesse
I Can Build a House by Shigeo Watanabe
I Like Books by Anthony Browne
I Like to Play by Marilyn J. Shearer
I Want to Whistle by Anne Alexander
Into The Napping House by Audrey Wood
Let's Play House by Lois Lenski
Like Jake and Me by Mavis Jukes
Lili at Ballet by Rachel Isadora
Listen to the Rain by Bill Martin, Jr. and John Archambault
Look at Your Eyes by Paul Showers
Look! Look! Look! by Tana Hoban
Mama, Do You Love Me? by Barbara M. Joosse
Mouths by Jill Bailey
Mr. Brown Can Moo! Can You? by Dr. Seuss
Mufaro's Beautiful Daughters: An African Tale by John Steptoe
My Father's Hands by Joanne Ryder
My Feet by Aliki
My Hands by Aliki
My Mom Travels a Lot by Caroline Bauer
The Nose Book by Al Perkins
Not Yet, Yvette by Helen Ketteman
Owl Moon by Jane Yolen
Peanut Butter and Jelly: A Rhyme Play by Nadine Bernard Westcott
Peter's Chair by Ezra Jack Keats
Playing Right Field by Willy Welch
Polar Bear, Polar Bear, What Do You Hear? by Bill Martin, Jr.
Relatives Came by Cynthia Rylant
Robby Visits the Doctor by Martine Davison

Sight by Sue Hurwitz
Smell by Sue Hurwitz
The Snowy Day by Ezra Jack Keats
Taste by Sue Hurwitz and Franklin Watts
The Three Bears (Traditional)
Touch by Sue Hurwitz
We Are Best Friends by Aliki
Why Mosquitoes Buzz in People's Ears by Verna Aardema
Will I Have a Friend? by Miriam Cohen

Other Books About Self-Concept

A House Is a House for Me by Mary Ann Hoberman
ABC I Like Me by Nancy Carlson
All About Alfie by Shirley Hughes
All About All of You: Bodies by Sue Clark
All About Me by Debbie MacKinnon
Best Friends by Miriam Cohen
El Chino by Allen Say
I Can Do It Myself by Lessie Jones Little
I Smell Honey by Andrea Pinkney
Jessica by Kevin Henkes
The Me I See by Barbara Shook Hazen
My Five Senses by Aliki
No Nap by Eve Bunting
Skip to My Lou by Nadine Bernard Westcott
Swimmy by Leo Lionni
Today I Feel Silly & Other Moods That Make My Day by Jamie Lee Curtis
Vera's First Day of School by Vera Rosenberry
What's Inside?: My Body by Angela Royston
Who's in a Family? by Robert Skutch
Why Am I Different? by Norma Simon
William's Doll by Charlotte Zolotow
You Smell and Taste and Feel and See and Hear by Mary Murphy

Colors All Around

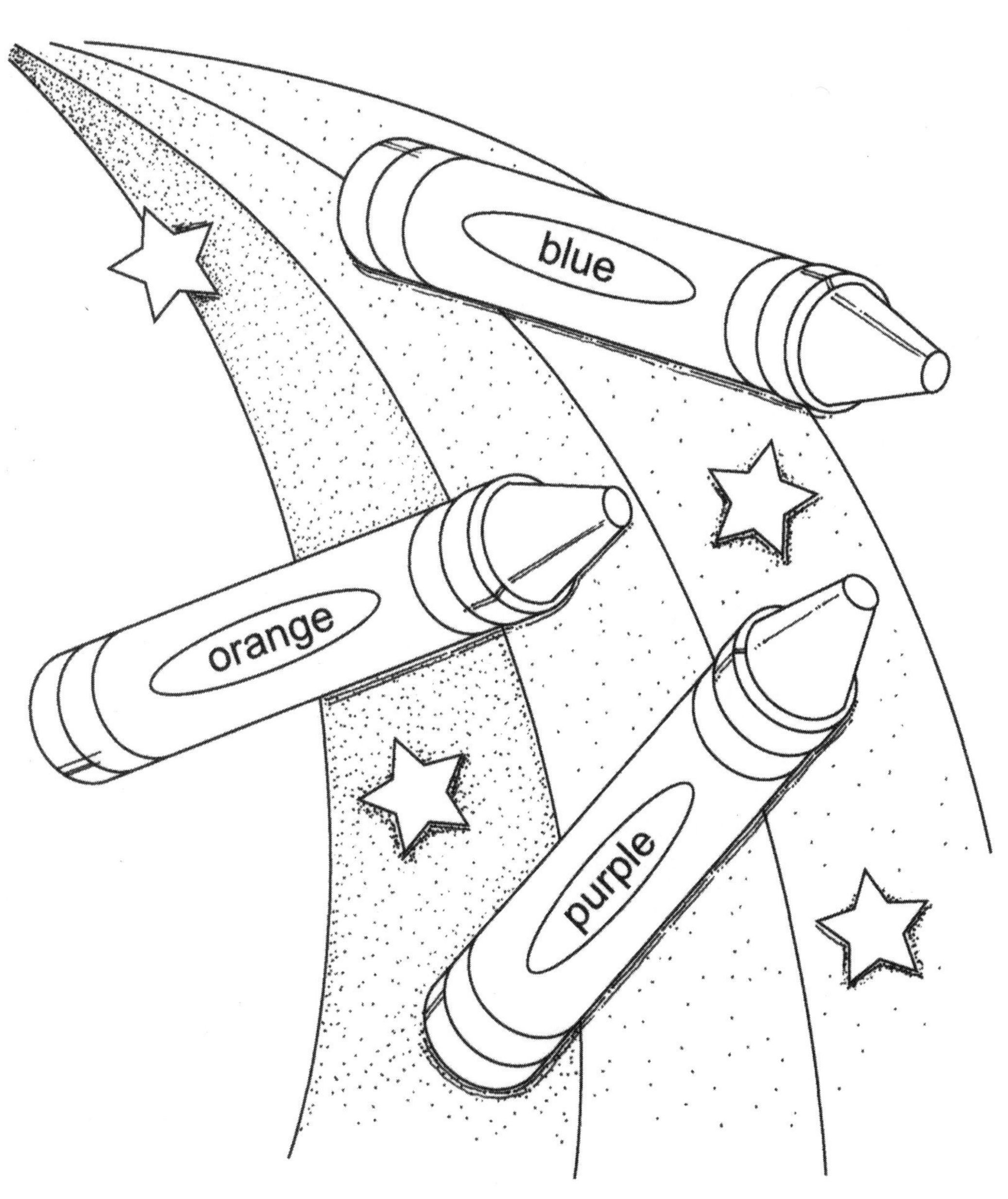

Red

Morning Circle

1. Wear red. Instead of dressing in all red, try wearing something odd that is red such as a hat, scarf, or special tie. This will help the children see red in contrast to other colors.
2. Encourage the children to look around the room for other red things. Make a list of the things that the children find. Count the items on the list.
3. Ask the children to think of something that is red but that is not within their sight. Perhaps they will think of an apple or a flower.
4. Discuss how colors affect us emotionally. Invite children to discuss how red makes them feel. (Red is a warm color and it usually makes us feel alert.)
5. Tell the children that red is said to increase our appetites. You may want to experiment and eat on red placemats (pieces of construction paper) today.
6. Teach the children the "I Like Red" cheer (Appendix p. 320).
7. Tell the children that today's activities will be about the color red.

Story Circle

Hello, Red Fox by Eric Carle
The Little Red Hen (Traditional)
"The Little Red Hen" flannel board story (Appendix p. 340)
Mary Wore a Red Dress, Henry Wore Green Sneakers by Merle Peek
Red by Mary Elizabeth Salzmann
Red in My World by Joanne Winne
Ted in a Red Bed by Jenny Tyler
Who Said Red? by Mary Serfozo

Music and Movement

Sing "The Color Song" (Appendix p. 295) or "My Little Red Wagon" (Appendix p. 297).

Sing "This Is Tiffany" (Appendix p. 303) and focus on the color of children's clothing.

Recite the poem "Little Red Apple" (Appendix p. 322).

*If children eat lunch at school, think about serving a "red meal." You might have red jelly or gelatin, apples, strawberries, or spaghetti. You can add food coloring to mashed potatoes, eggs, or fettuccini to make them red.

Learning Centers

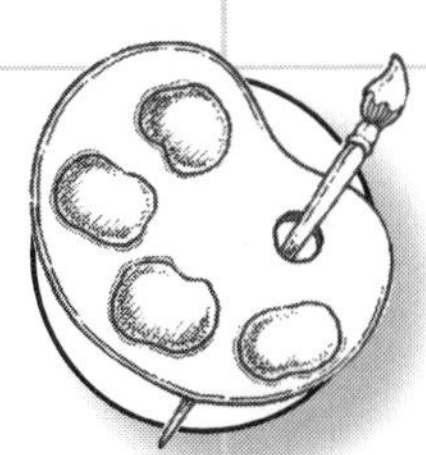

Art (Spatial)

Provide red paper, ribbon, beads, sequins, and other materials for making a red collage. Try coloring the glue red with tempera paint for extra fun!

Gross Motor (Bodily-Kinesthetic)

Toss red beanbags into a red box.

Language (Linguistic, Interpersonal)

Provide "The Little Red Hen" flannel board patterns (Appendix p. 437). Invite the children to tell the story of "The Little Red Hen."

Math (Logical-Mathematical)

Create patterns using only red items such as red crayons, red blocks, red stringing beads, and other red objects.

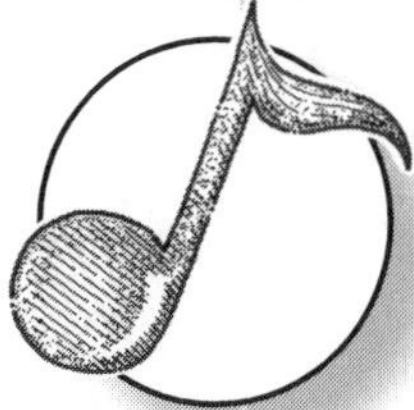

Music (Musical, Intrapersonal)

Paint to classical music using red fingerpaint.

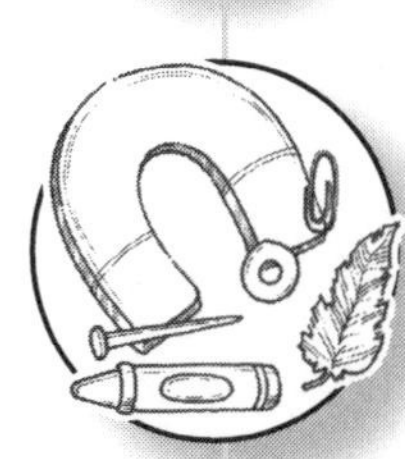

Science (Naturalist)

Look through magazines and books for red insects and bugs. Circle them with a red marker.

Closing Circle (Reflections on the Day)

Ask the children:

1. What have you learned about the color red?
2. What is your favorite red thing? Why?
3. Which insects or bugs are red?
4. Can you think of words that often go with the word "red", like red rose, red bug, red light, Red Lobster, red spot, and red mark?

Blue

Morning Circle

1. Hang blue crepe paper streamers in the doorway the children use to enter the room.
2. Have a basket full of multicolored items in the middle of the Morning Circle. Invite a volunteer to find all the blue items in the basket.
3. Encourage the children to help you arrange the blue items from darkest to lightest.
4. Count the number of blue items that were found.
5. Discuss the phrase "I feel blue." Ask children how blue makes them feel. Tell the children that blue is considered a cool color and that it is generally a color that makes us feel calm.
6. Teach the children the "I Like Blue" cheer (Appendix p. 319).
7. Tell the children that today's activities will be about the color blue.

Story Circle

Blueberries for Sal by Robert McCloskey
Blue Frogs by Margaret Campilonga
Blue Sea by Robert Kalan
Mary Lou Likes Blue by Lyn Hester
Olmo the Blue Butterfly by Alma Flor Ada

Music and Movement

Invite the children to dance a rendition of "Blue Suede Shoes" or to Blues music.

Sing "Lavender Blue" (Appendix p. 292).

Invite the children to dance with blue streamers.

*If children eat lunch at school, think about serving a "blue meal." You might have blueberries, blue gelatin, or cake with blue icing. You can add food coloring to fettuccini, mashed potatoes, or eggs to make them blue.

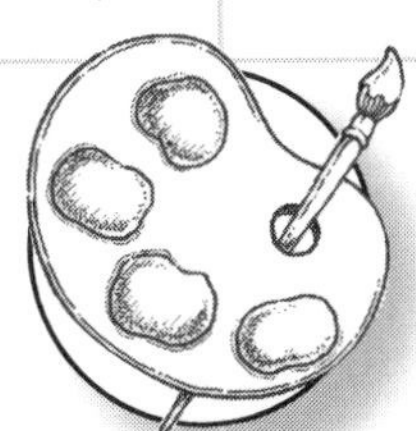

ART (SPATIAL, INTRAPERSONAL)

Provide blue tempera paint and encourage the children to paint "blue pictures."

DRAMATIC PLAY (NATURALIST)

Challenge the children to create a "blue meal." Provide magazines that feature food and invite the children to cut out pictures of blue foods, such as blueberries, blue corn chips, or blueberry yogurt and glue them to a paper plate.

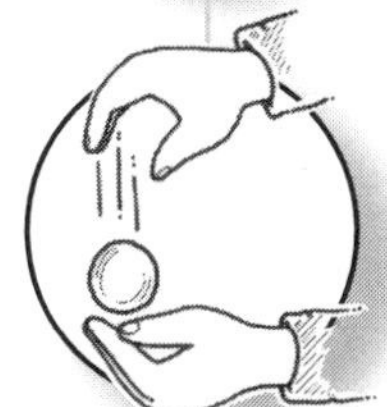

FINE MOTOR (SPATIAL, LOGICAL-MATHEMATICAL)

Provide blue rubber bands (in several shades, if possible) for creating blue designs on geoboards. (SUPERVISE CLOSELY AT ALL TIMES!)

GROSS MOTOR (SPATIAL, BODILY-KINESTHETIC, INTERPERSONAL)

Build a Blue City. Encourage the children to build a city with blue construction paper, blue pipe cleaners, blue cellophane, glue, and tape.

LANGUAGE (LINGUISTIC)

Write the word "blue" on several 4" x 6" index cards. Invite the children to trace the word "blue" onto tracing paper using a blue marker. Or write the word "blue" on copy paper and invite children to trace over it with a blue felt-tip marker.

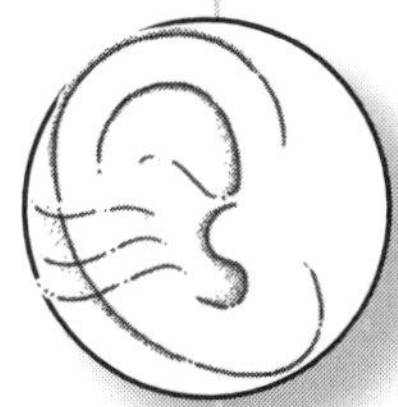

LISTENING (MUSICAL, INTRAPERSONAL)

Provide Blues music and invite the children to listen. Challenge them to come up with a reason this kind of music is called "the Blues."

Closing Circle (Reflections on the Day)

Ask the children:

1. What have you learned about the color blue?
2. Why do you think Blues music is called "the Blues"?

Yellow

Morning Circle

1. Cut yellow circles from large sheets of construction paper and write each child's name on a circle. Place the circles in the Morning Circle and invite children to find their names and sit down.
2. Show the children a collection of pictures of yellow things that you have cut from magazines. Discuss each item. Ask the children if they have seen the item in another color. For example, has anyone seen blue butter?
3. Ask the children to find classmates who are wearing yellow today.
4. Invite the children to make a human graph. Show them how to arrange themselves into two lines—one that represents children who are wearing yellow and one that represents children who are not wearing yellow. Which line is longer?
5. Ask the children how the color yellow makes them feel. Tell the children that yellow is a warm color and encourages creativity.
6. Teach the children the "I Like Yellow" cheer (Appendix p. 320).
7. Tell the children that today's activities will be about the color yellow.

Story Circle

Fuzzy Yellow Ducklings by Matthew Van Fleet
Little Blue and Little Yellow by Leo Lionni
Yellow by Mary Elizabeth Salzmann
Yellow in My World by Joanne Winne
The Yellow Lion by Margaret Camplilonga

Music and Movement

Play rhythm band instruments to "The Yellow Rose of Texas" (Appendix p. 308).

Play "Drop the Handkerchief" (Appendix p. 358). Use a yellow scarf for a handkerchief.

Invite the children to dance with yellow streamers.

Encourage the children to make yellow shadows outdoors with yellow cellophane.

*If children have lunch at school, think about serving a "yellow meal." You might have macaroni and cheese, eggs, pineapple, yellow gelatin, yellow cookies, or yellow cake with yellow icing.

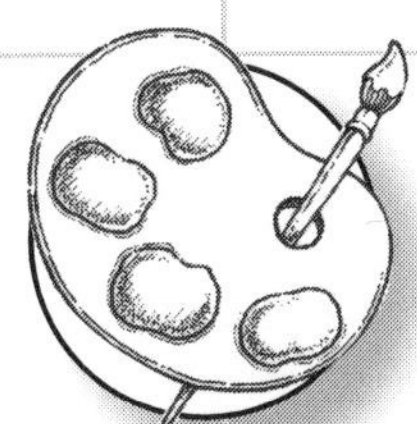

Art (Spatial)

Give the children yellow playdough (Appendix p. 377) to create a yellow sun and yellow pipe cleaners to add sun rays.

Dramatic Play (Interpersonal)

Provide lemons, strainers, water, and sugar. Invite the children to make lemonade for their friends in another class or for their families.

Gross Motor (Intrapersonal, Musical, Bodily-Kinesthetic)

Encourage the children to dance to classical music using yellow streamers for expression.

Language (Linguistic)

Retell the story of *Little Blue and Little Yellow* using blue and yellow cellophane on the overhead projector or with a flashlight on the wall.

Math (Logical-Mathematical, Naturalist)

Classify a box of buttons or beads into sets of "yellow" and "not yellow."

Science (Logical-Mathematical)

Examine lemon peels with magnifying glasses.

Learning Centers

Closing Circle (Reflections on the Day)

Ask the children:

1. What would you think about calling lemonade "yellowade?"
2. What is your favorite yellow thing? Why?

GREEN

MORNING CIRCLE

1. Hold Morning Circle outdoors if weather permits. Have the children look around for green things.
2. Sing "The Green Grass Grew All Around" (Appendix p. 288) or "Great Green Gobs" (Appendix p. 288).
3. Discuss the way the grass feels on your hands. If weather permits, take off your shoes and see how the grass feels on your feet.
4. Ask the children how the color green makes them feel.
5. Teach the children the "I Like Green" cheer (Appendix p. 320).
6. Tell the children that today's activities will be about the color green.

STORY CIRCLE

Green by Mary Elizabeth Salzmann
Green Eggs and Ham by Dr. Seuss
The Green Giraffe by Margaret Campilonga
Green in My World Joanne Winne
Little Blue and Little Yellow by Leo Lionni

MUSIC AND MOVEMENT

Play "Red Light! Green Light!" (Appendix p. 366).
Sing "Five Little Speckled Frogs" (Appendix p. 286) or "Over in the Meadow" (Appendix p. 298).

*If children have lunch at school, think about serving a "green meal." You might have green eggs and ham, green gelatin, jalapeño jelly, green beans, spinach, green apples, or lime yogurt. You can add food coloring to mashed potatoes, fettuccini, or macaroni and cheese to make them green.

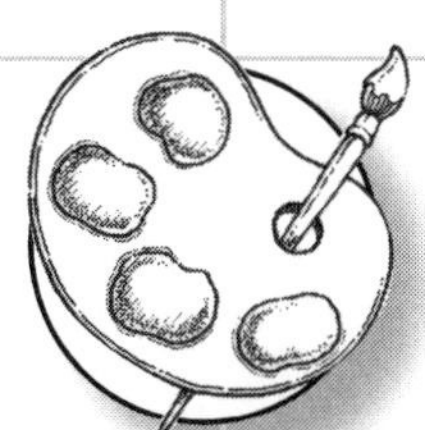

Art (Spatial)

Sponge paint with green tempera paint.

Dramatic Play (Interpersonal, Linguistic, Intrapersonal)

Provide props for acting out the story, *Green Eggs and Ham.* Discuss how it feels to have someone keep forcing something on you that you don't want.

Gross Motor (Bodily-Kinesthetic)

Cut large green lily pads and lay them on the floor a few feet apart. Encourage the children to leap from lily pad to lily pad like frogs.

Language (Musical)

Provide "Five Little Speckled Frogs" Puppets (Appendix p. 478) and encourage the children to move the frogs to the song "Five Little Speckled Frogs" (Appendix p. 286).

Science (Naturalist)

Sort a box of green leaves into as many categories as you can come up with, such as big/little, rough/smooth edges, big veins/little veins.

Snack (Logical-Mathematical)

Help the children prepare green eggs and ham or provide green cream cheese (food coloring and cream cheese) to spread on celery.

Closing Circle (Reflections on the Day)

Ask the children:

1. What would the world be like without green? What if everything was green?
2. What are some of the green things you saw today?

Purple

Morning Circle

1. Bring a large box to Morning Circle that is filled with purple things, such as crayons, scarves, shoes, or bows.
2. Encourage the children to find other purple things in the room and add them to the box.
3. Recite the poem, "I Never Saw a Purple Cow" (Appendix p. 321) with the children. Would it make a difference if the cow in the poem was orange instead of purple?
4. How does the color purple make you feel? Do you know someone whose favorite color is purple?
5. Tell the children that today's activities will be about the color purple.

Story Circle

"The Great Big Turnip" flannel board story (Appendix p. 336)

Harold and the Purple Crayon by Crockett Johnson

Mr. Pine's Purple House by Leonard Kessler

Purple by Mary Elizabeth Salzmann

A Purple Cow: How to Learn Colors by Betsy Lee

Purple Is Best by Dana Meachen Rau

Music and Movement

Invite the children to dance creatively with purple streamers to a favorite tune. If you can, locate a copy of "Purple People Eater"—it will tickle the children's funnybones.

Invite the children to make purple shadows outdoors with purple cellophane.

*If children have lunch at school, think about serving a purple lunch. You might serve grapes, grape juice, red cabbage, purple gelatin, or plums. You can add food coloring to fettuccini, eggs, mashed potatoes, and many other foods to make them purple.

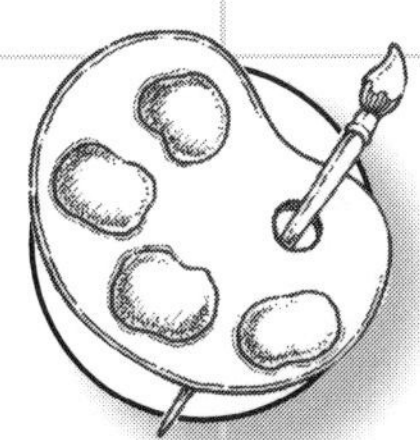

Art (Spatial, Linguistic, Intrapersonal)

Provide several shades of purple crayons and invite the children to create a picture from their own imagination. With permission, transcribe a description of what they have drawn on their picture.

Dramatic Play (Musical, Spatial, Interpersonal)

Cover flashlights with purple cellophane. Put on a piece of upbeat music and invite the children to work together to create a light show on the wall.

Math (Logical-Mathematical)

Provide several shades of purple crayons. Encourage the children to make patterns with the crayons.

Science (Naturalist)

Provide a flower catalog and encourage the children to circle the flowers that are purple. If you don't have a flower catalog, provide plastic or silk flowers to sort into categories of "purple" and "not purple."

Snack (Interpersonal, Linguistic, Logical-Mathematical)

Encourage the children to follow the rebus recipe to make Purple Cow Shakes (Appendix p. 372).

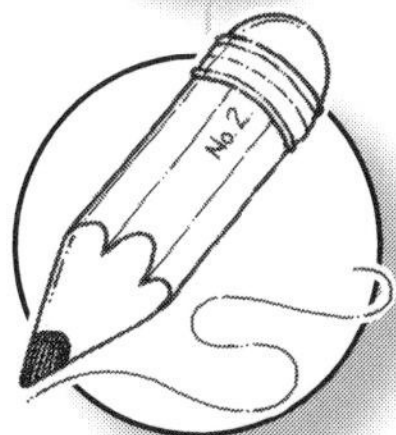

Writing (Linguistic)

Write the words "Purple Cow" on an index card. Encourage the children to use a purple crayon or marker to copy the words. Children who aren't comfortable making letters can draw a picture of a purple cow.

Closing Circle (Reflections on the Day)

Ask the children:

1. What have you learned about purple today?
2. In what ways is the color purple like the color blue?

ORANGE

MORNING CIRCLE

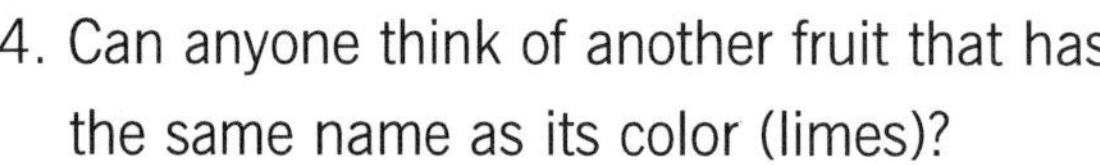

1. Bring a tray of oranges cut into wedges to the circle and allow each child to have one.
2. Ask the children to think of things that are made from oranges (gelatin, drinks, candy).
3. Encourage the children to find other orange things in the room. On a piece of chart paper, make a list of other things they find.
4. Can anyone think of another fruit that has the same name as its color (limes)?
5. (Optional) In the fall, include orange leaves and carving pumpkins in your activities.
6. Tell the children that today's activities will be about the color orange.

STORY CIRCLE

The Carrot Seed by Ruth Krauss
Each Orange Had 8 Slices by Paul Giganti
Just Enough Carrots by Stuart Murphy
Orange by Mary Elizabeth Salzmann
Orange in My World by Joanne Winne
Pumpkin, Pumpkin by Jeanne Titherington
Too Many Pumpkins by Linda White

MUSIC AND MOVEMENT

Play "Apple, Apple, Orange" as you would "Duck, Duck, Goose" (Appendix p. 359).

*If children have lunch at school, think about serving an orange lunch. You might have oranges, carrots, orange marmalade jelly, orange gelatin, orange yogurt, or orange juice.

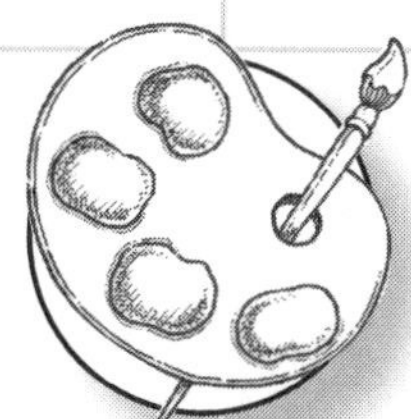

Art (Spatial, Musical, Interpersonal)

Cut the sides of a large box (approximately 24" x 30") to create a flat box with 2" - 3" sides. Cut a sheet of butcher paper to fit inside the bottom of the box. Place marbles that have been dipped in orange paint inside the box. Invite the children to work in pairs with one child holding each end of the box. Play music and have the children roll the marbles to the beat.

Dramatic Play (Interpersonal)

Provide orange playdough (Appendix p. 377) to roll into pumpkins and oranges. You may want to scent your playdough with allspice or with orange extract.

Gross Motor (Bodily-Kinesthetic, Linguistic)

Create a maze filled with orange detour signs. Invite the children to navigate the maze.

Gross Motor (Linguistic, Interpersonal)

Make construction zone signs for the block center. Encourage the children to create a building site.

Science (Naturalist, Logical-Mathematical)

Provide a variety of orange fruits and vegetables such as carrots, oranges, gourds, or pumpkins for the children to examine. You can add a balancing scale and magnifying glass to make the examination more interesting. You might also bring in a goldfish for observation.

Snack (Interpersonal)

Provide carrots and a peeler. Encourage the children to peel their carrot before eating it for snack. Or provide Gold Fish crackers and have children count out five fish to eat for snack. (Supervise closely at all times!)

Closing Circle (Reflections on the Day)

Ask the children:

1. What are some orange things?
2. Is orange a bright color or a dark color? Is it a hot color or a cool color?
3. What is your favorite orange thing? Why?

Black

Morning Circle

1. Dress in black and white.
2. Find black items in the classroom.
3. Sing or recite the fingerplay "Two Little Blackbirds" (Appendix p. 313).
4. Discuss phrases like "black as night," "black cats are bad luck," "black-balled," and "bad guys wear black hats."
5. Discuss the perception that black has a negative or bad connotation (meaning).

   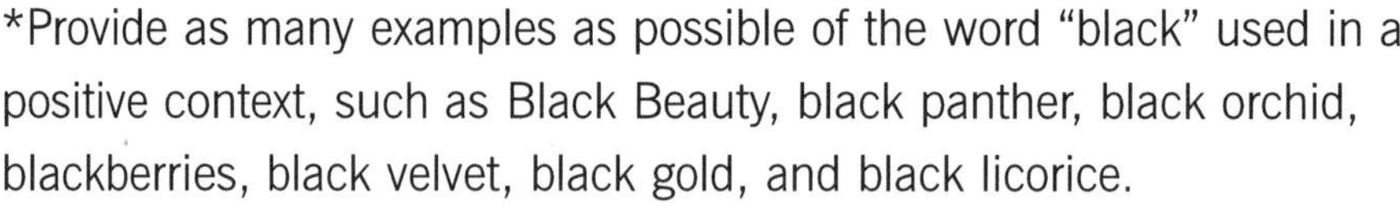

   *Provide as many examples as possible of the word "black" used in a positive context, such as Black Beauty, black panther, black orchid, blackberries, black velvet, black gold, and black licorice.
6. Teach the children the "I Like Black" cheer (Appendix p. 319).
7. Tell the children that today's activities will be about the color black.

Story Circle

Black and White Rabbit's ABC by Alan Baker

Black on White by Tana Hoban

Black, White, Just Right by Marguerite W. Davol

Blanco en Negro by Tana Hoban

Bold and Bright, Black-and-White Animals by Dorothy Hinshaw Patent

Ten Black Dots by Donald Crews

Music and Movement

Provide black scarves. Play "stormy" classical music. Suggest that the children pretend to be thunderclouds in a stormy sky.

Give the children black streamers and invite them to dance creatively to some heavy classical music.

Play "Drop the Handkerchief" (Appendix p. 358) using a black scarf.

Art (Spatial)

Encourage the children to make a color design on a piece of paper and then color over it with a black crayon. Provide toothpicks and show the children how to scratch a design on their picture.

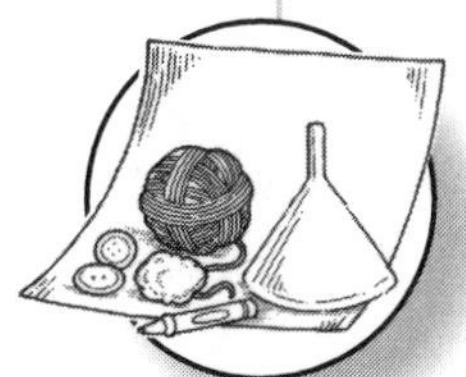

Discovery (Spatial, Logical-Mathematical)

Give the children 10 black dots. Encourage them to create a design or picture of their choice.

Gross Motor (Bodily-Kinesthetic)

Cover potato chip cans with black construction paper to make bowling pins. Provide a black ball for a bowling ball and encourage the children to try their hands at bowling.

Language (Linguistic)

Provide children's magazines or newspaper comic strips. Encourage the children to use black crayons to circle words they recognize.

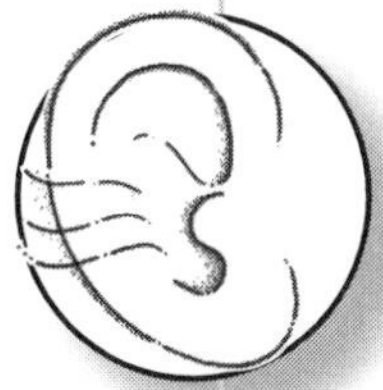

Listening (Musical)

Provide stormy weather (environmental) music for the children. Ask the children how the music makes them feel.

Math (Spatial, Logical-Mathematical, Intrapersonal)

Provide black paper cut into strips, squares, circles, triangles, and squiggles. Encourage the children to arrange the cutouts on white paper to make a design.

Learning Centers

Closing Circle (Reflections on the Day)

Ask the children:

1. What new thing have you learned about the color black today?
2. Is there anything that is black that you haven't thought of before?
3. What would the world be like without the color black?

White

Morning Circle

1. Hold Morning Circle outdoors if weather permits. Have the children lie on their backs and watch the clouds in the sky. Look for shapes that resemble familiar objects. Play music if you have a battery-powered tape or CD player.
2. Look for other white things outdoors.
3. Encourage the children to brainstorm a list of white things that might be seen outdoors.
4. Discuss how the color white makes you feel.
5. Tell the children that today's activities will be about the color white.

Story Circle

Frosty the Snowman flannel board patterns and song (Traditional) (Appendix p. 418 and 287)

It Looked Like Spilt Milk by Charles Shaw

Little White Dog by Laura Godwin

White in My World by Joanne Winne

White on Black by Tana Hoban

Music and Movement

Use a large white sheet as a parachute and play parachute games or just toss a ball up and down in the sheet.

Fold paper into fans and do a fan dance to soft music.

*If children are at school for lunchtime you can serve a white meal. You might have mashed potatoes, fettuccini, milk, pudding, or rice.

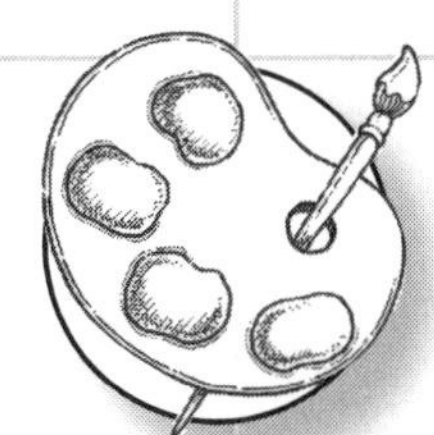

Art (Spatial, Musical, Intrapersonal)

Provide Puff Paint (Appendix p. 377). Encourage the children to fingerpaint with the fluffy paint. Play music while they paint.

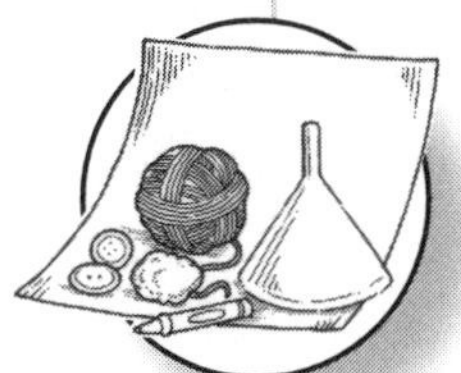

Discovery (Naturalist)

Provide a box of white items such as a tissue, Styrofoam chips, cotton ball, piece of paper, button, scarf, string, crayon, and feather. Invite the children to experiment with the items to see which ones float when they are dropped and which ones just drop.

Fine Motor (Linguistic, Logical-Mathematical, Interpersonal)

Invite the children to help you make a recipe of Gak using a rebus chart (Appendix p. 492). When the Gak is ready, invite the children to play with it.

Gross Motor (Bodily-Kinesthetic)

Provide cotton balls and a bowl. Challenge the children to toss the cotton balls into the bowl.

Language (Spatial, Interpersonal)

Provide several different shapes cut from white pelon or felt. Encourage the children to create a cloudy sky by placing the cutouts on a large piece of blue or black felt.

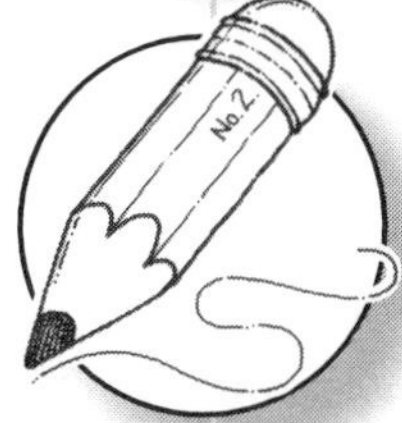

Writing (Linguistic)

Provide a tray of salt. Encourage the children to use their fingers to make letters or designs in the salt.

Closing Circle (Reflections on the Day)

Ask the children:

1. What have you learned about the color white today?
2. What is your favorite white thing? Why?

Pink

Morning Circle

1. Hang pink crepe paper streamers over the door where children enter the classroom or cut a large heart out of the middle of a pink sheet and hang it over the door. Invite the children to enter the room through the crepe paper or through the heart.
2. Play "I Spy" (Appendix p. 362), focusing on pink things.
3. Recite the chant, "I Love Pink Bubble Gum" (Appendix p. 320) with the children.
4. Point out that when babies are born, their birth announcements and clothes are often chosen using pink to designate a girl and blue for a boy. Discuss the traditional view that pink is for girls and blue is for boys. Ask the children what they think about the color designation.
5. What does it mean when people say they are "tickled pink"?
6. Tell the children that today's activities will be about the color pink.

Story Circle

First Pink Light by Eloise Greenfield
Hannah and the Pink Balloon by Mary Beckett
Little Pink Ballerina by Ronne Randall
Little Pink Pig by Pat Hutchins
The Pink House by Kate Salley Palmer
Pink Is Perfect for Pigs by Barbara and Cindy Ruiter
Think Pink by Olga Cossi and Lea Anne Clarke
What Is Pink? by Christina Rossetti

Music and Movement

Provide pink cellophane and encourage children to create pink shadows on the playground.

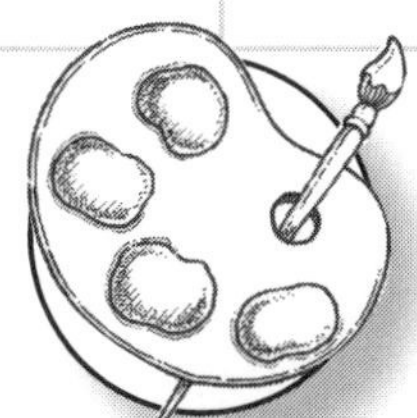

ART (Spatial)

Fill a shallow tub with water and detergent. Add approximately three tablespoons of pink tempera paint and beat with a hand beater or whip to create large bubbles. Invite the children to press their papers on top of the bubbles to create a pink bubble gum picture.

DRAMATIC PLAY (Spatial, Interpersonal)

Provide pink peppermint-scented playdough (Appendix p. 377) and encourage the children to create confections.

FINE MOTOR (Bodily-Kinesthetic)

Teach the children how to make pink pig tails either by using a pair of scissors to curl pink paper ribbon or by twisting a pink pipe cleaner around a pencil. (Supervise closely at all times!)

LANGUAGE (Interpersonal, Musical, Intrapersonal, Linguistic)

Using the patterns, provide Pig and Wolf Puppets (Appendix p. 488). Encourage the children to create a musical version of *The Three Little Pigs*.

MATH (Logical-Mathematical)

Cut pink construction paper to look like several different sizes of pink cotton candy. Roll brown construction paper to look like sticks and glue the "candy" to the sticks. Encourage the children to arrange the candy from smallest to largest.

SNACK (Interpersonal, Linguistic)

Invite the children to make pink Peppermint Baggie Ice Cream. Provide rebus directions (Appendix p. 496).

Closing Circle (Reflections on the Day)

Ask the children:

1. What was your favorite activity today? Why?
2. Of all the colors we have studied, which one do you think is most like pink? Why?

Brown

Morning Circle

1. Build a tunnel with large cardboard boxes for the children to crawl through to enter the classroom.
2. Have the children look at each other for articles of brown clothing, hair, or eyes.
3. Look around the room for other brown things. Make a list of the items the children find on chart paper or a chalkboard.
4. Sing "I'm a Little Acorn Brown" (Appendix p. 291). Talk about other brown things in nature.
5. Tell the children that today's activities will be about the color brown.

Story Circle

"Brown Bear, Brown Bear" story cards (Appendix p. 458-460)

Brown Bear, Brown Bear, What Do You See? by Bill Martin, Jr. and Eric Carle

Moo, Moo, Brown Cow by Jacki Wood

We're Going on a Bear Hunt by Michael Rosen

Music and Movement

Act out "Going on a Bear Hunt" (Appendix p. 317).

Go on a nature hike and look for brown things.

Sing "There Once Were Three Brown Bears" (Appendix p. 302).

Art (Spatial)

Provide watercolors, brushes, and paper. Encourage the children to mix all the colors together. What color do they get?

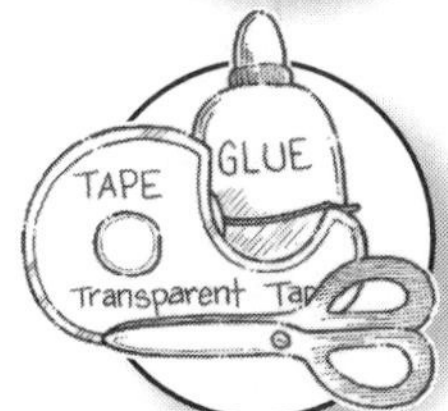

Construction (Spatial, Interpersonal, Intrapersonal)

Provide brown cardboard boxes for building.

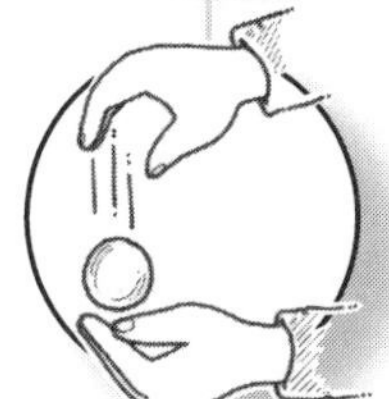

Fine Motor (Interpersonal)

Invite the children to help mix up a recipe of Peanut Butter Playdough (Appendix p. 374). Let the children play with their dough and then eat it when they are finished. (Check for allergies)

Gross Motor (Bodily-Kinesthetic)

Give the children a bowl of acorns. Have them remove their shoes and use their toes to remove the acorns from the bowl and drop them into a box.

Math (Logical-Mathematical, Linguistic)

Invite the children to tell the story of "Goldilocks and the Three Bears" (Appendix p. 421-425) on the flannel board. Challenge them to arrange bears, bowls, chairs, and beds in small to large order.

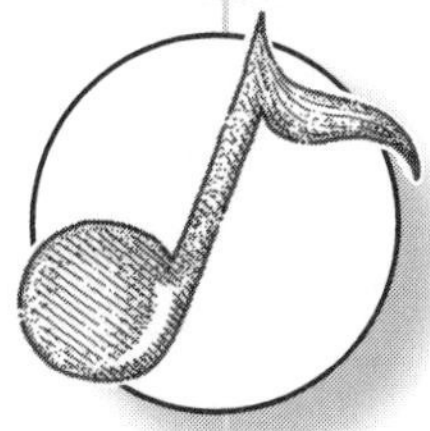

Music (Musical, Intrapersonal)

Provide cardboard boxes (drums) and wooden spoons (drumsticks). Encourage the children to play their drums.

Closing Circle (Reflections on the Day)

Ask the children:

1. What brown things have you played with today?
2. What is your favorite brown thing? Why?

Assessment for "Colors all Around"

Intellectual Strength	Assessment
Linguistic	Hold up construction paper squares or circles and ask the children to make up a sentence using the color of the square (or circle) in the sentence. For example, they may say, "My friend, Gabrielle, has a pretty red dress" or "I like red roses."
Spatial	Invite the children to paint a red dog, yellow flower, blue house, green sun, purple cloud, and orange person. Make up any items that seem interesting to the children.
Musical	Invite the children to sing "If You're Happy and You Know It" (Appendix p. 290). Instead of clapping their hands, stomping their feet, or other suggested movement, have them point to objects of each color they have learned.
Interpersonal Bodily-Kinesthetic Logical-Mathematical	Create a human graph. Invite the children to interview their classmates to determine each friend's favorite color. Then place construction paper squares on the floor representing all colors and invite children stand behind their favorite color.
Intrapersonal	Challenge the children to think of a feeling that each color elicits or provide a list of feelings and invite children to assign a color to the feeling.
Naturalist	Encourage the children to identify an item in nature that is representative of each color. For example, the grass is green, apples are red, the sun is yellow, and so on.

Books Used in "Colors All Around"

A Purple Cow: How to Learn Colors by Betsy Lee
Black and White Rabbit's ABC by Alan Baker
Black on White by Tana Hoban
Black, White, Just Right by Marguerite W. Davol
Blanco en Negro by Tana Hoban
Blue Frogs by Margaret Campilonga
Blue Sea by Robert Kalan
Blueberries for Sal by Robert McCloskey
Bold and Bright, Black-and-White Animals by Dorothy Hinshaw Patent
Brown Bear, Brown Bear, What Do You See? by Bill Martin, Jr. and Eric Carle
The Carrot Seed by Ruth Krauss
Each Orange Had 8 Slices by Paul Giganti
First Pink Light by Eloise Greenfield
Fuzzy Yellow Ducklings by Matthew Van Fleet
Green by Mary Elizabeth Salzmann
Green Eggs and Ham by Dr. Seuss
The Green Giraffe by Margaret Campilonga
Green in My World Joanne Winne
Hannah and the Pink Balloon by Mary Beckett
Harold and the Purple Crayon by Crockett Johnson
Hello, Red Fox by Eric Carle
It Looked Like Spilt Milk by Charles Shaw
Just Enough Carrots by Stuart Murphy
Little Blue and Little Yellow by Leo Lionni
Little Pink Ballerina by Ronne Randall
Little Pink Pig by Pat Hutchins
The Little Red Hen (Traditional)
Little White Dog by Laura Godwin
Mary Lou Likes Blue by Lyn Hester
Mary Wore a Red Dress, Henry Wore Green Sneakers by Merle Peek
Moo, Moo, Brown Cow by Jacki Wood
Mr. Pine's Purple House by Leonard Kessler
Olmo the Blue Butterfly by Alma Flor Ada
Orange by Mary Elizabeth Salzmann
Orange in My World by Joanne Winne

The Pink House by Kate Salley Palmer
Pink Is Perfect for Pigs by Barbara and Cindy Ruiter
Pumpkin, Pumpkin by Jeanne Titherington
Purple by Mary Elizabeth Salzmann
Purple Is Best by Dana Meachen Rau
Red by Mary Elizabeth Salzmann
Red in My World by Joanne Winne
Ted in a Red Bed by Jenny Tyler
Ten Black Dots by Donald Crews
Think Pink by Olga Cossi and Lea Anne Clarke
Too Many Pumpkins by Linda White
We're Going on a Bear Hunt by Michael Rosen
What Is Pink? by Christina Rossetti
White in My World by Joanne Winne
White on Black by Tana Hoban
Who Said Red? by Mary Serfozo
Yellow by Mary Elizabeth Salzmann
Yellow in My World by Joanne Winne
The Yellow Lion by Margaret Camplilonga

Other Books About Colors

Color by Ruth Heller
Color Dance by Ann Jonas
A Color of His Own by Leo Lionni
Growing Colors by Bruce McMillan
Is It Red? Is It Blue? Is It Yellow? by Tana Hoban
Mouse Magic by Ellen Stoll Walsh
Mouse Paint by Ellen Stoll Walsh
My Crayons Talk by Patricia Hubbard
Nature's Paintbrush: The Patterns and Colors Around You by Susan Stockdale
Of Colors and Things by Tana Hoban
Planting a Rainbow by Lois Ehlert
A Song of Colors by Judy Hindley

The Shape of Things

Circles

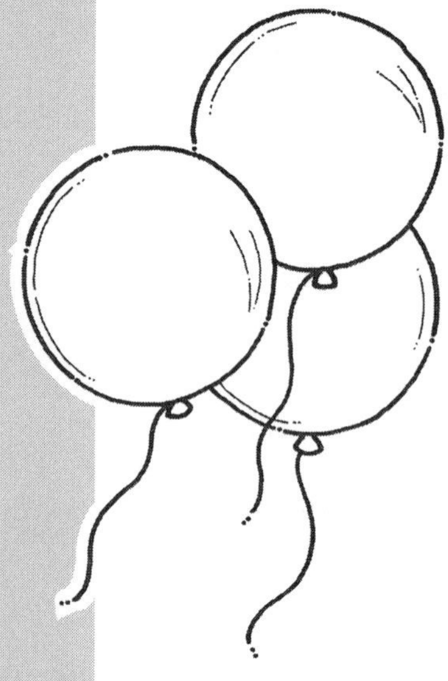

Morning Circle

1. Make a big masking tape circle in the Morning Circle area and encourage the children to sit on it when they come to the circle.
2. Have the children stand and hold hands. Encourage them to look at the shape they are making. Ask if they know the name of the shape. Tell them that a circle is a shape that is made up of curved lines and that circles have no sides or corners.
3. Sing "The Wheels on the Bus" (Appendix p. 306) with the children.
4. Invite the children to make circles with their individual bodies. They can make a circle with their arms or with their fingers. They can also make a circle with their whole body if they so choose.
5. Look for circles in the classroom. On chart paper, make a list of what you find.
6. Tell the children that today's activities will be about circles.

Story Circle

Alphonse Knows . . . a Circle Is Not a Valentine by H. Werner Zimmermann
Circles by Janie Spaht Gill
Circles by Jennifer Burke
If You Give a Mouse a Cookie by Laura Joffe Numeroff (circular story)
Round, Round, Round by Tana Hoban
"Smart Cookie's Best Friend, Greta Graham" flannel board story (Appendix p. 343)
The Wheels on the Bus by Paul O. Zelinsky

Music and Movement

Play "Circle 'Round the Zero" (Appendix p. 357) or "Ring Around the Rosie" (Appendix p. 367).
Dance with streamers and twirl them in circles.
Play any circle game.
Play with hula hoops.
Play with a Pendulum (Appendix p. 398). See if children can make different shapes on the floor by guiding the swing of the pendulum.

*If children have lunch at school, think about serving a "circular" meal. You might have hamburgers, round pasta, apples sliced horizontally, banana slices or grapes, and round cookies.

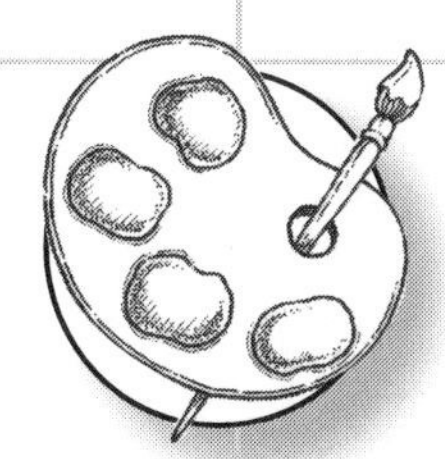

Art (Spatial)

Provide spools or large-size bubble wrap and tempera paint. Invite the children to make circle prints. Call attention to the shape of the spool and the shape of the print on the paper.

Discovery (Naturalist)

Give the children eyedroppers, water, and wax paper. Show them how to use the eyedropper to squeeze drops of water onto the wax paper. Provide a magnifying glass for an up-close look at the water circles.

Gross Motor (Naturalist, Logical-Mathematical, Bodily-Kinesthetic)

Provide several round objects such as an oatmeal box, bowl lids, a ball, and a paper plate. Also provide objects that are not round such as a book, a block, and a puzzle piece. Invite the children to predict which items will roll. Then have them test each item to see if it will roll. Ask them to sort the items into "will roll" and "will not roll." What do the items that roll have in common?

Language (Linguistic, Intrapersonal)

Give the children Circle Surprises (Appendix p. 385). Encourage them to open the circles one section at a time and use what they see to guess what the circle is.

Math (Logical-Mathematical, Naturalist)

Give the children pennies, nickels, dimes, and quarters to sort.
(Supervise closely at all times!)

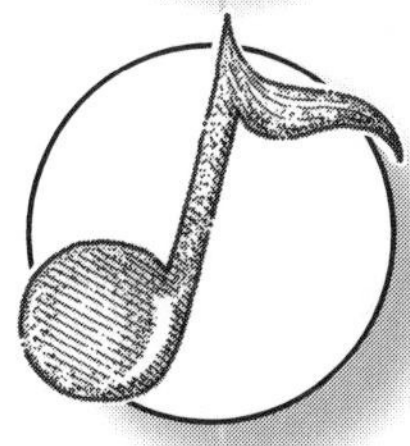

Music (Musical, Interpersonal)

Provide Music Makers (Appendix p. 395). Encourage the children to play the Music Makers to music. What shapes are the Music Makers? Make rhythm band instruments available to the children. Which instruments are circular?

Closing Circle (Reflections on the Day)

Ask the children:

1. What have you learned about circles today?
2. Which items were able to roll in your science experiment today? Why are they able to roll?

(Suggest children look for circles on the way home today. Suggest they start by looking at the outside of cars.)

Ovals

Morning Circle

1. Make a masking tape oval on the floor. When the children come to the circle, have them sit on the lines of the tape.
2. Have the children stand and hold hands. Encourage them to look at the shape they are making. Ask if they know the name of the shape. The children should say circle, which is a correct answer. Now tell the children that they are going to make a shape that is similar to a circle but is not a circle. Help them stretch their circle into an oval. Point out that an oval is similar to a circle because it is made up of curved lines and has no corners or sides, but it is different because it is not round like a circle.
3. Give the children a pipe cleaner and encourage them to shape it into an oval.
4. Teach the children "My Head" (Appendix p. 324). Point out that many people have faces that are oval-shaped.
5. Tell the children that today's activities will be about ovals.

Story Circle

Ovals by Jennifer Burke

Ovals: What Shape Is It? by Mary Elizabeth Salzmann

Music and Movement

Blow Bubbles (Appendix p. 375). Show the children how to blow slowly to create an oval before the bubble leaves the wand. What shape are the bubbles after they leave the wand?

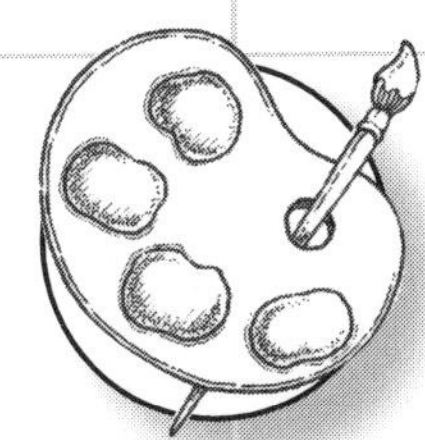

ART (Spatial)

Give the children playdough (Appendix p. 377). Have them roll the dough into snakes and then connect the ends to make first a circle and then an oval.

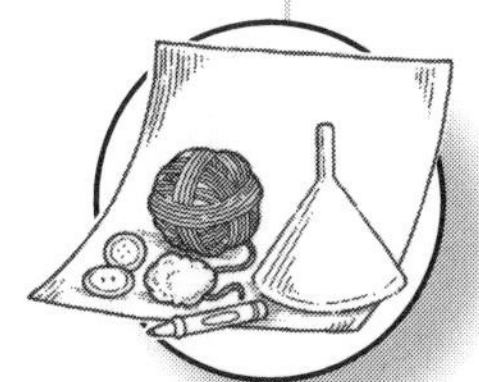

DISCOVERY (Musical, Linguistic)

Provide several small mirrors or one large one. Have the children look into the mirror and say "oo" and "o." What shapes do their mouths make for each sound?

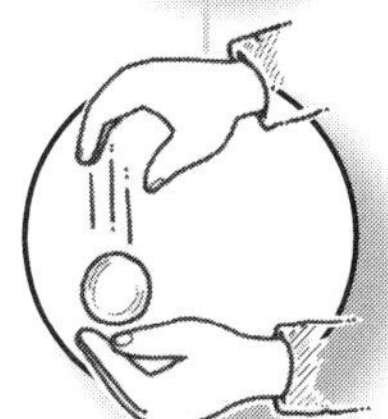

FINE MOTOR (Interpersonal, Spatial)

Encourage the children to string 1" pieces of straws onto yarn to make a necklace. Wrap masking tape around the needle end of the yarn to make stringing easier. When the children are finished, have them lay their necklace on the table as a circle and then change it to be an oval. How does it hang on their necks?

GROSS MOTOR (Bodily-Kinesthetic, Naturalist, Logical-Mathematical)

Give the children ovals and circles cut from poster board. Invite them to experiment rolling each shape. Which shape rolls the easiest?

LANGUAGE (Interpersonal, Spatial)

Cut ovals from pink and tan felt to represent faces. Provide a variety of felt eyes, mouths, noses, and ears. Invite the children to create a face.

WRITING (Linguistic, Bodily-Kinesthetic)

Provide a tray of sand or salt. Encourage children to use their index fingers to make ovals in the sand or salt. What letter of the alphabet looks like an oval? What number looks like an oval?

Closing Circle (Reflections on the Day)

Ask the children:

1. What have you learned about ovals today?
2. What new things have you learned about circles?
3. How are ovals and circles alike?

(Suggest that the children look for ovals at home.)

Rectangles

Morning Circle

1. Use masking tape to make a large rectangle on the floor. When the children come to the circle have them sit on the rectangle. Ask them if Morning Circle should now be called something else. What? (Morning Rectangle!)
2. Have the children stand to get a better feel for the rectangular shape of their seating arrangement. Tell them that a rectangle has four sides and four corners. Count them with the children.
3. Play "I Spy" (Appendix p. 362). Encourage the children to use only rectangular items in the game.
4. Encourage the children to select a partner. How many ways can they put their bodies together to make a rectangle?
5. Tell the children that today's activities will be about rectangles.

Story Circle

Rectangles by Jennifer Burke

"Smart Cookie's Best Friend, Greta Graham" flannel board story (Appendix p. 343)

Music and Movement

Go on a Shape Walk. Look for rectangles first; then look for circles and squares.

Recite "Window Watching" (Appendix p. 327).

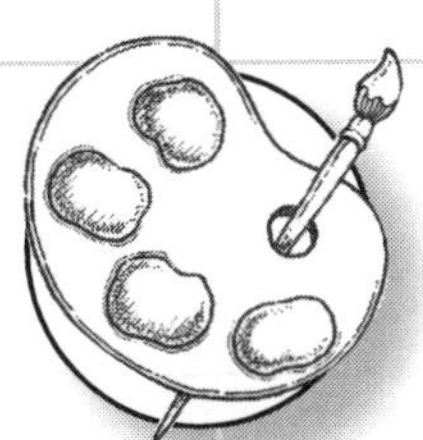

ART (SPATIAL)

Provide rectangles cut from different textures of sandpaper. Encourage the children to make rubbings.

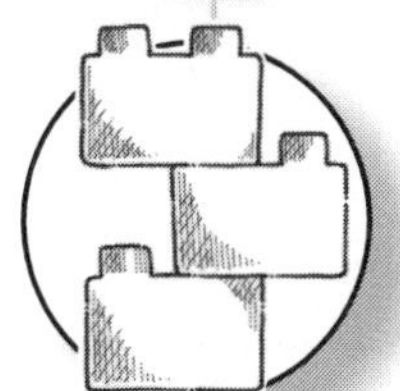

Blocks (SPATIAL, BODILY-KINESTHETIC, INTRAPERSONAL)

Challenge the children to build a structure using only the rectangular blocks.

DRAMATIC PLAY (LINGUISTIC, INTERPERSONAL)

Show the children how to make Animal Face Paper Bag Puppets (Appendix p. 381). Point out that the bodies of these puppets are rectangles. Invite them to create a puppet show using their puppets.

LANGUAGE (SPATIAL, LINGUISTIC)

Laminate magazine pictures or posters and then cut into puzzle pieces to create rectangular puzzles for the children to put together.

MATH (LOGICAL-MATHEMATICAL, NATURALIST)

Provided several rectangular boxes of varying sizes. Encourage the children to place the boxes inside each other.

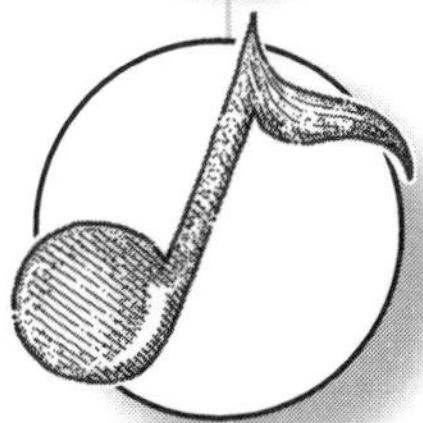

Music (MUSICAL)

Make a Shoebox Guitar (Appendix p. 400) with the children. Let the children experiment playing a tune on the guitar.

Closing Circle (Reflections on the Day)

Ask the children:

1. What have you learned about rectangles today?
2. Can you think of something in your room or home that is a rectangle (doorway, bed)?

(Suggest that the children look for rectangles on the way home from school today.)

Squares

Morning Circle

1. Use masking tape to make a large square on the floor. When the children enter the room, ask them to sit on the square.
2. Invite the children to stand up and look at the shape they are forming. Tell them that a square is a rectangle with four equal (same size) sides and four corners. Count the sides and corners. If children are old enough to understand, match the children one-to-one on all four sides of the square.
3. Say the rhyme, "A Square Is a Square" (Appendix p. 325) with the children.
4. Serve each child a graham cracker. Discuss its shape. You may want to start with a full cracker and have the children break the rectangle in half to make two squares.

5. Encourage the children to find squares in the classroom.
6. Tell the children that today's activities will be about squares.

Story Circle

So Many Circles, So Many Squares by Tana Hoban
Squares by Jennifer Burke
There's a Square by Mary Serfozo
What Is Square? by Rebecca Kai Dotlich

Music and Movement

Teach the children a simple Square Dance (Appendix p. 368).
Play Hopscotch (Appendix p. 361).

*If the children have lunch at school, think about serving a "square" meal. You might have a sandwich or ravioli, gelatin cut into squares, and graham crackers.

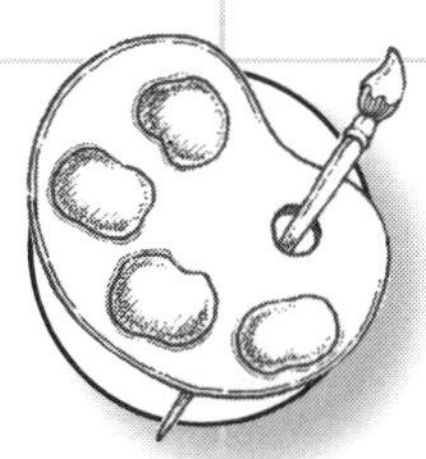

Art (Spatial)

Provide square-shaped stencils and encourage the children to make designs using the stencils.

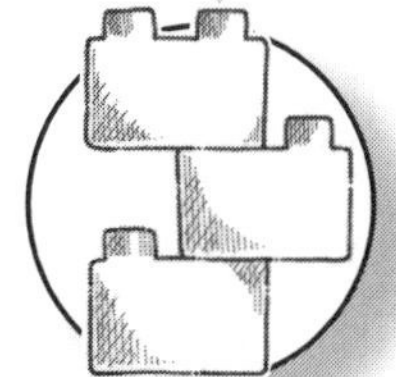

Blocks (Spatial, Interpersonal, Bodily-Kinesthetic)

Encourage the children to build a structure using only the square blocks.

Gross Motor (Bodily-Kinesthetic)

Provide square beanbags and a square box. Invite the children to toss the beanbags in the box.

Library (Linguistic)

Fill the library with square-shaped books such as *The Paper Bag Princess*, *Thomas' Snowsuit,* or *Moira's Birthday*. You may want to make blank square-shaped books. Encourage the children to draw illustrations for their square books, which were made using the directions for a Felt Book (Appendix p. 382) or Baggie Book (Appendix p. 382).

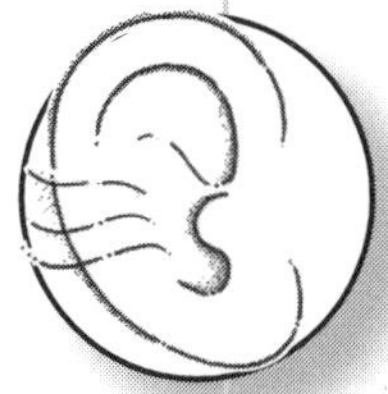

Listening (Musical)

Provide square boxes (with lids) and jingle bells. Encourage the children to make a musical instrument by placing the bells inside the boxes and shaking them.

Math (Logical-Mathematical)

Photocopy and enlarge photos of children. Cut them into a square and mount them on a piece of construction paper. Cut each photo into four smaller squares to create a square puzzle.

Closing Circle (Reflections on the Day)

Ask the children:

1. What have you learned about squares today?
2. What was your favorite activity today? Why?

(Suggest that children look for squares on their way home today.)

Triangles

Morning Circle

1. Place masking tape on the floor in a triangular shape. Encourage the children to sit on the triangle as they come to Morning Circle.
2. Invite the children to stand and take a look at the shape they are making. Tell them this is a triangle. Tell them that a triangle has three sides and three corners. Count the sides and corners with the children.
3. In advance, collect triangular objects including blocks, a Triangle (rhythm band instrument), triangular stencils, and triangle-shaped chips or crackers. Place the items in a box or a bag. Take the items out one at time to show them to the children. Lay each object on the floor in front of you after you have introduced it. Point out that each item has three sides and three corners.
4. Show the children how you can fold a square in half to make a triangle. Provide construction paper squares and invite the children to try folding their squares into a triangle.
5. Tell the children that today's activities will be about triangles.

Story Circle

"Tillie Triangle" chalk story (Appendix p. 352)
Triangles by Jennifer Burke

Music and Movement

Play the Hopscotch variation (Appendix p. 361).

Sing and do the motions to "My Hat, It Has Three Corners" (Appendix p. 297).

Show children how to build a Pyramid (Appendix p. 366). Make sure children are on a safe surface like the grass or a mat. (Supervise closely at all times!)

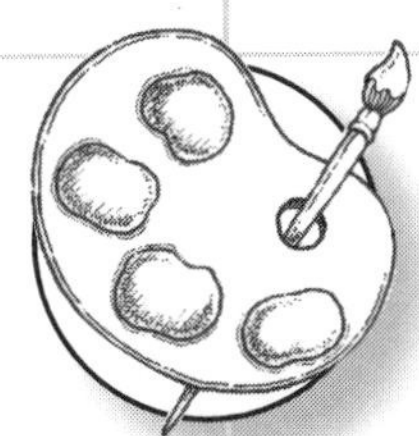

Art (Spatial)

Cut easel paper into triangles and encourage the children to paint a triangle picture.

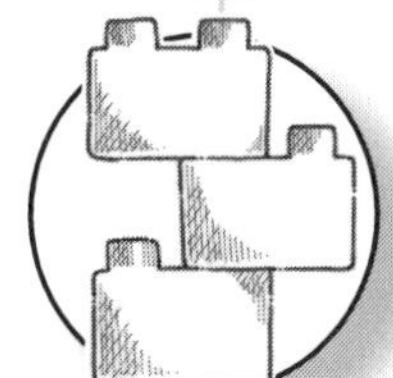

Blocks (Spatial, Interpersonal)

Challenge the children to build a structure using only the triangular blocks.

Discovery (Intrapersonal, Naturalist)

Encourage the children to arrange the picture cards on the "My Favorite Things" Pyramid (Appendix p. 531-532). Place the cards on the pyramid with their favorite activity on the top and the cards arranged from top to bottom by the degree to which they enjoy the activity. Lay a piece of yarn around the outside edges of the pyramid to illustrate the triangle shape.

Language (Linguistic)

Help the children to fill in the Story Pyramid (Appendix p. 538) for a familiar story.

Math (Logical-Mathematical, Musical)

Challenge the children to make up a pattern of sounds using triangles (instruments).

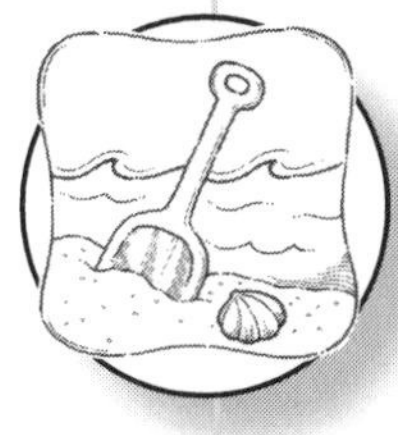

Sand and Water (Spatial, Bodily-Kinesthetic)

Provide Sand Combs (Appendix p. 400) with V-shape cuts. Encourage the children to make trails in the sand. Can they make triangles?

Learning Centers

Closing Circle (Reflections on the Day)

Ask the children:

1. What have you learned about triangles today?
2. What shape is a pizza? What shapes are the pieces when you cut them? (Suggest that children look for triangles at home tonight.)

Assessment for "The Shape of Things"

Intellectual Strength	Assessment
Linguistic	Hold up construction paper shapes and ask the children to make up a sentence using each shape. For example, they may say, "My friend, Austin, has a square block" or "I like circles."
Spatial	Invite the children to use playdough to shape a circle, oval, rectangle, square, and triangle.
Musical	Invite the children to sort through rhythm band instruments to find as many shapes as they can. For example, they may decide that a tambourine is circular, the triangle is triangular, or the harmonica is rectangular. Ask them which shapes are not represented by the rhythm instruments?
Interpersonal Bodily-Kinesthetic Logical-Mathematical Intrapersonal	Encourage the children to work in pairs to create a circle, oval, rectangle, square, and triangle with their bodies.
Naturalist	Encourage the children to sort and classify construction paper shapes into various colors and sizes.

Books

Books Used in "The Shape of Things"

Alphonse Knows . . . a Circle Is Not a Valentine by H. Werner Zimmermann
Circles by Janie Spaht Gill
Circles by Jennifer Burke
If You Give a Mouse a Cookie by Laura Joffe Numeroff (circular story)
Ovals by Jennifer Burke
Ovals: What Shape Is It? by Mary Elizabeth Salzmann
Rectangles by Jennifer Burke
Round, Round, Round by Tana Hoban
So Many Circles, So Many Squares by Tana Hoban
Squares by Jennifer Burke
There's a Square by Mary Serfozo
Triangles by Jennifer Burke
What Is Square? by Rebecca Kai Dotlich
The Wheels on the Bus by Paul O. Zelinsky

Other Books about Shapes

Book of Shapes by Christopher Santoro
Brian Wildsmith's 1, 2, 3's by Brian Wildsmith
Circles, Triangles, and Squares by Tana Hoban
Let's Look for Shapes by Bill Gillham
My First Book of Shapes by Eric Carle
My First Look at Shapes by Dorling Kindersley
Round Is a Moon Cake: A Book of Shapes by Roseanne Thong
Shape by Henry Pluckrose (editor)
The Shape of Me and Other Stuff by Dr. Seuss
Shapes by Dorling Kindersley (editor)
Shapes, Shapes, Shapes by Tana Hoban
What Shape? by Debbie MacKinnon

Sing a Song of Opposites

Big and Little

Morning Circle

1. Wear a pair of shoes that are too *big* for you as you greet children at the door.
2. When you move to Morning Circle, tell the children you are having a problem with your shoes. Ask them if they know what the problem might be.
3. When someone says that your shoes are too *big,* say, "Oh, my! I think you are right. May I try on one of your shoes?" When you can't get the shoe on your foot, ask again, "What's the problem?" When someone says that the shoe is too *little*, respond again, "Oh, my! I think you are right."
4. Ask children to help you think of things that are *big* and things that are *little*. Tell them that *big* and *little* refer to size.
5. Tell the children that today's activities will be about *big* and *little*.

Story Circle

Big by Keith Haring
Big and Little by Ruth Krauss
Big Dog, Little Dog by Margaret Wise Brown
Big Ones, Little Ones by Tana Hoban
Big Puppy and Little Puppy by Irma Black
George Shrinks by William Joyce
"Goldilocks and the Three Bears" flannel board story (Appendix p. 421-425)
"The Great Big Pumpkin" flannel board story (Appendix p. 426-427)
"The Great Big Turnip" flannel board story (Appendix p. 427-428)
Hey Little Ant by Phil and Hannah Hoose
I'm Too Small, You're Too Big by Judi Barrett
Is It Large? Is It Smaller? by Tana Hoban
"The Lion and the Mouse" (Appendix p. 338)
Too Little, Too Big by Colette Hellings

Music and Movement

Sing "Sing a Song of Opposites" (Appendix p. 301).
Have a Parade. Take big marching steps and little marching steps.
Play "Mother, May I?" (Appendix p. 364).
Play "One Elephant" (Appendix p. 365), recite "Big and Small" (Appendix p. 314), or sing "The Ants Go Marching" (Appendix p. 283).

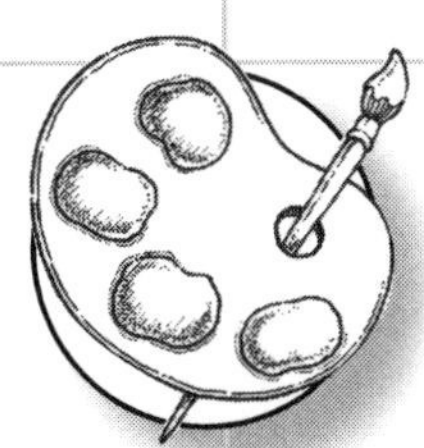

ART (SPATIAL)

Provide a *big* piece of easel paper and a *little* (3" x 3") piece of paper. Invite the children to draw a picture on each piece of paper.

LIBRARY (LINGUISTIC)

Invite the children to sort the library books into *big* books and *little* books. (You may want to pre-select books to sort.)

MATH (LOGICAL-MATHEMATICAL, BODILY-KINESTHETIC, NATURALIST)

Provide both *big* and *little* stringing beads. Challenge the children to create a necklace with a pattern, such as one *big* bead, one *little* bead pattern, and so on.

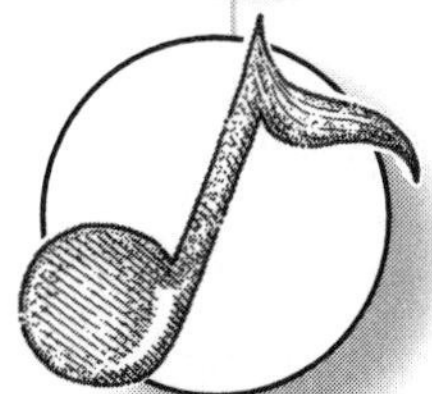

MUSIC (MUSICAL, BODILY-KINESTHETIC)

Make a Drum (Appendix p. 387) or provide one. Give the children *big* drumsticks, such as wooden spoons or tubes from coat hangers, and some *little* drumsticks, such as unsharpened pencils and paintbrushes.

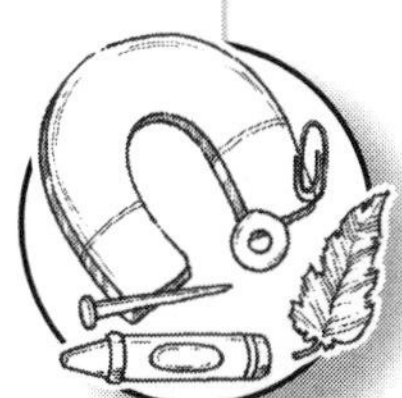

SCIENCE (NATURALIST)

Provide a pile of leaves. Encourage the children to sort the leaves into categories of *big* and *little*. If leaves are unavailable, supply assorted items such as different sizes of boxes, cans, tubes (toilet paper, paper towel, wrapping paper), and so on.

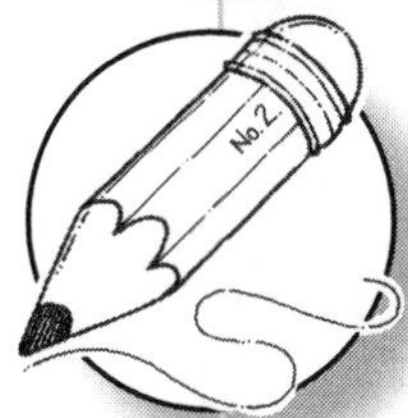

WRITING (INTERPERSONAL, INTRAPERSONAL, LINGUISTIC)

Challenge the children to think about how it feels to be an ant in a world of people. Invite them to draw a picture or dictate a sentence about how they decide it might feel.

LEARNING CENTERS

Closing Circle (Reflections on the Day)

Ask the children:

1. What have you learned today about *big* and *little*?
2. Which was the easiest piece of paper to draw on—the *big* sheet or the *little* sheet? Why?
3. Which drumsticks work best? What is the difference?
4. How do you think it feels to be an ant in the world of humans?

Tall and Short

Morning Circle

1. Before Morning Circle, gather pairs of *tall* and *short* items (for example, food boxes, bottles, blocks, and so on). Show them to the children. Use the *tall* and *short* verse from "Sing a Song of Opposites" (Appendix p. 301) to introduce each pair of items. Tell the children that *tall* and *short* refer to height.
2. Say and do the action rhyme, "Sometimes" (Appendix p. 325) with the children.
3. Tell the children that today's activities will be about *tall* and *short*.

Story Circle

I Am by Rita Milios
Jack and the Beanstalk (Traditional)
Mouse Tales by Arnold Lobel
Paul Bunyan by Steven Kellogg
Short and Tall (Animal Opposites) by Rod Theodorou and Carol Telford
Tall Bodies, Short Bodies, Everybody's Somebody by Mary Hollingsworth

Music and Movement

Take a walk outdoors and look for tall and short things.

Act out "I Measure Myself" (Appendix p. 321), "Tiny Seeds" (Appendix p. 326), or "Big and Small" (Appendix p. 314).

Sing "Where Is Thumbkin?" (Appendix p. 307).

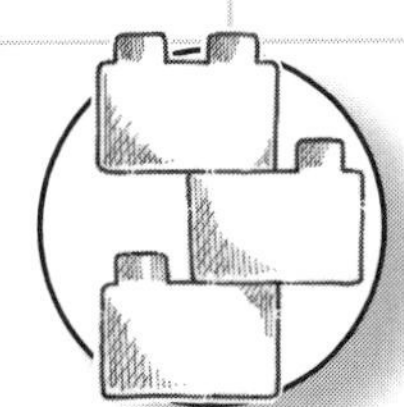

Blocks (Bodily-Kinesthetic, Spatial)

Build *tall* and *short* towers. Challenge the children to build a tower that is as *tall* as they are.

Discovery (Naturalist)

Give the children your pairs of *tall* and *short* items. Invite them to sort the items into pairs. Encourage them to search for other pairs of *tall* and *short* items.

Dramatic Play (Interpersonal, Intrapersonal)

Challenge the children to look at the furnishings in the center and think about which things might be good to adjust for *taller* or *shorter* heights (for example, chairs, mirrors, height of counters). Help the children make a list of things that might be nice to adjust to someone's height.

Language (Linguistic, Naturalist)

Encourage the children to line up lower-case magnetic or felt alphabet letters to determine which letters are *tall* and which are *short*.

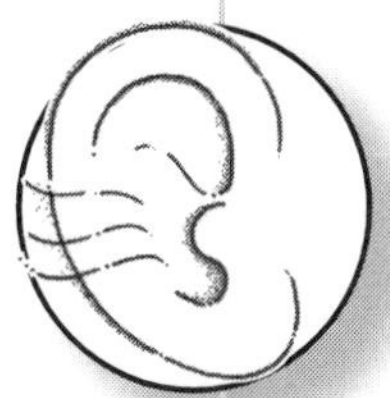

Listening (Musical)

Make *tall* (use paper towel tubes) and *short* (use toilet paper tubes) Kazoos (Appendix p. 392). Encourage the children to play both types of kazoos and determine if they hear a difference in the sounds made by each.

Science (Logical-Mathematical, Intrapersonal)

Measure the children to determine their height. Cut a streamer to the same length as their height measurement and challenge them to find something in the room that is as *tall* as they are.

Closing Circle (Reflections on the Day)

Ask the children:

1. Are there things in the dramatic play center that might be better at different heights?
2. Do the *tall* and *short* kazoos make different sounds?
3. What have you learned today about *tall* and *short*?

Long and Short

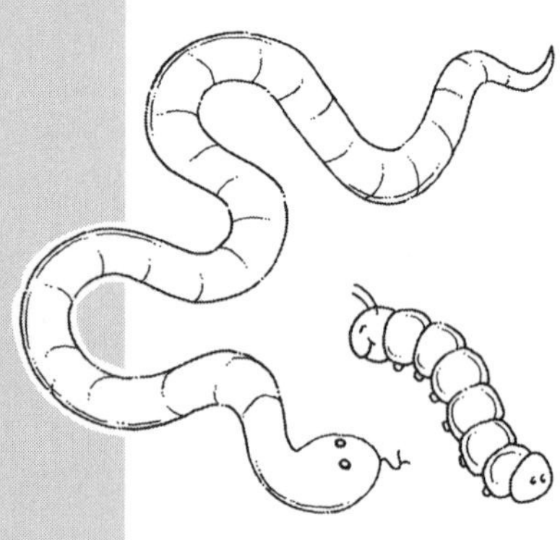

Morning Circle

1. Bring two pieces (or enough for everyone to sample a piece, if possible) of string licorice to the Morning Circle. If you can't find string licorice, you can use a licorice twist or a stick of hard candy. Make one piece *long* and the other noticeably *shorter.*
2. Ask the children which piece of candy they would choose if you offered it to them. They will likely all choose the *longer* piece. Ask them why.
3. Discuss *long* and *short*. Tell the children that *long* and *short* refer to length. Look for things in the classroom that are *long* and/or *short.*
4. Teach the children how to draw for straws. Make several of the straws *short*.
5. Encourage the children to measure their straws against their classmates' straws and to divide themselves into groups based on the size of their straws. Which group has the *longer* straws? Explain how this game is used to decide which member or members of a group will do a specific task. Use the game during the day if you need to select someone for a specific task.
6. Tell the children that today's activities will be about *long* and *short* things.

Story Circle

"The Lion's Haircut" prop story (Appendix p. 339)
The Long and Short of It by Cheryl Nathan and Lisa McCourt
The Long and Short of Mother Goose: The Long Book by Beverly Smith
The Long and Short of Mother Goose: The Short Book by Beverly Smith
Mop Top by Don Freeman
"The Strange Visitor" prop story (Appendix p. 346)

Music and Movement

Sing a long song such as, "The Green Grass Grew All Around" (Appendix p. 288) and a short song such as, "Make New Friends" (Appendix p. 294).

Sing "Where, Oh Where, Has My Little Dog Gone?" (Appendix p. 307) or "Sing a Song of Opposites" (Appendix p. 301).

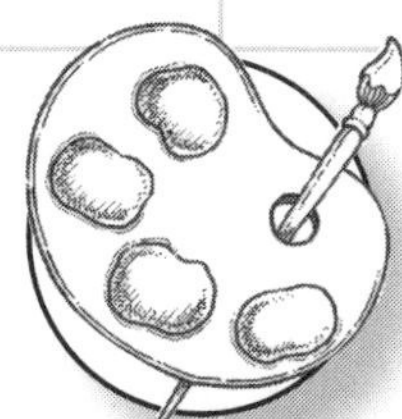

ART (SPATIAL)

Provide *long* and *short* brushes for the children to use to paint.

DRAMATIC PLAY (INTERPERSONAL)

Give the children *long* and *short* Pantyhose Wigs (Appendix p. 396) to play with.

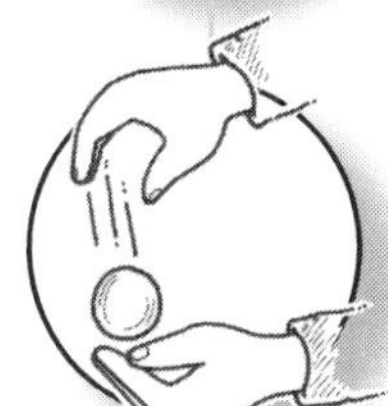

FINE MOTOR (BODILY-KINESTIC, INTERPERSONAL, INTRAPERSONAL)

Provide playdough (Appendix p. 377) and show the children how to roll long and short snakes. What other things can the children think of to make *long* and *short*?

LANGUAGE (LINGUISTIC, NATURALIST)

Write several *long* words (words with more than six letters) such as "Mississippi" and "supercalifragilisticexpialidocious" on sentence strips or large index cards and several *short* words (words with less than three letters) such as "a," "I," and "an" on sentence strips or index cards. Encourage the children to sort the words into stacks of *long* words and *short* words.

MATH (LOGICAL-MATHEMATICAL)

Provide long straws and short straws and encourage the children to sort them.

Give the children wrapping paper tubes, paper towel tubes, and toilet paper tubes. Ask them to stand the tubes up and arrange them from shortest to *longest*.

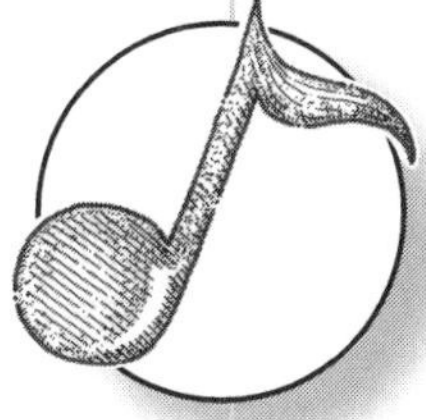

MUSIC (MUSICAL)

Make a Rubber Band Harp (Appendix p. 399). Encourage the children to listen for the differences between the *long* rubber bands and the *short* rubber bands. (SUPERVISE CLOSELY AT ALL TIMES!)

Closing Circle (Reflections on the Day)

Ask the children:

1. What have you learned about *long* and *short* today?
2. What things did you make from the playdough?
3. What is the *longest* word you found?
4. Can you think of a time when drawing straws might be a good way to decide who will do something (for example, clean up the block center, be the helper or leader for the day, and so on)?

Up and Down

Morning Circle

1. Let the children help you tell the story of "Mr. Wiggle and Mr. Waggle" (Appendix p. 341).
2. Ask them if they think Mr. Wiggle and Mr. Waggle get tired of going *up* and *down* the hills by their houses. Ask if any of the children have experienced going *up* and *down* a hill. If no one has experienced a hill, ask about steps. If there are steps close, you can let the children walk *up* and *down* them. Tell the children *up* and *down* are direction words.
3. Tell the children that today's activities are about *up* and *down*.

Story Circle

All Falling Down by Gene Zion
A Great Day for Up by Dr. Seuss
Inside, Outside, Upside Down by Stan and Jan Berenstain
Look Up, Look Down by Tana Hoban
Sun Up, Sun Down by Gail Gibbons
Up and Down on the Merry-Go-Round by Bill Martin, Jr. and John Archambault
Up, Up, Down by Robert Munsch
Ups and Down by Ethel S. Berkley
Upside Down by Crockett Johnson

Music and Movement

Sing "The Grand Old Duke of York" (Appendix p. 288). Discuss the up and down motion of the legs when marching.

Sing "Itsy Bitsy Spider" (Appendix p. 291), "London Bridge" (Appendix p. 293), "This Is the Way We Clean Our Teeth" (Appendix p. 303), or "My Little Red Wagon" (Appendix p. 297). Do the motions to "See-Saw Millie McGraw" (Appendix p. 325) or "Jack-in-the-Box" (Appendix p. 312).

Discovery (Bodily-Kinesthetic, Intrapersonal)

Provide Bubble Soap (Appendix p. 325). Invite children to blow bubbles and challenge them to find ways to keep the bubbles *up* in the air. How do you think the bubbles might feel, if they could feel, after they leave the wand?

Fine Motor (Bodily-Kinesthetic, Logical-Mathematical)

Tie a string to the ceiling. Challenge children to string beads *up* the string. Why do they keep falling back *down*?

Language (Linguistic, Naturalist)

Invite children to straighten the books in the library. Encourage them to check that all the books are placed on the shelf with the right side up.

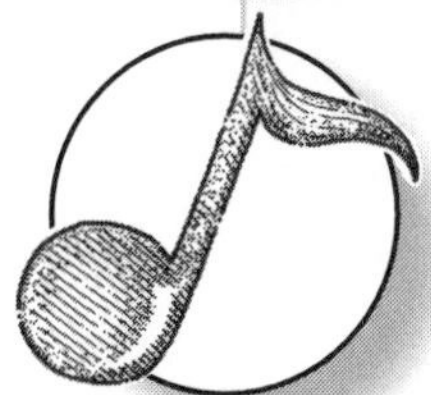

Music (Musical)

Position a xylophone in a vertical position. Invite the children to play notes *up* and *down* the xylophone. Position it in a horizontal position and invite the children to play notes *up* and *down* the scale.

Science (Logical-Mathematical)

Attach a pulley to ceiling. Use a rope to attach a bucket or a tub to the pulley. Invite children to put items in the pulley and raise it *up* and lower it *down*. (Supervise closely at all times!)

Snack (Spatial, Interpersonal)

Invite children to make toast in a toaster. Talk about how the toast goes *down* and pops back *up*. Provide jellies and sprinkles for children to decorate their toast before they eat it. (Check for allergies) (Supervise closely at all times!)

Learning Centers

Closing Circle (Reflections on the Day)

Ask the children:

1. What was your favorite activity today? Why?
2. What have you learned about *up* and *down*?
3. How did you keep the bubbles *up* in the air?

In and Out

Morning Circle

1. Play "Simon Says" (Appendix p. 368). Use only commands that include *in* and *out*. For example, put your finger *in* the air, breathe *in*, breathe *out*, stand *out* of the Circle, get *in* a line, put your finger *in* your ear, and so forth. Tell the children that *in* and *out* are position words. They tell us where something is.
2. Do the fingerplay, "Jack-in-the-Box" (Appendix p. 312) with the children.
3. Tell the children that today's activities will be about *in* and *out*.

Story Circle

Cat in the Hat by Dr. Seuss
Elephant Buttons by Noriko Ueno
Inside, Outside, Upside Down by Stan and Jan Berenstain
The Mitten by Jan Brett
Over in the Meadow by Ezra Jack Keats (illustrator)
What Lives in a Shell? by Kathleen Weidner Zoehfeld

Music and Movement

Move to "Go In and Out the Windows" (Appendix p. 360) or the Hokey Pokey (Appendix p. 361).

Sing "Sing a Song of Opposites" (Appendix p. 301).

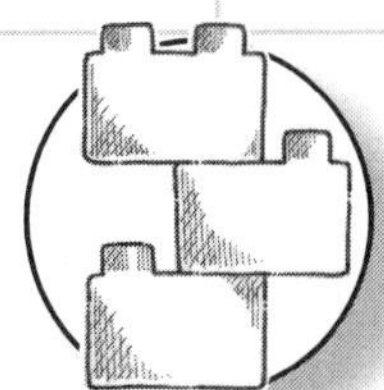

Blocks (Interpersonal, Bodily-Kinesthetic)

Provide trucks and invite the children to put blocks *in* (fill) the truck at one location and drive them to another location to take them *out* (unload).

Dramatic Play (Spatial)

Provide burlap, yarn, and large plastic needles. Show the children how to move the needle *in* and *out* of the fabric to sew a design.
(Supervise closely at all times!)

Gross Motor (Spatial, Bodily-Kinesthetic, Logical-Mathematical)

Provide rope, paper towel tubes, and toilet paper tubes to string. Challenge them to make a pattern of tubes on the rope. Talk about putting the string *in* one end of the tube and watching it come *out* the other end.

Language (Linguistic, Intrapersonal)

Challenge the children to draw a picture of or write a sentence about something that gets them *in* trouble. Have them turn their paper over and draw a picture of, or write a sentence about something that gets them *out* of trouble.

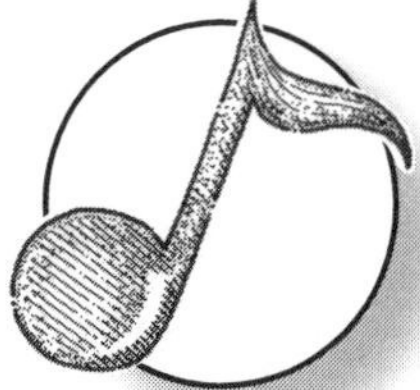

Music (Musical, Logical-Mathematical)

Try to teach the children to whistle. Can they whistle blowing both *in* and *out*?

Science (Naturalist)

Provide two boxes (approximately 8" x 11" in size). Draw a tree *in* the bottom of one box and leave the other as it is. Provide magazines and challenge the children to look for animals that live *in* trees and animals that don't live *in* trees. Invite the children to cut out the animals and sort them into the boxes.

Closing Circle (Reflections on the Day)

Ask the children:

1. What have you learned about *in* and *out* today?
2. Which animals live *in* trees?
3. Did you learn how to whistle?

Inside and Outside

Morning Circle

1. Bring an apple to Morning Circle. Invite the children to tell you everything about the *outside* of the apple that they can think of. It is red. It is round. It is shiny. It has a stem.
2. Ask the children what the apple looks like on the *inside*. Let them provide descriptions.
3. Let the children know that you have a special story for them about a surprise *inside* the apple. Tell the prop story, "A Special Surprise" (Appendix p. 344).
4. Explain that *inside* and *outside* are location words. They tell us where something is located.
5. Tell the children that today's activities will be about *outside* and *inside*. You may want to hold your centers *outside* today if weather permits.

Story Circle

Inside, Outside, Upside Down by Stan and Jan Berenstain

"There Was an Old Lady Who Swallowed a Fly" puppet story song (Appendix p. 302, 485-487)

Music and Movement

Encourage children to blow bubbles *inside* and then *outside*. What do they notice about how the bubbles move in the different locations?

Do the motions to "Inside Out" (Appendix p. 321).

Sing "Sing a Song of Opposites" (Appendix p. 301).

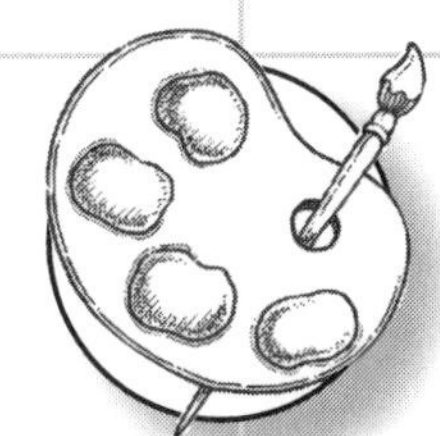

Art (Spatial, Intrapersonal)

Give the children a large cardboard box for a house. Encourage them to paint the *outside* of their house and decorate the *inside* of their house. Provide paint, carpet squares, and wallpaper samples.

Discovery (Logical-mathematical, Bodily-Kinesthetic)

Fill four empty coffee cans—two with heavy items, such as blocks and a can of food, and two with light items, such as paper and paperclips. Encourage the children to roll the cans down a ramp to determine which cans go faster—the ones with something heavy inside or the ones with something light inside.

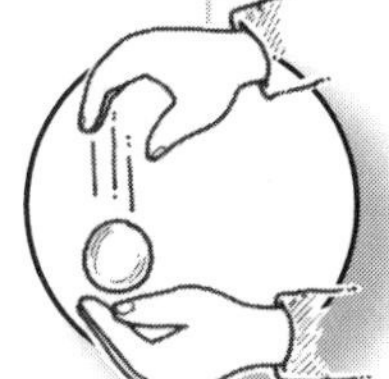

Fine Motor (Naturalist, Intrapersonal)

Encourage children to look through magazines for activities they can do *outside* and ones they can do *inside*. Have them cut out the pictures that they find and sort them into activities that can be done *inside*, *outside,* or both.

Library (Linguistic, Interpersonal)

Build a Sheet Tent or an Air Tent (Appendix p. 379) and let the children look at books *inside* the tent.

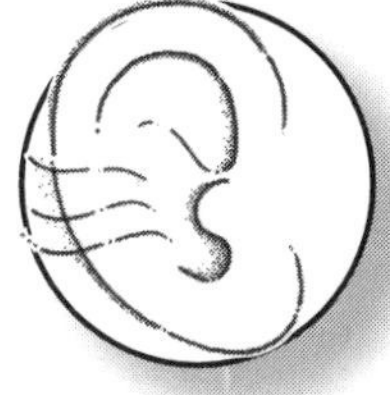

Listening (Music)

Cut a 1" - 1 ½" slice into three or four old tennis balls and fill them with noisemaking items such as jingle bells, gravel, paper clips, and buttons. Place a piece of masking tape or duct tape over the cut. Encourage the children to bounce the ball and guess what is *inside*.

Science (Naturalist, Interpersonal)

Provide a mirror and a flashlight. Encourage the children to look *inside* each other's mouths. What do they see? (Supervise closely at all times!)

Closing Circle (Reflections on the Day)

Ask the children:

1. What have you learned about *inside* and *outside* today?
2. Can you guess what is *inside* the rolling cans?
3. What's *inside* our mouths?

Over and Under

Morning Circle

1. Use pairs of chairs to make a pathway from your doorway to the Morning Circle. Tie crepe paper or yarn to each set of chairs. When the children arrive, have them follow the path, going *over* one piece of crepe paper/yarn and *under* the next until they arrive at the circle area.
2. Discuss the concept of *over* and *under*. You may want to demonstrate using a box and a beanbag. Place the beanbag *over* the box and then *under* the box. Let a volunteer assist you. Tell the children that *over* and *under* are both position and direction words.
3. Tell the children that today's activities will be about *over* and *under*.

Story Circle

The Good Bad Cat by Nancy Antle
Opposites by Tedd Arnold
Over the River and Through the Woods by Lydia Marie Child
Over, Under and Through, and Other Spatial Concepts by Tana Hoban
We're Going on a Bear Hunt by Michael Rosen

Music and Movement

Play "Follow the Leader" (Appendix p. 360). Use all the spatial concepts in the game but focus on *over* and *under.*

Act out "Going on a Bear Hunt" (Appendix p. 317).

Sing "The Bear Went Over the Mountain" (Appendix p. 284), "Over in the Meadow" (Appendix p. 298), or "Five Little Ducks" (Appendix p. 286).

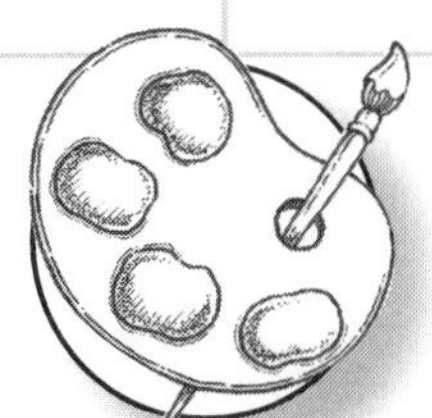

Art (Spatial, Bodily-Kinesthetic)

Tape a piece of drawing paper *under* the table and encourage the children to lie on their backs and draw a picture *under* the table.

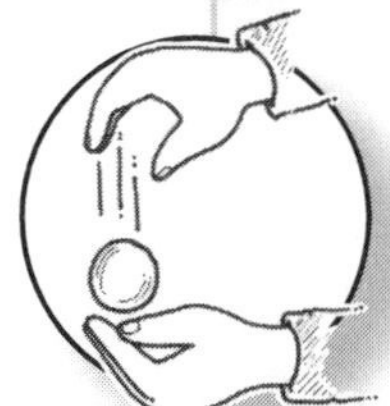

Fine Motor (Logical-Mathematical, Bodily-Kinesthetic, Naturalist)

Make a Meat Tray Loom or a Forked Branch Loom (Appendix p. 404). Encourage the children to weave lace, pipe cleaners, and ribbon into a pattern on the looms.

Gross Motor (Bodily-Kinesthetic, Intrapersonal)

Make a maze using yarns, sheets, boxes, and furniture. Ask the children to talk about going *over* and *under* the obstacles.

Gross Motor (Bodily-Kinesthetic, Intrapersonal, Interpersonal)

Play a game of Twister. If you don't have a commercial game, make one (Appendix p. 403).

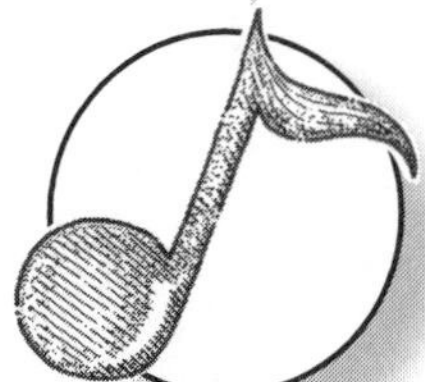

Music (Musical)

Give the children a music box or musical toy. Challenge them to listen to the music when it is placed *under* a box. Does the music sound different when it is heard out in the open?

Writing (Linguistic)

Provide tracing paper and a design to trace. Invite the children to place the tracing paper *over* the design and trace it.

Learning Centers

Closing Circle (Reflections on the Day)

Ask the children:

1. What was your favorite activity today? Why?
2. Does the music sound different when it comes from *under* the box?
3. How is drawing under the table different from drawing on top of the table?

Back and Front/ Backward and Forward

Morning Circle

1. Wear your clothes *backward* today. Invite the children to do the same. Discuss the *front* and *back* of clothing. How are they different? Do you ever accidentally put your clothes on *backward*? How can you tell the difference between the *front* and *back* of clothing? (check the labels, doesn't fit right)
2. Ask the children to stand. Have every other child turn around to create a pattern of facing *front*, facing *back*. Tell the children that *back* and *front* are description words. They are also both direction and position words. *Backward* and *forward* are direction words. They tell us which direction something is moving or facing.
3. Tell the children that today's activities will be about *front* and *back* and *backward* and *forward*.

Back

Front

Story Circle

Annos Counting House by Mitsumasa Anno
The Backward Day by Ruth Krauss
Backwards Day by Joan Holub
Becca Backward, Becca Frontward by Bruce McMillan
Front Frog Fred and Back Frog Jack by Mr. Sunshine
The Little Engine That Could by Wally Piper
Push, Pull, Empty, Full: A Book of Opposites by Tana Hoban
Thomas' Snowsuit by Robert Munsch

Music and Movement

Play "Circle 'Round the Zero" (Appendix p. 357).

Play "Simon Says" (Appendix p. 368). Ask "Simon" to use directions that include forward and backward.

Sing "Sing a Song of Opposites" (Appendix p. 301).

ART (Spatial)

Invite the children to draw a picture on the *front* of their paper and then turn their paper over to draw a picture on the *back* of their paper.

DRAMATIC PLAY (Intrapersonal, Interpersonal)

Provide dress-up clothes and invite children to try them on *backward.*

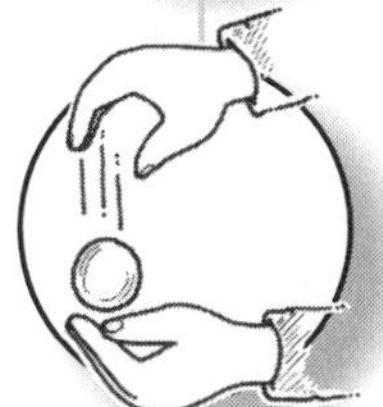

GROSS MOTOR (Bodily-Kinesthetic)

Provide a Bowling Game (Appendix p. 383). Invite the children to bowl facing *forward* and then facing *backward* (bending and rolling the ball through their legs). Which is easiest? Which is the most fun?

LANGUAGE (Linguistic)

Provide a book that can be read *front* to *back* and then turned over and read *back* to *front* such as *Wake Up and Good Night* by Charlotte Zolotow. Encourage the children to explore the book.

MATH (Logical-Mathematical)

Encourage the children to make patterns with puzzles pieces that are facing *forward* and *backward*.

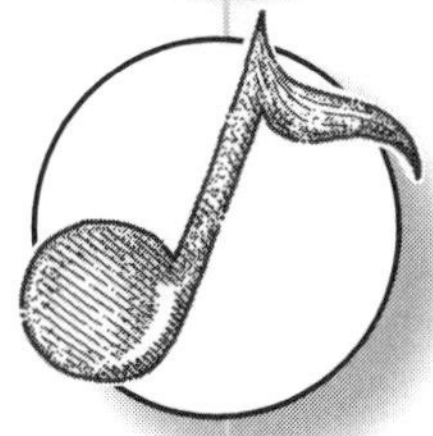

MUSIC (Musical, Naturalist)

Provide Two-Sided Frog Puppets (Appendix p. 475). Make up a story about Front Frog Fred and Back Frog Jack using the puppets. Create a frog song for the frogs to sing. Will they sing the same song or a different song? Who is Fred and who is Jack?

Closing Circle (Reflections on the Day)

Ask the children:

1. What was your favorite activity today? Why?
2. How did you do with the game of *backward* bowling? Which bowling is the easiest?
3. Who can sing the song that we made up for Fred and Jack?

Wide and Narrow/Fat and Skinny

Morning Circle

1. Hold Morning Circle with the children sitting in two parallel lines. Begin with the lines close together (with a *narrow* space between them). Have the children back up several steps to create a *wide* space between the lines. Tell the children that the space between them can also be described as *skinny* and *fat* or *narrow* and *wide*.
2. Sing "Five Fat Turkeys Are We" (Appendix p. 316) with the children.
3. Tell the children *wide* and *narrow* and *fat* and *skinny* are description (or descriptive) words. They describe things. Lay two red crayons that are different sizes (regular and chunky) on the floor in front of you. Ask someone to hand you a red crayon. When he hands you one of the crayons say you wanted the other one. Ask the children how you could have made sure you got the right crayon the first time you asked.
4. Ask the children to name *wide/fat* things and *narrow/skinny* things. Be aware that children may bring up body weight. If they do, explain that being called *fat* or *skinny* can hurt someone's feelings. (Note: Be especially sensitive if you have heavy and/or thin children in your class. You may want to use *wide* and *narrow* and not include *fat* and *skinny* in this lesson.)
5. Tell the children that today's activities will be about *wide/fat* and *narrow/skinny*.

Story Circle

Anansi's Narrow Waist: An African Folk Tale by Len Cabral
Dragon's Fat Cat by Dav Pilkey
Fat Cat Sat on the Mat by Nurit Karlin
Fat Cat: A Danish Folktale by Margaret Read MacDonald
"Fat Cat: A Danish Folktale" flannel board story (Appendix p. 333)
"Tillie Triangle" chalk story (Appendix p. 352)

Music and Movement

Play music and dance like *fat* animals (e.g., an elephant, hippo, and a gorilla), and then dance like *skinny* animals (e.g., an ant, a tiger, and a spider monkey).

Sing "My Dog Rags" (Appendix p. 296) or "Annie Mae" (Appendix p. 283).

Learning Centers

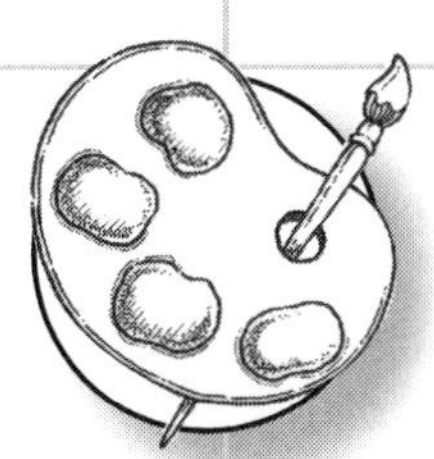

Art (Spatial, Logical-Mathematical)

Provide *wide* and *narrow* brushes and encourage the children to paint a pattern using the different brush widths. You may want to use thicker paint.

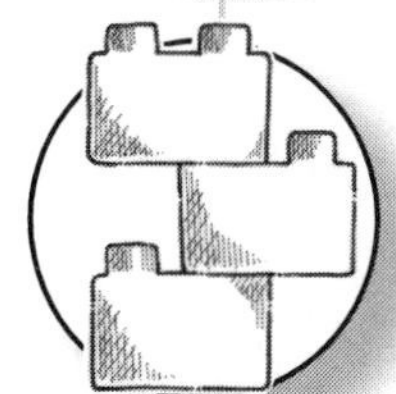

Blocks (Bodily-Kinesthetic, Naturalist)

Challenge the children to build *wide* and *narrow* streets and *wide* and *narrow* buildings. Encourage them to use cars on their roads and to think about the difference the size of the road might make to the drivers.

Language (Linguistic, Intrapersonal)

Give the children the "Fat Cat" flannel board story (Appendix p. 333, 411-417) and encourage them to retell the story. Ask them how they think the cat might feel about being called *fat*. Ask them how the old woman might feel about the way her cat behaved.

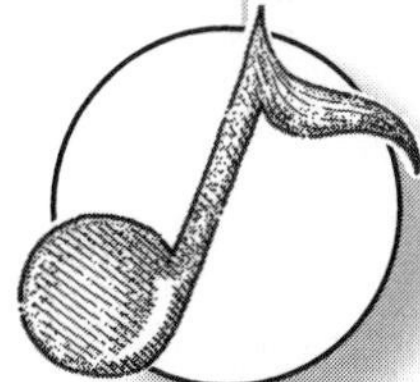

Music (Musical)

Let the children play with the xylophone. How are the sounds made by striking the bars on the *wide* end of the instrument different from the sounds made by striking the bars on the *narrow* end?

Snack (Interpersonal, Naturalist)

Provide *skinny* snacks such as pretzels and crackers, and *fat* snacks including fat pretzels and croutons. Encourage the children to sort and then eat the snacks.

Writing (Linguistic, Spatial)

Provide chunky crayons and regular crayons for the children to write with.

Closing Circle (Reflections on the Day)

Ask the children:

1. Do you like the story we heard today? Why? What was the funniest part?
2. What have you learned about *wide/fat* and *narrow/skinny*?

Day and Night

Morning Circle

1. Invite the children to come to school in their pajamas. Ask, "What is wrong with having your pajamas on now?"
2. Make a list of *night* things and *day* things. Tell the children that *day* and *night* are description words.
3. Ask the children what they think is the biggest difference between *day* and *night*.
4. Sing "Mister Sun" (Appendix p. 295) and "Mister Moon" (Appendix p. 295) with the children. Ask what things are alike in the songs and what things are different.
5. Tell the children that today's activities will be about *day* and *night*.

Story Circle

City Night by Eve Rice
Dark Day, Light Night by Jan Carr
Good Morning, Good Night by Michael Grejniec
Goodnight Moon by Margaret Wise Brown
Grandfather Twilight by Barbara Berger
Into the Napping House by Audrey Wood
It Looked Like Spilt Milk by Charles Shaw
The Napping House Wakes Up by Audrey Wood
Night in the Country by Cynthia Rylant
Owl Moon by Jane Yolen
Petey's Bedtime Story by Beverly Cleary
Shine Sun by Carol Greene
What the Sun Sees, What the Moon Sees by Nancy Tafuri

Music and Movement

Sing "Twinkle, Twinkle Little Star" (Appendix p. 306) or "Itsy Bitsy Spider" (Appendix p. 291).

Do morning exercises.

Take children outdoors in the sunlight to chase their shadows.

Sing "Sing a Song of Opposites" (Appendix p. 301).

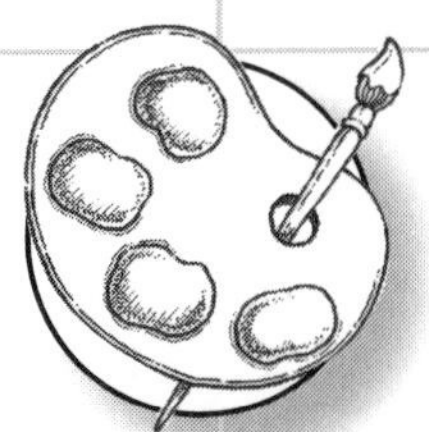

Art (Spatial, Intrapersonal)

Place white butcher paper on the top of a table shiny side up. Spray with shaving cream and invite the children to mix in blue tempera paint to create a blue (*day*) sky. Show them how to use their fingers to make designs (skywriting). (Supervise closely at all times!)

Fine Motor (Bodily-Kinesthetic)

Provide tweezers and rock salt (stars). Using a piece of black felt, encourage the children to use the tweezers to move the stars from a small bowl to the *night* sky.

Provide white chalk and a chalkboard and invite the children to design a *night* sky.

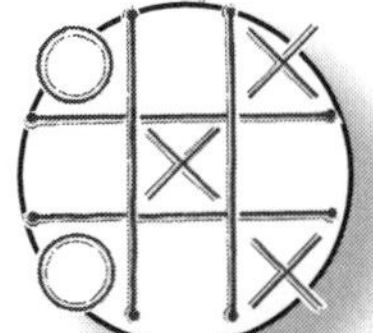

Games (Logical-Mathematical, Naturalist, Interpersonal)

Provide a large set of wiggle eyes. Have the children take turns tossing the eyes into a box. Are there more sleepy eyes (eyes facing down) or more wakeful eyes (eyes facing up)? Show the children how to match them one-to-one.

Language (Spatial)

Provide felt suns, clouds, moons, and stars. Encourage the children to create *night* skies and *day* skies.

Language (Linguistic, Intrapersonal)

Invite the children to make a list of things they like to do during the *day*, and a list of things they like to do at *night.* Transcribe their list into a book (folded sheets of drawing paper stapled together) and encourage them to illustrate the activities.

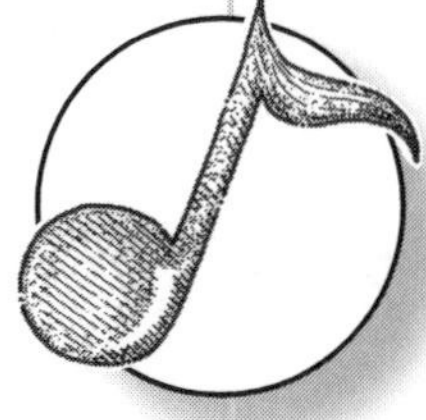

Music (Musical, Linguistic)

Provide lullabies for the children to listen to and bedtime storybooks for them to enjoy.

Closing Circle (Reflections on the Day)

Ask the children:

1. Do you enjoy the *day* or the *night* best? Why?
2. What is the first thing you think of when you think of the *day*? What about the *night*?
3. What was your favorite activity today? Why?

Assessment for "Sing a Song of Opposites"

Intellectual Strength	Assessment
Linguistic	Give the children several pairs of opposites and have them select a pair about which they can make up a story. Encourage them to record their stories or dictate their stories to you.
Spatial	Have the children fold a piece of drawing paper in half and draw pairs of opposites, one item on each side of the paper.
Musical	Have the children find concrete examples for all the verses (pairs of opposites) of "Sing a Song of Opposites" (Appendix p. 301).
Interpersonal Bodily-Kinesthetic	Have the children make up a new verse to "Hokey Pokey" (Appendix p. 361). Encourage them to describe all the opposites in the dance.
Logical-Mathematical	Give the children sets of three items and have them identify the two things in the set that make a pair of opposites.
Intrapersonal	Have the children identify two or three things about themselves and then point out a friend who is the opposite from each of the things they named.
Naturalist	Provide a basket of items that include several pairs of items that might be opposites. Encourage the children to make pairs of opposites from the items in the basket.

Books Used in "Sing a Song of Opposites"

A Great Day for Up by Dr. Seuss
All Falling Down by Gene Zion
Anansi's Narrow Waist: An African Folk Tale by Len Cabral
Annos Counting House by Mitsumasa Anno
The Backward Day by Ruth Krauss
Backwards Day by Joan Holub
Becca Backward, Becca Frontward by Bruce McMillan
Big and Little by Ruth Krauss
Big by Keith Haring
Big Dog, Little Dog by Margaret Wise Brown
Big Ones, Little Ones by Tana Hoban
Big Puppy and Little Puppy by Irma Black
Cat in the Hat by Dr. Seuss
City Night by Eve Rice
Dark Day, Light Night by Jan Carr
Dragon's Fat Cat by Dav Pilkey
Elephant Buttons by Noriko Ueno
Fat Cat Sat on the Mat by Nurit Karlin
Fat Cat: A Danish Folktale by Margaret Read MacDonald
Front Frog Fred and Back Frog Jack by Mr. Sunshine
George Shrinks by William Joyce
The Good Bad Cat by Nancy Antle
The Little Engine That Could by Wally Piper
Good Morning, Good Night by Michael Grejniec
Goodnight Moon by Margaret Wise Brown
Grandfather Twilight by Barbara Berger
Hey Little Ant by Phil and Hannah Hoose
I Am by Rita Milios
I'm Too Small, You're Too Big by Judi Barrett
Inside, Outside, Upside Down by Stan and Jan Berenstain
Into the Napping House by Audrey Wood
Is It Larger? Is It Smaller? by Tana Hoban
It Looked Like Spilt Milk by Charles Shaw
Jack and the Beanstalk (Traditional)
The Long and Short of It by Cheryl Nathan and Lisa McCourt
The Long and Short of Mother Goose: The Long Book by Beverly Smith
The Long and Short of Mother Goose: The Short Book by Beverly Smith
Look Up, Look Down by Tana Hoban
The Mitten by Jan Brett

Books

Mop Top by Don Freeman
Mouse Tales by Arnold Lobel
The Napping House Wakes Up by Audrey Wood
Night in the Country by Cynthia Rylant
Opposites by Tedd Arnold
Over in the Meadow by Ezra Jack Keats (illustrator)
Over the River and Through the Woods by Lydia Marie Child
Over, Under and Through, and Other Spatial Concepts by Tana Hoban
Owl Moon by Jane Yolen
Paul Bunyan by Steven Kellogg
Petey's Bedtime Story by Beverly Cleary
Push, Pull, Empty, Full: A Book of Opposites by Tana Hoban
Shine Sun by Carol Greene
Short and Tall (Animal Opposites) by Rod Theodorou and Carol Telford
Sun Up, Sun Down by Gail Gibbons
Tall Bodies, Short Bodies, Everybody's Somebody by Mary Hollingsworth
Thomas' Snowsuit by Robert Munsch
Too Little, Too Big by Colette Hellings
Up and Down on the Merry-Go-Round by Bill Martin, Jr. and John Archambault
Up, Up, Down by Robert Munsch
Ups and Down by Ethel S. Berkley
Upside Down by Crockett Johnson
We're Going on a Bear Hunt by Michael Rosen
What Lives in a Shell? by Kathleen Weidner Zoehfeld
What the Sun Sees, *What the Moon Sees* by Nancy Tafuri

Other Books About Opposites

The Best Bug Parade by Stuart Murphy
Colors, Shapes, and Sizes by Delores Bonwit
Exactly the Opposite by Tana Hoban
Fat Cat: A Danish Folktale by Jack Kent (out of print but available in libraries)
Green Eggs and Ham by Dr. Seuss
In and Out, Up and Down by Jim Henson (editor)
Opposites by Sandra Boynton
Up, Down, All Around; A Story About Opposites by Matt Mitter, et al

World of Animals

Dinosaurs

Morning Circle

1. Cut a dinosaur footprint (4' x 3') (1.2m x .9m) out of bulletin board paper. Lay it in the middle of the Morning Circle area. Explain to the children that the paper is the size of a brontosaurus' foot. Invite the children to see how many of them can stand inside the footprint.
2. Encourage the children to compare their foot to the dinosaur's foot.
3. Explain that a brontosaurus could grow to a length of 80' (24.4m). Convert 80' to the number of widths of the classroom. You may want to use a piece of yarn or string 80' long to demonstrate.
   - The brontosaurus was an herbivore (it ate plants and grass). Other dinosaurs, such as the Tyrannosaurus Rex, were carnivores (they ate meat).
   - See what other dinosaur names children know.
4. Ask the children to think of reasons why dinosaurs are extinct.
5. Tell the children that today's activities will be about dinosaurs.

Story Circle

Dinosaurs: All Shapes and Sizes by Sarah Corona
How Big Were the Dinosaurs? by Bernard Most

Music and Movement

Act out "Five Huge Dinosaurs" (Appendix p. 309).
Sing "One Elephant" (Appendix p. 365). Change the word "elephant" to "dinosaur."

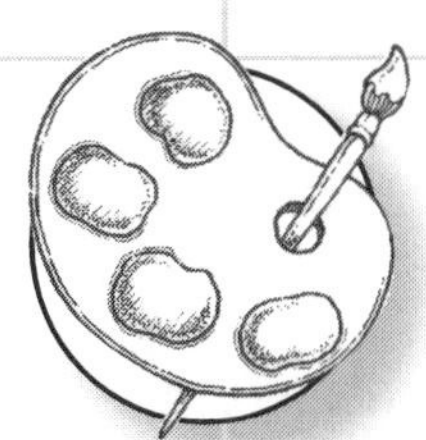

Art (Spatial, Intrapersonal)

Provide clay. Encourage the children to create dinosaurs and dinosaur eggs. Challenge them to create new specimens.

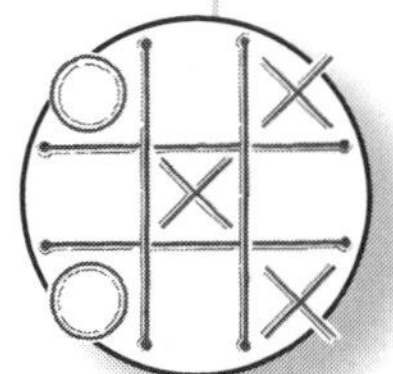

Games (Bodily-Kinesthetic, Interpersonal)

Use the Dinosaur Footprint from the Morning Circle activity to create a jumping game. Tape the footprint to the floor with masking tape, and use another piece of tape to make a starting line. Challenge the children to jump from the starting line into the dinosaur footprint. When they have mastered that activity, challenge them to try to jump over the footprint.

Math (Logical-Mathematical)

Match plastic dinosaurs one-to-one with dinosaur eggs (large plastic eggs).

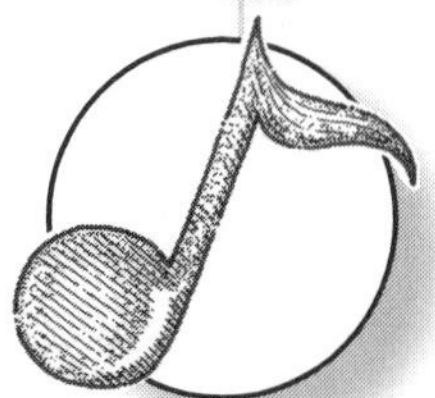

Music (Musical, Bodily-Kinesthetic)

Provide baritone music and invite the children to make up a dance called "The Dinosaur Romp."

Science (Naturalist)

Provide pictures of dinosaurs (some carnivorous and herbivorous). Invite the children to sort the dinosaurs according to diet.

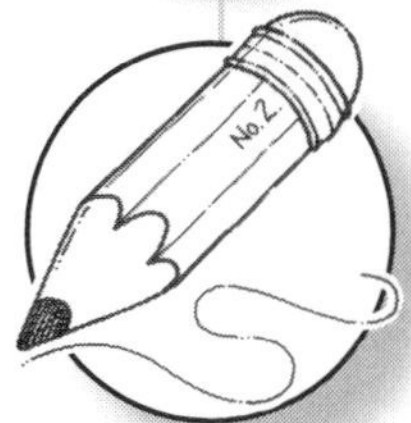

Writing (Linguistic)

Write the names of several dinosaurs on 4" x 6" index cards. Provide tracing paper and encourage the children to trace the dinosaur names.

Closing Circle (Reflections on the Day)

Ask the children:

1. What new thing have you learned about dinosaurs today?
2. Can someone show me "The Dinosaur Romp?"
3. Do you think there are any animals living today that are as large as dinosaurs were?

Big Mammals

Morning Circle

1. An adult elephant's foot size is typically 2' (.6m) in diameter. Cut a replica of an elephant's footprint from butcher paper. Place it on the floor beside the dinosaur's footprint.
2. When children come to Morning Circle, encourage them to compare the two footprints.
3. Tell the children that the elephant is the largest living land animal today. Male elephants (bulls) grow to be 9' to 13' (3 to 4.5m) high (at shoulders), will have ears that are 4' x 6' (2m x 1.5m) wide and will weigh 9,000 to 13,000 pounds (4,500 to 6,000kg). Female elephants (cows) will be slightly smaller—7' to 9' high at the shoulder and will weigh between 4,500 and 7,000 pounds (2,200 to 3,000kg).
4. Discuss how the elephant uses its trunk. The elephant's trunk is an elongated nose that the elephant uses for trumpeting, smelling, drinking, grasping, and communicating.
5. The blue whale is the largest living marine (water) animal. It is one of the most intelligent of all animals, although it has no sense of taste or smell and very poor eyesight. It depends on its sense of touch and sound for survival. The whale can grow to a length of 100' and can weigh 220 short tons (200 metric tons). Use a piece of yarn to demonstrate the length of the whale. Ask the children to compare the whale's length to the dinosaur's length (see p. 108).
6. The whale and the elephant are mammals (warm-blooded animals that nurse their young). Show pictures of elephants and whales.
7. Tell the children that today's activities will be about elephants and whales.

Story Circle

Blind Men and the Elephant by Karen Blackstein
Horton Hears a Who by Dr. Seuss
Horton Hatches an Egg by Dr. Seuss
Never Mail an Elephant by Mike Thaler
The Whales' Song by Dylan Sheldon
Whales: The Gentle Giants by Joyce Milton

Music and Movement

Sing and move to "One Elephant" (Appendix p. 365), "Going on a Whale Watch" (Appendix p. 317), or "The Elephant" (Appendix p. 315).

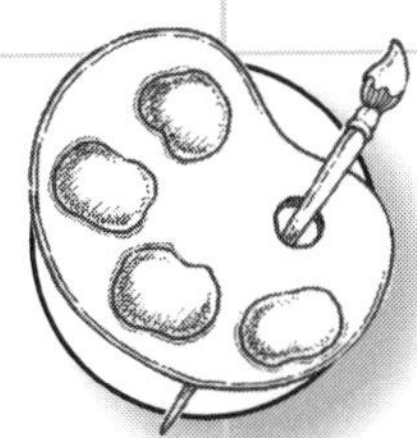

Art (Spatial, Intrapersonal, Linguistic)

Provide gray paint and invite the children to paint an elephant or a whale. Ask the children to think about what it would feel like to be gray, and invite them to dictate a sentence about their thoughts for you to transcribe onto the back of their pictures. If you have gray modeling clay, give it to the children and invite them to mold a whale or an elephant.

Games (Bodily-Kinesthetic, Interpersonal)

Invite the children to play "Pin the Tail on the Whale," the same as they would play "Pin the Tail on the Donkey."

Gross Motor (Bodily-Kinesthestic, Intrapersonal)

Provide a "Feed the Elephant Game" (Appendix p. 388) and peanuts in the shell. Encourage children to feed the elephant. Invite children to remove one shoe and sock and to use their bare foot the same way an elephant uses its trunk. Remind them how the elephant uses its nose. Provide a bowl of peanuts and see if children can pick the peanuts up with their toes and deliver it to the elephant's trunk. (Supervise closely at all times!)

Language (Linguistic)

Write the words "elephant" and "whale" on a piece of chart paper. Give the children the magnetic letters and encourage them to spell the animals' names on the magnetic board or on the table.

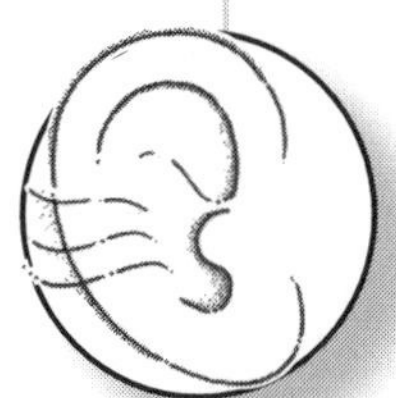

Listening (Musical)

Provide a tape of whale sounds for the children to listen to or provide paper towel tubes and encourage the children to use the tubes as elephants' trunks. Show them how to make elephant trumpeting sounds.

Science (Naturalist, Logical-Mathematical)

Invite the children to crack open peanuts and graph the results of how many peanuts they find in each shell—1, 2, or 3.
(Supervise closely at all times!)

Closing Circle (Reflections on the Day)

Ask the children:

1. How are whales and elephants alike? How are they different?
2. What is the most interesting thing you learned about elephants?
3. What is the most interesting thing you learned about whales?

Smaller Mammals

Morning Circle

1. Locate pictures of smaller mammals (for example, rabbits, squirrels, skunks, and so on) or use Animal Puppet Patterns (Appendix p. 463-467). Show the pictures to the children. Tell them that these animals are mammals just like whales and elephants. You may want to pass around a box of animal-shaped cookies/crackers and invite children to pick out their favorite animal.
2. Ask the children to share information with you about any of the animals they have seen. Where did they see them? What were the animals doing?
3. Tell the children that today's activities will be about other animals that are mammals.

Story Circle

"Brown Bear, Brown Bear" story cards (Appendix p. 458-460)
"The Lion's Haircut" prop story (Appendix p. 339)
Katy No-Pocket by Emmy Payne
A Squirrel's Tale by Richard Fowler

Music and Movement

Do the Bunny Hop (Appendix p. 357).

Sing and move to "Five Little Monkeys" (Appendix p. 316), "Three Little Monkeys" (Appendix p. 326), "Animal Fair" (Appendix p. 283), "Gray Squirrel" (Appendix p. 288), or "This Little Monkey" (Appendix p. 326).

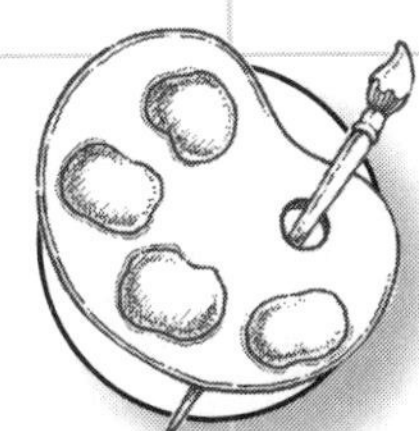

ART (SPATIAL, BODILY-KINESTHETIC)

Provide playdough (Appendix p. 377) and encourage the children to shape an animal of their own choice or creation.

DISCOVERY (NATURALIST)

Provide animal magazines and invite children to look for mammals. Invite them to cut out the pictures they find and make a big classroom collage of mammals.

DRAMATIC PLAY (MUSIC, INTERPERSONAL, INTRAPERSONAL)

Make animal puppets (Appendix p. 463-467). You might want to make a squirrel, rabbit, and skunk in advance of this activity. Encourage children to create an animal puppet show.

FINE MOTOR (BODILY-KINESTHETIC)

Give the children a box of squirrel food (acorns and other kinds of nuts still in the shell). Encourage them to sort the nuts into a muffin tin using a pair of tongs.

LANGUAGE (LINGUISTIC)

Allow the children to use the "Brown Bear, Brown Bear" story cards (Appendix p. 458-460) to retell the story. You may want to help them sort the cards as to which animals in the story are mammals. Remember, people are mammals, too.

MATH (LOGICAL-MATHEMATICAL)

Make multiple copies in seriated sizes of the carrots in the Fruit and Vegetable Patterns (Appendix p. 529). Give the carrots to the children to arrange from smallest to largest and largest to smallest. Ask them which bunch of carrots they think bunnies would prefer to eat.

Closing Circle (Reflections on the Day)

Ask the children:

1. What new thing have you learned about animals today?
2. Which animals in the "Brown Bear, Brown Bear" story aren't mammals?
3. What animal did you make out of playdough?

Reptiles

Morning Circle

1. Use a ribbon or a trail of paper to create a snake from the doorway to the circle area. Have the children follow the snake to the circle area.
2. Make a Snake Sock Puppet (Appendix p. 400). Use it to introduce the information about reptiles. Show pictures of reptiles.
3. Explain to the children that reptiles are different from mammals. They have cold blood and their babies hatch from eggs. Explain that snakes, lizards, turtles, frogs, crocodiles, and alligators are all reptiles.
4. Encourage the children to tell you what they know about reptiles.
5. Do the fingerplay, "There Once Was a Turtle" (Appendix p. 312) with the children. Talk about what reptiles eat.
6. Tell the children that today's activities will be about reptiles.

Story Circle

The Day Jimmy's Boa Ate the Wash by Trinka Hakes Noble
DK Readers: Slinky, Scaly, Snakes by Jennifer Dussling
The Iguana Brothers: A Tale of Two Lizards by Tony Johnston
Komodo by Peter Sis
Look Out for Turtles by Melvin Berger
Lyle, Lyle, Crocodile by Bernard Waber
The Tortoise and the Hare (Aesop Fable)
Yertle the Turtle and Other Stories by Dr. Seuss

Music and Movement

Sing and move to "Three Little Monkeys" (Appendix p. 312), "Crocodile Song" (Appendix p. 285), "Crocodile" (Appendix p. 314), or "Five Little Speckled Frogs" (Appendix p. 286).

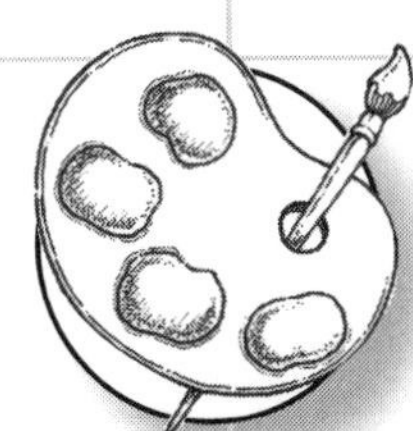

Art (Spatial, Bodily-Kinesthetic)

Provide playdough (Appendix p. 377) and invite the children to roll snakes. Provide a toothpick for etching facial features.

(Supervise closely at all times!)

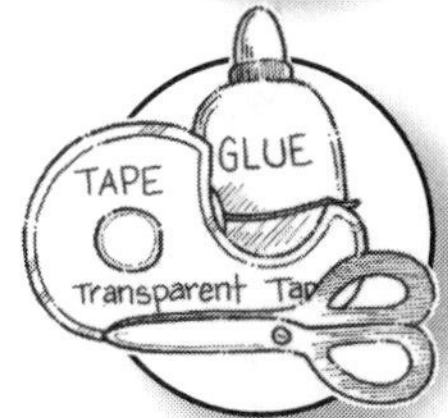

Construction (Spatial)

Invite the children to make Spiral Snakes (Appendix p. 401).

Dramatic Play (Linguistic, Musical, Intrapersonal)

Encourage the children to re-enact "Three Little Monkeys" (Appendix p. 312). Ask the children to think about why the monkeys ended up being eaten. Challenge them to make up a new chant that would allow the monkeys to escape.

Fine Motor (Bodily-Kinesthetic)

Give the children a Clothespin Alligator (Appendix p. 386). Encourage the children to use the alligators to pick up plastic flies or monkeys cut from felt.

Games (Logical-Mathematical, Naturalist, Interpersonal)

Encourage the children to play Reptile Concentration using the game patterns (Appendix p. 509).

Math (Logical-Mathematical)

Give the children Reptile Puzzles (Appendix p. 399) to work.

Closing Circle (Reflections on the Day)

Ask the children:

1. How are reptiles different from mammals?
2. Which reptile did you like the best?
3. What new rhyme or chant did you make up about the monkeys?

Birds

Morning Circle

1. Try to borrow a bird for the day, but if none is available use, photos of birds.
2. Find out what the children know about birds. Ask them:
   - What do birds eat?
   - How do they get around (hop, fly, walk, float, glide)?
   - Where do birds live?
   - With what are they covered?
3. Tell the children that today's activities will be about birds.

Story Circle

Are You My Mother? by P.D. Eastman
Best Nest by P.D. Eastman
Little Green by Keith Baker
Make Way for Ducklings by Robert McCloskey
My Spring Robin by Anne F. Rockwell
Silly Little Goose by Nancy Tafuri

Music and Movement

Sing and move to "Two Little Blackbirds" (Appendix p. 313), "White Wings" (Appendix p. 307), or "Be Kind to Your Web-Footed Friends" (Appendix p. 284).

Give children feathers and invite them to toss them in the air and then blow them to keep them aloft.

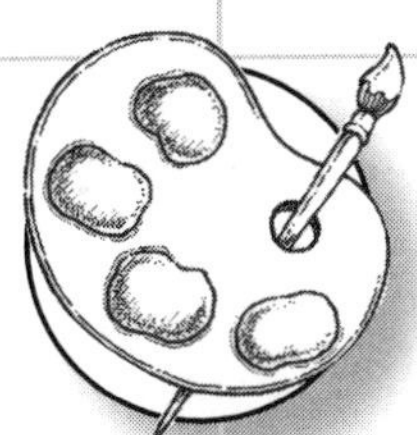

ART (Spatial)

Show the children how to use feathers as brushes and invite them to paint a picture.

DRAMATIC PLAY (Interpersonal, Naturalist)

Set up a bird-watching center close to the windows. Make binoculars by gluing or taping two empty toilet paper tubes together. Encourage the children to look for birds. How many different kinds can they find? How many different colored birds can they find?

FINE MOTOR (Bodily-Kinesthetic)

Cut pipe cleaners into 1" strips to make worms. Provide tweezers for the children to use as bird beaks and challenge the children to pick up the "worms."

GROSS MOTOR (Bodily-Kinesthetic, Intrapersonal, Logical-Mathematical)

Use masking tape to make a start and finish line about 4' apart. Invite children to have a Feather Race (Appendix p. 359). The first child to get her feather across the line is the winner and can then face a new challenger.

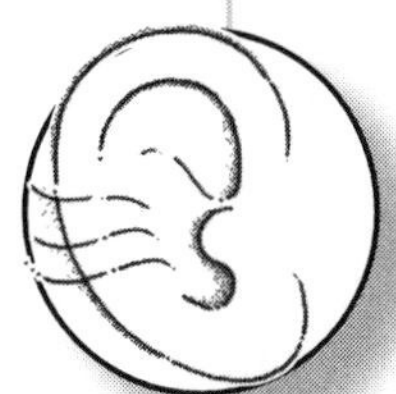

LISTENING (Musical, Naturalist)

Play nature tapes with birdcalls on them. Invite the children to try to hear the differences in the sounds of the calls.

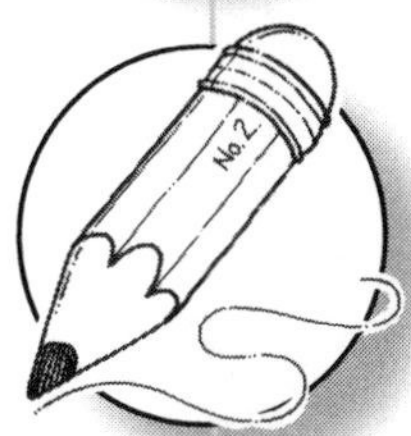

WRITING (Linguistic)

Encourage the children to use a feather as a writing instrument. Provide tempera paint to dip the "quill" in and invite the children to draw or write.

Closing Circle (Reflections on the Day)

Ask the children:

1. How is a bird like a turtle or a snake? How are birds different from turtles and snakes?
2. How many birds did you see today? Where were they?
3. What new thing did you learn about birds today?

Fish

Morning Circle

1. If you do not have a fish in your classroom, try to find a fish you can borrow for the day. If no fish are available, use photos of fish.
2. Show the children the fish. Talk about what fish eat and how they move.
3. Discuss the parts of the fish: fins, gills, tail (moves side to side, not up and down like the whale's tail), scales, and eyes (no eyelids).
4. Serve goldfish crackers for the children to eat.
5. Tell the children that today's activities will be about fish.

Story Circle

Fish Out of Water by Helen Palmer

In the Small, Small Pond by Denise Fleming

Over in the Meadow by Ezra Jack Keats

Swimmy by Leo Lionni

Music and Movement

Sing and move to "Over in the Meadow" (Appendix p. 298) or "Michael Finnegan" (Appendix p. 295).

Swim like fish to music with varied tempos.

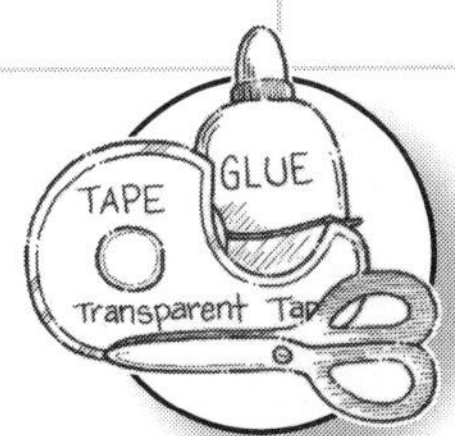

Construction (Interpersonal)

Help the children make Twirly Fish (Appendix p. 403). Encourage them to race their fish.

Dramatic Play (Interpersonal, Bodily-Kinesthetic, Logical-Mathematical, Naturalist)

Give the children a Fishing Game (Appendix p. 388). Invite them to take a pretend fishing trip. When they have caught all the fish, challenge them to arrange the fish in order of size from the largest to the smallest.

Language (Spatial, Linguistic)

Cut fish out of colored acetate and invite the children to play with them on the overhead projector. Encourage them to make up a story about these fish.

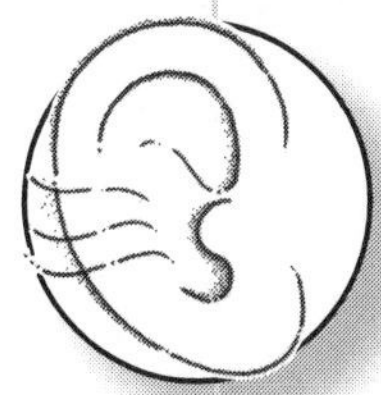

Listening (Music, Naturalist)

Use large clear sequins to represent fish scales. Provide a scoop, funnel, and several different surfaces such as a cookie tray, piece of felt, piece of cardboard, or plastic plate onto which the children will drop the sequins. How many different sounds can they create?

Math (Logical-Mathematical)

Use the fish in the Fishing Game (Appendix p. 388) to make two sets of fish for matching. Encourage the children to find the fish that look alike and sort them into pairs.

Science (Naturalist, Intrapersonal)

Provide a real fish or pictures of fish and a magnifying glass. Invite the children to take a close look at the fish. Challenge them to think about how it might feel to be a goldfish swimming all day in the same small space.

Closing Circle (Reflections on the Day)

Ask the children:

1. How are fish like whales? How are they different?
2. What would a fish need to be able to live on land?
3. How are fish different from birds? How are they alike?

Farm Animals

Morning Circle

1. Dress like a farmer in overalls or jeans, an old shirt, boots, and a straw hat. Greet children at the door.
2. Sing "Old MacDonald Had a Farm" (Appendix p. 298). Remind the children that females can be farmers, too. You may want to change the words in the song to reflect Old MacDonald as a woman farmer.
3. Find out what children know about farms. Ask them:
   - Who has been to a farm?
   - What animals live on a farm?
   - Who cares for the animals?
   - Why do farmers have animals on the farm?
   - What does each animal produce? (chicken—eggs, cows—milk, pigs— meat, and so on)
4. Tell the children that today's activities will be about farm animals.

Story Circle

Barnyard Banter by Denise Fleming

Big Red Barn by Margaret Wise Brown

"The Great Big Turnip" flannel board story (Appendix p. 336)

"Old MacDonald's Farm" song and flannel board patterns (Appendix p. 298, 439-440)

Once Upon MacDonald's Farm by Stephen Gammell

Music and Movement

Move like farm animals—walk like a chicken, gallop like a pony, hop like a bunny, sway like a pig, waddle like a duck.

Sing and move to "Five Little Ducks" (Appendix p. 286), "Old Gray Mare" (Appendix p. 297), "Tiny Seeds" (Appendix p. 326), "Over in the Meadow" (Appendix p. 298), "This Little Piggy" (Appendix p. 312), "Bingo" (Appendix p. 284), or "Mary Middling Had a Pig" (Appendix p. 323).

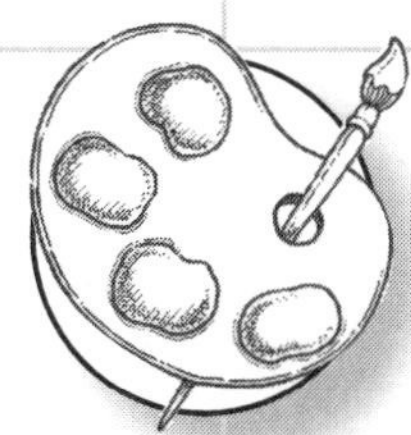

Art (Spatial)

Provide buttermilk in a shallow bowl, drawing paper, and colored chalk. Encourage the children to dip the chalk into the buttermilk and draw a picture. What happens to the chalk? Where does buttermilk come from?

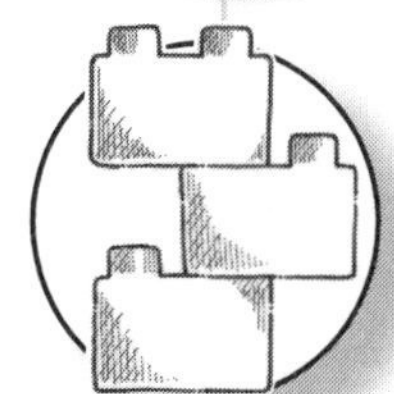

Blocks (Interpersonal, Bodily-Kinesthetic, Spatial, Intrapersonal)

Make a Farmyard Ground Cover (Appendix p. 387) and a Silo (Appendix p. 400). Provide plastic farm animals and encourage the children to build a farm.

Discovery (Naturalist)

Provide plastic farm and zoo animals and invite the children to sort the animals by where the animals live. If plastic animals are unavailable, use magazine pictures or patterns (Appendix p. 526-527).

Language (Linguistic)

Provide the Homemade Butter Rebus Recipe (Appendix p. 493). Encourage the children to follow the directions and make butter. Provide crackers so they can sample the butter.

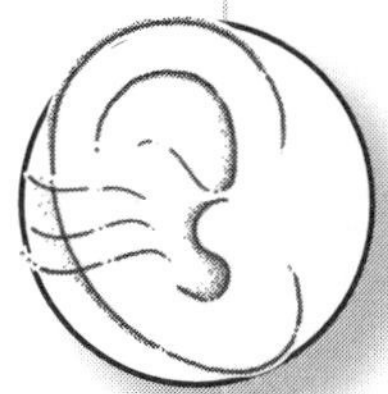

Listening (Musical, Naturalist)

Make a tape of animal noises. Make animal picture cards from the animals in the "Old MacDonald Had a Farm" flannel board story (Appendix p. 439-440), and invite the children to match the sound on the tape to the animal on the card.

Math (Logical-Mathematical)

Make a "Feed the Chickens" Game (Appendix p. 388). Encourage the children to count five corn kernels into each chicken's mouth.

Learning Centers

Closing Circle (Reflections on the Day)

Ask the children:

1. What did you learn about farm animals?
2. Did you find that some of the same animals that live on the farm also live in the zoo?

Zoo Animals

Morning Circle

1. Dress like a zookeeper. You may want to wear khakis, a vest, boots and a cap. Carry a broom and put a sign around your neck that says "Zookeeper."
2. Talk about the care of zoo animals. Ask the children:
   - Who feeds and cleans up after zoo animals?
   - How would the animals get food if they were in the wild instead of zoo cages?
   - Who's been to the zoo?
3. Encourage the children to talk about their experiences.
4. Tell the children that today's activities will be about zoo animals.

Story Circle

1,2,3 to the Zoo: A Counting Book by Eric Carle
Color Zoo by Lois Ehlert
Curious George Visits the Zoo by Margaret Rey
Going to the Zoo by Tom Paxton
If I Ran the Zoo by Dr. Seuss
Put Me in the Zoo by Robert Lopshire

Music and Movement

Play Monkey See, Monkey Do (Appendix p. 364) or One Elephant (Appendix p. 365).

Sing and move to "Three Little Monkeys" (Appendix p. 312), "Five Little Monkeys" (Appendix p. 310), "This Little Monkey" (Appendix p. 326), or "The Elephant" (Appendix p. 315).

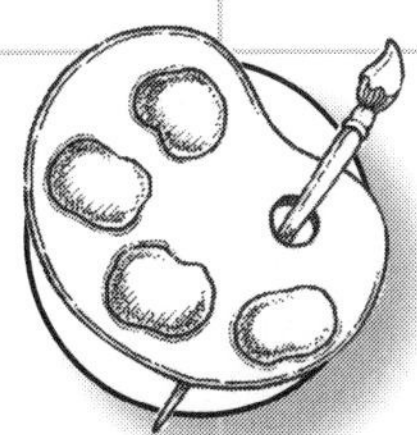

Art (Spatial)

Provide yellow construction paper, oval sponges, and brown tempera paint. Invite the children to create giraffe skin patterns by sponging the brown paint onto the yellow paper in a design of their choice.

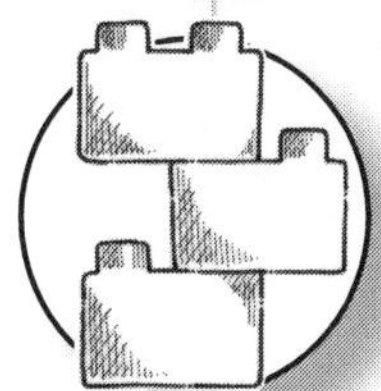

Blocks (Interpersonal, Naturalist)

Provide plastic animals and berry baskets to use as cages. Encourage the children to build a zoo and to sort the animals into cages by those that are alike. For example, all monkeys in one cage, all birds into another, and so on.

Dramatic Play (Intrapersonal, Musical, Bodily-Kinesthetic)

Provide Animal Masks (Appendix p. 511-517) and encourage the children to imitate the animal whose mask they are wearing.

Language (Linguistic)

On chart paper, print names of the different animal houses at the zoo, such as Aviary, Reptiles, Monkeys, Aquarium, or Lions. Encourage the children to copy the names and label zoo cages in the block center.

Math (Logical-Mathematical)

Give the children a "Feed the Seal" game (Appendix p. 360) and encourage them to feed each seal the requested number of fish (fish crackers). Use the zoo animals patterns (Appendix p. 510) to prepare a concentration game. Invite the children to play zoo concentration.

Snack (Interpersonal)

Invite the children to eat the monkey's favorite food—bananas. Give them plastic knives to slice a banana into quarter-size slices or let them enjoy it the way a monkey does—just peel it and eat it.

Learning Centers

Closing Circle (Reflections on the Day)

Ask the children:

1. What is your favorite zoo animal? Why?
2. Would you like to work in the zoo? Why?

Forest Animals

Morning Circle

1. Turn the classroom, or at least the doorway area, into a forest. Use brown and green bulletin board paper to make trees with leafy branches. Add mushrooms, flowers, and grass cut out of construction paper. Place stuffed animals around the trees.

2. Sing "Little Rabbit" (Appendix p. 293) with the children.
3. Discuss forest animals. What do the children know about the forest? Make a list on chart paper of animals found in the forest.
4. Tell the children that today's activities will be about forest animals.

Story Circle

"Goldilocks and the Three Bears" flannel board story (Appendix p. 335, 421-425)

"The Great Big Pumpkin" flannel board story (Appendix p. 335, 426-427)

The Great Kapok Tree by Lynne Cherry

The Gruffalo by Julia Donaldson

Play with Me by Marie Hall Ets

Who Is the Beast? by Keith Baker

Why Mosquitoes Buzz in People's Ears by Verna Ardena

Music and Movement

Sing and move to "Going on a Bear Hunt" (Appendix p. 317), "Gray Squirrel" (Appendix p. 288), "Little Skunk's Hole" (Appendix p. 293), "Little Bunny Foo-Foo" (Appendix p. 292), or "Do Your Ears Hang Low?" (Appendix p. 285).

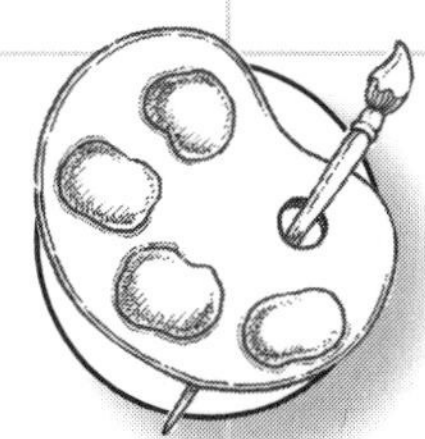

ART (Spatial, Intrapersonal)

Place a large sheet of bulletin board paper or butcher paper on the wall. Provide green and brown tempera paints and encourage the children to paint a forest. Provide construction paper cutouts of mushrooms and flowers. Encourage the children to look through magazines for animals to add to their mural.

DISCOVERY (Naturalist)

Provide leaves, twigs, mushrooms, and moss for the children to look at with a magnifying glass. As a safety precaution, place the moss and mushrooms in zippered plastic bags as there might be tiny creatures living in both.

DRAMATIC PLAY (Linguistic, Interpersonal, Musical)

Use tongue depressors to make stick puppets from the Forest Animal Concentration game patterns (Appendix p. 505). Encourage the children to re-enact a forest animal story they know or challenge them to create a new story or song about forest animals.

FINE MOTOR (Bodily-Kinesthetic)

Provide nuts and nutcrackers. Invite the children to crack the nuts and sample them. Ask them how the squirrels crack their nuts.
(Supervise closely at all times!) (Check for allergies)

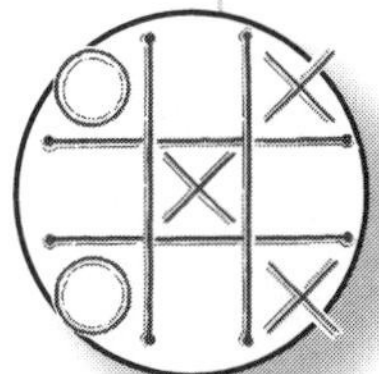

GAMES (Naturalist, Linguistic)

Encourage the children to play Forest Animal Concentration using the game patterns (Appendix p. 505).

SNACK (Logical-Mathematical)

Give each child six Teddy Grahams. Encourage the children to count the correct number of bears into a set of numbered Bear Caves (Appendix p. 382). When they have finished, invite them to eat the Teddy Grahams.

Closing Circle (Reflections on the Day)

Ask the children:

1. Would you like to live in a forest? Why or why not?
2. What animals do we find in the forest? Do any of the zoo animals also live in the forest? Which ones?
3. What new thing have you learned about forest animals?

Circus Animals

Morning Circle

1. Sing "The Calliope Song" (Appendix p. 284) with the children.
2. Find out what the children know about circus animals. Discuss which animals appear in the circus. Ask the children:
   - Who cares for the animals?
   - What do the animals eat?
3. Explain that the elephants often help put up the big tent. Do the children know what the big tent is called?
4. Tell the children that today's activities will be about circus animals.

Story Circle

Circus Train by Joseph A. Smith
The Circus Surprise by Ralph Fletcher
Clifford at the Circus by Norman Bridwell
If I Ran the Circus by Dr. Seuss
Little Engine That Could by Watty Piper

Music and Movement

Chant and move to "Fido" (Appendix p. 316), "Five Little Monkeys" (Appendix p. 316), "Three Little Monkeys" (Appendix p. 326), "The Elephant" (Appendix p. 315), or "This Little Monkey" (Appendix p. 326).

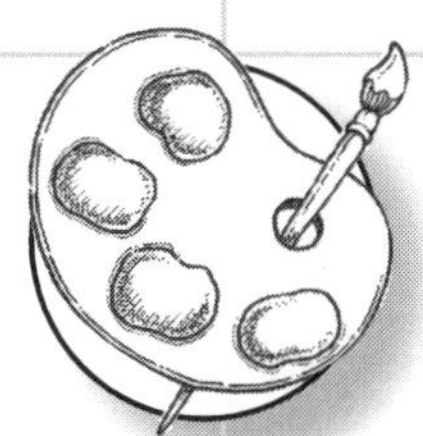

ART (Spatial)

Provide tempera paint, brushes, and paper. Invite the children to paint their favorite circus animal. Ask why the animal is their favorite. Write children's responses on the back of their papers.

DRAMATIC PLAY (Intrapersonal, Musical, Linguistic, Bodily-Kinesthetic)

Help each child construct a Dancing Bear (Appendix p. 521). Provide crayons for coloring and decorating. Encourage the children to create a performance for the bears.

GROSS MOTOR (Bodily-Kinesthetic)

Give the children small balls and challenge them to balance a ball on their nose just as the circus seal does.

GROSS MOTOR (Bodily-Kinesthetic, Interpersonal, Spatial, Musical)

Let the children try tricks on the balance beam. Show them how to stand on one foot and how to turn around. Ask them to imagine doing these activities on the back of a moving horse. Add music to the performance. (Supervise closely at all times!)

LIBRARY (Linguistic, Interpersonal)

Use striped sheets or a large piece of striped fabric to create a circus tent in the center. Fill the tent with books about circus animals.

MATH (Logical-Mathematical)

Give the children the "Feed the Elephant" game using the patterns (Appendix p. 388). Encourage them to match the correct number of peanuts to each elephant using the numbers on the animal saddles as a guide. (Supervise closely at all times!) (Check for allergies)

Closing Circle (Reflections on the Day)

Ask the children:

1. Would you like to work in the circus? Why or why not?
2. Which job would you like?
3. Are any of the farm animals that we talked about also circus animals?

Pets

Morning Circle

1. In advance, invite the children to bring a stuffed animal to school. Have a show-and-tell in the form of a "Pet Show." Invite the children to show their pets and tell something about them.
2. Discuss real pets that children may have. Talk about feeding and caring for pets. Discuss the role of the veterinarian.
3. Tell the children that today's activities will be about pets.

Story Circle

Can I Keep Him? by Steven Kellogg
Good Dog, Carl by Alexandra Day
Hamster Chase by Anastasia Suen
Pet Show by Ezra Jack Keats
Whistle for Willie by Ezra Jack Keats

Music and Movement

Play "Dog, Dog, Cat" the way you would play "Duck, Duck, Goose" (Appendix p. 359).

Play the game "Whose Dog Art Thou?" (Appendix p. 369) or do the action rhyme "Old Gray Cat" (Appendix p. 324).

Do the Bunny Hop (Appendix p. 357).

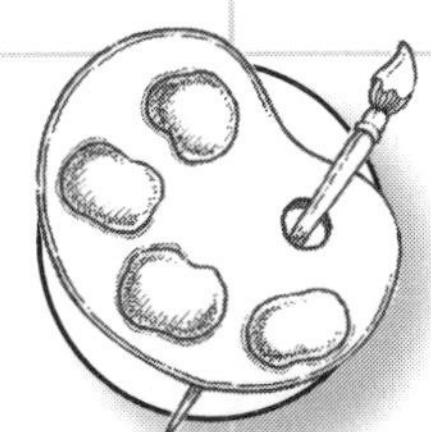

ART (SPATIAL)

Provide fishing line for whiskers and paper and tempera paint. Encourage the children to paint a picture using the cat whiskers for a brush.

DRAMATIC PLAY (INTERPERSONAL, INTRAPERSONAL)

Set up a vet's office with a stethoscope, white coat (old shirt), bowls, tweezers, and bandages. Use the stuffed animals as patients. Ask the children how they are taking care of the pets. Which pet is their favorite to treat?

GROSS MOTOR (BODILY-KINESTHETIC)

Provide a plastic fish bowl. Give the children beanbags to toss into the fish bowl.

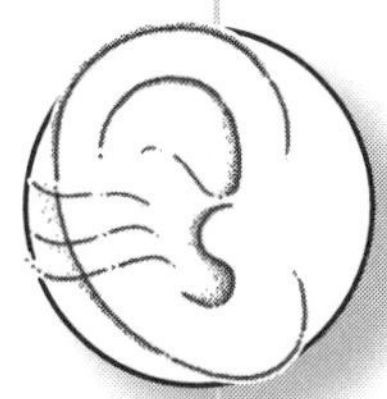

LISTENING (MUSICAL, NATURALIST)

Teach the children to whistle and encourage them to practice. Give them a couple of different examples of ways you might whistle for a dog. Does anyone know a different whistle?

MATH (LOGICAL-MATHEMATICAL)

Use the patterns in the Appendix to make the "Dog and Bone" game (Appendix p. 501-502). Encourage the children to match bones to dogs by matching dots on the bones to numbers on the dog collars.

WRITING (LINGUISTIC)

Write the words "dog" and "cat" on a piece of paper. Provide a tray of sand and encourage the children to use their fingers to write the words in the sand.

Closing Circle (Reflections on the Day)

Ask the children:

1. Which pet would you choose if you could have any pet you wanted?
2. What responsibilities come with owning a pet?

Assessment for "World of Animals"

Intellectual Strength	Assessment
Linguistic	Ask the children to dictate descriptions of three or four of their favorite animals. Have them include the group to which the animal belongs in their description.
Spatial	Provide playdough and encourage the children to shape one animal for each animal type that has been studied. For example, they might shape a turtle to represent the reptile group, a cat for the mammals, and a chicken for the birds.
Musical	Have the children identify songs that mention animals. Ask them to describe which animal group the animal or animals in the song belong to.
Interpersonal Bodily-Kinesthetic	Have the children demonstrate how the following animals move: turtles, snakes, elephants, bunnies, cats, monkeys, ducks, and robins.
Logical-Mathematical	Have the children dictate a list of animals who have a pattern in their skin such as zebras, turtles, tigers, Dalmatians, and skunks.
Intrapersonal	Have the children think of an animal they would most like to be and then describe why they would like to be that particular animal. Ask the children which animal they think is most like them and why.
Naturalist	Provide photographs of several different types of animals and have the children sort them by type, how they move, and what they eat.

Books Used in "World of Animals"

1,2,3 to the Zoo: A Counting Book by Eric Carle
A Squirrel's Tale by Richard Fowler
Are You My Mother? by P.D. Eastman
Barnyard Banter by Denise Fleming
Best Nest by P.D. Eastman
Big Red Barn by Margaret Wise Brown
Blind Men and the Elephant by Karen Blackstein
Can I Keep Him? by Steven Kellogg
The Circus Surprise by Ralph Fletcher
Circus Train by Joseph A. Smith
Clifford at the Circus by Norman Bridwell
Color Zoo by Lois Ehlert
Curious George Visits the Zoo by Margaret Rey
The Day Jimmy's Boa Ate the Wash by Trinka Hakes Noble
Dinosaurs: All Shapes and Sizes by Sarah Corona
DK Readers: Slinky, Scaly, Snakes by Jennifer Dussling
Fish Out of Water by Helen Palmer
Going to the Zoo by Tom Paxton
Good Dog, Carl by Alexandra Day
The Great Kapok Tree by Lynne Cherry
The Gruffalo by Julia Donaldson
Hamster Chase by Anastasia Suen
Horton Hatches an Egg by Dr. Seuss
Horton Hears a Who by Dr. Seuss
How Big Were the Dinosaurs? by Bernard Most
If I Ran the Circus by Dr. Seuss
If I Ran the Zoo by Dr. Seuss
The Iguana Brothers: A Tale of Two Lizards by Tony Johnston
In the Small, Small Pond by Denise Fleming
Katy No-Pocket by Emmy Payne
Komodo by Peter Sis
Little Engine That Could by Watty Piper
Little Green by Keith Baker
Look Out for Turtles by Melvin Berger
Lyle, Lyle, Crocodile by Bernard Waber
Make Way for Ducklings by Robert McCloskey
My Spring Robin by Anne F. Rockwell
Never Mail an Elephant by Mike Thaler
Once Upon MacDonald's Farm by Stephen Gammell

Over in the Meadow by Ezra Jack Keats
Pet Show by Ezra Jack Keats
Play with Me by Marie Hall Ets
Put Me in the Zoo by Robert Lopshire
Silly Little Goose by Nancy Tafuri
Swimmy by Leo Lionni
The Tortoise and the Hare (Aesop Fable)
The Whales' Song by Dylan Sheldon
Whales: The Gentle Giants by Joyce Milton
Whistle for Willie by Ezra Jack Keats
Who Is the Beast? by Keith Baker
Why Mosquitoes Buzz in People's Ears by Verna Ardena
Yertle the Turtle and Other Stories by Dr. Seuss

Other Books About Animals

Baby Animals by Margaret Wise Brown
Brown Bear, Brown Bear, What Do You See? by Bill Martin, Jr.
Come to the Meadow by Anna Grossnickle Hines
The Cow that Went Oink! by Bernard Most
Deep in the Forest by Brinton Turkle
Early Morning in the Barn by Nancy Tafuri
Emma's Pet by David McPhail
Endangered Animals by John Wexo
For the Love of Earth by P.K. Hallinan
Frogs, Toads, Lizards, and Salamanders by Joan Wright and Nancy Winslow Parker
Hop Jump by Ellen Stoll Walsh
Life in the Pond by Eileen Curran
Little Critter's These Are My Pets by Mercer Mayer
Moo, Moo Brown Cow by Jakki Wood
The Mouse and the Potato by Thomas Berger
Nature Spy by Shelley Rotner and Ken Kreisler
Polar Bear, Polar Bear, What Do You Hear? by Bill Martin, Jr.
Rabbits and Raindrops by Jim Arnosky
Sammy the Seal by Syd Hoff
When the Elephant Walks by Keiko Kasza
Where Once There Was a Wood by Denise Fleming

Little Things
(Insects and Bugs)

ANTS

MORNING CIRCLE

1. Collect ants (non-biting type) from an ant bed and place them in a jar with a secure lid. Be sure to get the queen if you can find her. The queen ant is larger than the other ants. Her thorax (mid-section) is particularly larger, generally four times larger than that of the worker ants.
2. When the children arrive at school, invite them to crawl on their hands and knees in a line (pretending to be ants) to the Morning Circle. Have a plate of cookies waiting for them. Ants are always looking for food… especially something that is sweet.
3. Find out what the children know about ants. Show them the ants that you have collected.
4. Explain that ants are insects, which have six legs and three body parts (head, thorax and abdomen) and two antennae. Sing "The Insect Song" (Appendix p. 291).
   - Ants live in colonies. They are social insects like bees. They spend their whole life working to build their home (they can tunnel 15' under the ground) and gathering and storing food.
   - Has anyone seen ants carrying something bigger than they are? People who study insects are known as entomologists. Explain that for the next few days they will be entomologists.
5. Tell the children that today's activities will be about ants.

STORY CIRCLE

The Ant Bully by John Nickle
Ant Cities by Author Durros
Hey, Little Ant by Phillip Hoose
Inside an Ant Colony by Allan Fowler
The Little Red Ant and the Great Big Crumb: A Mexican Fable by Shirley Climo
One Hundred Hungry Ants by Bonnie MacKain
Two Bad Ants by Chris Van Allsburg

MUSIC AND MOVEMENT

Sing "The Ants Go Marching" (Appendix p. 283).
Play fast-tempo music and invite the children to scurry like ants.

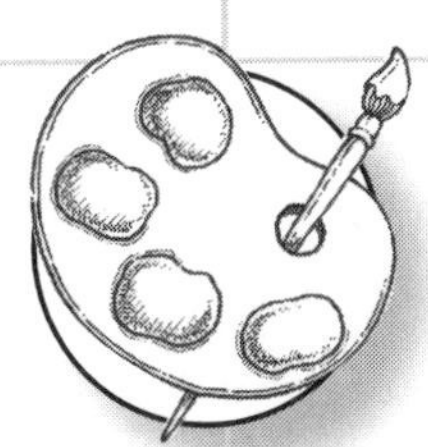

ART (Spatial, Logical-Mathematical)

Provide an inkpad, pencils, and crayons. Encourage the children to make an ant by connecting three of their thumbprints to make the body and then adding legs and antennae with a crayon or pencil.

FINE MOTOR (Bodily-Kinesthetic)

Make a Magnetic Maze (Appendix p. 394). Encourage the children to move the ant from its hill to the cookie.

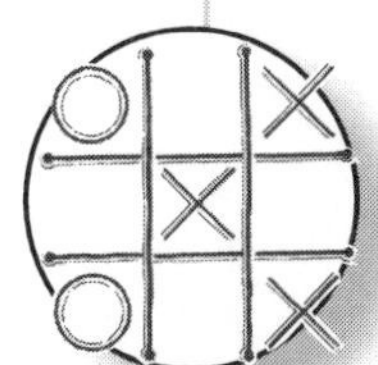

GAMES (Interpersonal, Linguistic)

Use the patterns to make the Insect Concentration game (Appendix p. 506). Encourage the children to match pairs of insects.

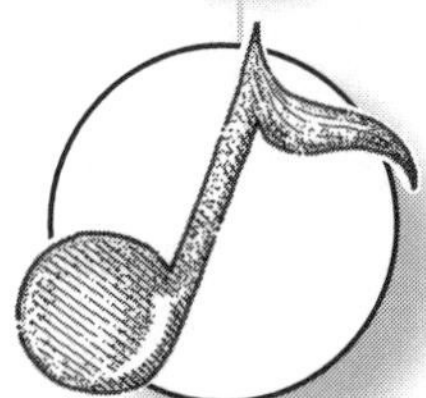

MUSIC (Musical, Intrapersonal)

Give the children rhythm band instruments. Challenge them to create a musical beat that matches the quick pace of ants' movements.

SCIENCE (Naturalist, Intrapersonal)

Place a jar of ants in the center and encourage the children to observe the behavior of the ants. Provide a magnifying glass for a close look. Encourage them to watch for ants to talk to each other (which they do by touching antennae). Ask the children how they think it would feel to work all the time.

SNACK (Interpersonal, Spatial)

Provide celery strips, peanut butter, and raisins. Invite children to make "Ants on a Log" (Appendix p. 371).
(Check for allergies)

Closing Circle (Reflections on the Day)

Ask the children:

1. What have you learned about ants today?
2. What would be different about the way ants move if they were big instead of little?
3. How do you think we look to ants?

Busy Bees

Morning Circle

1. Sing "Baby Bumblebee" (Appendix p. 283) with the children. Are any of the children familiar with another version of this song? How are the two songs different? Why does the child in this song talk to the bee instead of smashing it? Ask the children if a bee has ever stung them. How did it make them feel?
2. Discuss being kind to animals and bugs. Explain that all animals and bugs are nature's creatures.
3. Find out what the children know about bees. Have photos of bees or live bees available to show, if possible.
4. Explain that bees come in different types: worker bees, guard bees, and queen bees.
   - Worker bees collect nectar and pollen from flowers. Bees make honey from the nectar and use pollen for food. Have honey available for the children to sample. Guard bees watch the nest and protect it from intruders. The queen bee helps reproduce new bees.
   - Bees communicate with each other by their movements. They do what is called a Waggle Dance (Appendix p. 369). In this dance, the directions in which the bee moves in relationship to the hive communicates the location of food and pollen to the rest of the bees.
5. Ask the children if bumblebees are insects. Have them count the body parts, legs, and antennae. What does a bee have that most ants do not have? (Answer: wings). Sing "The Insect Song" (Appendix p. 291).
6. Tell the children that today's activities will be about bees.

Story Circle

Buzz by Janet Wong

The Honeybee and the Robber by Eric Carle

Honeybees Busy Day by Richard Fowler

"Ms. Bumblebee Gathers Honey" puppet story (Appendix p. 343)

Music and Movement

Give each child two plastic or paper plates. Play classical music and invite the children to move like bumblebees, using the plates for wings. Have them try out the Waggle Dance (Appendix p. 369).

Do the motions to "Here Is the Beehive" (Appendix p. 312).

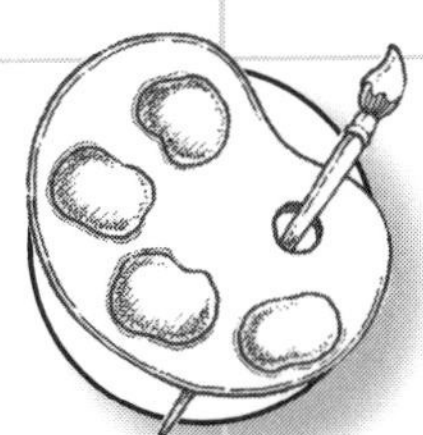

Art (Spatial)

Provide yellow and black tempera paint. Encourage the children to paint bumblebees.

Fine Motor (Bodily-Kinesthetic, Linguistic)

Place bee pollen (sand or salt colored with powder yellow tempera paint) on a cookie sheet. Encourage the children to draw designs in the pollen.

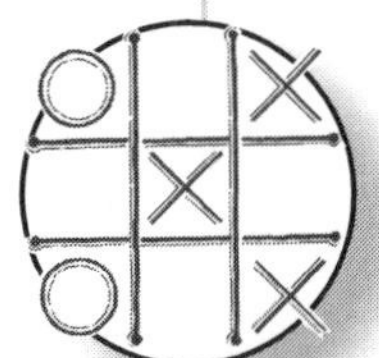

Games (Interpersonal, Naturalist)

Invite the children to play the Insect Concentration game (Appendix p. 506).

Language (Linguistic, Interpersonal)

Give the children the puppets from "Ms. Bumblebee Gathers Honey" (Appendix p. 468). Encourage them to re-enact the story or make up a new story.

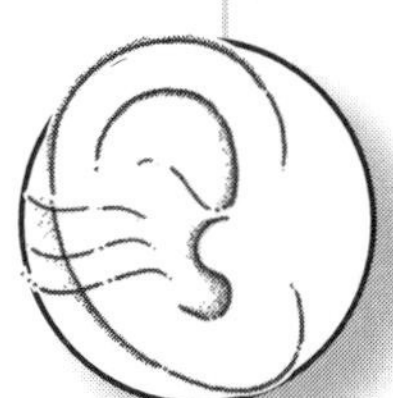

Listening (Musical, Intrapersonal)

Invite children to listen to "Flight of the Bumblebees" by Rimsky-Korsakov. How does the music make them feel?

Math (Logical-Mathematical)

Provide several 1" x 8" strips of both yellow and black construction paper. Challenge the children to make yellow and black striped patterns to match the patterns on the bumblebee's back.

Closing Circle (Reflections on the Day)

Ask the children:

1. What have you learned about bees today?
2. How are bees like ants? How are they different?
3. Can someone demonstrate the Waggle Dance?

Grasshoppers and Crickets

Morning Circle

1. Invite the children to hop to the Morning Circle like grasshoppers. Read "Grasshopper Three" (Appendix p. 318) to the children.
2. Find out what the children know about grasshoppers. Show pictures or photos of grasshoppers if at all possible or, better yet, show them a live grasshopper.
3. Explain that grasshoppers are insects. Crickets are a type of grasshopper.
   - Grasshoppers are vegetarians, which means they eat mostly grass and leaves. They can do enormous damage to flowers and crops (for example, corn and beans).
   - When grasshoppers move in a group it is called a swarm. When they hop they use a catapulting motion similar to when we bounce and jump or when we wind up to throw a ball.
   - Grasshoppers lay eggs in the moist ground. The eggs hatch in about three weeks' time.
   - When grasshoppers grow they shed their skin. This is called molting. It will happen four or five times before the grasshopper is fully-grown. Fully-grown grasshoppers reach sizes up to 3" in length.
   - Grasshoppers sing using two different mechanics—rubbing the teeth-like ridges on their legs against a ridge on their wing or rubbing together the teeth-like ridges on their forewings.
4. Tell the children that today's activities will be about grasshoppers.

Story Circle

"The Ant and the Grasshopper" (Appendix p. 329)

Grasshoppers and Crickets by Theresa Greenaway

Leaping Grasshoppers by Christine Zuchora-Walske

Quick as a Cricket by Audrey Wood

The Very Quiet Cricket by Eric Carle

Music and Movement

Sing "Grasshopper" (Appendix p. 288).

Discovery (Naturalist)

Grasshoppers can grow to be 3" long. Give each child a piece of yarn that is 3" long and challenge him or her to use the piece of yarn to find things in the room that are 3" long.

Fine Motor (Bodily-Kinesthetic, Logical-Mathematical, Naturalist, Spatial)

Give the children Grasshopper Puzzles (Appendix p. 390) to work.

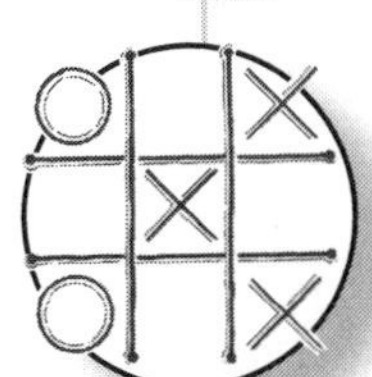

Games (Bodily-Kinesthetic, Interpersonal, Logical-Mathematical)

Give the children Grasshopper Hoppers (Appendix p. 390). Challenge the children to see if they can make the hoppers bounce only once before going into a cardboard box or plastic tub.

Gross Motor (Bodily-Kinesthetic, Intrapersonal)

Create a maze of small boxes. Challenge the children to jump their way through the maze as a grasshopper would. Invite the children to try "grasshopper jumps." Show the children how to run a few steps, bounce (catapult), and then jump. If this is too challenging for some children, encourage them to try broad jumping. Place a piece of masking tape on the ground. Take a running start and jump from the masking tape line as far as possible.

Language (Linguistic)

Provide the story of "The Ant and the Grasshopper" on tape (Appendix p. 329) for the children to enjoy. Have the children illustrate the story after they have listened to it.

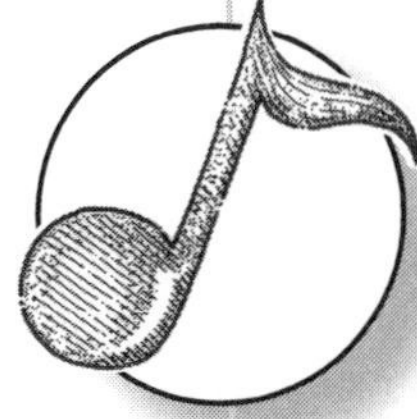

Music (Musical)

Provide several plastic combs and Popsicle sticks. Challenge the children to make the chirping sound of a grasshopper singing by running the stick along the teeth of the comb or by rubbing the teeth of one comb against the teeth of another comb.

Closing Circle (Reflections on the Day)

Ask the children:

1. What did you learn about grasshoppers today?
2. How are grasshoppers the same as bumblebees and ants?

Ladybugs

Morning Circle

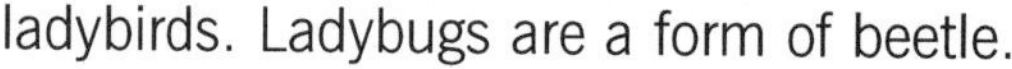

1. Show the children photos of ladybugs or live ladybugs, if available (they are often sold in nurseries).
2. Find out what the children know about ladybugs.
3. Explain that ladybugs are sometimes called lady beetles or ladybirds. Ladybugs are a form of beetle.
   - Farmers and gardeners like ladybugs because they eat aphids. Aphids are harmful to crops and to flowers. Ladybugs can eat up to 25 aphids a day.
   - Ladybugs are usually red with black spots but often fade with age, which makes them look orange.
   - Ladybugs were sent up on a 1999 space mission to see how they would do in space. There were four ladybugs aboard the shuttle. The astronauts named them after the Beatles: John, Paul, George and Ringo.
4. Tell the children that today's activities will be about ladybugs.

Story Circle

Are You a Ladybug? by Judy Allen
Five Little Ladybugs by Karyn Henley
Ladybug on the Move by Richard Fowler
Ladybug, Ladybug by Ruth Brown
Ladybug's Birthday by Steven Metzger
A Ladybug's Life by John Himmelman
The Grouchy Ladybug by Eric Carle

Music and Movement

Do the fingerplay "Five Little Ladybugs" (Appendix p. 310).

Give each child two red plastic plates and invite them to fly like ladybugs to classical music.

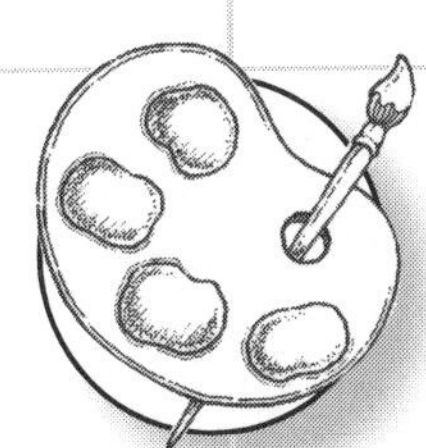

ART (SPATIAL)

Give children a smooth rock and red and black paints. Encourage them to paint the rock to look like a ladybug.

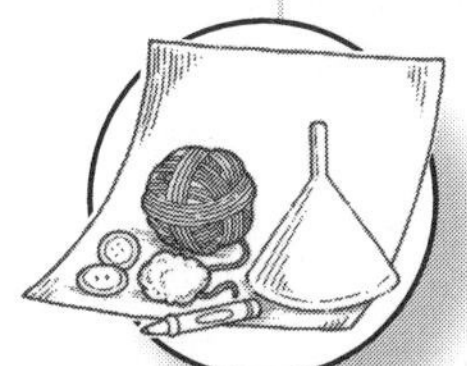

DISCOVERY (NATURALIST)

Place ladybugs and aphids (available in nurseries or feed stores, or by mail at Planet Natural, 1612 Gold Avenue, PO Box 3146, Bozeman, MT 59772, 1-800-289-6656) in an empty, clean plastic peanut butter jar for children to observe. Cut a piece of netting to fit over the mouth of the jar and secure with a rubber band. Provide a magnifying glass for a close look. Do the ladybugs eat the aphids?

DRAMATIC PLAY (INTERPERSONAL, MUSICAL, INTRAPERSONAL, LINGUISTIC)

Teach the children "Ladybird" (Appendix p. 322). Provide props and encourage the children to re-enact the rhyme. Ask how they think the ladybug might feel when she hears the message. What does she find when she gets home?

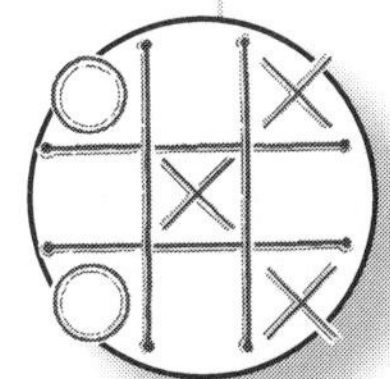

GAMES (INTERPERSONAL, NATURALIST, LINGUISTIC)

Invite the children to play the Insect Concentration game (Appendix p. 506).

GROSS MOTOR (BODILY-KINESTHETIC, INTERPERSONAL)

Make a big, red ladybug out of construction paper. Do not put spots on the insect. Use black spray paint on plastic milk carton lids or buttons to make the ladybug's spots. Challenge the children to toss the lids/buttons onto the ladybug.

MATH (LOGICAL-MATHEMATICAL)

Use the patterns to make the Ladybug Dot Match Game (Appendix p. 393). Encourage the children to put the ladybugs together by matching the dots.

Closing Circle (Reflections on the Day)

Ask the children:

1. What did you learn about ladybugs today?
2. Would farmers like to have ladybugs or grasshoppers on their farm? Why?

Flies and Mosquitoes

Morning Circle

1. Show the children photos of flies and mosquitoes or, if possible, the live insects.
2. Find out what the children know about flies and mosquitoes.
3. Explain that both flies and mosquitoes are insects. Count the legs, antennas and body parts. Sing "The Insect Song" (Appendix p. 291).
   - Flies have compound eyes; they see multiples of a single object. This is like looking through a broken glass. Flies have four wings.
   - Mosquitoes eat by sucking, much like a syringe.
4. Tell the children that today's activities will be about flies and mosquitoes.

Story Circle

Old Black Fly by Jim Aylesworth

There Was an Old Lady Who Swallowed a Fly by Simms Taback

"There Was an Old Lady Who Swallowed a Fly" puppet song (Appendix p. 302)

Why Mosquitoes Buzz in Peoples Ears: A West African Tale by Verna Aardema

Music and Movement

Act out "Shoo Fly" (Appendix p. 367).

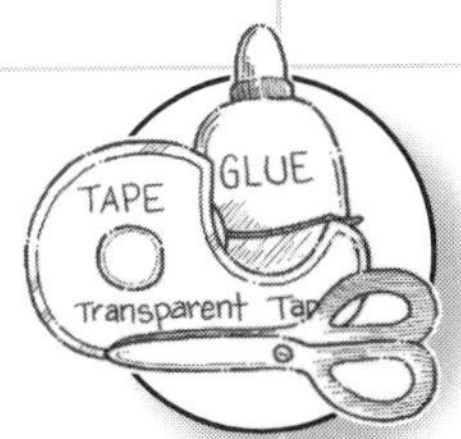

CONSTRUCTION (SPATIAL)

Invite the children to make Bug Eyes (Appendix p. 383).

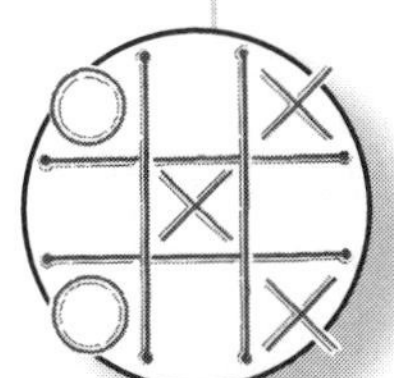

GAMES (INTERPERSONAL)

Encourage the children to play the Insect Concentration game (Appendix p. 506). Make the match of the fly a bonus and count as two points.

MATH (LINGUISTIC, MUSICAL)

Make an Old Lady Floor Mat (Appendix p. 395). Photocopy the patterns from the Old Lady Puppet patterns and invite the children to sequence the things the old lady swallowed. What did she swallow first?

MATH (LOGICAL-MATHEMATICAL)

Give the children the "Flies on Pies" matching game (Appendix p. 389). Encourage them to match the flies to the pies.

SCIENCE (NATURALIST)

Provide prisms. Encourage the children to try to look through the prisms at pictures or something in the room. What happens? How is this like the vision of the fly?

SNACK (NATURALIST, BODILY-KINESTHETIC)

Provide eyedroppers, a large container of juice, and individual cups. Invite the children to use the eyedroppers to serve themselves a cup of juice.

Closing Circle (Reflections on the Day)

Ask the children:

1. What did you learn about flies and mosquitoes today?
2. How long did it take you to serve yourself a cup of juice?
3. How are flies and mosquitoes like ladybugs?

Caterpillars

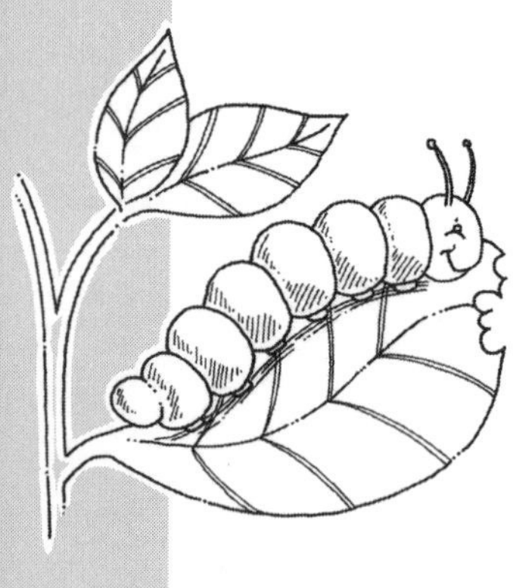

Morning Circle

1. Cut leaves from green construction paper and make a trail of them from the doorway to the Morning Circle area. Encourage the children to follow the leaves from the door to the Circle.
2. Make a Caterpillar/Butterfly Puppet (Appendix p. 384). Use it to introduce caterpillars to the children.
3. Find out what the children know about caterpillars. Show the children any photos of caterpillars, or live ones, if possible.
4. Explain that caterpillars are worms that will become butterflies (which are insects). Look at the caterpillar. Is it an insect? Does it have three body parts, six legs, and antennae? Not yet.
   - Tell the children about *metamorphosis*. Don't worry about how long this word is; children love to say it.
   - Explain that there are four stages and that the caterpillar is the second stage. Before the caterpillar is a caterpillar it is an egg.
   - Invite the children to act out each stage of metamorphosis, beginning with the egg. *Have children hold out a fist to represent an egg.*
   - When the egg hatches, out comes a caterpillar. *Have children wiggle their index finger to represent this stage.*
   - Next, the caterpillar makes a cocoon and wraps itself inside. *Have the children wrap their opposite hand around the caterpillar (their index finger).*
   - Finally, one day out of the cocoon comes a beautiful butterfly. *Encourage the children to flap their arms like wings.*
   - You can use your puppet to demonstrate the stages of metamorphosis.
   - Explain that during the time the butterfly is a caterpillar, it will do nothing but eat and eat. It will eat lots of leaves.
5. Tell the children that today's activities will be about caterpillars.

Story Circle

Charlie Caterpillar by Dom Deluise
Creepy, Crawly Caterpillars by Mary Facklam
The Very Hungry Caterpillar by Eric Carle
Waiting for Wings by Lois Elhert

Music and Movement

Do the motions to "Metamorphosis" (Appendix p. 323), "Fuzzy Caterpillar" Appendix p. 316), or "Caterpillar" (Appendix p. 309).

Gross Motor (Bodily-Kinesthetic, Interpersonal)

Give the children clean, old towels, sheets, or tablecloths. Encourage them to wrap each other in a cocoon. How does it feel inside the cocoon? (Supervise closely at all times!)

Language (Logical-Mathematical, Linguistic)

Give the children the patterns for *The Very Hungry Caterpillar* (Appendix p. 543-546). Challenge them to arrange the pieces into the order in which the caterpillar ate them.

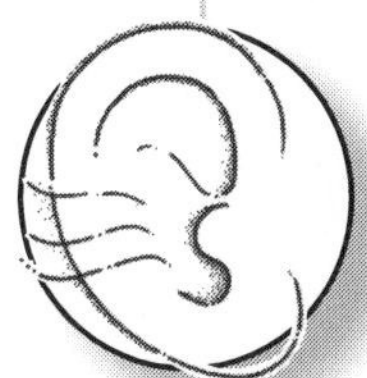

Listening (Musical, Intrapersonal)

Provide lullaby music. Encourage the children to select a lullaby for the caterpillar to listen to while it is in the cocoon.

Math (Logical-Mathematical, Spatial, Bodily-Kinesthetic)

Provide black, fuzzy pipe cleaners cut into 2" segments to represent caterpillars. Give the children "leaves" cut from green construction paper that are numbered 1 through 5. Invite the children to use tweezers to place the correct number of caterpillars on each leaf.

Science (Naturalist)

Provide a live caterpillar or photos of caterpillars for children to observe.

Science (Naturalist, Linguistic)

Provide the Metamorphosis Sequence Cards (Appendix p. 530). Invite the children to arrange the cards into the correct sequence. Encourage the children to describe each stage.

Closing Circle (Reflections on the Day)

Ask the children:

1. What did you learn about caterpillars today? Are they insects?
2. What was your favorite activity today?

Butterflies

Morning Circle

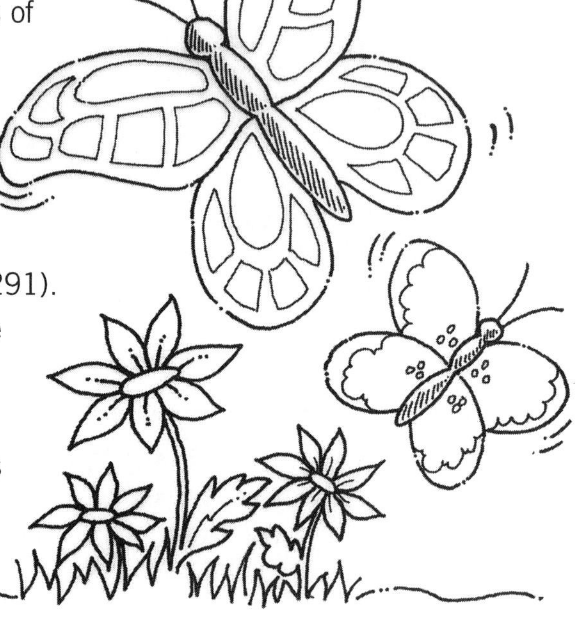

1. Use the Caterpillar/Butterfly Puppet (Appendix p. 384) again and review the stages of metamorphosis.
2. Explain that butterflies are insects. Count the body parts, antennae, and legs. Sing "The Insect Song" (Appendix p. 291).
3. Discuss how butterflies, like bumblebees, pollinate the flowers.
4. Tell the children that today's activities will be about butterflies.

Story Circle

From Caterpillar to Butterfly by Deborah Heiligman
I Wish I Were a Butterfly by James Howe
A New Butterfly: My First Look at Metamorphosis by Pamela Hickman
Waiting for Wings by Lois Elhert
Where Butterflies Grow by Joanne Ryder

Music and Movement

Provide scarves. Play classical music and encourage the children to dance like butterflies.

Take a walk outdoors and look for butterflies.

Act out "Metamorphosis" (Appendix p. 323).

Play "Caterpillar, Caterpillar, Butterfly" as you would "Duck, Duck, Goose" (Appendix p. 359).

Learning Centers

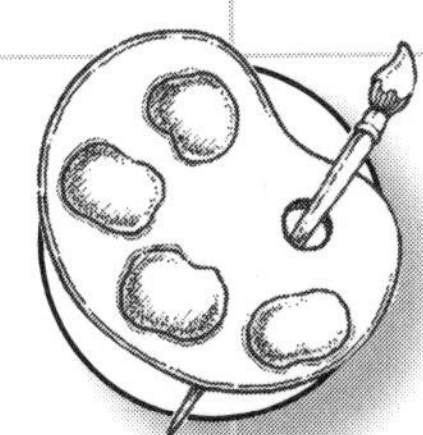

Art (Spatial, Bodily-Kinesthetic)

Fold sheets of white drawing paper in half and draw one half of a butterfly using the fold as the center. Encourage the children to cut around the lines, then open their paper and find a butterfly. Invite the children to place teaspoons of two or three different colors of thick tempera paint on the butterfly's wings. Show them how to fold the paper and smooth the wings to create a nice blotto design on the inside.

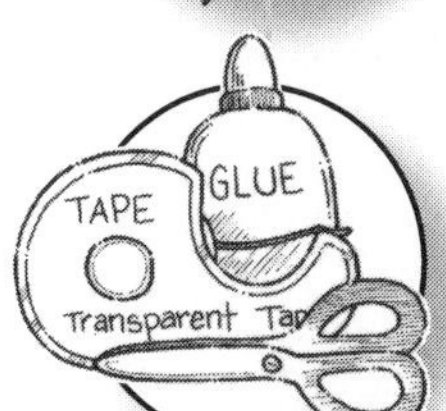

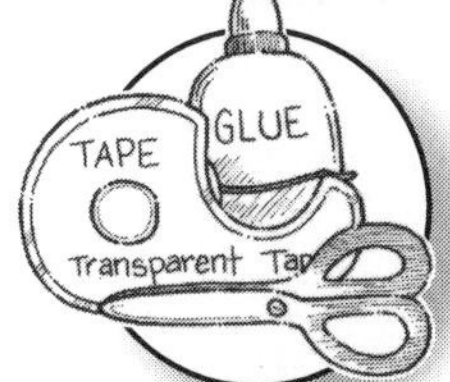

Construction (Bodily-Kinesthetic)

Invite the children to use an eyedropper to drop watered-down food coloring onto a coffee filter to create a colorful design. Be sure to call attention to the spread of the colors (absorption). When the filters are dry, help the children thread the filter into the slot of a non-spring wooden clothespin to make a butterfly. A marker can be used to add eyes. A small piece of pipe cleaner makes a great pair of antennae when wrapped around the head of the clothespin.

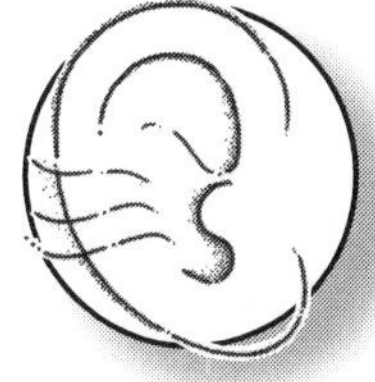

Listening (Musical, Intrapersonal, Interpersonal)

Provide classical music, perhaps "Madame Butterfly." Invite the children to use the scarves to create a butterfly dance.

Math (Logical-Mathematical, Spatial)

Give the children the Butterfly Match Game (Appendix p. 383) and challenge them to match the butterflies by wing pattern.

Science (Naturalist)

Provide the Metamorphosis Sequence Cards (Appendix p. 530). Encourage the children to arrange the cards in the correct sequence. As they arrange the cards, encourage them to talk about each step.

Writing (Linguistic)

Provide a tray of sand or salt that has been colored yellow with powdered tempera paint to resemble pollen. Invite the children to write the word "butterfly" in the pollen.

Closing Circle (Reflections on the Day)

Ask the children:

1. What did you learn about butterflies today?
2. How are butterflies and bees alike? How are they different?

Worms

Morning Circle

1. Sing "Nobody Likes Me" (Appendix p. 297). Serve gummy worm candy for the children to eat.
2. Find out what the children know about worms. Show them live worms or photos of worms.
3. Ask the children if worms are insects. Count the body parts. The worm has no legs. It has many body parts or segments.
   - Worms belong to a family of bugs called anthropoids (meaning no legs).
   - Worms help keep the dirt and soil loose. They make tunnels under the ground.
   - Birds and fish eat worms.
   - Worms eat decaying things. They also eat corn, apples, and pasta.
4. Tell the children that today's activities will be about worms.

Story Circle

There's a Hair in My Dirt: A Worm's Story by Gary Larson

Music and Movement

Invite the children to get into a line, hold on to each other's waists, and "worm" their way around the classroom.

Art (Spatial)

Give the children Styrofoam packing chips (the ones that look like worms). Provide tempera paint and invite them to paint worms.

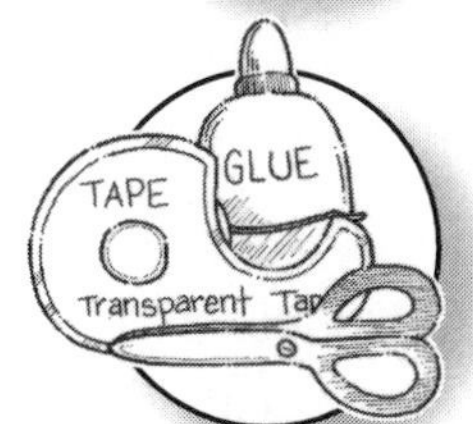

Construction (Spatial, Linguistic, Bodily-Kinesthetic)

Give each child one leg cut from a pair from pantyhose. Provide newspaper for stuffing. Encourage the children to wad up the newspaper and stuff their worm. When the worm is all stuffed, tie off the open end. Provide felt to glue on eyes. When the children have finished making their worm invite them to give their worm a name.

Discovery (Naturalist, Interpersonal)

Place a shovel full of dirt in a plastic tub and encourage the children to look through the dirt for worms. Make compost. Dig up the dirt to create a moist starting spot. Stack leaves and decaying materials over the dirt. Leftover lunch scraps (no meat) will help feed the inhabitants of your compost.

Fine Motor (Bodily-Kinesthetic)

Give the children playdough (Appendix p. 377) and encourage them to make worms by pressing the dough through a meat or garlic press.

Math (Logical-Mathematical)

Invite the children to match worms to apples in the Apple and Worm Match Game (Appendix p. 381).

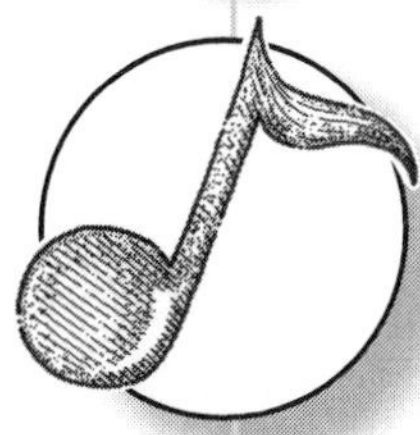

Music (Musical, Bodily-Kinesthetic)

Lay out all the rhythm band instruments. Challenge the children to figure out which instruments a worm might be able to play despite the fact that it has no arms or legs. How would a worm play the instrument? How would it sound? Invite the children to form their own worm band playing the instruments as worms might.

Closing Circle (Reflections on the Day)

Ask the children:

1. What have you learned about worms today?
2. Which band instruments did you decide a worm could play?
3. Where do you think the term "wiggle worm" comes from?

Pill Bugs

Morning Circle

1. Encourage those who wish to participate to do front rolls to the Morning Circle area. Encourage the children to take a few steps in between rolls if the distance is too great. Be sure to supervise closely.
2. Show the children live pill bugs or photos of pill bugs if available. Find out what they know about these bugs. Children in damp climates will probably have had some experiences. These bugs live in moist areas and are harmless and fascinating to children.
3. Discuss pill bugs.
   - Explain that these bugs are not bugs at all but are *Isopoda*, a class separate from other bugs and insects. Long ago, pill bugs lived only in water but now they have completely adapted to land. They still have gills just like fish.
   - Pill bugs are sometimes called "Roly Polys" because they can roll into a ball. They usually roll into a ball when they feel frightened or threatened.
   - They have oval bodies with seven pairs of legs and seven overlapping plates over their backs.
   - They are active mostly at night. They often live in damp places such as underneath logs and rocks.
   - Pill bugs are related to snails and slugs.
4. Tell the children that today's activities will be about pill bugs.

Story Circle

Pill Bugs and Sow Bugs by Elaine Pascoe
(You will probably want to show the pictures and tell the text in your own words.)

Music and Movement

Do Roly Poly Relay Races
(Appendix p. 367).

Take a walk outdoors in search of pill bugs. Look under logs and rocks.

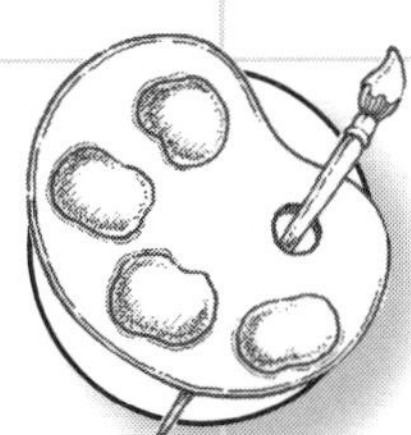

Art (Spatial, Bodily-Kinesthetic)

Provide tempera paint, Ping-Pong balls, paper, and a shallow box (10" x 15" or larger). Put the paper in the bottom of the box. Invite the children to dip the Ping-Pong balls in the tempera paint, place them in the box, and roll them around to create "roly-poly" art.

Gross Motor (Bodily-Kinesthetic, Interpersonal)

Provide an exercise mat or cushioned surface. Encourage the children to practice front rolls.

Math (Logical-Mathematical)

Give the children gray ovals (about 3" x 4" in size) cut from construction paper to represent the body of the pill bug. Provide several 1" segments of pipe cleaners. Challenge the children to place seven legs on each side of the pill bug's body.

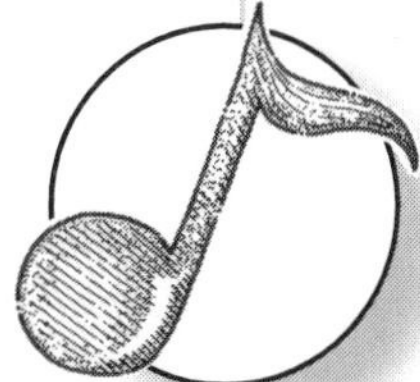

Music (Musical, Interpersonal)

Give the children Musical Balls (Appendix p. 395) that you have painted gray to represent pill bugs. You can enhance the pill bug by adding thread to represent antennae and drawing a pair of eyes with a marker. Invite the children to roll the "pill bugs" around in a box to create buggy bell tones.

Science (Naturalist)

Provide live pill bugs or pictures of pill bugs for children to study.

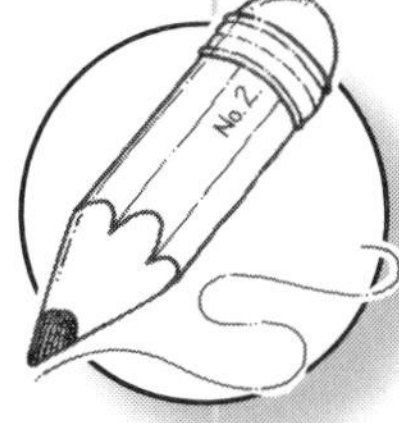

Writing (Linguistic, Intrapersonal, Logical-Mathematical)

Provide an inkpad, paper and pencils. Encourage the children to make thumbprint pill bugs. Challenge them to add the seven pairs of legs and antennae with a pencil or pen. Invite them to name their bug and to dictates a sentence about what might cause the pill bug to roll into a ball.

Closing Circle (Reflections on the Day)

Ask the children:

1. What have you learned about pill bugs today?
2. How are pill bugs like other bugs we have studied? How are they different?
3. How are pill bugs like fish?

Spiders

Morning Circle

1. Read "The Spider and the Fly" (Appendix p. 325). Why was the fly afraid to go into the spider's parlor?
2. Discuss spiders. Explain that spiders are not insects, but belong to a class of animals called arthropods.
   - Spiders have two body parts: the cephalothorax and the abdomen. They have eight legs.
   - Most spiders spin sticky webs (using their spinnerets) to use as traps to catch their prey. They kill their prey by biting them with poisonous fangs.
   - Insects are the main food source of spiders.
   - Some spiders live in holes in the ground and in the bark of trees.
   - Spiders come in all sizes. The bird-eating spider can have a leg span of one foot. Other spiders are so small you can barely see them.
3. Tell the children that today's activities will be about spiders.

Story Circle

Be Nice to Spiders by Margaret Bloom Graham
"Itsy Bitsy Spider" song cards (Appendix p. 291)
Miss Spider's Tea Party by David Kirk
Silly Spider by David Wood
"There Was an Old Lady Who Swallowed a Fly" puppet song (Appendix p. 302)
The Very Busy Spider by Eric Carle

Music and Movement

Teach the children how to do the Spider Walk (Appendix p. 368). Ask questions. Is it difficult to move? Why? Why does the spider not have any trouble moving with eight legs?

Sing "Itsy Bitsy Spider" using the song cards (Appendix p. 291, 461-462).

Take a nature hike in search of spider webs.

Act out "Little Miss Muffet" (Appendix p. 322), "Little Miss Spider" (Appendix p. 322), or "There Was an Old Lady Who Swallowed a Fly" (Appendix p. 302).

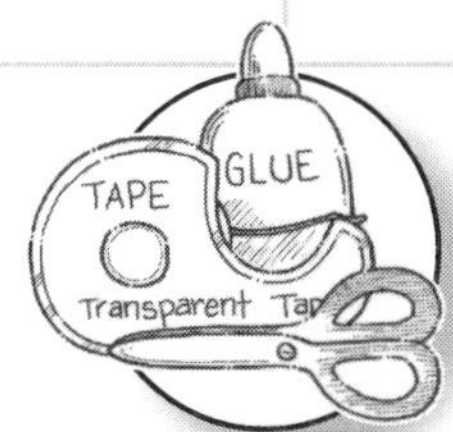

Construction (Spatial, Bodily-Kinesthetic)

Invite the children to make Spider Hats (Appendix p. 401).

Dramatic Play (Spatial, Musical, Interpersonal, Bodily-Kinesthetic)

Invite the children to make Dancing Spiders (Appendix p. 386). Encourage them to use the spiders as puppets and make up a puppet show. Suggest they might want to act out "Little Miss Muffet" (Appendix p. 322). Why was Miss Muffet frightened? Was the spider afraid?

Gross Motor (Bodily-Kinesthetic)

Make a maze with yarn to resemble a spider web. Invite the children to pretend to be flies. Encourage them to navigate their way through the web without touching any part of it.

Language (Linguistic, Intrapersonal)

Encourage the children to use the Itsy Bitsy Spider song cards (Appendix p. 461-462) to sequence the events in the song. Ask the children to make a list of reasons why the spider went up the spout again. Was she determined?

Math (Logical-Mathematical, Spatial)

Give the children playdough (Appendix p. 377) and pipe cleaners (cut into 3" segments). Challenge the children to use the playdough to fashion the body of a spider and then use the pipe cleaners to add the eight legs.

Science (Naturalist, Spatial, Bodily-Kinesthetic)

Invite the children to make web rubbings using Three-D Glue Designs (Appendix p. 402) as a surface. Give them paper and crayons to rub over the dried glue web design.

LEARNING CENTERS

Closing Circle (Reflections on the Day)

Ask the children:

1. What did you learn about spiders today?
2. How are spiders like the other insects we have studied? How are they different?
3. Why was it difficult to move in a specific direction when we were doing the "Spider Walk?"

Assessment for "Little Things"

Intellectual Strength	Assessment
Linguistic	Show the children pictures of insects and ask them to tell you something they know about each insect. Ask the children how insects are different from bugs.
Spatial	Have the children draw insects and bugs and describe the difference in the characteristics of each.
Musical Bodily-Kinesthetic	Have the children match the movement of insects and bugs to selections of classical music. Ask them to demonstrate the movement of the insect or bug with the music.
Logical-Mathematical	Ask the children to describe in numbers the body parts of insects, spiders, and worms.
Intrapersonal Interpersonal	Invite the children to describe how insects and bugs might feel when surrounded or captured by people.
Naturalist	Have the children classify insects and bugs into two categories and then make subcategories of each that are determined by how the insects or bugs move.

Books

Books Used in "Little Things"

A Ladybug's Life by John Himmelman
A New Butterfly: My First Look at Metamorphosis by Pamela Hickman
The Ant Bully by John Nickle
Ant Cities by Author Durros
Are You a Ladybug? by Judy Allen
Be Nice to Spiders by Margaret Bloom Graham
Buzz by Janet Wong
Charlie Caterpillar by Dom Deluise
Creepy, Crawly Caterpillars by Mary Facklam
Five Little Ladybugs by Karyn Henley
From Caterpillar to Butterfly by Deborah Heiligman
Grasshoppers and Crickets by Theresa Greenaway
The Grouchy Ladybug by Eric Carle
Hey, Little Ant by Phillip Hoose
The Honeybee and the Robber by Eric Carle
Honeybee's Busy Day by Richard Fowler
I Wish I Were a Butterfly by James Howe
Inside an Ant Colony by Allan Fowler
Ladybug on the Move by Richard Fowler
Ladybug, Ladybug by Ruth Brown
Ladybug's Birthday by Steven Metzger
Leaping Grasshoppers by Christine Zuchora-Walske
The Little Red Ant and the Great Big Crumb: A Mexican Fable by Shirley Climo
Miss Spider's Tea Party by David Kirk
Old Black Fly by Jim Aylesworth
One Hundred Hungry Ants by Bonnie Mac Kain
Pill Bugs and Sow Bugs by Elaine Pascoe
Quick as a Cricket by Audrey Wood
Silly Spider by David Wood
The Very Busy Spider by Eric Carle
The Very Hungry Caterpillar by Eric Carle
The Very Quiet Cricket by Eric Carle
There Was an Old Lady Who Swallowed a Fly by Simms Taback
There's a Hair in My Dirt: A Worm's Story by Gary Larson
Two Bad Ants by Chris Van Allsburg

Books

Waiting for Wings by Lois Elhert
Where Butterflies Grow by Joanne Ryder
Why Mosquitoes Buzz in Peoples Ears: A West African Tale by Verna Aardema

Other Books About Insects and Bugs

Alpha Bugs: A Pop-Up Alphabet by David Carter
Bug! Bugs! Bugs! by Jennifer Dussling
Creepy Crawlies by Cathy Kilpatrick
Icky Bug Alphabet Book by Jerry Pallotta
Icky Bug Counting Book by Jerry Pallotta
In the Tall, Tall Grass by Denise Fleming
It's a Good Thing There Are Insects Big Book by Allan Fowler

Things That Go Together

Clothing and Accessories

Morning Circle

1. Prepare a box of clothing items that go together such as pairs of socks, mittens, socks and shoes, or shorts and belt. When the children come to circle, take the pairs of items out of the box one at a time and discuss the relationship between the items. You may want to make a game of this. Place three items on the floor, two that go together and one that doesn't. Ask the children which two items go together.
2. Ask the children to think of other clothing items that go together. Make a list of the items they suggest.
3. Sing "Cap, Mittens, Shoes, and Socks" (Appendix p. 284).
4. Tell the children that today's activities will be about clothing items that go together.

Story Circle

Caps, Hats, Socks, and Mittens by Louise Bordon
The Mitten by Jan Brett

Music and Movement

Act out "Dressed for Play" action story (Appendix p. 332).

Do the motions to "I Can Do It Myself" (Appendix p. 319).

Play "Drop the Mitten" the same as you would "Drop the Handkerchief" (Appendix p. 358).

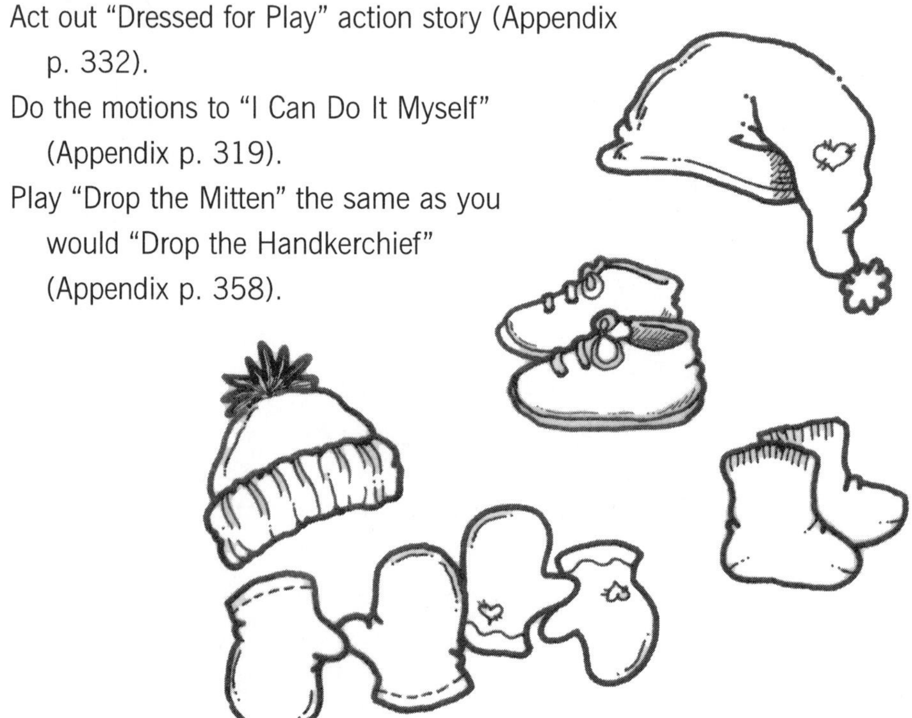

Discovery (Naturalist)

Provide nature items such as leaves, flowers, or acorns and a roll of masking tape. Encourage the children to create Nature Bracelets (Appendix p. 395) for their arms.

Dramatic Play (Interpersonal, Spatial, Intrapersonal)

Provide a large variety of hats for the children to explore. Which hat do they think looks best on them?

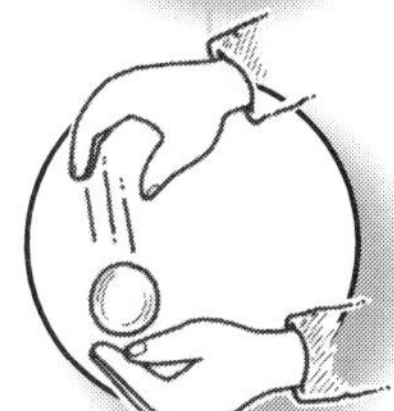

Fine Motor (Bodily-Kinesthetic)

Provide shoes with laces. Invite the children to lace the shoes.

Gross Motor (Musical)

Tape quarters on the bottoms of old shoes to make tap shoes. Play music and let the children try out the tap shoes.
(Supervise closely at all times!)

Language (Linguistic)

Cut several pairs of mittens out of the same color of construction paper. Place an upper- and lower-case alphabet letter on each pair of mittens. Mix the mittens up and challenge the children to put the mittens back into matching pairs.

Math (Logical-Mathematical)

Write the numerals 1 through 5 on five index cards. Provide play rings (or make rings with pipe cleaners). Invite the children to choose a card and then place the number of rings on their fingers that match the number they drew.

Closing Circle (Reflections on the Day)

Ask the children:

1. Which activity was your favorite today? Why?
2. Can you name two things that go with a shoe?

Food and Food Things

Morning Circle

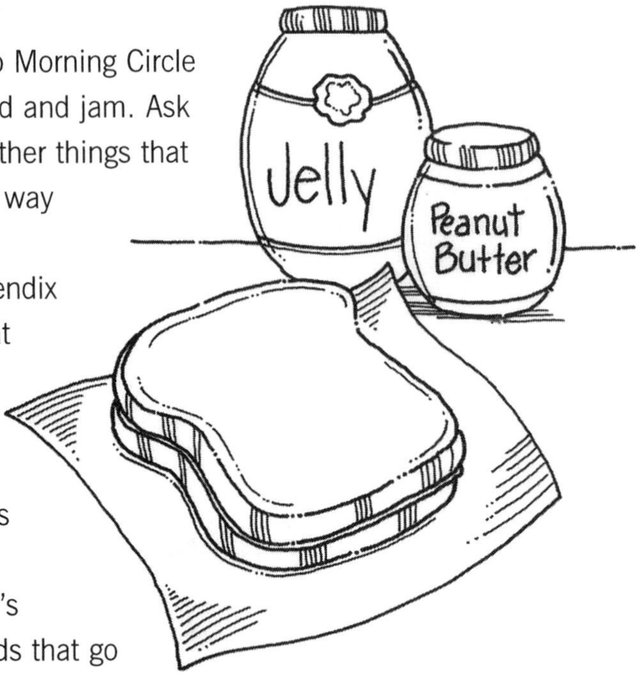

1. When the children come to Morning Circle serve them a piece of bread and jam. Ask them if they can think of other things that go with bread in the same way that jam does.
2. Sing "Peanut Butter" (Appendix p. 299). Discuss foods that go together. Are cookies better when they are served with milk? Do you like pancakes without syrup?
3. Tell the children that today's activities will be about foods that go together.

Story Circle

Bread and Jam for Frances by Russell Hoban
Green Eggs and Ham by Dr. Seuss
If You Give a Mouse a Cookie by Laura Joffe Numeroff
Pancakes for Breakfast by Tomie dePaola

Music and Movement

Sing "Peanut Butter" (Appendix p. 299) or "Who Stole the Cookie from the Cookie Jar?" (Appendix p. 369).

Learning Centers

Discovery (Logical-Mathematical, Musical, Naturalist)

Invite the children to place matched pairs of Sound Maker Eggs (Appendix p. 400) side by side in an egg carton.

Dramatic Play (Interpersonal, Musical, Intrapersonal, Linguistic)

Provide milk and cookies, a bedtime storybook, lullaby tape, blanket, rocker, and a baby doll. Invite the children to pretend to put the baby to bed.

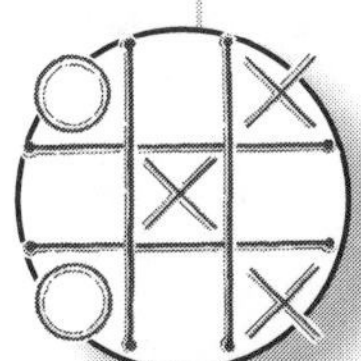

Games (Naturalist)

Provide food containers that can be matched, such as a milk carton and cereal box, a syrup bottle and a pancake mix box, or a milk carton and a cookie box. Invite the children to pair the containers.

Gross Motor (Bodily-Kinesthetic)

Make cookies by cutting circles out of playdough (Appendix p. 377), foam, or cardboard. Invite the children to toss the cookies into a cookie jar.

Math (Spatial, Logical-Mathematical)

Give the children cakes cut from brown (chocolate) and yellow (vanilla) felt and icing cut from several different colors of felt. Provide candles also cut from felt. Invite the children to create birthday cakes and then put candles on their creations.

Snack (Interpersonal, Linguistic, Logical-Mathematical)

Invite the children to use rebus directions to make Homemade Peanut Butter (Appendix p. 494). Provide crackers so the children can have peanut butter and crackers for snack.
(Check for allergies)

Closing Circle (Reflections on the Day)

Ask the children:

1. What is your favorite pair of food items?
2. What is the first thing you do when making a peanut butter and jelly sandwich?

Playthings

Morning Circle

1. Blow bubbles (Appendix p. 375) as the children are coming to Morning Circle.
2. Ask the children how to blow the bubbles without a wand.
3. Talk about toys that have two parts, such as a ball and bat, drum and drumstick, or tape player and tape. Would any of those toys be as much fun if a part were missing?

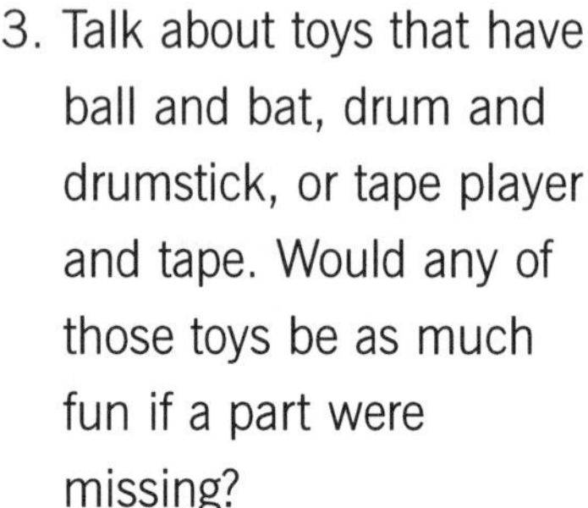

4. Do the "Jack-in-the-Box" fingerplay (Appendix p. 312) with the children. Would a Jack-in-the-Box be as much fun if there was no Jack?
5. Tell the children that today's activities will be about playthings that go together.

Story Circle

Geraldine's Blanket by Holly Keller
Harold and the Purple Crayon by Crockett Johnson
Playing Right Field by Willy Welsh

Music and Movement

Blow bubbles outdoors. What do you need to go with the bubble solution?

Play baseball outdoors. Talk about the equipment you need: a ball, a bat, and a glove.

Sing "Say, Say, My Playmate" (Appendix p. 300).

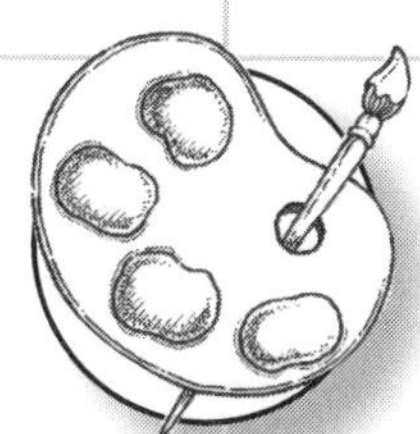

ART (SPATIAL)

Provide crayons and coloring books and invite the children to color in the books. Ask the children if they can use the coloring books without crayons. Would it be as much fun without crayons?

DRAMATIC PLAY (INTERPERSONAL, INTRAPERSONAL)

Give the children the Dress Me Dolls (Appendix p. 522-525) to play with. Would the dolls be as much fun to play with if they didn't have clothes to put on?

GROSS MOTOR (BODILY-KINESTHETIC, NATURALIST, LOGICAL-MATHEMATICAL)

Provide bubbles (Appendix p. 375) and a wand. Invite the children to blow bubbles. Show the children how to blow bubbles using their hand as a wand. What do you think it would feel like to be a bubble?

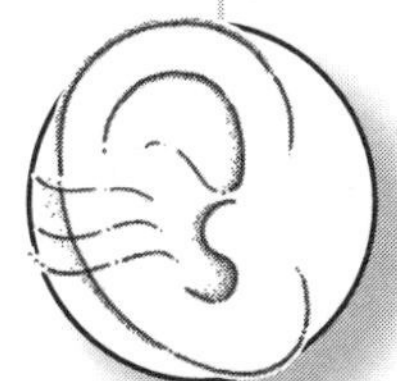

LANGUAGE (LINGUISTIC, SPATIAL)

Provide a chalkboard and chalk. Invite the children to write or draw on the chalkboard. Is there anything else you could use if you didn't have chalk?

LISTENING (MUSICAL)

Provide a tape player and cassette tapes for the children. What would you do with the tape player if you didn't have tapes? Provide a Drum and Drumsticks (Appendix p. 387) and a xylophone and mallets for the children to play.

SAND AND WATER (BODILY-KINESTHETIC, SPATIAL)

Provide sand pails and shovels. Invite the children to build with and explore the sand. Does using the sand pails and shovel make the play more fun? Does it make building easier?

Closing Circle (Reflections on the Day)

Ask the children:

1. What did you learn about playthings that go together?
2. Which activity was your favorite? Why?

Animal Homes and Animal Things

Morning Circle

1. Cut a honeycomb out of gold or tan bulletin board paper. Use a marker to make the sections of the honeycomb. Place the honeycomb in the circle area. When the children arrive at school, have them fly like bumblebees to the Morning Circle.
2. Show the children animals' homes (a bird's nest, a hermit crab's home, a dirt dauber's mud home, wasp nest, or honeycomb).
3. Invite the children to think of other animal homes.
4. Read the chant "Birdie, Birdie, Where Is Your Nest?" (Appendix p. 314) with the children.
5. Tell the children that today's activities will be about animals and their homes...things that go together.

Story Circle

Animal Homes by Brian Wildsmith

"Ms. Bumblebee Gathers Honey" puppet story (Appendix p. 343, 468)

Music and Movement

Go on a nature walk in search of animal homes.

Act out "Going on a Bear Hunt" (Appendix p. 317).

Sing "The Ants Go Marching" (Appendix p. 283) or recite "The Spider and the Fly" (Appendix p. 325).

FINE MOTOR (Bodily-Kinesthetic, Spatial)

Give the children a Magnetic Maze (Appendix p. 394). Use an ant hill for the finishing touch of the maze. Use an ant magnet for the traveler on the maze. Or, give the children clay to make dirt dauber homes.

GROSS MOTOR (Bodily-Kinesthetic, Spatial, Intrapersonal)

Make a large spider web in the classroom out of yarn or string. Invite the children to attempt going through the web like a maze without touching the yarn or string.

LANGUAGE (Linguistic, Interpersonal, Bodily-Kinesthetic)

Give the children the "Ms. Bumblebee Gathers Honey" puppets (Appendix p. 468). Invite the children to re-enact the story or make up a new story.

LANGUAGE (Linguistic, Musical, Logical-Mathematical)

Invite the children to re-enact "Going on a Bear Hunt" (Appendix p. 317). Provide sound makers for them to use to create sound effects. For example, provide a canister of paper clips to shake to make the sound of going through the wheat field, a bottle of water to slosh for swimming across the river, a couple of sticks to tap together, or a squeaky hinge for climbing the tree.

MATH (Logical-Mathematical)

Give the children the Frog Count Game (Appendix p. 389). Invite them to match the frogs to lily pads.

SNACK (Interpersonal, Linguistic, Logical-Mathematical)

Invite the children to make Bird Nest Candy using the rebus recipe (Appendix p. 490). Serve the candy for snack.

Closing Circle (Reflections on the Day)

Ask the children:

1. Which animal has the best home?
2. What kinds of homes do people have?

Transportation

Morning Circle

1. Place a collection of transportation toys on the floor in the circle area (cars, buses, airplanes, trains, and so on).
2. Pass the toys around for children to examine. Talk about the parts of the vehicle that make it possible for the vehicle to move. For example, cars, trains, and buses need wheels; airplanes need wings; and horses and people need legs.
3. Sing "The Wheels on the Bus" (Appendix p. 306). Talk about the parts of the bus mentioned in the song—wheels, wipers, horn, and driver.
4. Tell the children that today's activities will be about transportation vehicles and their parts.

Story Circle

A Bicycle for Rosaura by Daniel Barbot
The Blueberry Train by C.L.G. Martin
Freight Train by Donald Crews
Planes by Anne Rockwell
School Bus by Donald Crews
The Wheels on the Bus by Paul O. Zelinsky

Music and Movement

Use the riding toys outdoors today. Point out the parts of the vehicle that make it move.

Sing "My Little Red Wagon" (Appendix p. 297), "Down by the Station" (Appendix p. 286), "Little Hunk of Tin" (Appendix p. 293), "Row, Row, Row Your Boat" (Appendix p. 300), "Little Red Caboose" (Appendix p. 293), or "A Sailor Went to Sea" (Appendix p. 300).

Do the fingerplay, "My Airplane" (Appendix p. 312).

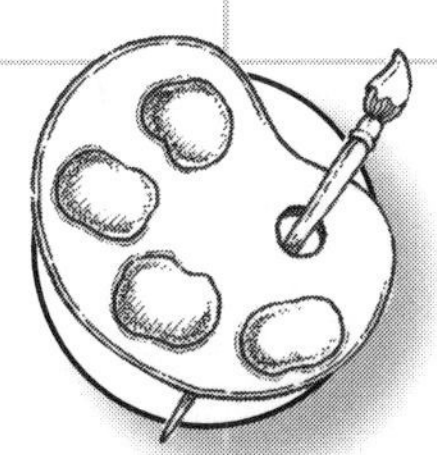

ART (SPATIAL)

Provide a shallow tray of tempera paint, paper, and small cars. Invite the children to run the cars through the tempera paint and then over their paper to make car track designs.

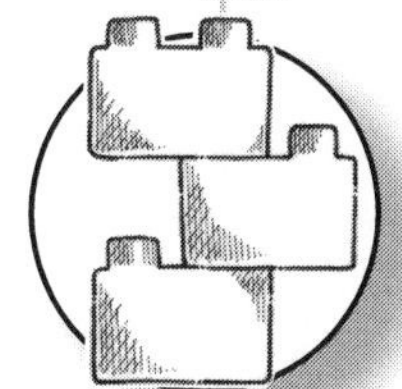

Blocks (LINGUISTIC, NATURALIST)

Make Garages (Appendix p. 390). Use masking tape to label the garages with the names of children and label a set of small cars with the same names. Invite the children to park the cars in the corresponding garages.

DRAMATIC PLAY (INTERPERSONAL, BODILY-KINESTHETIC)

Give the children a variety of shoes to explore including high heels, slippers, boots, and sandals. Which shoes fit their feet the best? Which shoes allow them to move quickly? Which shoes would be best for walking?

GROSS MOTOR (BODILY-KINESTHETIC, LOGICAL-MATHEMATICAL, NATURALIST)

Help the children construct an inclined plane using a plank. Invite them to roll a variety of cars and trucks down the ramp. Which ones move more quickly? Why?

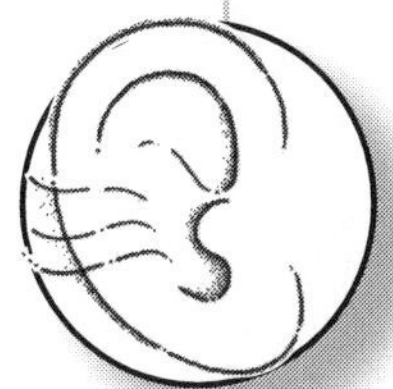

LISTENING (MUSICAL)

Invite the children to use empty toilet paper or paper towels tubes as train whistles. Encourage them to try to make a sound through the tube that sounds like a train whistle.

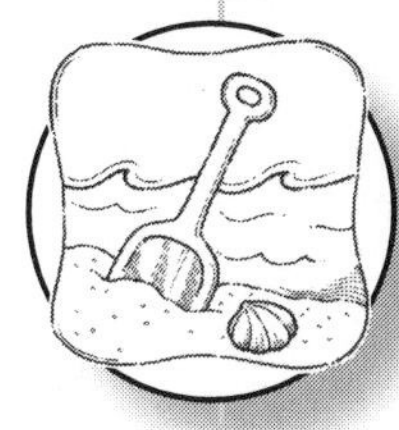

SAND AND WATER (NATURALIST, INTERPERSONAL, LOGICAL-MATHEMATICAL)

Invite the children to make Walnut Shell Boats (Appendix p. 404). Have them first try to get their boats to move on the water by blowing on them without a sail, then with a sail. Does the boat need a sail to float? Does the boat need a sail to go faster?

Closing Circle (Reflections on the Day)

Ask the children:

1. What is your favorite way to travel? Why?
2. How are all the transportation vehicles alike? How are they different?

Assessment for "Things That Go Together"

Intellectual Strength	Assessment
Linguistic Intrapersonal Logical-Mathematical	Give the children pairs of items that go together and ask them to describe the relationship of each pair. For example, a fork and a spoon go together because they are both silverware.
Spatial	Have the children draw pictures of items that go together.
Musical	Invite the children to use the structure of "Sing a Song of Opposites" (Appendix p. 301) and the tune to "Mary Had a Little Lamb" (Appendix p. 294) to make up several verses of a song about things that go together. For example, in the case of shoes and socks, the words might be: *"These are socks, and these are shoes,* *These are socks, these are shoes,* *These are socks and these are shoes,* *I wear them on my feet."*
Interpersonal Bodily-Kinesthetic Naturalist	Provide a box of items that go together and ask the children to match the items. Then ask the children to describe how or why the items go together. You might also ask the children if any of the sets of items that go together might also go with another set of items. For example, if you have a cup and saucer, will they go with a knife and fork? How/why?

Books

Books Used in "Things That Go Together"

A Bicycle for Rosaura by Daniel Barbot
Animal Homes by Brian Wildsmith
The Blueberry Train by C.L.G. Martin
Bread and Jam for Frances by Russell Hoban
Caps, Hats, Socks, and Mittens by Louise Bordon
Freight Train by Donald Crews
Geraldine's Blanket by Holly Keller
Green Eggs and Ham by Dr. Seuss
Harold and the Purple Crayon by Crockett Johnson
If You Give a Mouse a Cookie by Laura Joffe Numeroff
The Mitten by Jan Brett
Pancakes for Breakfast by Tomie dePaola
Planes by Anne Rockwell
Playing Right Field by Willy Welsh
School Bus by Donald Crews
The Wheels on the Bus by Paul O. Zelinsky

Other Books About Things That Go Together

Love and Kisses by Sarah Wilson
Pooh's Go Together Game
Some Things Go Together by Charlotte Zolotow
They Go Together by Peter Spizzirri
Where Does It Go? by Margaret Miller
Who Uses This? by Margaret Miller

It's Chow Time!

Breads, Cereals, Rice, and Pastas

Morning Circle

1. Sing "The Muffin Man" (Appendix p. 295) with the children.
2. Discuss breads, cereals, and pastas with children. Find out how many types of foods the children can name from this food group. Explain to the children that they need to eat something from this food group every day. The US Department of Agriculture recommends 6–11 servings each day.
3. Invite the children to sample dry cereal.
4. Tell the children that today's activities will be about breads, cereals, and pastas.

Story Circle

Bread, Bread, Bread by Ann Morris
Daddy Makes the Best Spaghetti by Anna Grossnickle Hines
Everybody Cooks Rice by Norah Dooley
Jalapeño Bagels by Natasha Wing
"The Little Red Hen" puppet story (Appendix p. 340, 437)
Minnie Maloney and MacAroni by Mark Alan Stamaty
Noodles by Sarah Weeks
Pancakes for Breakfast by Tomie De Paola
Pancakes, Pancakes by Eric Carle
Spaghetti for Suzy by Peta Coplans
This is the Bread I Baked for Ned by Crescent Dragonwagon
Wednesday is Spaghetti Day by Maryann Cocca-Leffler

Music and Movement

Sing "The Donut Song" (Appendix p. 286) or "Oats, Peas, Beans, and Barley Grow" (Appendix p. 297)

*If the children are at school for lunch, be sure to serve some bread, cereal, rice, or pasta. Are the children able to recognize which foods on their plates belong to this group?

Dramatic Play (Interpersonal, Intrapersonal)

Provide props such as rolling pins, cookie cutters, bowls, aprons, and playdough. Invite the children to set up a bakery.

Fine Motor (Bodily-Kinesthetic, Naturalist)

Provide magazines, paper, scissors, and glue. Invite the children to find pictures of breads, cereals, and pastas, cut them out and glue them to their paper.

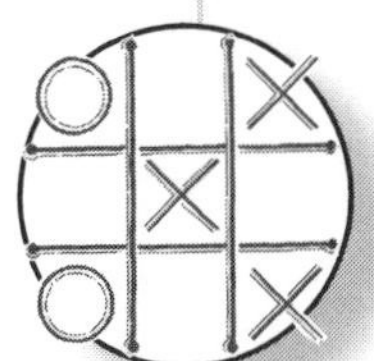

Games (Spatial, Logical-Mathematical)

Cut 6 to 8 yellow yarn strips varying in length from 3" to 12" to represent spaghetti. Encourage the children to arrange the strips from shortest to longest. Or, use yellow straws cut in various lengths.

Language (Linguistic, Spatial)

Make puzzles out of the sides of cereal boxes. Invite the children to put the puzzles together.

Library (Interpersonal, Intrapersonal, Linguistic, Musical)

Provide "The Little Red Hen" puppets (Appendix p. 437). Invite the children to create a puppet show.

Snack (Spatial)

Give the children a slice of bread for snack. Invite them to take bites around the edges of the bread to create a special design.

Learning Centers

Closing Circle (Reflections on the Day)

Ask the children:

1. What is your favorite food from this group of foods—cereal, bread, rice, or pasta?
2. What was your favorite activity today? Why?

Milk, Yogurt, and Cheese

Morning Circle

1. Teach the children "Ice Cream" (Appendix p. 321).
2. Discuss milk, yogurt, and cheese with children. Find out how many types of foods the children can name from this food group. Explain that the children need to eat something from this food group every day. The US Department of Agriculture recommends two to three servings a day.

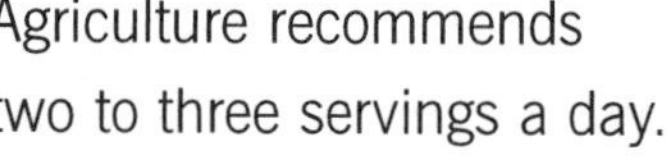

3. Invite the children to sample cheese. (Check for allergies)
4. Tell the children that today's activities will be about milk, yogurt, and cheese.

Story Circle

Extra Cheese Please! by Cris Peterson
It Looked Like Spilt Milk by Charles Shaw
Milk by Donald Carrick
The Milk Makers by Gail Gibbons

Music and Movement

Play "Mouse and Cheese" as you would "Dog and Bone" (Appendix p. 358).
Play Twist dance music and pretend to be milk shakes shaking.

*If the children are at school for lunch, be sure to serve some of this food group. Are the children able to recognize which foods on their plates belong to this group?

ART (Spatial)

Mix Puff Paint (Appendix p. 377). Invite the children to paint it onto cardboard circles to simulate putting whipped cream on pies.

DISCOVERY (Naturalist)

Give the children milk cartons of various sizes. Invite them to arrange the cartons from the smallest to the largest.

Look at cheese under a magnifying glass.

FINE MOTOR (Bodily-Kinesthetic, Naturalist)

Provide magazines, paper, scissors, and glue. Invite the children to find pictures of milk, ice cream, and cheese. Then encourage the children to cut them out and glue them to their papers.

MATH (Logical-Mathematical)

Give the children the Ice Cream Cone Match Game (Appendix p. 391). Invite them to match cones to ice cream.

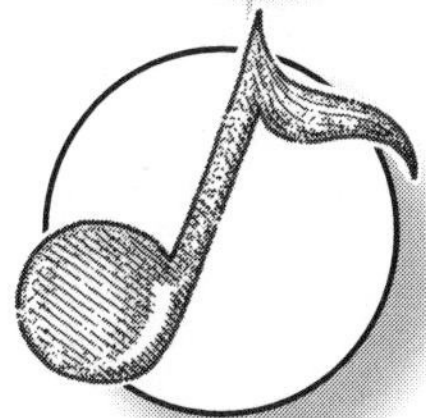

MUSIC (Musical, Naturalist)

Give the children Milk Carton Shakers (Appendix p. 394). Invite them to play the shakers in rhythm to music.

SNACK (Logical-Mathematical, Linguistic, Interpersonal)

Invite the children to make and sample Frozen Yogurt using the rebus directions (Appendix p. 491). Or let the children help mix and then enjoy one of the Blender Drinks made from milk (Appendix p. 371-372). (Check for allergies)

Closing Circle (Reflections on the Day)

Ask the children:

1. Which food from this group do you like best?
2. What was you favorite activity today?

Meat, Poultry, Fish, Beans, Eggs, and Nuts

Morning Circle

1. Sing "Peanut Butter" (Appendix p. 299) with the children.
2. Discuss meats, poultry, fish, beans, eggs, and nuts. Find out how many types of foods the children can name from this food group. Explain that the children need to eat something from this food group every day. The US Department of Agriculture recommends two to three servings a day.
3. Invite the children to sample nuts. (Check for allergies)
4. Tell the children that today's activities will be about meats, poultry, fish, beans, eggs, and nuts.

Story Circle

Cloudy with a Chance of Meatballs by Judi Barrett
Don't Forget the Bacon! by Pat Hutchins
Fish Fry Tonight by Jackie French Koller
Green Eggs and Ham by Dr. Seuss
Too Many Tamales by Gary Soto

Music and Movement

Play "Duck, Duck, Goose" (Appendix p. 359).

Sing "Oats, Peas, Beans, and Barley Grow" (Appendix p. 297), "Found a Peanut" (Appendix p. 287), or "Five Fat Turkeys Are We" (Appendix p. 316).

Suggest that the children perform Egg Rolls (front rolls) across the floor. If the children are not skilled in rolling, have them roll on a mat or on the grass outdoors for safety. (Supervise closely at all times!)

*If the children are at school for lunch, be sure to serve some of this food group. Are the children able to recognize which foods on their plates belong to this group?

LEARNING CENTERS

DRAMATIC PLAY (INTERPERSONAL, LOGICAL-MATHEMATICAL)

Give the children a Fishing Game (Appendix p. 388). Invite them to take a pretend fishing trip. When they have caught all the fish, challenge them to arrange the fish in order of size from the largest to the smallest.

FINE MOTOR (NATURALIST)

Provide a bowl of several different types of nuts and a pair of tongs. Encourage children to use the tongs to sort the nuts into a muffin tin. (CHECK FOR ALLERGIES)

LANGUAGE (BODILY-KINESTHETIC, LINGUISTIC, NATURALIST, INTRAPERSONAL)

Provide magazines, paper, scissors, and glue. Invite the children to find pictures of milk, ice cream, and cheese. Then cut them out and glue them to their paper. Suggest that the children glue the foods they like on one side of their paper and those they don't care for on the other side of their paper.

LIBRARY (LINGUISTIC, INTERPERSONAL, MUSICAL)

Give the children the Five Fat Turkey Puppets (Appendix p. 473-474). Encourage the children to create a puppet show with the turkeys.

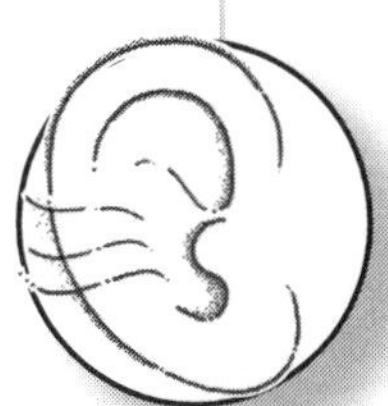

LISTENING (MUSICAL, NATURALIST)

Invite the children to place matched pairs of Sound Maker Eggs (Appendix p. 400), side by side in an egg carton.

SNACK (INTERPERSONAL)

Help the children prepare green eggs and ham (add food coloring to eggs before cooking). Invite them to sample their unusual dish.

Closing Circle (Reflections on the Day)

Ask the children:

1. Which food from this group do you like best? Why?
2. What was your favorite activity today? Why?

Fruits and Vegetables

Morning Circle

1. Sing "Apples and Bananas" (Appendix p. 283) with the children.
2. Discuss fruits and vegetables. Find out how many types of foods the children can name from this food group. Explain to the children that they need to eat something from this food group every day. The US Department of Agriculture recommends two to four servings a day.

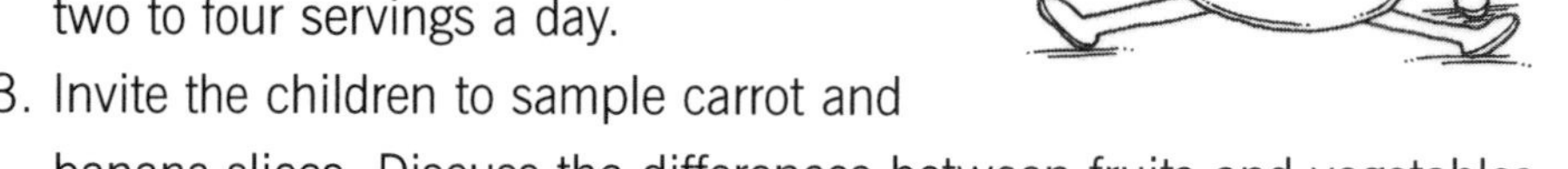

3. Invite the children to sample carrot and banana slices. Discuss the differences between fruits and vegetables.
4. Tell the children that today's activities will be about fruits and vegetables.

Story Circle

An Apple a Day by Judi Barrett
Cabbage Moon by Tim Chadwick
Corn-On and Off the Cob by Allan Fowler
Grandma's Latkes by Malka Drucker
"The Great Big Pumpkin" flannel board story (Appendix p. 335, 426-427)
"The Great Big Turnip" flannel board story (Appendix p. 336, 427-428)
Growing Vegetable Soup by Lois Ehlert
No Peas for Nellie by Chris L. Demarest
Oliver's Vegetables by Vivian French
The Vegetables Go to Bed by Christopher L. King
Watermelon Day by Kathi Appelt

Music and Movement

Play Fruit Basket Turnover (Appendix p. 360).

Sing "Little Red Apple" (Appendix p. 322), "Down by the Bay" (Appendix p. 286), or do the fingerplay "Five Little Pumpkins" (Appendix p. 310).

*If the children are at school for lunch, be sure to serve some of this food group. Are the children able to recognize which foods on their plates belong to this group?

LEARNING CENTERS

Discovery (Naturalist, Linguistic)

Provide fruits and vegetables for the children to explore. Cut the fruits and vegetables so children can see both the inside and outside. Provide magnifying glasses for up-close viewing. Encourage the children to describe what they see.

Fine Motor (Bodily-Kinesthetic, Linguistic, Naturalist)

Provide magazines, paper, scissors, and glue. Invite the children to find pictures of fruits and vegetables, cut them out, and glue them to their paper. Suggest the children glue fruits on one side of their paper and vegetables on the other side.

Fine Motor (Musical, Bodily-Kinesthetic, Spatial)

Provide apple seeds and small containers such as orange juice cans or lemonade cans. Invite the children to use tweezers to pick up apple seeds and place them in the containers. Provide paints, glue, and paper. Encourage the children to decorate their seed shakers.

Gross Motor (Bodily-Kinesthetic)

Provide corn cobs or peach pits. Invite the children to toss the cobs or pits into a basket. Challenge them to take a step away from the basket each time they throw in order to increase the difficulty of hitting the target.

Math (Logical-Mathematical)

Give the children the Corny Counting Game (Appendix p. 386). Encourage them to use tweezers to place the correct number of corn kernels into each container. Give the children the Apple and Worm Match Game (Appendix p. 381). Encourage them to match worms to the holes in the apples.

Snack (Spatial, Interpersonal, Intrapersonal)

Invite the children to make Fruit Kabobs (Appendix p. 372). Challenge them to try new, unfamiliar fruits instead of just the fruits they know they like. Make Homemade Applesauce (Appendix p. 372).

Closing Circle (Reflections on the Day)

Ask the children:

1. What are some differences between fruits and vegetables?
2. What was your favorite activity today? Why?

Junk Food versus Healthy Foods

Morning Circle

1. Sing the "Raindrop Song" (Appendix p. 300) with the children.
2. Talk about junk food. Explain to the children why the food is called junk food. Remind the children why nutritious foods are important to the body. Help the children make a list of junk foods.
3. Discuss the importance of drinking water instead of sweetened juices and punch. Tell the children that water helps them feel and think better.
4. Invite the children to sample carrot sticks, yogurt, orange slices, or apple wedges. Explain that this is a healthy snack. See if the children can think of other healthy snacks.
5. Tell the children that today's activities will be about junk food and healthy foods.

Story Circle

Animal Snackers by Betsy Lewin
Curious George Goes to an Ice Cream Shop by Margret Rey
Hot Fudge by James Howe
Little Nino's Pizzeria by Karen Barbour
Mmmm . . . Cookies! by Monica Weiss
"Smart Cookie's Best Friend, Greta Graham" (Appendix p. 343, 446)
Who Stole the Cookies? by Judith Moffatt

Music and Movement

Act out "Candy Land Journey" action story (Appendix p. 329).
Sing "The Donut Song" (Appendix p. 286) or "Who Stole the Cookie from the Cookie Jar?" (Appendix p. 369)
Play the song "The Candy Man" if available and let children dance to the music.

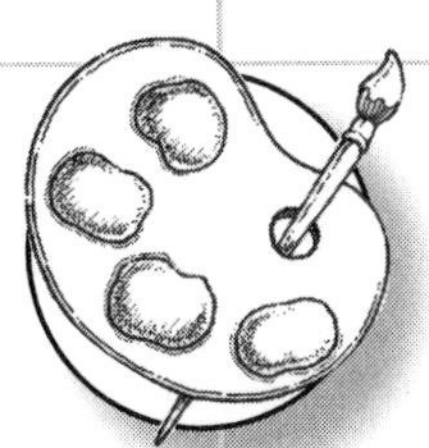

Art (Spatial, Logical-Mathematical)

Cut easel paper into big circles. Offer red and white paints and invite the children to paint peppermint wheels. Point out the red and white pattern.

Fine Motor (Bodily-Kinesthetic, Linguistic, Naturalist)

Provide magazines, paper, scissors, and glue. Invite the children to find pictures of junk food and healthy food, cut them out, and glue them to their paper. Suggest the children glue junk food on one side of their paper and healthy food on the other side.

Gross Motor (Bodily-Kinesthetic)

Make cookies by cutting circles out of playdough (Appendix p. 377), foam, or cardboard. Invite the children to toss the cookies into a cookie jar.

Math (Logical-Mathematical)

Invite the children to put the Corn Candy Puzzles (Appendix p. 386) together.

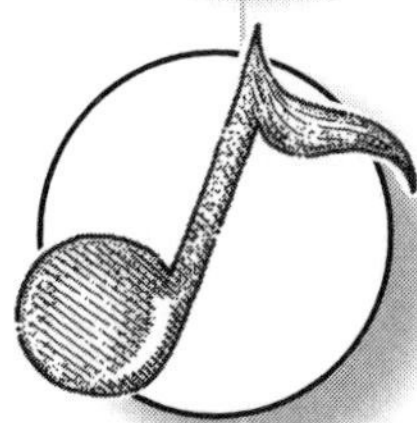

Music (Musical)

Challenge the children to think of healthy items to replace the lemon drops and gumdrops in the "Raindrop Song." For example, replacements might be tangerines and apples, or granola bars and rice cakes.

Snack (Interpersonal, Linguistic)

Invite the children to make Donuts (Appendix p. 372). Talk to them about why donuts are considered junk food.
(Supervise closely at all times!)

Closing Circle (Reflections on the Day)

Ask the children:

1. What did you learn about junk food today?
2. What healthy snack will you try?
3. How do you plan to start drinking more water?
4. What healthy things did you decide the "raindrops" could be?

Assessment for "It's Chow Time!"

Intellectual Strength	Assessment
Linguistic	Ask the children to describe a meal that would include all the food groups.
Spatial Bodily-Kinesthetic	Have the children use a magazine to find pictures of food, cut them out, and then make a collage of a meal that would include all the food groups.
Musical	Ask the children to think of songs about food and then classify the songs into food groups. For example, "Apples and Bananas" would be classified with fruit. "The Muffin Man" would be classified as a bread and cereal.
Interpersonal	Invite the children to use magazine pictures to create a meal for their family. Have them think of foods that each member likes and then figure out how to make a meal that appeals to everyone.
Intrapersonal	Have the children identify their favorite meal and then assess it as to how many food groups it represents.
Naturalist Logical-Mathematical	Provide food pictures and have the children sort them into food groups.

Books

Books Used in "It's Chow Time!"

An Apple a Day by Judi Barrett
Animal Snackers by Betsy Lewin
Bread, Bread, Bread by Ann Morris
Cabbage Moon by Tim Chadwick
Cloudy with a Chance of Meatballs by Judi Barrett
Corn-On and Off the Cob by Allan Fowler
Curious George Goes to an Ice Cream Shop by Margret Rey
Daddy Makes the Best Spaghetti by Anna Grossnickle Hines
Don't Forget the Bacon! by Pat Hutchins
Everybody Cooks Rice by Norah Dooley
Extra Cheese Please! by Cris Peterson
Fish Fry Tonight by Jackie French Koller
Grandma's Latkes by Malka Drucker
Green Eggs and Ham by Dr. Seuss
Growing Vegetable Soup by Lois Ehlert
Hot Fudge by James Howe
It Looked Like Spilt Milk by Charles Shaw
Jalapeño Bagels by Natasha Wing
Little Nino's Pizzeria by Karen Barbour
Milk by Donald Carrick
The Milk Makers by Gail Gibbons
Minnie Maloney and MacAroni by Mark Alan Stamaty
Mmmm . . . Cookies! by Monica Weiss
No Peas for Nellie by Chris L. Demarest
Noodles by Sarah Weeks
Oliver's Vegetables by Vivian French
Pancakes for Breakfast by Tomie De Paola
Pancakes, Pancakes by Eric Carle
Spaghetti for Suzy by Peta Coplans
This is the Bread I Baked for Ned by Crescent Dragonwagon
Too Many Tamales by Gary Soto
The Vegetables Go to Bed by Christopher L. King
Watermelon Day by Kathi Appelt
Wednesday is Spaghetti Day by Maryann Cocca-Leffler
Who Stole the Cookies? by Judith Moffatt

Other Books About Food

Apples and Pumpkins by Anne Rockwell
The Carrot Seed by Ruth Krauss
Chicken Soup with Rice by Maurice Sendak
From Seed to Pear by Ali Mitgutsch
Gregory, the Terrible Eater by Mitchell Sharmat
I Need a Lunch Box by Jeannette Caines
Learning Your ABC's of Nutrition by Caroline A. Glyman
Lunch by Denise Fleming
Stone Soup by Marcia Brown
This Year's Garden by Cynthia Rylant
Today Is Monday by Eric Carle
What Do I Eat? by Shirley Greenway
What's On My Plate? by Ruth Belov Gross
Who Eats What? by Patricia Lauber

Mother Goose on the Loose (Nursery Rhymes)

Humpty Dumpty

Morning Circle

1. Scatter broken eggshells along the pathway from the classroom door to the circle area. When the children arrive, have them follow the eggshells to the circle area.
2. Ask the children where they think the eggshells came from. If they don't guess Humpty Dumpty, give them some clues. For example, you might say, "I think these shells belong to an egg that fell off the wall."
3. Recite "Humpty Dumpty" (Appendix p. 318) with the children. Explain that "Humpty Dumpty" is a Mother Goose nursery rhyme and that there is a collection of these rhymes. Point out the rhyming words in the rhyme.
4. Ask the children if they can think of a way to get Humpty back together. Read them the alternative verse of the rhyme in the Appendix (p. 318). Invite the children to write another verse that reflects their ideas.
5. Tell the children that today's activities will be about the nursery rhyme, "Humpty Dumpty."

Story Circle

Humpty Dumpty by Colin Hawkins

Humpty Dumpty by Daniel Kirk

Humpty Dumpty by Kin Eagle

"Humpty Dumpty" flannel board rhyme (Appendix p. 318, 429-431)

Music and Movement

Suggest that the children perform Egg Rolls (front rolls) across the floor. If the children are not skilled in rolling, have them roll on a mat or on the grass outdoors for safety.

Act out "The Grand Old Duke of York" (Appendix p. 288).

Have a plastic egg hunt outdoors.

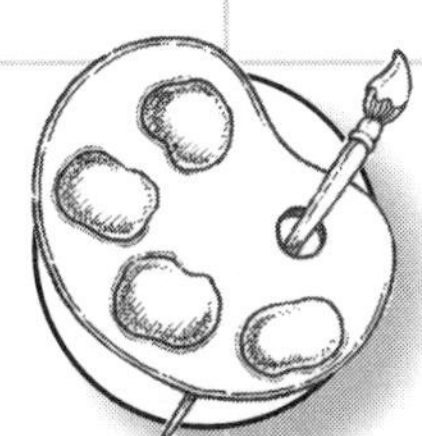

Art (Spatial)

Cut easel paper into an egg shape. Provide tempera paint and brushes and invite the children to paint Humpty Dumpty.

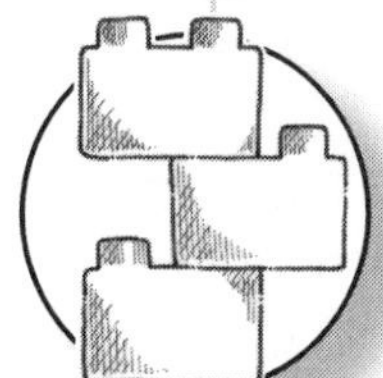

Blocks (Bodily-Kinesthetic, Spatial, Logical-Mathematical, Intrapersonal, Interpersonal)

Invite the children to build a wall with blocks. Provide plastic eggs and ask the children to see if they can balance the eggs on the wall. What makes this a difficult task?

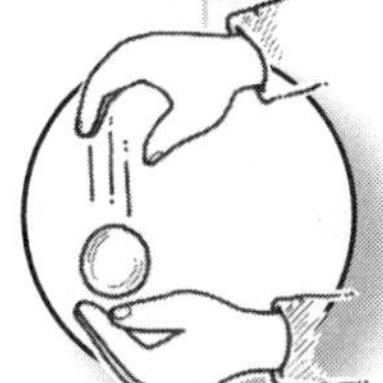

Fine Motor (Linguistic, Spatial)

Make some Humpty Dumpty Puzzles (Appendix p. 391). Invite the children to put Humpty Dumpty together.

Language (Linguistic, Interpersonal)

Give the children the "Humpty Dumpty" flannel board rhyme (Appendix p. 318, 429-431) and encourage them to re-tell the rhyme.

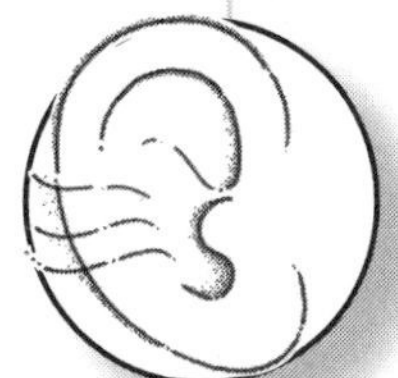

Listening (Musical, Naturalist)

Give the children the Sound Maker Eggs (Appendix p. 400). Invite them to arrange the shakers into pairs.

Snack (Interpersonal, Bodily-Kinesthetic)

Invite the children to make Humpty Dumpty Eggs (Appendix p. 373).
(Check for allergies)

LEARNING CENTERS

Closing Circle (Reflections on the Day)

Ask the children:

1. Why do you think Humpty Dumpty fell off the wall?
2. What made him so hard to put back together?

Little Miss Muffet

Morning Circle

1. Write "Little Miss Muffet" (Appendix p. 322) on a piece of chart paper or on a chalkboard. Say the rhyme with the children. Tell the children that "Little Miss Muffet" is another Mother Goose rhyme.
2. Ask the children why they think Miss Muffet was frightened. Talk about things that are scary. Introduce Verse 2 of "Little Miss Muffet" (Appendix p. 322) to the children.
3. Ask the children what "curds and whey" are. Who has eaten cottage cheese? Do they like it?
4. Tell the children that today's activities will be about the nursery rhyme, "Little Miss Muffet."

Story Circle

Little Miss Muffet and Other Nursery Rhymes by Lucy Cousins
"Little Miss Muffet" flannel board rhyme (Appendix p. 322, 435-436)
Little Miss Muffet's Count-Along Surprise by Emma Chichester Clark
Some Things Are Scary by Florence Parry Heide

Music and Movement

Invite the children to do the Spider Walk (Appendix p. 368).
Dance like a spider.
Sing "Itsy Bitsy Spider" (Appendix p. 291) or "There Was an Old Lady Who Swallowed a Fly" (Appendix p. 302).

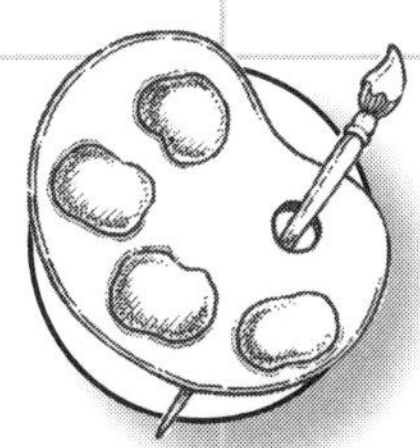

Art (Spatial, Intrapersonal, Linguistic)

Invite children to draw a picture of something that scares them. Ask about their picture. Encourage them to dictate a sentence or two telling about their picture.

Dramatic Play (Spatial, Musical, Interpersonal, Bodily-Kinesthetic)

Invite children to make Dancing Spiders (Appendix p. 386). Encourage them to use the spiders as puppets and make up a puppet show. Suggest they might want to act out "Little Miss Muffet" (Appendix p. 322). Why was Miss Muffet frightened? Was the spider afraid?

Fine Motor (Bodily-Kinesthetic)

Make Little Miss Muffet Lacing Cards (Appendix p. 393). Encourage the children to use a shoestring to lace the card.

Language (Linguistic)

Give children the "Little Miss Muffet" flannel board rhyme (Appendix p. 322, 435-436) and encourage them to re-tell the rhyme.

Math (Logical-Mathematical)

Give children Peanut Butter Playdough (Appendix p. 374), pretzels, and raisins. Show them how to make a spider's body by rolling two balls of Peanut Butter Playdough and putting them together. Encourage them to count out eight pretzels to stick in the body for legs and to add two raisins for eyes. After the spider is made invite the children to eat it.
(Check for allergies)

Snack (Interpersonal, Naturalist)

Invite children to sample some "curds and whey" (cottage cheese). You may want to serve it with fruit. Who likes it? What does it taste like? Is it smooth or lumpy? (Check for allergies)

Closing Circle (Reflections on the Day)

Ask the children:

1.What did you learn about Miss Muffet today?

2. Do you think Miss Muffet would be afraid of the Itsy Bitsy Spider?

Sing a Song of Sixpence

Morning Circle

1. Write "Sing a Song of Sixpence" (Appendix p. 325) on chart paper or a chalkboard. Read it to the children. Tell the children that this is another Mother Goose rhyme.
2. Talk about the rhyme. What is sixpence? What is the king doing? What is the queen doing? What is the maid doing?
3. Tell the children that today's activities will be about the nursery rhyme, "Sing a Song of Sixpence."

Story Circle

Sing a Song of Sixpence by Pam Adams
"Sing a Song of Sixpence" flannel board rhyme (Appendix p. 325, 443)
Songs of Sixpence; Rhymes for Reading Readiness by Arnold Cheyney

Music and Movement

Invite the children to fly like blackbirds just released from a pie.
Act out "Two Little Blackbirds" (Appendix p. 313).
Sing "I've Got Sixpence" (Appendix p. 291).

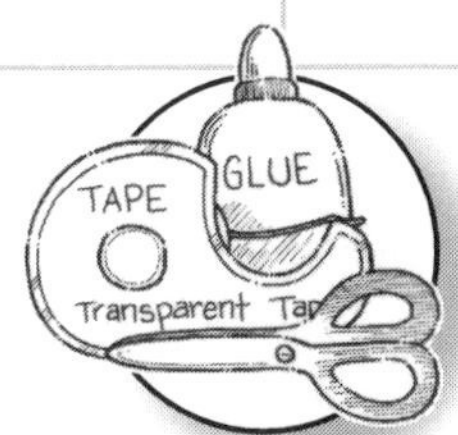

Construction (Spatial, Intrapersonal)

Cut construction paper or tagboard crowns out for the children. Provide sequins, glitter, paint, and glue and let the children decorate their crowns. How does it make them feel to wear a crown on their heads?

Dramatic Play (Interpersonal, Bodily-Kinesthetic)

Provide a clothesline, clothespins, and a basket of clothes. Invite the children to hang the clothes on the line. Tell them to watch out for their noses!

Fine Motor (Bodily-Kinesthetic, Musical)

Provide playdough (Appendix p. 377), rolling pins, and small pie tins. Encourage the children to pretend to make pies. Provide blackbird cutouts to fill the pies and challenge the children to make up a song for the blackbirds to sing.

Language (Linguistic)

Give the children the "Sing a Song of Sixpence" (Appendix p. 325) flannel board rhyme. Invite them to re-tell the rhyme or make up a new one.

Math (Logical-Mathematical, Naturalist, Intrapersonal)

Give the children several different types of coins such as pennies, nickels, dimes, and quarters to sort. Which coins do they like best?
(Supervise closely at all times!)

Snack (Interpersonal, Intrapersonal)

Serve bread and honey for snack. Let the children wear their crowns while they eat. Do they feel like queens and kings?
(Check for allergies)

Closing Circle (Reflections on the Day)

Ask the children:

1. What was your favorite activity today? Why?
2. What do you think it would feel like to be a king or a queen?
3. Would you want to eat blackbird pie? Why or why not?

Jack and Jill

Morning Circle

1. Write "Jack and Jill" (Appendix p. 321) on a piece of chart paper. Read it to the children. Explain to them that "Jack and Jill" is a Mother Goose nursery rhyme.
2. Discuss the strange vocabulary in the rhyme. What does "broke his crown?" mean? What is a nob? What does caper mean?

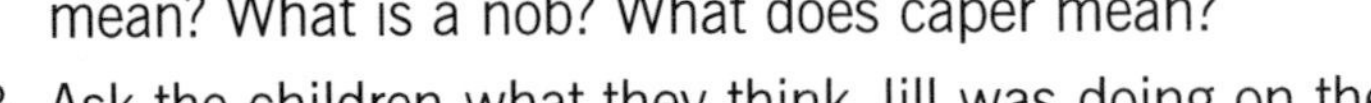

3. Ask the children what they think Jill was doing on the hill. Was she helping Jack or just keeping him company?

4. Tell the children that today's activities will be about the nursery rhyme, "Jack and Jill."

Story Circle

Jack and Jill by James Patterson

Jack and Jill by Louisa May Alcott

"Jack and Jill" flannel board rhyme (Appendix p. 321, 431-434)

Jack and Jill and other Nursery Rhymes by Lucy Cousins

Jack and Jill's Spill by Lisa Ann Marsoli

Music and Movement

Teach the children how to do a few tumbles. Be sure to work on a soft surface such as a mat or the grass outdoors.

Act out "Two Little Blackbirds" (Appendix p. 313).

Sing "The Grand Old Duke of York" (Appendix p. 288) or "The Itsy Bitsy Spider" (Appendix p. 291).

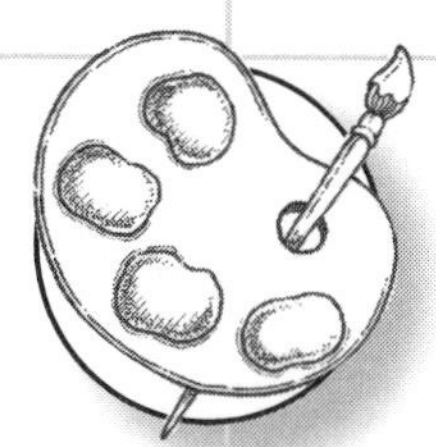

Art (Spatial, Naturalist)

Provide green tempera paint and encourage the children to paint green hills.

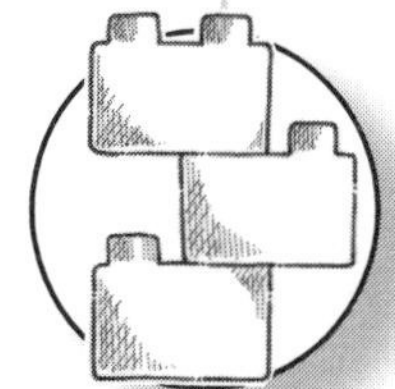

Blocks (Bodily-Kinesthetic, Interpersonal)

Create hills in the block center with bunched up fabric or sheets. Spread a Farmyard Ground Cover (Appendix p. 387) over the hills. Give the children plastic people, vehicles, and animals to encourage dramatic play.

Dramatic Play (Interpersonal, Intrapersonal)

Provide props for a doctor's office or Dame Dob's house. Encourage the children to pretend to be doctors, nurses, or Dame Dob. Be sure to include bandages for a "broken crown."

Language (Linguistic, Interpersonal)

Give the children the "Jack and Jill" flannel board rhyme (Appendix p. 321, 431-434) and invite them to re-tell the rhyme.

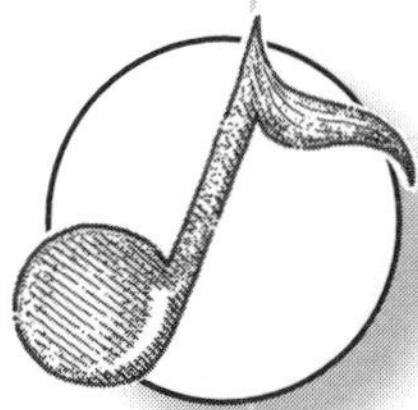

Music (Musical)

Provide a nursery rhyme tape or CD for the children to listen to. Which rhyme is their favorite?

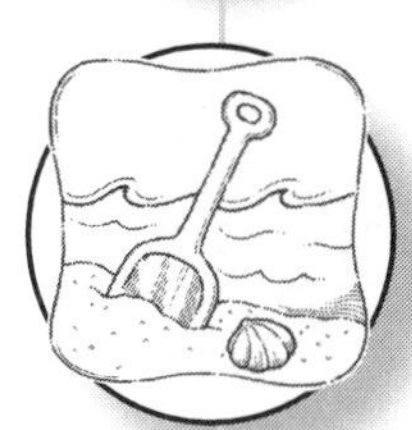

Sand and Water (Interpersonal, Logical-Mathematical)

Provide pails to use in the water play table. How heavy are the pails when they are full? What would happen if you dropped a pail full of water?

Learning Centers

Closing Circle (Reflections on the Day)

Ask the children:

1. What made Jack fall?
2. How was his fall different from Humpty Dumpty's fall?

One, Two, Buckle My Shoe

Morning Circle

1. Make a pathway of numbered sheets of construction paper (1 to 10) from the doorway to the circle area. Have the children walk the number line to the circle.
2. Recite "One, Two, Buckle My Shoe" (Appendix p. 324) with the children. Tell the children that this is another Mother Goose nursery rhyme.
3. Invite the children to help you make up another counting rhyme. Write 1, 2 on chart paper and challenge the children to think of rhyming words to use for the next sentence. Continue up to 10. Can the children think of other counting rhymes?
4. Tell the children that today's activities will be about the nursery rhyme, "One, Two, Buckle My Shoe."

Story Circle

Big Fat Hen by Keith Baker
One, Two, Buckle My Shoe by Heather Collins
"One, Two, Buckle My Shoe" flannel board rhyme (Appendix p. 324, 441-442)
One, Two, Buckle My Shoe: Songs and Games for Children by Friedman Fairfax

Music and Movement

Sing "This Old Man" (Appendix p. 304) or "The Ants Go Marching" (Appendix p. 283).
Chant "Counting Rhyme" (Appendix p. 314) or "One Potato, Two Potato" (Appendix p. 325).

LEARNING CENTERS

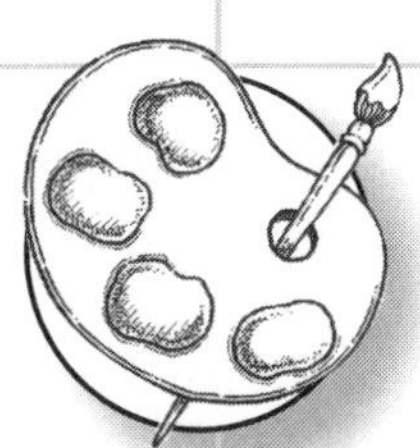

ART (Spatial)

Provide old baby shoes, tempera paint, and paper. Invite the children to make shoe prints on their paper.

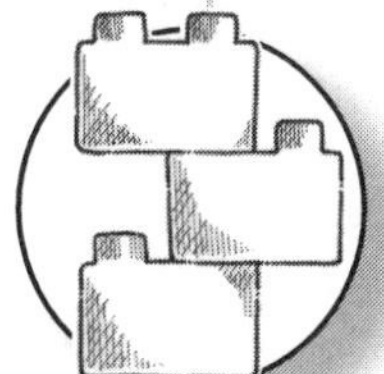

Blocks (Bodily-Kinesthetic, Logical-Mathematical)

Invite the children to lay the blocks out in a straight line like the sticks in the rhyme.

DRAMATIC PLAY (Bodily-Kinesthetic, Interpersonal, Naturalist)

Collect shoes that buckle and put them in the dramatic play center. Invite the children to explore the shoes. How many types of buckles do they see on the shoes?

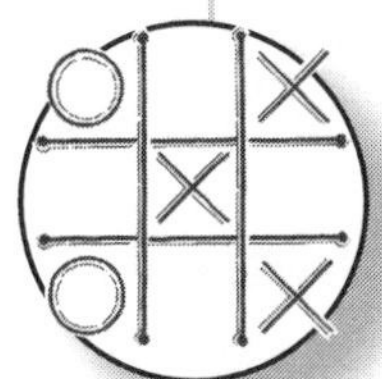

GAMES (Interpersonal, Bodily-Kinesthetic)

Give the children Pick-Up-Sticks. If you don't have Pick-Up-Sticks, use drinking straws.

LANGUAGE (Linguistic, Musical)

Give the children the "One, Two, Buckle My Shoe" flannel board rhyme (appendix page 324, 441-442). Invite them to use the flannel board pieces to re-tell the rhyme or make up a new one.

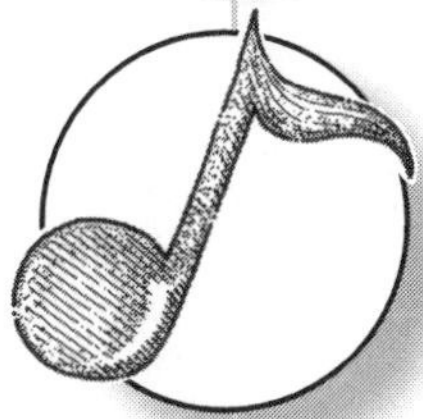

Music (Musical)

Provide a nursery rhyme tape or CD for the children. Which rhyme is their favorite?

Closing Circle (Reflections on the Day)

Ask the children:

1. What was your favorite activity today? Why?
2. Which of the nursery rhymes that we have studied is your favorite? Why?

Assessment for "Mother Goose on the Loose"

Intellectual Strength	Assessment
Linguistic	Have the children teach two or three of the nursery rhymes to another class of children.
Spatial	Ask the children to illustrate two or three of the nursery rhymes.
Musical	Have the children sing each of the nursery rhymes either to tunes they know or to tunes they make up.
Interpersonal Bodily-Kinesthetic	Have the children act out each of the nursery rhymes.
Logical-Mathematical	Have the children come up with solutions for how Humpty Dumpty could have kept from falling off the wall, how Jack and Jill could have gotten the water without falling, and how Miss Muffet could have held her ground against the spider.
Intrapersonal	Have the children describe how they think Humpty Dumpty felt when the King's horses and King's men couldn't fix him. Ask them how the spider might have felt when Miss Muffet ran away.
Naturalist	Have the children classify the nursery rhymes into categories of things that could really happen and things that could not really happen. For example, "Miss Muffet" and "Jack and Jill" are about situations that could actually happen. "Humpty Dumpty" and "Sing a Song of Sixpence" are fanciful.

Books Used in "Mother Goose on the Loose"

Big Fat Hen by Keith Baker
Humpty Dumpty by Kin Eagle
Humpty Dumpty by Colin Hawkins
Humpty Dumpty by Daniel Kirk
Jack and Jill by Louisa May Alcott
Jack and Jill by James Patterson
Jack and Jill and other Nursery Rhymes by Lucy Cousins
Jack and Jill's Spill by Lisa Ann Marsoli
Little Miss Muffet and Other Nursery Rhymes by Lucy Cousins
Little Miss Muffet's Count-Along Surprise by Emma Chichester Clark
One, Two, Buckle My Shoe by Heather Collins
One, Two, Buckle My Shoe: Songs and Games for Children by Friedman Fairfax
Some Things Are Scary by Florence Parry Heide
Sing a Song of Sixpence by Pam Adams
Songs of Sixpence; Rhymes for Reading Readiness by Arnold Cheyney

Other Books About Mother Goose

Animal Crackers by Jane Dyer
Animal Crackers: Nursery Rhymes by Jane Dyer
The Arnold Lobel Book of Mother Goose by Arnold Lobel
The Children's Treasury of Virtues by William J. Bennett
Fee Fi Fo Fum by Raymond Briggs
The Glorious Mother Goose by Cooper Edens
Humpty Dumpty and Other Nursery Rhymes by Lucy Cousins
Jeepers Creepers by Foster & Erickson
Little Bo Peep by Paul Galdone
Little Boy Blue and Other Rhymes by Iona Opie
Little Miss Muffet and Other Nursery Rhymes by Lucy Cousins
Lullabies: An Illustrated Songbook by Richard Kapp
The Mammoth Book of Fairy Tales by Michael Ashley
Mother Goose by Eulalie Osgood Grover
The Mother Goose Video Treasury (vol. 2): The Little Bo Peep Collection by Frank Brandt

Over the Hills and Far Away: A Book of Nursery Rhymes by Alan Marks
Say, Sing & Sign Mother Goose Rhymes (video) by Production Associates
There Was an Old Woman Who Lived in a Glove by Bernard Lodge

Sing Me a Song
(Traditional Songs)

Twinkle, Twinkle Little Star

Morning Circle

1. Sing "Twinkle, Twinkle Little Star" (Appendix p. 306) with the children. Typically, children sing only the first verse of the song. Teach them another verse or the whole song. Use the Flannel Board Rhyme (Appendix p. 454-455) with the song. Point out that sailors often use stars to tell the direction in which they are sailing.
2. Explain that "Twinkle, Twinkle, Little Star" is a traditional children's song. Almost everyone knows this song. Encourage the children to ask their parents if they know the song. How many verses do they know? "Twinkle, Twinkle, Little Star" was originally a Mother Goose rhyme.
3. Ask the children why they think stars appear to be twinkling? Explain that stars are dazzling balls of burning gases, which is why they flicker like candles.
   - Stars are very far away. That is why they look so small.
   - The sun is a star. It is the nearest, most important star to Earth. It gives us light and warmth.
4. Tell the children that today's activities will be about things in the song, "Twinkle, Twinkle, Little Star."

Story Circle

Twinkle, Twinkle Little Star by Iza Trapani

Twinkle, Twinkle Little Star by Jeanette Winter

"Twinkle, Twinkle Little Star" flannel board rhyme (Appendix p. 306, 454-455)

Music and Movement

Cut out a star from poster board and use it to play "Star Hide and Seek."

Cut out a star from poster board and play "Drop the Star" as you would "Drop the Handkerchief" (Appendix p. 358).

Play "Planet, Planet, Star" as you would "Duck, Duck, Goose" (Appendix p. 359).

ART (Spatial, Naturalist)

Cut stars and moons out of white felt and give them to the children. Encourage them to create a night sky on the flannel board using the felt cutouts.

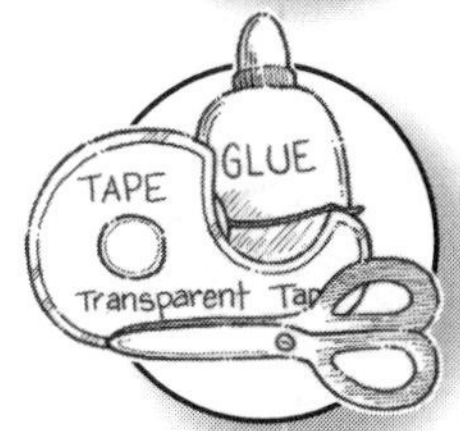

CONSTRUCTION (Logical-Mathematical)

Cut several star shapes out of construction paper, varying the sizes of the stars. Punch a hole in the middle of each star. Give the children a straw and encourage them to string the stars onto their straws to create a design.

FINE MOTOR (Bodily-Kinesthetic)

Provide rock salt in a bowl, a piece of black felt, and tweezers. Encourage the children to use the tweezers to pick up the diamonds (rock salt) and place them in the sky (black felt).

GROSS MOTOR (Bodily-Kinesthetic)

Provide a service bell and a white star cut out of felt (about 8" in diameter). Cut a small hole in the middle of the star and lay it over the finger press of the service bell. Give the children a beanbag and challenge them to toss it at the star to make the star ring.

LANGUAGE (Linguistic, Musical, Interpersonal)

Give the children the flannel board pieces (Appendix p. 454-455) to the song and encourage them to sequence the events in the song.

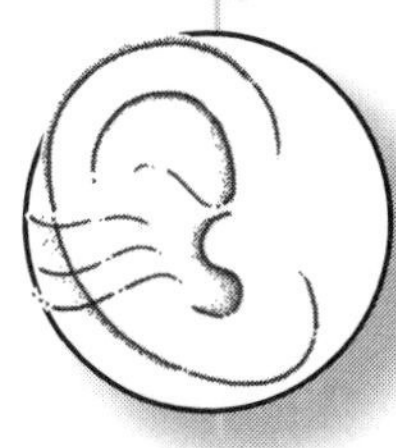

LISTENING (Musical, Intrapersonal, Naturalist)

Remind the children that the stars are very far away. Ask them if they think the stars make a sound when they twinkle. Provide several instruments and items, like an xylophone, jingle bell, tambourine, or two spoons for the children to use to replicate the noise a twinkling star might make.

LEARNING CENTERS

Closing Circle (Reflections on the Day)

Ask the children:

1. What did you learn about stars today?
2. What sound did you create for the stars?

Itsy Bitsy Spider

Morning Circle

1. Sing "Itsy Bitsy Spider" (Appendix p. 291) with the children. Use the song cards (Appendix p. 461-462) or puppets to accompany the song.
2. Explain that "Itsy Bitsy Spider" is a traditional song. Next to "Happy Birthday to You," it is the most well-known children's song.
3. Discuss the spider's reaction to the rain. Did she give up or continue her journey?
4. Talk about the determination and persistence of the spider. Encourage the children to think of things they do that require them to be persistent such as learning to tie a shoe or learn to throw a ball. Make a list of the things they name. Point out that persistence is a good thing.
5. Tell the children that today's activities will be about things that happen in the song of the "Itsy Bitsy Spider."

Story Circle

Itsy Bitsy Spider by Pam Schiller (editor)
Itsy Bitsy Spider by Iza Trapani (illustrator)
"Itsy Bitsy Spider" song cards (Appendix p. 291, 461-462)
Miss Spider's Tea Party by David Kirk
Silly Spider! by David Wood
"There Was an Old Lady Who Swallowed a Fly" puppet song (Appendix p. 302, 485-487)
The Very Busy Spider by Eric Carle

Music and Movement

Dance to Little Richard's rendition of "Itsy Bitsy Spider."
Dance like spiders.
Do the Spider Walk (Appendix p. 368) or have a Spider Walk race.
Take a nature hike and look for signs of spiders.

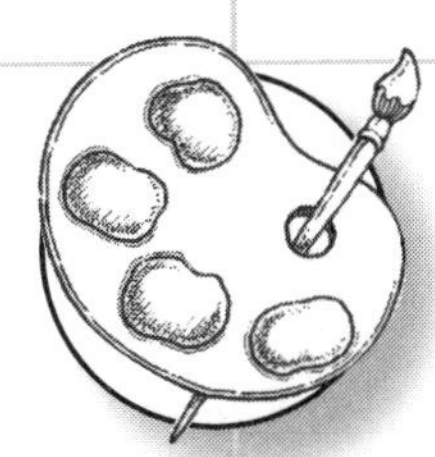

Art (Spatial)

Provide straws (cut in half), tempera paint, and paper. Place paint on the paper and invite the children to blow through the straws to move the paint into dancing spiders.

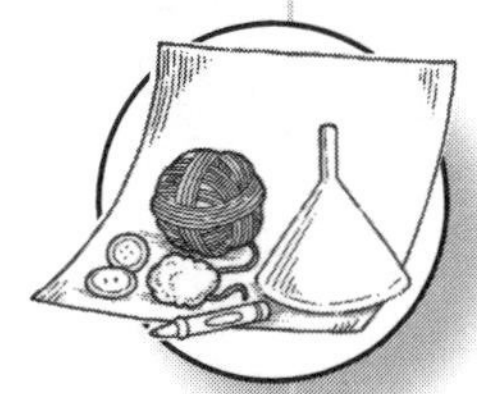

Discovery (Logical-Mathematical)

Place a plastic spider in a bucket and attach the bucket to one end of a rope. Put the other end of the rope over a pulley and let children move the spider up and down via the pulley.

Fine Motor (Bodily-Kinesthetic)

Provide small plastic spiders and tweezers. Encourage the children to use the tweezers to move the spiders from a puddle of water (blue construction paper) to a sun (yellow construction paper sun). If plastic spiders are unavailable, make spiders by twisting black or brown pipe cleaners together.

Language (Linguistic, Intrapersonal)

Encourage the children to use the Itsy Bitsy Spider song cards (Appendix p. 461-462) to sequence the events in the song. Ask the children to make a list of reasons why the spider might be so persistent about going up the waterspout. Why was the spider so determined?

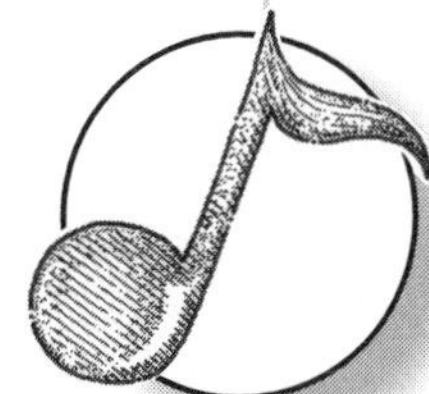

Music (Musical, Linguistic)

Give the children an "Itsy Bitsy Spider" Cup Puppet (Appendix p. 484). Let them activate the puppet while listening to a recording of the song.

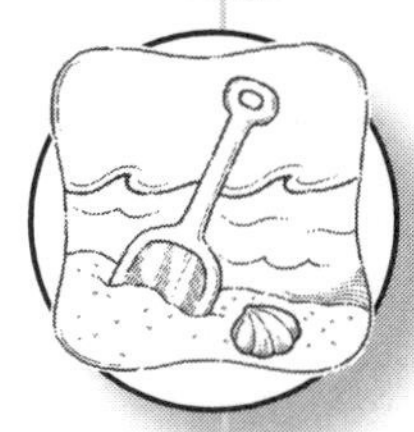

Sand and Water (Bodily-Kinesthetic, Interpersonal)

Give the children colanders and strainers and encourage them to make rain.

Closing Circle (Reflections on the Day)

Ask the children:

1. What was your favorite activity today? Why?
2. Why do you think the spider was so persistent?

This Old Man

Morning Circle

1. Sing "This Old Man" (Appendix p. 304) with the children. Record the song to use later in the Music Center.
2. Explain that "This Old Man" is a traditional song. It is a counting song. Sing and record the variation of "This Old Man." Use the flannel board patterns (Appendix p. 305, 451-453) with the song. Ask the children which version they like best. Explain that people often make up new words to traditional songs.
3. Tell the children that today's activities will be about things mentioned in the song, "This Old Man."

Story Circle

Give a Dog a Bone by Steven Kellogg
This Old Man by Pam Adams (illustrator)
This Old Man by Carol Jones (illustrator)
"This Old Man" flannel board song (Appendix p. 305, 451-453)
This Old Man: A Musical Counting Book by Tony Ross (illustrator)

Music and Movement

Play "Dog and Bone" (Appendix p. 358).

Invite the children to make up hand jives. Provide appropriate music.

LEARNING CENTERS

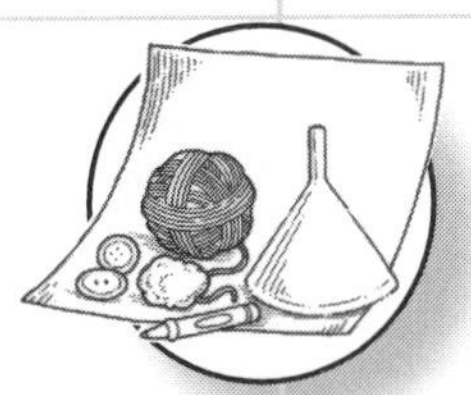

Discovery (Logical-Mathematical, Naturalist)

Make a photocopy of the Old Man from the flannel board pieces (Appendix p. 451). Color, cut out, and laminate him. Invite the children to put the old man inside a variety of objects like an empty paper towel tube, tin can, a metal mint box, matchbox, or a liter bottle and see if he will roll.

Gross Motor (Bodily-Kinesthetic)

Give the children a basket and a nylon dog bone. Encourage them to toss the bone into the basket. After they get progressively better at hitting the basket, suggest they toss the bone over their shoulder into the basket.

Language (Linguistic, Logical-Mathematical)

Give the children the "This Old Man" flannel board song (Appendix p. 305, 451-453). Invite them to match the objects to the numbers.

Math (Logical-Mathematical)

Give the children the "Dog and Bone Match Game" (Appendix p. 386). Invite them to match dogs to bones.

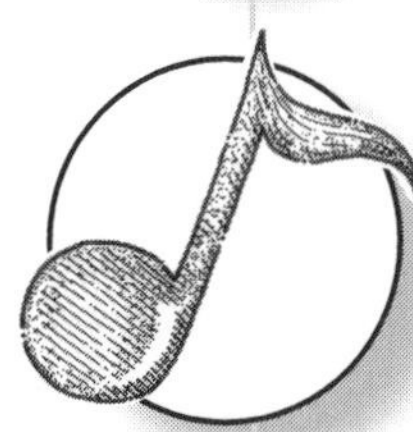

Music (Musical, Intrapersonal)

Give the children the two versions of the song recorded during Morning Circle. Encourage them to listen to both versions and then to vote for their favorite version.

Science (Logical-Mathematical, Naturalist)

Provide a stamp pad and paper. Invite the children to make thumbprints and then examine them through a magnifying glass.

Closing Circle (Reflections on the Day)

Ask the children:

1. How is "This Old Man" like "The Ants Go Marching"?
2. Which version of the song do you like best?

Old MacDonald Had a Farm

Morning Circle

1. Sing "Old MacDonald Had a Farm" (Appendix p. 298) with the children. Use the flannel board illustrations (Appendix p. 439-440) with the song.
2. Tell the children that "Old MacDonald Had a Farm" is a traditional song. Does anyone remember when they first learned the song?
3. Talk about farms and farmers. Has anyone ever visited on a farm? What do farmers do (e.g., plant crops, care for animals, provide food for us)? Point out that the flannel board illustrations show a female farmer. Tell the children that there are many farmers who are women.
4. Sing "Old MacDonald Had a Band" (Appendix p. 298) with the children. Tell them this is a variation of the original song. Which one do the children like best?
5. Tell the children that today's activities will be about things that happen in the song, "Old MacDonald Had a Farm."

Story Circle

Old MacDonald Had a Farm by Pam Adams (illustrator)
Old MacDonald Had a Farm by Carol Jones (illustrator)
"Old MacDonald Had a Farm" flannel board song (Appendix p. 298, 439-440)
Old MacDonald Had an Apartment House by Judi Barrett
Once Upon MacDonald's Farm by Stephen Gammel

Music and Movement

Sing and play "The Farmer in the Dell" (Appendix p. 359) or sing "Five Little Ducks" (Appendix p. 286).

LEARNING CENTERS

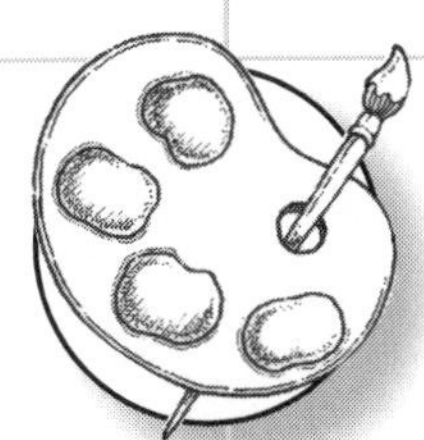

ART (Spatial, Intrapersonal)

Give the children playdough (Appendix p. 377) and animal cookie cutters. Invite them to cut out their favorite farm animals.

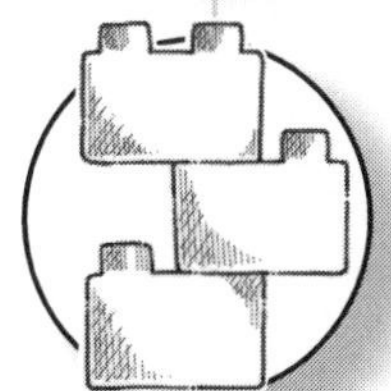

Blocks (Bodily-Kinesthetic, Naturalist, Interpersonal, Logical-Mathematical)

Provide props such as a Farmyard Ground Cover (Appendix p. 387), a Silo (Appendix p. 400), plastic animals, and cages (berry baskets) to build a farm. Invite the children to sort the animal into cages.

DRAMATIC PLAY (Bodily-Kinesthetic, Interpersonal)

Give the children the Animal Face Paper Bag Puppets (Appendix p. 381). Encourage them to put on an animal puppet show or to act out the song, "Old MacDonald Had a Farm."

FINE MOTOR (Bodily-Kinesthetic, Linguistic, Logical-Mathematical)

Give the children Farm Puzzles (Appendix p. 387) to work.

LANGUAGE (Linguistic, Musical)

Give the children the "Old MacDonald Had a Farm" flannel board song (Appendix p. 439-440). Invite them to sing the song and add the appropriate animals as they are mentioned.

SCIENCE (Naturalist)

Provide rye grass seed or beans for the children to plant in cups of potting soil. Or, plant a garden outdoors.

Closing Circle (Reflections on the Day)

Ask the children:

1. Which animal on Old MacDonald's farm is your favorite? Why?
2. Would you like to be a farmer? Why or why not?

Five Little Ducks

Morning Circle

1. Make duck footprints from the doorway to the Morning Circle area. Sing "Five Little Ducks" (Appendix p. 286) with the children. Use the puppets (Appendix p. 471-472) with the song.
2. Explain to the children that "Five Little Ducks" is a traditional song.
3. Talk about listening to parents. Why didn't the ducks come back when they were called? Do you listen to one parent better than you do another? It is important to listen to adults around you. They are making sure you are safe.
4. Tell the children that today's activities will be about things that happen in the song, "Five Little Ducks."

Story Circle

Five Little Ducks by Raffi
Five Little Ducks by Jose Aurego (Illustrator)
"Five Little Ducks" puppets (Appendix p. 471-472)
Five Little Ducks: An Old Rhyme by Pamela Paparone (Illustrator)
Five Little Ducks (Five Little Ducks and Mother) by Penny Dann

Music and Movement

Sing and move to "Six White Ducks" (Appendix p. 301) or "Over in the Meadow" (Appendix p. 298).
Play "Duck, Duck Goose" (Appendix p. 359).
Hide a duck and play "Duck Hide and Seek."

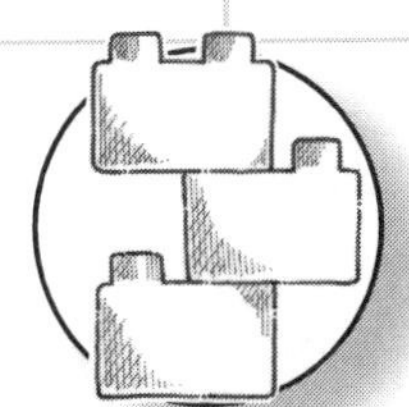

Blocks (Bodily-Kinesthetic, Spatial)

Cut a piece of blue bulletin board paper to represent a pond and crumple a green sheet or piece of fabric to represent a hill. Give the children rubber ducks and encourage them to re-enact the song. Invite them to build houses around the pond and to use their binoculars (see Construction, below) to search for lost ducks.

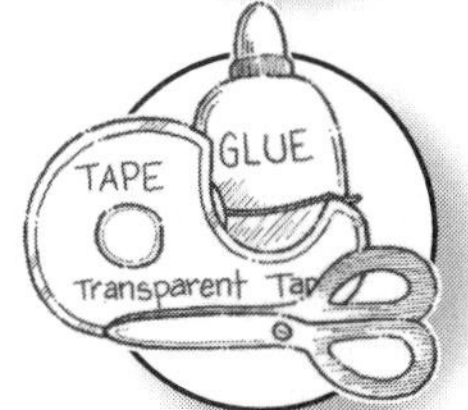

Construction (Spatial)

Help the children make binoculars by taping two empty toilet paper tubes together. Provide markers, crayons, and paint to decorate their binoculars. Can they find the ducks by using the binoculars?

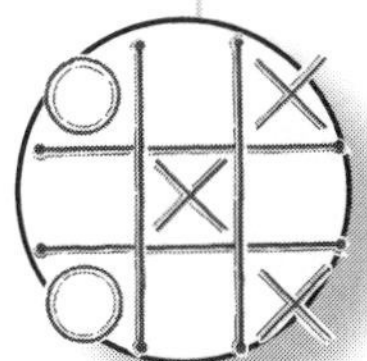

Games (Naturalist)

Give the children the Animal Footprint Concentration Game (Appendix p. 381). Invite them to match the footprints. How are the ducks' footprints different from the other animals?

Gross Motor (Bodily-Kinesthetic, Logical-Mathematical, Interpersonal)

Use masking tape to create a maze on the floor. Give the children a rubber duck and encourage them to take the duck through the maze.

Language (Linguistic, Musical, Intrapersonal, Interpersonal)

Give the children the "Five Little Ducks" puppets (Appendix p. 471-472). Encourage them to sing the song using the ducks. Can they make up a new song? Encourage the children to think of reasons why the ducks might not have come back when they were called. What were they doing?

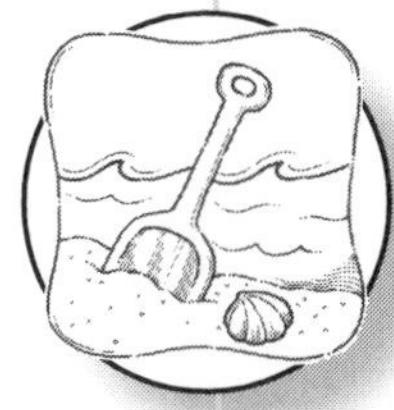

Sand and Water (Interpersonal, Logical-Mathematical)

Place several rubber ducks in the water table. Put matching colored dots on the bottom in sets of two. Challenge the children to pick up one duck, look at the colored dot on the bottom and attempt to pick up the other duck with the matching dot.

Closing Circle (Reflections on the Day)

Ask the children:

1. Why do you think the ducks didn't come the first time they were called?
2. What have you learned today about listening?

Assessment for "Sing Me a Song"

Intellectual Strength	Assessment
Linguistic	Challenge the children to make up a new verse to the song they like the best.
Spatial	Invite the children to design a record cover for each song.
Musical	Have the children select a rhythm band instrument to accompany each of the songs they have studied.
Interpersonal Bodily-Kinesthetic	Challenge the children to make up a dance or new hand motions to each of the songs they have studied.
Logical-Mathematical	Have the children identify the songs that have a number mentioned in them. Ask them to think of a way that "Old MacDonald Had a Farm," "Itsy Bitsy Spider," and "Twinkle, Twinkle, Little Star" could use numbers.
Intrapersonal	Invite the children to select their favorite song and then find a classmate who also likes that song the best. For example, if Madison likes "Twinkle, Twinkle Little Star," she will be a good match for Kenny who also likes that song the best.
Naturalist	Have the children name the songs that have animals in them. For example, "Old MacDonald Had a Farm" and "Five Little Ducks."

Books Used in "Sing Me a Song"

Five Little Ducks by Jose Aurego (Illustrator)
Five Little Ducks (Five Little Ducks and Mother) by Penny Dann
Five Little Ducks by Raffi
Five Little Ducks: An Old Rhyme by Pamela Paparone (Illustrator)
Give a Dog a Bone by Steven Kellogg
Itsy Bitsy Spider by Iza Trapani (illustrator)
Itsy Bitsy Spider by Pam Schiller (editor)
Miss Spider's Tea Party by David Kirk
Old MacDonald Had a Farm by Carol Jones (illustrator)
Old MacDonald Had a Farm by Pam Adams (illustrator)
Old MacDonald Had an Apartment House by Judi Barrett
Once Upon MacDonald's Farm by Stephen Gammel
Silly Spider! by David Wood
This Old Man by Carol Jones (illustrator)
This Old Man by Pam Adams (illustrator)
This Old Man: A Musical Counting Book by Tony Ross (illustrator)
Twinkle, Twinkle Little Star by Iza Trapani
Twinkle, Twinkle Little Star by Jeanette Winter
The Very Busy Spider by Eric Carle

Books About Favorite Songs

All Fall Down by Helen Oxenbury
Cat Goes Fiddle-I-Fee by Paul Galdone
Diane Goode's Book of Silly Stories & Songs by Diane Goode
Down by the Bay by Raffi
Fox Went Out on a Chilly Night by Peter Spier
Go Tell Aunt Rhody by Aliki
Hush, Little Baby by Jeanette Winter
If You're Happy and You Know It by Nicki Weiss
Itsy Bitsy Spider by Iza Trapani (Illustrator)
Jane Yolen's Old MacDonald Songbook by Jane Yolen
The Kingfisher Nursery Rhyme Songbook by Sally Emerson
Little Bo Peep by Paul Galdone
London Bridge is Falling Down by Peter Spier (Illustrator)

Books

Mary Had a Little Lamb by Sarah Hale
Over the River and Through the Woods by Lydia Maria Child
Peanut Butter and Jelly by Nadine Bernard Wescott
The Song by Charlotte Zolotow
There Was an Old Lady Who Swallowed a Fly by Nadine Bernard Westcott
There Was an Old Lady Who Swallowed a Fly by Simms Taback
There Was an Old Lady Who Swallowed a Trout by Teri Sloat
A Treasury on Songs for Little Children by Esther Botwin
The Three Little Kittens by Lorinda Bryan Cauley
The Twelve Days of Christmas by Jan Brett
We Wish You a Merry Christmas by Tracey Campbell Pearson
The Wheels on the Bus by Maryann Kovalski
The Wheels on the Bus by Paul O. Zelinsky (Illustrator)
Yankee Doodle by Edward Bangs

Tell Me a Tale

(Favorite Stories)

Goldilocks and the Three Bears

Morning Circle

1. Sing "The Three Bears Rap" with the children (Appendix p. 305). Use the Glove Puppet (Appendix p. 481) with the rap.
2. Ask the children what they know about the story of *Goldilocks and the Three Bears?*
3. Tell them the story is a traditional one, meaning that it has been around a long time. Tell them that this story is one that was told to their mommies and daddies when they were little and even to their grandparents when they were little.
4. Tell the story of Goldilocks and the Three Bears (Appendix p. 335).
5. Tell the children that today's activities will be about things that happen in the story of *Goldilocks and the Three Bears.*

Story Circle

Deep in the Forest by Brinton Turkle
Goldilocks and the Three Bears by James Marshall
Goldilocks and the Three Bears by Jan Brett
Goldilocks and the Three Bears/Bears Should Share by Alvin Granowsky
Goldilocks Returns by Lisa Cambell Ernst
"Goldilocks and the Three Bears" flannel board story (Appendix p. 335, 421-425)
The Three Bears Rhyme Book by Jane Yolen
Yours Truly, Goldilocks by Alma Flor Ada

Music and Movement

Act out "Walk-on Nursery Rhyme" (Appendix p. 326) or "There Once Were Three Brown Bears" (Appendix p. 302).

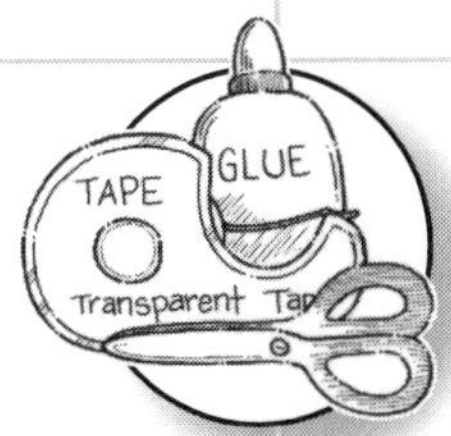

CONSTRUCTION (SPATIAL)

Using the patterns provided, invite the children to make Goldilocks Puppets (Appendix p. 481). When they have finished their puppet, encourage them to think of something the puppet can say to apologize to the Bear family.

DRAMATIC PLAY (INTERPERSONAL, INTRAPERSONAL)

Provide props and encourage the children to pretend the Homemaking Center of the classroom is the cottage of the three bears.

LANGUAGE (LINGUISTIC, INTERPERSONAL)

Give the children the "Goldilocks and the Three Little Bears" flannel board story (Appendix p. 421-425) and invite them to re-tell the story or make up a new one.

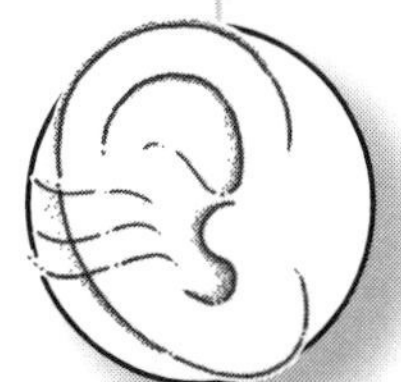

LISTENING (MUSICAL, BODILY-KINESTHETIC)

Make a tape of the children singing "The Three Bears Rap" (Appendix p. 305). Place it in the center for listening. Invite the children to make up a clapping pattern to accompany the rap.

MATH (LOGICAL-MATHEMATICAL, NATURALIST)

Invite the children to make place settings for three from a basket of bowls, spoons, cups, and napkins.

SNACK (INTERPERSONAL)

Invite the children to help prepare porridge (oatmeal). Encourage them to sample the porridge for snack. Have them decide if the temperature of the porridge is just right. (SUPERVISE CLOSELY AT ALL TIMES!)

Closing Circle (Reflections on the Day)

Ask the children:

1. Do you think that Goldilocks learned a lesson about going into people's houses uninvited?
2. How would the story be different if the bears had been home when Goldilocks arrived?

The Three Little Pigs

Morning Circle

1. Place sticks, straw, and a few bricks along the pathway from the classroom door to the circle area. When the children come to the circle area, ask them if they can guess what story might be the focus of the day by looking at the clues on the floor. Children should be able to guess but if they don't, give them more clues.
2. Tell the children that *The Three Little Pigs* is another traditional tale, one that their parents and grandparents listened to when they were children. Use the Glove Puppet (Appendix p. 483) to introduce the characters in the story.
3. Read or tell the story of "The Three Little Pigs."
4. Explain that most of the traditional tales taught a lesson. For example, the lesson in *The Three Bears* was—don't go inside someone's house uninvited. Does anyone know what the lesson is in the story of *The Three Little Pigs*? If the children know the lesson, talk about it for a minute.
4. Tell the children that today's activities will be about things that happen in the story of *The Three Little Pigs*. If the children are not able to identify the lesson in the story, then discuss the importance of doing things right.

Story Circle

The Fourth Little Pig by Teresa Celsi
The Three Little Pigs by Paul Galdone
The Three Little Pigs: An Old Story by Margot Zemach
"The Three Little Pigs" puppet story (Appendix p. 350, 488-489)
The Three Pigs by David Wiesner
The True Story of the Three Little Pigs by Jon Scieszka

Music and Movement

Do the motions to "This Little Piggy" (Appendix p. 312).
Play "Pig, Pig, Wolf" like you would "Duck, Duck, Goose" (Appendix p. 359).
Teach the children to do a "Pig Jig" to music that is appropriate for an Irish Jig.

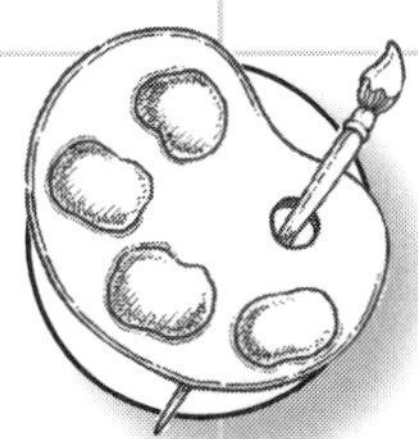

Art (Spatial)

Provide pink tempera paint, easel paper, and brushes. Invite the children to paint pink pictures.

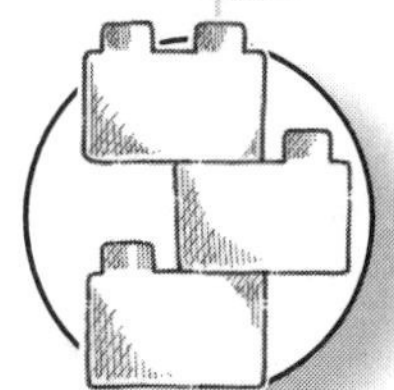

Blocks (Bodily-Kinesthetic, Spatial, Interpersonal, Intrapersonal, Naturalist)

Invite the children to build pig homes out of twigs, straw, and bricks (Paper Bag Blocks, Appendix p. 396). When they have finished building, ask them which house they might choose to live in and why.

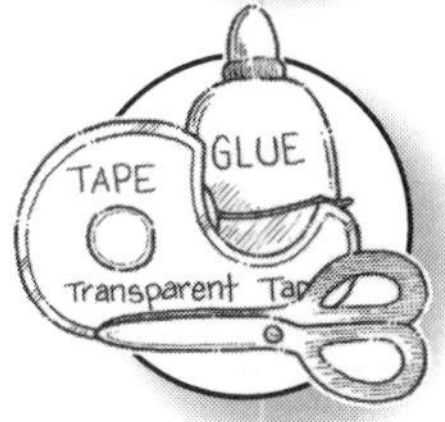

Construction (Musical)

In many versions of this traditional tale, the pigs play flutes and other musical instruments. Help the children construct a flute by punching holes in an empty paper towel tube. Teach the children the jingle, "You can't catch me. Oh no, you can't catch me."

Fine Motor (Bodily-Kinesthetic)

Invite the children to make pigtails. Show them how to curl paper ribbon using the flat edge of a pair of children's scissors or the straight edge of a ruler. You can also make pigtails by curling pink pipe cleaners around a pencil. (Supervise closely at all times!)

Language (Linguistic, Interpersonal)

Give the children "The Three Little Pigs" puppet story (Appendix p. 350, 488-489) and encourage them to re-tell the story or to make up a new one.

Math (Logical-Mathematical, Spatial)

Provide some sticks (straws) for the children to use to build a house. After the house is built, encourage them to blow it down. Ask them to count the number of times they have to blow to get the house to fall and record the number using tally marks or bean counters.

Closing Circle (Reflections on the Day)

Ask the children:

1. What did you learn today about the story of *The Three Little Pigs*?
2. What mistake did the first two pigs make when they were building their houses?
3. What things in today's story are like the things in yesterday's story? (Number 3, Lesson, Animals)

The Three Billy Goats Gruff

Morning Circle

1. Build a bridge from your classroom door to the circle area. Use blocks, boxes, or draw a bridge on brown bulletin board paper.
2. Ask the children if the bridge makes them think of a story they know. If no one says *The Three Billy Goats Gruff,* give them more clues until they guess correctly.
3. Tell the children that this story is another traditional tale, one that their parents and grandparents listened to when they were children. Use the Glove Puppets (Appendix p. 482) to introduce the characters in the story.
4. Tell the story using the glove puppet.
5. Tell the children that today's activities will be about things that happen in the story of *The Three Billy Goats Gruff.*

Story Circle

The Three Billy Goats Gruff by Paul Galdone

The Three Billy Goats Gruff by Janet Stevens

The Three Billy Goats Gruff by Steven Carpenter (Illustrator)

"The Three Billy Goats Gruff" flannel board story (Appendix p. 348, 447-449)

The Three Billy Goats Gruff/Just a Friendly Troll by Alvin Granowsky

Music and Movement

Invite the children to try several different kinds of steps that might be used by different-sized goats—small steps, medium steps, and large steps; light steps, normal steps, and heavy steps; slow steps, regular speed steps, and fast steps. Don't forget to say the "trip, traps" with each set of steps.

Sing "Mary Had a Little Goat" (Appendix p. 294).

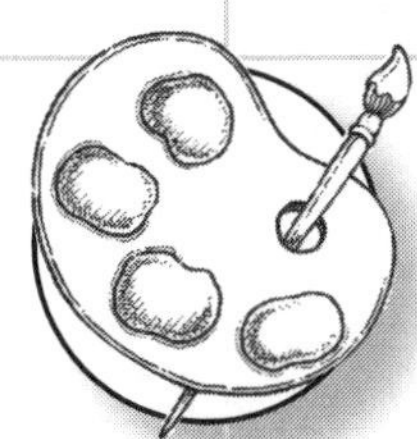

ART (Spatial)

Provide paint, brushes, and paper and invite the children to paint a troll.

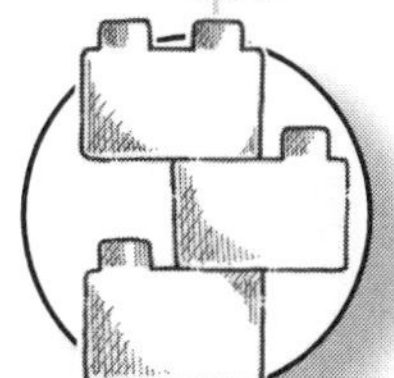

Blocks (Bodily-Kinesthetic, Interpersonal)

Invite the children to build a bridge using blocks.

LANGUAGE (Linguistic, Interpersonal)

Give the children "The Three Billy Goats Gruff" flannel board story (Appendix p. 348, 447-449). Invite them to re-tell the story or make up a new one.

MATH (Logical-Mathematical, Naturalist)

Provide an assortment of materials that come in small, medium, and large, such as soda cups, cups, or plates. Invite the children to arrange the items in order from the smallest to the largest. After they have arranged all the items, encourage them to sort the items into small, medium, and large categories.

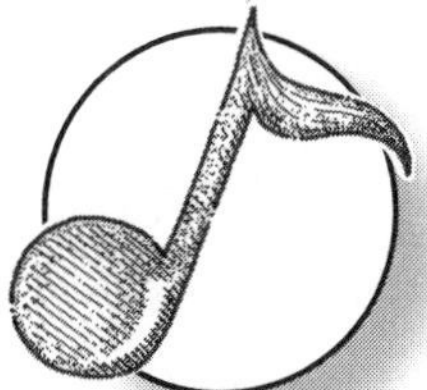

Music (Musical, Naturalist)

Challenge the children to find materials to create the "trip, trap" sound that the goats made when they crossed the bridge. If necessary, suggest using two blocks, drums and drumsticks, plastic cups, hands, and mouths.

WRITING (Spatial, Linguistic, Intrapersonal)

Invite the children to draw a picture of a sibling or a friend who is older than they are. Encourage them to dictate a sentence that tells why it is fun to have a bigger brother, sister, or friend.

Closing Circle (Reflections on the Day)

Ask the children:

1. How would the story be different if the troll had said, "Come on across my bridge?"
2. Which parts of the story could really happen?

The Little Red Hen

Morning Circle

1. Bake bread or rolls (cinnamon rolls would be great) in a toaster oven and time the process to coincide with the arrival of the children to school.
2. Talk about the wonderful aroma in the room.
3. Tell the children that today's story is *The Little Red Hen* (Appendix p. 340). Find out what children know about the story.
4. Tell the story.
5. Discuss helping. Ask children what things they help with at home. Talk about helping each other at school. Point out how much easier it is to pick up the blocks when everyone is helping.
6. Tell the children that today's activities will be about things that happen in the story of *The Little Red Hen.*

Story Circle

The Little Red Hen by Paul Galdone (Illustrator)
"The Little Red Hen" flannel board story (Appendix p. 340, 437)
Little Red Hen: An Old Story by Margo Zemach
The Little Red Hen Makes a Pizza by Philemon Sturges
The Little Red Hen, Help Yourself, Little Red Hen by Alvin Granowsky

Music and Movement

Teach children to dance like a chicken.

Play "Duck, Duck, Hen" as you would "Duck, Duck, Goose" (Appendix p. 359).

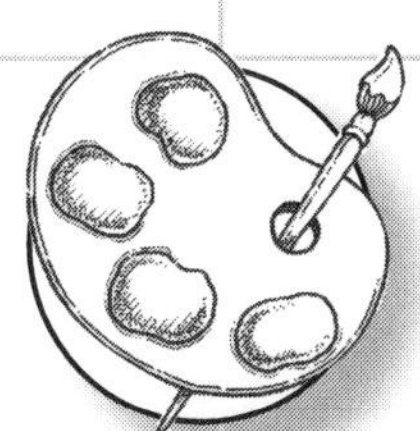

Art (Spatial, Intrapersonal)

Invite the children to draw or paint their favorite character from the story. Ask the children why they like the character they chose the best.

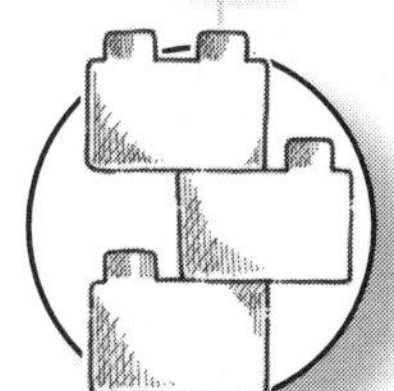

Blocks (Bodily-Kinesthetic, Logical-Mathematical, Naturalist)

Provide props like a Farmyard Ground Cover (Appendix p. 387), a Silo (Appendix p. 400), plastic animals, and cages (berry baskets) to build a farm. Invite the children to sort the animals into cages.

Discovery (Naturalist)

Provide several different grains, such as barley, wheat, corn, or rye. Invite the children to examine the grains. Provide a mortar and pestle. Invite the children to grind the grains.

Dramatic Play (Interpersonal)

Provide rolling pins, playdough, aprons, baker hats, cups, and spoons. Invite the children to create a "Little Red Hen Bake Shop."

Language (Linguistic, Interpersonal, Musical)

Give the children the "Little Red Hen" flannel board story (Appendix p. 437). Invite them to re-tell the story or make up a new one. Provide materials for sound effects, such as shakers, rhythm band instruments, pots, and pans.

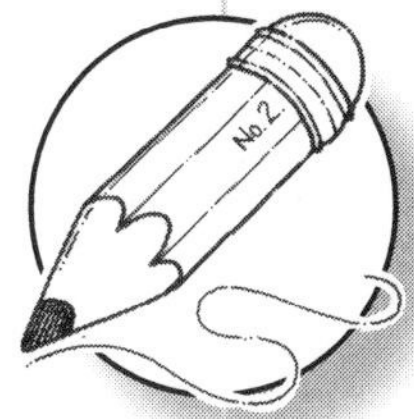

Writing (Spatial, Linguistic)

Write the names of the characters in the story on 4" x 6" index cards. Invite the children to trace over the names with markers.

Closing Circle (Reflections on the Day)

Ask the children:

1. What is your favorite part of the story? Why?
2. Do you think it is okay that the hen decides not to share her bread with the animals that didn't help her?

Caps for Sale

Morning Circle

1. Invite the children to wear caps to school today. Encourage them to tell something about the hat they are wearing. What kind of hat is it? Where did it come from? What made them choose that hat to wear?
2. Tell the children that today's story is about hats. Tell them that monkeys are also in the story. Can anyone guess which story it is? If not, tell them that it is *Caps for Sale*.
3. Tell the story.
4. Explain that *Caps for Sale* is a traditional tale. It has been around a long time, but not as long as *Goldilocks and the Three Bears, The Three Little Pigs, The Three Billy Goats Gruff*, and *The Little Red Hen.* Tell the children that their parents probably heard the story when they were young but their grandparents probably didn't. Tell the children that a traditional tale is one that remains popular over a long period of time. *Caps for Sale* is a modern day traditional tale.
5. Tell the children that today's activities will be about things that happen in the story *Caps for Sale*.

Story Circle

Caps for Sale by Esphyr Slobodkina

"Caps for Sale" flannel board story (Appendix p. 330, 409-410)

Music and Movement

Play "Copycat" (Appendix p. 358), "Follow the Leader" (Appendix p. 360), or play "Drop the Hat" as you would "Drop the Handkerchief" (Appendix p. 358).

Do the motions to "Five Little Monkeys" (Appendix p. 316), "Three Little Monkeys" (Appendix p. 312), or "My Hat, It Has Three Corners" (Appendix p. 297).

Dramatic Play (Interpersonal, Naturalist, Logical-Mathematical, Intrapersonal)

Give the children a variety of hats to try on. Encourage them to sort the hats by color and type. Which hat do they like best?

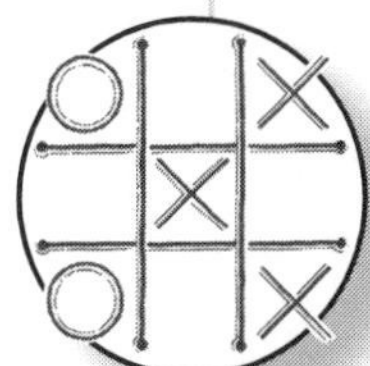

Games (Interpersonal, Bodily-Kinesthetic, Intrapersonal)

Give the children a cap. Encourage them to make a game out of removing the hat from each other's heads. The object of the game is to take the hat off of each other without the one who is wearing the hat feeling it when it is removed. Suggest that one child sit down and the other child come from behind to try to remove the hat.

Gross Motor (Bodily-Kinesthetic)

Give the children hats and encourage them to walk with the hats stacked on their heads. Can they walk the balance beam with the hats? If you don't have hats, use a beanbag.

Language (Linguistic, Interpersonal)

Give the children the "Caps for Sale" flannel board story (Appendix p. 409-410). Invite them to re-tell the story or to make up a new story.

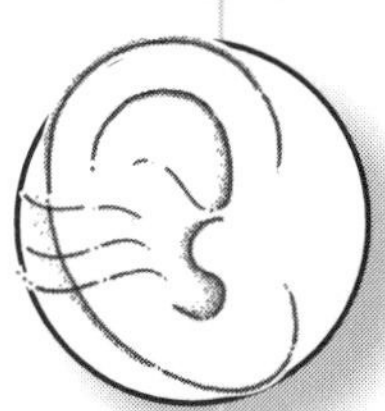

Listening (Musical, Bodily-Kinesthetic, Linguistic)

Invite the children to think of other noises the monkeys could have made other than "tsk, tsk, tsk." Suggest the children record their new sounds. Show the children how to say "no" in sign language (Appendix p. 537). Could the monkeys have done this?

Math (Logical-Mathematical, Naturalist)

Give the children fifty-cent pieces to explore. Explain that two quarters or five dimes also make fifty cents. Let the children make fifty cents out of quarters or dimes. Let younger children just trace the different sizes of coins onto a piece of paper. If coins are unavailable, copy the caps from the patterns for the flannel board story (Appendix p. 409-410) and invite the children to make a pattern out of them.

Closing Circle (Reflections on the Day)

Ask the children:

1. What is your favorite part of the story? Why?
2. Could this story really happen? Which parts could really happen?
3. Is there anything about this story that is similar to the other stories we studied this week?

Assessment for "Tell Me a Tale"

Intellectual Strength	Assessment
Linguistic	Have the children retell some of their favorite stories.
Spatial	Have the children draw a "map" of the route the three billy goats may have taken across the bridge or the path Goldilocks may have taken to the home of the bears.
Musical	Have the children select a musical instrument from the rhythm band set that would represent the way each of the three billy goats walk across the bridge. For example, they might select a bell for the baby billy goat, a cymbal for the medium billy goat, and a drum for the big billy goat.
Bodily-Kinesthetic	Have the children demonstrate the movements of the following characters: Papa Bear, Pig Number Three, the baby billy goat, the little red hen, and the peddler.
Interpersonal	Invite the children to role play one of their favorite stories. Have them work together to decide who should be each character.
Logical-Mathematical	Have the children identify all of the stories that had three primary characters in them.
Intrapersonal	Have the children identify their favorite story and then tell why the story is their favorite.
Naturalist	Help the children to fill out a Story Pyramid (Appendix p. 538) for their favorite story.

Books

Books About Traditional Tales

Chicka Chicka Boom Boom by Bill Martin, Jr.
Cinderella by Marcia Brown
Hansel and Gretel retold by Dom DeLuise
Jack and the Beanstalk by Matt Faulkner
Jack and the Beanstalk by Niamh Sharkey (Illustrator)
Jack and the Beanstalk by Steven Kellogg
Jan Lewis' Fairy Tales: The Ugly Duckling, Little Red Riding Hood, Cinderella, and the Three Little Pigs by Jan Lewis
Johnny Appleseed by Steven Kellogg
The Jolly Postman by Janet Ahlberg
Little Red Riding Hood by Brothers Grimm
Little Red Riding Hood by Paul Galdone
Little Red Riding Hood by Trina Schart
Paul Bunyan by Steven Kellogg
Rumpelstiltskin by Paul O. Zelinsky
Sleeping Beauty by Trina Schart Hyman
Snow White by Jane Yolen
The Three Little Kittens by Paul Galdone
The Three Wishes by Margot Zemach
The True Story of the Three Little Pigs by Jon Scieszka

More Modern Traditional Tales

Brown Bear, Brown Bear, What Do You See? by Bill Martin, Jr.
Katy No-Pocket by Emmy Payne
Leo the Late Bloomer by Robert Kraus
Little Blue and Little Yellow by Leo Lionni
The Little Engine that Could by Watty Piper
Rosie's Walk by Pat Hutchins
The Stone Soup by Marcia Brown
Swimmy by Leo Lionni

Whether the Weather

Sunny Days

Morning Circle

1. Invite the children to move the Weather Wheel (Appendix p. 547) to the appropriate reading.
2. Sing "You Are My Sunshine" with the children or read "My Shadow" (Appendix p. 324).
3. Ask the children to brainstorm a list of things they can do on a sunny day. Transcribe the list on chart paper.
4. Encourage the children to think about ways the sun is helpful to us—it keeps us warm, keeps us healthy, helps the plants grow, provides light, and so on.
5. Discuss sun safety. Tell the children they should never look directly at the sun or stay in the sun so long that it burns their skin. Explain that children who live in sunny areas of the country should always wear a sunscreen when they are outdoors.
6. Explain that there is an instrument used to measure the heat generated by the sun (temperature). The instrument is a thermometer. The thermometer tells us how hot or cold it is. Show the children a thermometer.
7. Tell the children that today's activities will be about sunny days.

Story Circle

Shine, Sun! by Carol Greene
Sunshine by Jan Ormerod
The Wind and the Sun by Tomie dePaola
"The Wind and the Sun" (Appendix p. 354)

Music and Movement

Give the children 4' strips of colored cellophane and encourage them to make colorful shadows on the playground.

Play Shadow Games (Appendix p. 367).

Read "April Clouds" (Appendix p. 309), and Sing "Mister Sun" (Appendix p. 295), "Itsy Bitsy Spider" (Appendix p. 291), "Over in the Meadow" (Appendix p. 298), or "Frosty the Snowman" (Appendix p. 287).

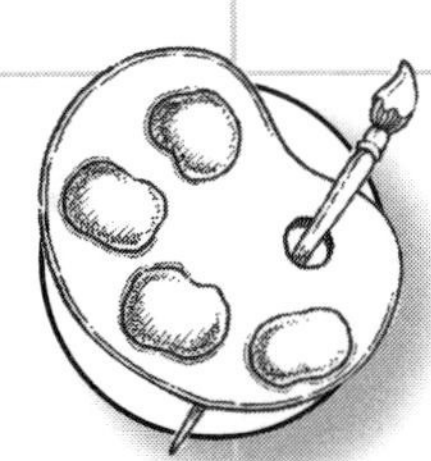

Art (Spatial)

Encourage the children to experiment with Sun Art (Appendix p. 402).

Discovery (Naturalist, Spatial)

Give the children several pairs of sunglasses and Colorscopes (Appendix p. 386) to explore. Can they use the sun coming through the window to make colored shadows on the floor with the Colorscopes?

Dramatic Play (Intrapersonal, Interpersonal)

Give the children Dress Me Dolls (Appendix p. 522-525). Encourage them to select appropriate clothing for the dolls to wear on a hot, sunny day or a cold, sunny day.

Fine Motor (Bodily-Kinesthetic, Spatial, Logical-Mathematical)

Provide scissors and paper. Invite the children to cut out different shapes and tape them to the windows to create shadows.

Language (Linguistic, Musical, Interpersonal)

Give the children the "Itsy Bitsy Spider" Puppets (Appendix p. 484) and encourage them to sing the song and then place the puppets in the sequence in which they are mentioned in the song. What role does the sun play in the song?

Science (Spatial, Logical-Mathematical, Intrapersonal)

Give the children prisms to place in sunny spots. How do the rainbows make them feel?

Closing Circle (Reflections on the Day)

Ask the children:

1. What did you learn about the sun today?
2. What was your favorite activity? Why?

Windy Days

Morning Circle

1. Invite the children to move the Weather Wheel (Appendix p. 547) to the appropriate reading.
2. Set a fan close to the Morning Circle area and position it to blow directly on the children. (Supervise closely at all times!) Ask the children how the wind feels. Read "The Wind" (Appendix p. 327), "Who Has Seen the Wind?" (Appendix p. 327), or "The March Wind" (Appendix p. 322)
3. Find out what children know about the wind. Ask them to think of ways they would know the wind was blowing just by looking out the window.
4. Explain that wind is moving air.
   - Wind blows the clouds across the sky. Clouds hold rain. Most rainstorms are accompanied by varying degrees of wind.
   - A hurricane is an intense storm made up of high winds and rain. Hurricanes can do a lot of damage.
   - A tornado is a spinning funnel of wind that races across the ground. As it spins, it sucks up rocks, trees, and even houses and cars in its path.
   - Weather vanes and windsocks tell us the direction the wind is blowing.
5. Help the children think of ways that wind is helpful to us—it helps pollinate the flowers, blows clouds away, brings the rain, and so on.
6. Tell the children that today's activities will be about the wind and windy days.

Story Circle

"Dressed for Play" action story (Appendix p. 332)
Gilberto and the Wind by Marie Hall Ets
Who Took the Farmer's Hat? by Joan Nodset
The Wind and the Sun by Tomie dePaola
"The Wind and the Sun" listening story (Appendix p. 354)
The Wind Blew by Pat Hutchins

Music and Movement

Act out "Fall Leaves" (Appendix p. 315).
Blow and chase bubbles.

Art (Spatial, Logical-Mathematical)

Invite the children to make Wind Catchers (Appendix p. 405). If possible, find a place outdoors to hang the Wind Catchers. What happens when the wind blows?

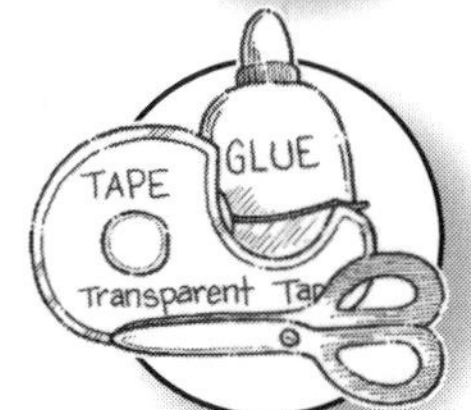

Construction (Spatial, Bodily-Kinesthetic)

Help the children make a Kite (Appendix p. 392). Let the children fly their kites during outdoor playtime. What role does the wind play in keeping their kites aloft?

Discovery (Logical-Mathematical, Intrapersonal)

Give the children a Tornado in a Bottle (Appendix p. 402), or use a bottle connector to make a tornado (available from school supply stores and catalogs). Invite the children to swirl the bottle to make a tornado. Ask the children to think about how it might feel to be caught in a tornado. Would it be scary or would it be fun like a carnival ride?

Gross Motor (Bodily-Kinesthetic, Logical-Mathematical)

Encourage the children to blow bubbles (Appendix p. 375) in front of the fan. What happens to the bubbles? Try blowing bubbles away from the fan. What happens?

Language (Linguistic, Naturalist, Interpersonal, Musical)

Provide a tape recorder and props for making wind sounds such as empty tubes, cups, or bottles. Challenge the children to make wind sounds using both their mouths and/or the props. Invite them to record the sounds. Do they sound like the wind when they are played back? Help the children think of some words used to describe the sound of the wind, such as "swoosh," "swirl," and "whoosh." Invite them to record the words. Do they sound like the wind?

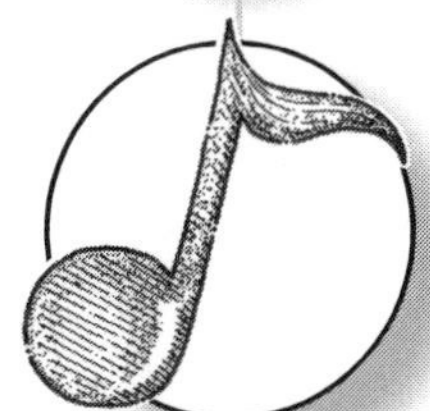

Music (Musical, Bodily-Kinesthetic)

Invite the children to make Wind Chimes (Appendix p. 405). If possible, find a place outdoors to hang them. What happens when the wind blows?

Closing Circle (Reflections on the Day)

Ask the children:

1. What have you learned today about the wind?
2. How is the wind the same as the air you use to blow bubbles?
3. Can you think of some things that can ride on the wind? (leaves, bubbles, paper, etc.)

Rainy Days

Morning Circle

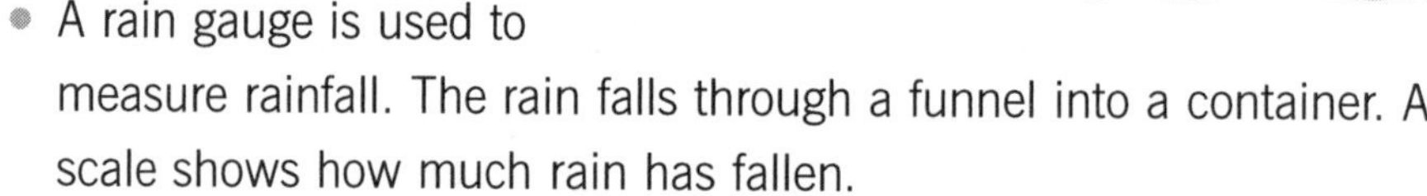

1. Invite the children to move the Weather Wheel (Appendix p. 547) to the appropriate reading.
2. Sing "The Raindrop Song" (Appendix p. 300) with the children.
3. Find out what children know about the rain.
    - Water in clouds falls as rain, hail, sleet, or snow depending on the temperature.
    - Clouds are made up of water that is absorbed from the earth.
    - A rain gauge is used to measure rainfall. The rain falls through a funnel into a container. A scale shows how much rain has fallen.
4. Encourage the children to think of ways that the rain is helpful—it makes plants grow, cleans the earth, refills the lakes, and so on.
5. Tell the children that today's activities will be about rain and rainy days.

Story Circle

Listen to the Rain by Bill Martin, Jr.
Rain by Peter Spier
Rain Talk by Mary Serfozo
The Tiny Seed by Eric Carle (Illustrator)

Music and Movement

Sing and move to "Rain, Rain, Go Away" (Appendix p. 299), "The Raindrop Song" (Appendix p. 300), or "The Ants Go Marching" (Appendix p. 283).
Act out "April Clouds" (Appendix p. 309) and "Thunderstorm" (Appendix p. 326).

Art (Spatial)

Invite the children to make a raindrop picture. Show them how to sprinkle their paper with dry tempera paint and then wet it with a spray bottle of water. If they turn their picture on its side while it is still wet, the water will make running trails.

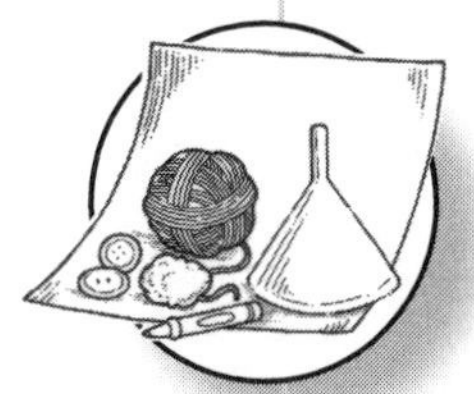

Discovery (Naturalist)

Help the children make a rain gauge. Show them how to mark a medium-size plastic jar with a Sharpie pen in ½" increments. Put a funnel in the mouth of the jar and then place it outdoors in a safe place to await the next rainfall.

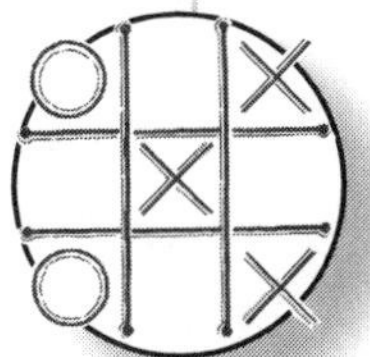

Games (Naturalist, Logical-Mathematical, Interpersonal)

Give the children an eyedropper. Invite them to place a drop of water on a cookie sheet beside a friend's drop of water. Then have them turn the cookie sheet up on edge and watch the drops of water race to the bottom of the sheet. Which drop wins? Is there a way to have a better chance of winning? (Note: larger drops fall more quickly.)

Language (Linguistic, Intrapersonal)

Provide paper and crayons. Challenge the children to make a "Things to Do on a Rainy Day" book. Transcribe their ideas. Encourage them to illustrate their ideas.

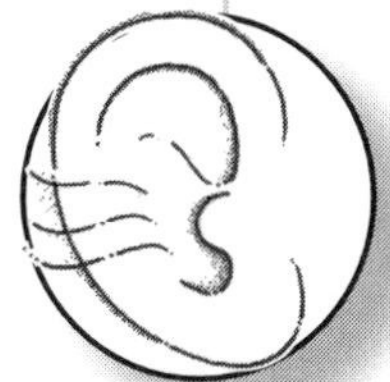

Listening (Musical, Interpersonal)

Give the children three or four spray bottles of water. Use bottles that have adjustments for the intensity of the spray. Invite the children to spray the bottles onto a cookie sheet and listen for the differences in sounds of water as it hits the tray. Challenge them to create a tune with the sounds.

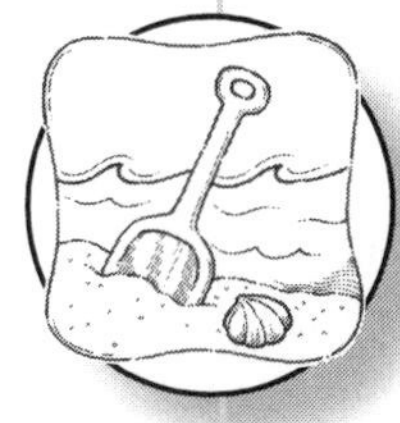

Sand and Water (Bodily-Kinesthetic)

Provide funnels, cups, basters, colanders, and strainers for water play. Encourage the children to make rain by pouring water through the colander.

Closing Circle (Reflections on the Day)

Ask the children:

1. How do the rain and the clouds work together?
2. What rainy day activities did you think of?
3. Can someone play the tune that was created with the spray bottles?

Cold Days

Morning Circle

1. Invite the children to move the Weather Wheel (Appendix p. 547) to the appropriate reading.
2. Read "Whether the Weather" (Appendix p. 327) or "Cold Fact" (Appendix p. 314) to the children.
3. Find out what children know about cold weather.
   - Talk about things you can do in cold weather.
   - Discuss cold-weather clothing.
   - Talk about ways of keeping warm.
   - Show the children how to rub their hands together and to blow into their hands to make them warm.
4. Tell the children that today's activities will be about cold days.

Story Circle

Fox Went Out on a Chilly Night by Peter Spier

"Frosty the Snowman" flannel board song (Appendix p. 287, 418-420)

Owl Moon by Jane Yolen

Music and Movement

Act out "Cold Fact" (Appendix p. 314).

Sing "Winter Is Coming" (Appendix p. 307).

Play "Hot and Cold Hide and Seek" (Appendix p. 362).

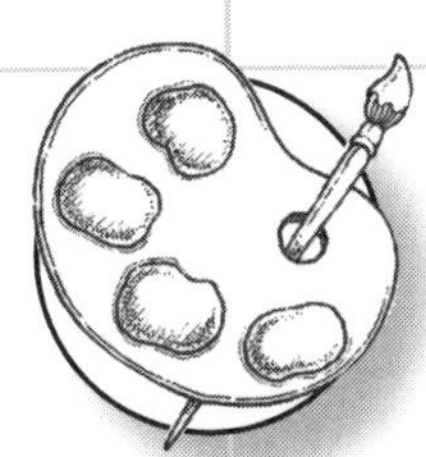

ART (Spatial)

Invite the children to try Ice Painting (Appendix p. 391).

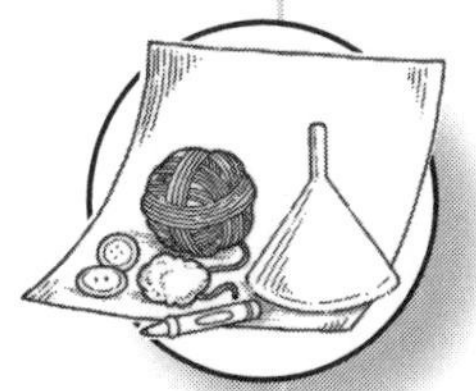

DISCOVERY (Logical-Mathematical)

Place ice in a resealable plastic bag and invite the children to watch it melt. You may want to freeze small toys inside the ice and challenge the children to think of ways to get the toys out.

DRAMATIC PLAY (Intrapersonal, Interpersonal)

Give the children the Dress Me Dolls (Appendix p. 522-525). Encourage them to select appropriate clothing for the dolls to wear on a cold day.

FINE MOTOR (Naturalist, Bodily-Kinesthetic)

Provide magazines and scissors. Invite the children to look through magazines for pictures of things they can do in cold weather. Encourage them to cut the cold day activity pictures out of the magazines.

GROSS MOTOR (Bodily-Kinesthetic, Musical)

Clear an uncarpeted area in the room. Invite the children to take off their shoes and ice skate (sock skate) to classical music.

SNACK (Interpersonal, Logical-Mathematical, Linguistic)

Invite the children to make Peppermint Baggie Ice Cream using the rebus recipe (Appendix p. 496).

Closing Circle (Reflections on the Day)

Ask the children:

1. What have you learned about cold days today?
2. What happens to rain when the weather is really cold?

Snowy Days

Morning Circle

1. Invite children to move the Weather Wheel (Appendix p. 547) to the appropriate reading.
2. Read "I'm a Frozen Icicle" (Appendix p. 321) to the children.
3. Find out what children know about snow.
4. Discuss snow.
   - Snow is frozen ice crystals.
   - You can build things out of snow.
   - Some people live in places where it snows most of the year; others live in places where it rarely or never snows.
5. Tell the children that today's activities will be about snow and snowy days.

Story Circle

"Frosty the Snowman" flannel board story (Appendix p. 287, 418-420)
Look! Snow! by Kathryn O. Galbraith
The Mitten by Jan Brett (Illustrator)
The Snowman by Raymond Briggs
The Snowy Day by Ezra Jack Keats

Music and Movement

Play "Musical Freeze" (Appendix p. 365).
Dance with white scarves and pretend to be snowflakes.
Sing "The Raindrop Song" (Appendix p. 300), "Jingle Bells" (Appendix p. 292), or "Over the River and Through the Woods" (Appendix p. 298).

LEARNING CENTERS

ART (SPATIAL)

Provide white tempera paint and blue and black paper for the children to use to create a snowy day picture.

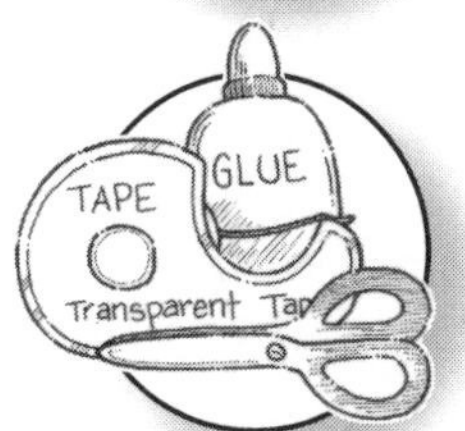

CONSTRUCTION (SPATIAL, INTRAPERSONAL, BODILY-KINESTHETIC)

Provide white playdough. Encourage the children to make snow people. Provide scraps of cloth, beads, and other materials to use as accessories for the snow people. What would it be like to be a snow person living outdoors in the snow?

DRAMATIC PLAY (SPATIAL, INTERPERSONAL, BODILY-KINESTHETIC)

Provide shaving cream and let the children make a snowy scene on a tabletop.

LANGUAGE (MUSICAL, INTRAPERSONAL, LINGUISTIC)

Give the children the "Frosty the Snowman" flannel board story (Appendix p. 418-420) to re-enact.

MATH (LOGICAL-MATHEMATICAL)

Cut snowflakes from coffee filters in a variety of sizes. Invite the children to arrange the snowflakes from smallest to largest.

SAND AND WATER (BODILY-KINESTHETIC)

Fill the sand and water table with snow, if available. If snow is not available, use pretend snow (Styrofoam chips).

Closing Circle (Reflections on the Day)

Ask the children:

1. How is snow like rain?
2. What would you do on a snowy day?

Assessment for "Whether the Weather"

Intellectual Strength	Assessment
Linguistic	Have the children make up a rhyme about a sunny day.
Spatial	Invite the children to paint a picture of a snowy day, a sunny day, a rainy day, and a windy day.
Musical	Challenge the children to think of songs that are appropriate to sing on rainy days, snowy days, and sunny days.
Bodily-Kinesthetic	Have the children demonstrate how they walk to the car on a sunny day, a rainy day, a chilly day, a snowy day, and a windy day.
Logical-Mathematical Interpersonal	Have the children interview their friends to determine which weather type is their favorite sleeping weather and then make a graph of their results by putting tally marks on the weather chart.
Intrapersonal	Have the children describe activities they enjoy doing on sunny days, rainy days, chilly days, snowy days, and windy days.
Naturalist	Have the children sort clothing according to the type of weather.

Books Used in "Whether the Weather"

Fox Went Out on a Chilly Night by Peter Spier
Gilberto and the Wind by Marie Hall Ets
Listen to the Rain by Bill Martin, Jr.
Look! Snow! by Kathryn O. Galbraith
The Mitten by Jan Brett (Illustrator)
Owl Moon by Jane Yolen
Rain by Peter Spier
Rain Talk by Mary Serfozo
Shine, Sun! by Carol Greene
The Snowman by Raymond Briggs
The Snowy Day by Ezra Jack Keats
Sunshine by Jan Ormerod
The Tiny Seed by Eric Carle (Illustrator)
The Wind and the Sun by Tomie dePaola
The Wind Blew by Pat Hutchins
Who Took the Farmer's Hat? by Joan Nodset

Other Books about Weather

Caps, Hats, Socks, and Mittens by Louise Borden
Elmer's Weather by David McKee
How's the Weather? by Melvin Berger
Something Is Going to Happen by Charlotte Zolotow
The Sun, The Wind and the Rain by Lisa Westberg Peters
Weather by Pascale De Bourgoing
What's the Weather Today? by Allan Fowler

'Tis the Season

Spring

Morning Circle

1. Cut a tree trunk and branches from brown bulletin board paper. Cut leaves from green construction paper. Put the tree and branches on the wall or bulletin board close to the Morning Circle area. Do not put the leaves on.
2. When the children arrive at school, give them each a leaf and help them put the leaves on the tree with masking tape or a stapler. Sing "Spring Is Here!" (Appendix p. 301) with the children.
3. Talk about spring. One of the first things we notice is green leaves returning to the trees. What are other signs of spring? Encourage the children to list the things they know about springtime. Ask them:
   - What does the weather feel like?
   - What clothes do you wear?
   - What animals do you see?
   - What vegetables do you see?
4. Tell the children that today's activities will be about spring.

Story Circle

The Boy Who Didn't Believe in Spring by Lucille Clifton
Flower Garden by Eve Bunting
Mud Makes Me Dance in the Spring by Charlotte Agell
My Spring Robin by Anne F. Rockwell
Spring Is Here by Lois Lenski
Spring Is Like the Morning by M. Jean Craig
Spring Story by Jill Barklem
The Sugar Snow Spring by Lillian Hoban
"The Three Billy Goats Gruff" flannel board story (Appendix p. 348, 447-449)
When Spring Comes by Robert Maass

Music and Movement

Sing the "Raindrop Song" (Appendix p. 300), "Little Bunny Foo-Foo" (Appendix p. 292), or "Over in the Meadow" (Appendix p. 298).

Read "Fuzzy Caterpillar" (Appendix p. 316), or "Birdie, Birdie, Where Is Your Nest?" (Appendix p. 314), or April Clouds" (Appendix p. 309).

Take a walk outdoors and look for signs of spring.

LEARNING CENTERS

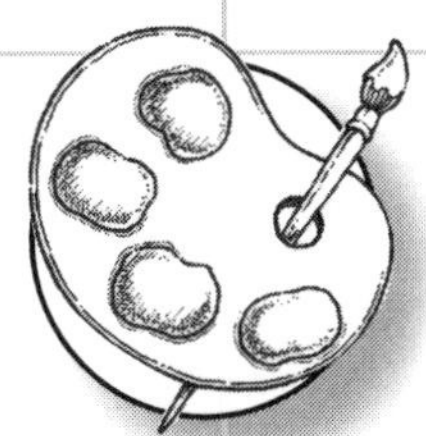

ART (Spatial)

Provide several spring colors of tissue paper. Show the children how to tear, wad, and glue it to their paper to make spring flowers.

Blocks (Bodily-Kinesthetic, Interpersonal, Spatial)

Provide Tree and Flower Props (Appendix p. 540-542). Invite the children to build a neighborhood and add the touches of spring.

FINE MOTOR (Bodily-Kinesthetic)

Lay a blue sheet of bulletin board paper or a blue shower curtain liner on the table and invite the children to use shaving cream to create clouds in a spring sky.

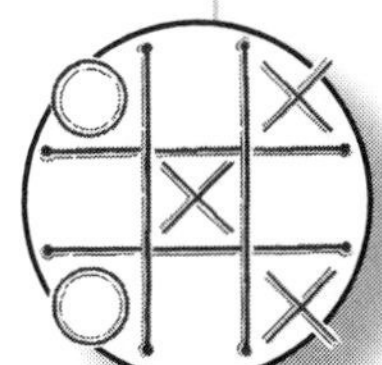

GAMES (Logical-Mathematical, Naturalist, Linguistic)

Give the children the Insect Concentration Game (Appendix p. 391) to play. Ask them why we see more insects in the spring.

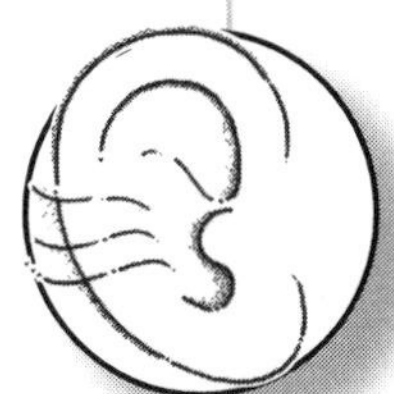

LISTENING (Musical, Intrapersonal, Naturalist)

Provide a nature tape with spring sounds such as the chirping of birds and pitter-patter of rain.

MATH (Logical-Mathematical)

Give the children the Bird and Nest Matching Game (Appendix p. 382) and invite them to match birds to nests. Ask the children why they think birds choose the spring season to build their nests.

Closing Circle (Reflections on the Day)

Ask the children:

1. Can you name some signs of spring?
2. What is your favorite thing about spring? Why?

Summer

Morning Circle

1. Make paper fans and give one to each child during Morning Circle. Ask the children what time of the year they will most likely need a fan.
2. Discuss summer. Ask the children:
   - What is the weather like?
   - What kind of clothes do you wear?
   - What activities do you do in the summer?
   - Are there special foods you might be more likely to eat during the summer?
   - Are there special places you might go?
3. Sing "Summer Is Coming" (Appendix p. 301).
4. Tell the children that today's activities will be about summer and things we do in the summertime.

Story Circle

"The Ant and the Grasshopper" listening story (Appendix p. 329)

One Hot Summer Day by Nina Crews

"The Wind and the Sun" (Appendix p. 354)

Music and Movement

Sing "This Is the Way We Dress for Summer" (Appendix p. 304), "She Waded in the Water" (Appendix p. 300), "Down by the Bay" (Appendix p. 286), "Ice Cream" (Appendix p. 321), "Mister Sun" (Appendix p. 295), or "Take Me Out to the Ball Game" (Appendix p. 302).

DRAMATIC PLAY (INTRAPERSONAL, NATURALIST, INTERPERSONAL)

Give the children Dress Me Dolls (Appendix p. 522-525). Invite them to dress the dolls in summer clothing.

GROSS MOTOR (Bodily-KINESTHETIC)

Provide a beach ball and encourage the children to roll it into a large basket or box.

LANGUAGE (LINGUISTIC, INTRAPERSONAL, LOGICAL-MATHEMATICAL, INTERPERSONAL, NATURALIST)

Give the children a rebus Vacation Packing List (Appendix p. 498), a suitcase, and the items on the rebus list. Encourage them to follow the list to pack their suitcase for vacation. Ask the children if they think everything they need is on the list. If not, what else will they need?

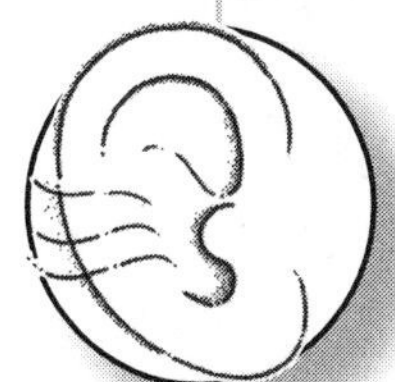

LISTENING (MUSICAL, NATURALIST)

Provide a nature sounds tape of ocean waves for the children.

MATH (LOGICAL-MATHEMATICAL, Bodily-KINESTHETIC)

Give the children the Watermelon Seed Transfer Game (Appendix p. 404) to explore. If watermelon seeds are unavailable, give them the Ice Cream Cone Match Game (Appendix p. 391).

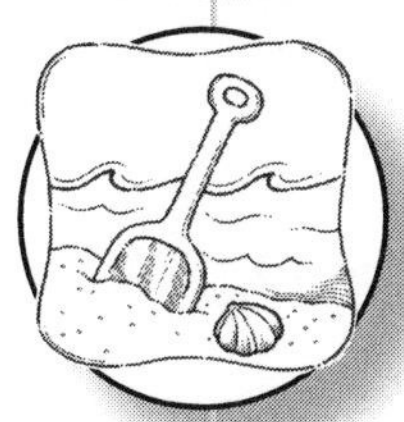

SAND AND WATER (INTERPERSONAL, SPATIAL)

Provide seashells, sand pails, and shovels for the children to play with. If the sand is damp, show the children how to make seashell prints in the sand.

Closing Circle (Reflections on the Day)

Ask the children:

1. What is your favorite summertime activity? Why?
2. How did you do packing the suitcase for vacation? Did you think of other things you would want to take along? What were they?

Fall

Morning Circle

1. Cut a tree trunk and branches from brown bulletin board paper. Cut leaves from orange, purple, red, yellow, and brown construction paper. Put the tree and branches on the wall or bulletin board close to the Morning Circle area. If the tree has green leaves on it, leave it as it is. If not, put a few green leaves on the tree.
2. When the children arrive at school, give them each a fall leaf and help them use masking tape or a stapler to put the leaves on the tree (and a few on the ground). Sing "Autumn Leaves" (Appendix p. 283) with the children or read "Fall" (Appendix p. 315).
3. Talk about fall. One of the first things we notice are the leaves turning brilliant colors. Can you think of some other signs of fall? Encourage the children to list the things they know about fall. Ask them:
   - What does the weather feel like?
   - What clothes do you wear?
   - What fruits/vegetables do you see?
   - What animals do you see?
4. Tell the children that today's activities will be about fall.

Story Circle

Apples and Pumpkins by Anne Rockwell
"The Ant and the Grasshopper" listening story (Appendix p. 329)
Every Autumn Comes the Bear by Jim Arnosky
Fall Leaves Fall! by Zoe Hall
"The Great Big Pumpkin" flannel board story (Appendix p. 335, 426-427)
Now It's Fall by Lois Lenski
The Seasons of Arnold's Apple Tree by Gail Gibbons
"A Special Surprise" (Appendix p. 344)
Why Do Leaves Change Color? by Betsy Maestro

Music and Movement

Sing and move to "Falling Leaves" (Appendix p. 315), "Five Waiting Pumpkins" (Appendix p. 316), "This Is the Way We Rake the Leaves" (Appendix p. 304), "Gray Squirrel" (Appendix p. 288), "I'm a Little Acorn Brown" (Appendix p. 291), or "Johnny Appleseed" (Appendix p. 292).

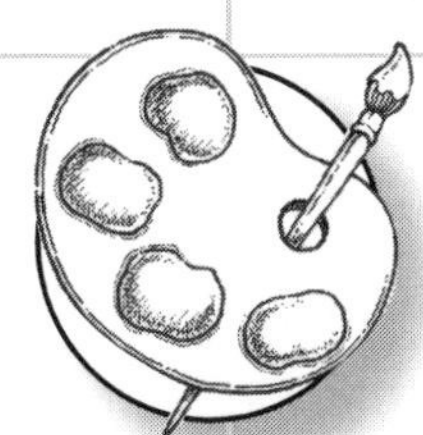

Art (Spatial, Musical, Intrapersonal)

Provide fall colors of tempera paint, brushes, and paper. Invite the children to paint to classical music.

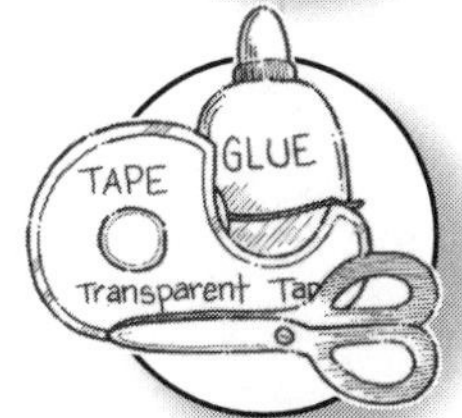

Construction (Naturalist, Linguistic, Interpersonal)

Provide materials and encourage the children to make Fall Observation Bottles (Appendix p. 387).

Discovery (Naturalist, Linguistic, Interpersonal)

Invite the children to examine a squash. Cut it open and provide a magnifying glass for a closer look.

Gross Motor (Bodily-Kinesthetic)

Provide corncobs and a basket. Challenge the children to toss the cobs into the basket. Gradually increase the distance between the basket and the thrower.

Snack (Logical-Mathematical, Interpersonal, Linguistic)

Allow the children to help you make Apple Cider (Appendix p. 371).

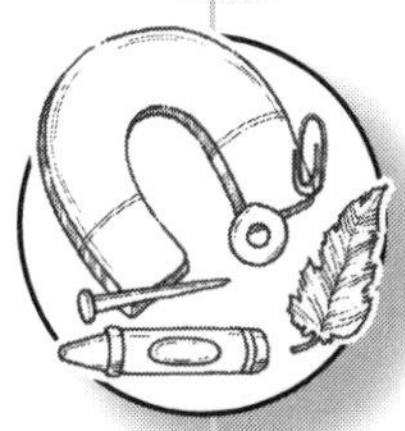

Science (Logical-Mathematical, Naturalist)

Provide a basket of leaves for the children to sort by color, shape, and size.

Closing Circle (Reflections on the Day)

Ask the children:

1. What did you learn about fall today?
2. Which color of fall leaf is your favorite? Why?
3. How is fall different from summer?

Winter

Morning Circle

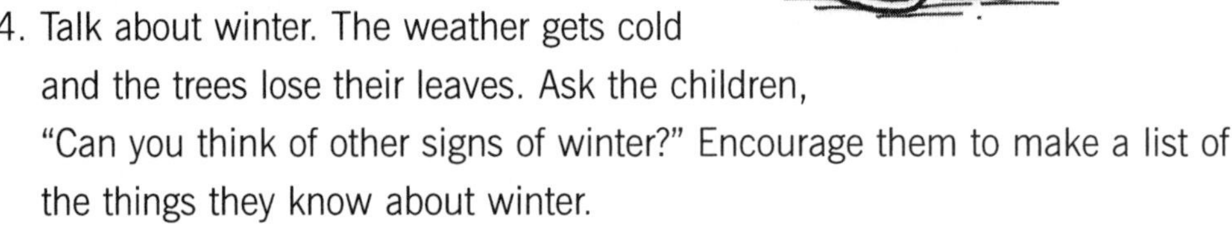

1. Cut a tree trunk and branches from brown bulletin board paper and place it on the wall or bulletin board close to the Morning Circle area.
2. When the children come to the Circle, ask them if they can tell the time of the year by looking at the bare tree.
3. Sing "Winter Is Coming" with the children (Appendix p. 307). Read the poems "Jack Frost" (Appendix p. 321) or "Cold Fact" (Appendix p. 314).
4. Talk about winter. The weather gets cold and the trees lose their leaves. Ask the children, "Can you think of other signs of winter?" Encourage them to make a list of the things they know about winter.
5. Tell the children that today's activities will be about winter.

Story Circle

"Frosty the Snowman" flannel board story (Appendix p. 287, 418-420)
Henrietta's First Winter by Robin Lewis
The Mitten by Jan Brett
The Snowy Day by Ezra Jack Keats
Winter by Ron Hirschi
When Winter Comes by Robert Maass

Music and Movement

Play classical music. Invite the children to take their shoes off and try ice skating (in socks) on the floor.

Sing "Over the River and Through the Woods" (Appendix p. 299), "Jingle Bells" (Appendix p. 292), or do the fingerplay "Five Little Snowmen" (Appendix p. 310).

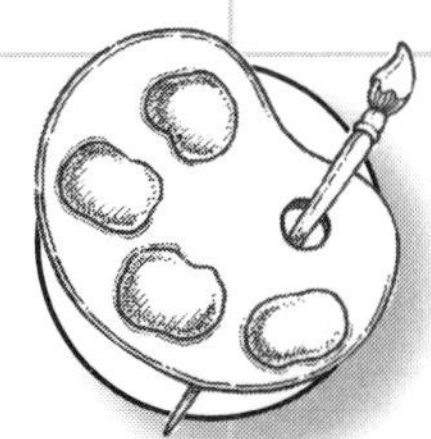

ART (Spatial, Interpersonal)

Invite the children to create snow pictures by using white crayons on blue paper. When they have finished, have them paint over their pictures with an Epsom Salt Solution (Appendix p. 375). It will create a glazed appearance when it dries.

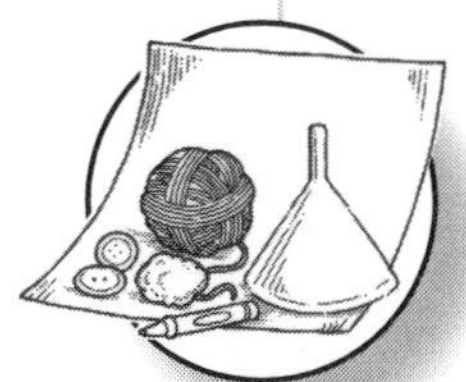

DISCOVERY (Naturalist)

Provide materials and encourage the children to make Winter Observation Bottles (Appendix p. 406).

DRAMATIC PLAY (Interpersonal, Naturalist)

Give the children Dress Me Dolls (Appendix p. 522-525). Invite them to dress the dolls for winter activities.

GROSS MOTOR (Bodily-Kinesthetic)

Spray shaving cream on the top of a table and invite the children to create a snowy scene with their hands.

LANGUAGE (Linguistic, Musical)

Give the children the "Frosty the Snowman" flannel board story (Appendix, p. 418-420) and encourage them to re-tell the story on the flannel board.

MATH (Logical-Mathematical)

Give the children white felt circles of varying sizes and felt hats and features to build snowmen. What arrangement of the circles is necessary to create a snowman?

Closing Circle (Reflections on the Day)

Ask the children:

1. What do you like about winter? Why?
2. What new thing have you learned about winter today?
3. How is winter different from fall?

The Calendar

Morning Circle

1. Display a calendar in the Morning Circle area. Sing "Good Morning" (Appendix p. 287) with the children.
2. Discuss calendars. Talk about the months of the year. Show the days and weeks. Talk about the seasons.
3. Read the children "Monday's Child" (Appendix p. 323).
4. Tell the children that today's activities will be about the calendar.

September

SUN	MON	TUE	WED	THU	FRI	SAT
1	2	3	4	5	6	7
8	9	10	11	12	13	14
15	16	17	18	19	20	21
22	23	24	25	26	27	28
29	30					

Reminders:
School Supplies: pencils, glue, ruler, paper

Story Circle

Around the Year by Tasha Tudor
Chicken Soup with Rice by Maurice Sendak
June 29, 1999 by David Wiesner
A Red Wagon Year by Kathi Appelt
Through the Year With Harriet by Betsy Maestro
Tuesday by David Wiesner
The Turning of the Year by Bill Martin, Jr.
The Very Hungry Caterpillar by Eric Carle

Music and Movement

Sing "The Mulberry Bush" (Appendix p. 364) or "Good Morning" (Appendix p. 287).

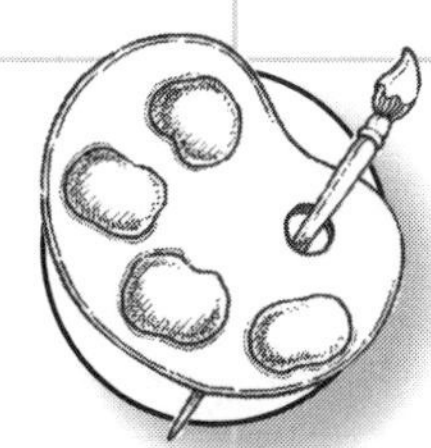

Art (Spatial, Intrapersonal)

Give each child a Calendar Page (Appendix p. 520) to illustrate. Talk to them about the months of the year. Invite them to pick their favorite month and draw a picture to reflect something that happens during that month. Help them put the dates on the calendar.

Discovery (Naturalist, Logical-Mathematical)

Give the children a set of seasonal photos (one photo to represent each season). You can use the photos from an old calendar. Challenge the children to place the photos in seasonal order.

Gross Motor (Bodily-Kinesthetic, Logical Mathematical, Naturalist)

Make a Calendar Walk (Appendix p. 384). Invite the children to walk the months of the year. As they pass each month, have them say the name of the month and place a representative cutout on the month.

Language (Linguistic, Interpersonal)

Cut up the seasonal photographs on an old calendar to make puzzles for the children to work.

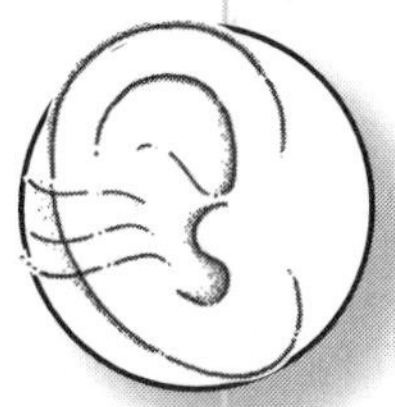

Listening (Musical)

Give the children Season Mats (Appendix p. 533-536). Make a cassette tape of seasonal songs such as "Frosty the Snowman," "Down by the Bay," or "Baby Bumblebee." Invite the children to listen to the tape and point to the mat that is the appropriate season for the song.

Math (Logical-Mathematical)

Give the children a "Calendar Number Match Game" (Appendix p. 383). Invite them to match the days from one calendar to another calendar.

Closing Circle (Reflections on the Day)

Ask the children:

1. Which is your favorite month of the year? Why?
2. Which season do you like best? Why?
3. What have you learned about calendars today?

Assessment for "'Tis the Season"

Intellectual Strength	Assessment
Linguistic Interpersonal	Have the children look at books in the library center and select books whose setting or activities fit each season of the year.
Spatial	Have the children help illustrate a calendar. They will need a drawing for each month of the year.
Musical	Ask the children to listen to several pieces of music and assign a season to each piece.
Bodily-Kinesthetic	Challenge the children to identify sports played or enjoyed during each season of the year. For example, football in the fall, swimming in the summer, soccer or baseball in the spring, and skiing in the winter.
Intrapersonal	Have the children identify their least favorite season and then tell why they like that season the least.
Naturalist Logical-Mathematical	Ask the children to match weather types to seasons. For example, during the summer the weather is generally sunny, in the winter it is snowy, in the fall it is chilly, and during the spring it is rainy.

Books Used in "'Tis the Season"

A Red Wagon Year by Kathi Appelt
Apples and Pumpkins by Anne Rockwell
Around the Year by Tasha Tudor
The Boy Who Didn't Believe in Spring by Lucille Clifton
Chicken Soup with Rice by Maurice Sendak
Every Autumn Comes the Bear by Jim Arnosky
Fall Leaves Fall! by Zoe Hall
Flower Garden by Eve Bunting
Henrietta's First Winter by Robin Lewis
June 29, 1999 by David Wiesner
The Mitten by Jan Brett
Mud Makes Me Dance in the Spring by Charlotte Agell
My Spring Robin by Anne F. Rockwell
Now It's Fall by Lois Lenski
One Hot Summer Day by Nina Crews
The Seasons of Arnold's Apple Tree by Gail Gibbons
The Snowy Day by Ezra Jack Keats
Spring Is Here by Lois Lenski
Spring Is Like the Morning by M. Jean Craig
Spring Story by Jill Barklem
The Sugar Snow Spring by Lillian Hoban
The Turning of the Year by Bill Martin, Jr.
Through the Year With Harriet by Betsy Maestro
Tuesday by David Wiesner
The Very Hungry Caterpillar by Eric Carle
When Spring Comes by Robert Maass
When Winter Comes by Robert Maass
Why Do Leaves Change Color? by Betsy Maestro
Winter by Ron Hirschi

Other Books about Seasons

The Earth Is Good by Michael DeMunn
Flower Fairies of the Seasons by Cicely Mary Barker
Four Stories for Four Seasons by Tomie De Paola

Books

My Favorite Time of Year by Susan Pearson

Ox Cart Man by Donald Hall

Seasons by John Burningham

The Seasons of Arnold's Apple Tree by Gail Gibbons

Snowy, Flowy, Blowy by Nancy Tafuri

Summer Coat, Winter Coat by Doe Boyle

Sunshine Makes the Seasons by Franklyn M. Branley

Thirteen Moons on Turtle's Back by Joseph Bruchac

The Tiny Seed by Eric Carle

The Turning of the Year by Bill Martin, Jr.

Celebrations
(Holidays)

Valentine's Day

Morning Circle

1. Cut a big heart out of butcher paper. Put the heart in the art area and tape the butcher paper over the door. Have the children walk through the heart to enter the room.
2. Use masking tape to make a large heart on the floor. Encourage the children to sit on the tape when they come to Morning Circle. Ask the children if they know what shape they are sitting in.
3. Tell the children that this shape is used to tell people we love them.
4. Say "Five Pink Valentines" (Appendix p. 311) or "Five Special Valentines" (Appendix p. 311) with the children. What shapes are most valentines?
5. Tell the children that today's activities will be about Valentine's Day traditions.

Story Circle

Bee My Valentine by Miriam Cohen
Little Mouse's Big Valentine by Thacher Hurd
Love and Kisses by Sarah Wilson
Love Is by Wendy Anderson Halperin
One Zillion Valentines by Frank Modell
The Valentine Bears by Eve Bunting
"Valencia Valentine" flannel board story (Appendix p. 353, 456-457)
Valentine Cats by Jean Marzollo
Valentine Mice! by Bethany Roberts

Music and Movement

Play "Drop the Heart" as you would "Drop the Handkerchief" (Appendix p. 359).

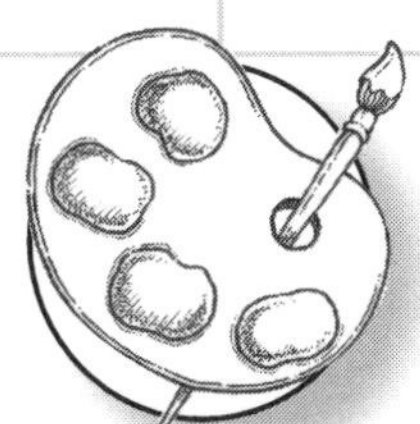

ART (Spatial, Intrapersonal)

Provide doilies, construction paper, markers, lace, sequins, and other materials for making valentines for someone special. Encourage the children to dictate a message to go on their valentine.

Provide crayons and invite the children to draw a picture or write a message on a big heart cut from butcher paper.

FINE MOTOR (Bodily-Kinesthetic, Linguistic)

Fold pieces of paper in half and draw half of a heart on the fold of the paper. Give children scissors and encourage them to cut out the heart. Write "I Love You" on a heart and let the children use it as a model to write their own "I Love You" message.

LANGUAGE (Linguistic)

Provide the "Valencia Valentine" flannel board story (Appendix p. 456-457) and encourage the children to re-tell it on the flannel board.

MATH (Logical-Mathematical, Naturalist)

Provide several different colors of hearts cut in many sizes. Challenge the children to sort the hearts by color or by size. Encourage them to arrange the hearts in patterns and to put them in order from smallest to largest.

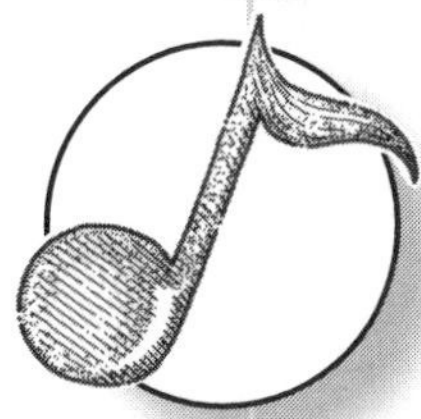

MUSIC (Musical)

Encourage the children to sing a valentine song they know or make one up. Provide a recorder so they can tape their songs.

SNACK (Interpersonal)

Let the children cut gelatin into heart-shaped Gelatin Jigglers (Appendix p. 372) and have them for snack.

Closing Circle (Reflections on the Day)

Ask the children:

1. What shape do you think of when you think of Valentine's Day? What colors do you think of?
2. What was your favorite activity today? Why?

St. Patrick's Day

Morning Circle

1. In advance of the day, remind the children to wear green. Have a few green shamrocks on hand in case someone forgets.
2. Before children arrive, make little green leprechaun footprints all over the classroom—over tables, up walls, and even inside the shelves. You may also want to put a few obvious things in the wrong places as well (you know leprechauns are mischievous). When the children comment, tell them that a leprechaun must be loose somewhere in the school. Pretend to see him dashing around all during the day.
3. Talk about leprechauns; their size, behavior, and their place in Irish history and folklore. Be sure to mention the pot of gold that the Leprechaun protects.
4. Discuss St. Patrick's Day with the children. Explain that St. Patrick's Day is an Irish Holiday. Its purpose is to celebrate the life of one of their religious patrons, St. Patrick. There are many legends about St. Patrick. The most famous legend is that he is said to have driven all the snakes out of Ireland. In this country, we celebrate the holiday by wearing green clothes or a shamrock emblem. Some cities hold parades. The parades consist of pipers, fiddlers, folk dancers, drums, and bagpipers. Ask if any of the children are Irish.
5. Tell the children that today's activities will be about St. Patrick's Day.

Story Circle

Leprechaun's Gold by Teresa Bateman

A Leprechaun's St. Patrick's Day by Sarah Kirwan Blazek

St. Patrick's Day by Gail Gibbons

St. Patrick's Day in the Morning by Eve Bunting

Music and Movement

Sing "MacNamara's Band" (Appendix p. 294).

Teach the children an Irish jig.

Do the movements to "Five Lively Leprechauns" (Appendix p. 311).

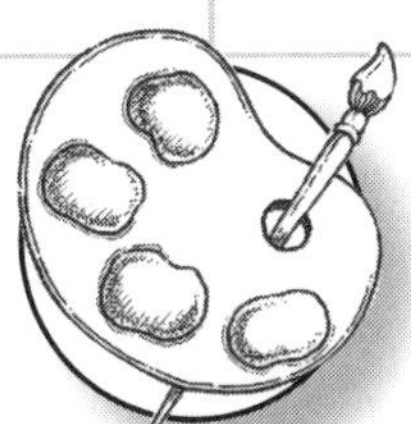

ART (Spatial)

Give the children shamrock stencils. Encourage them to trace the stencils and color the shamrocks they make.

LANGUAGE (Linguistic, Intrapersonal)

Encourage the children to make up a story about a mischievous leprechaun. What does the leprechaun do to get in trouble? What happens to him?

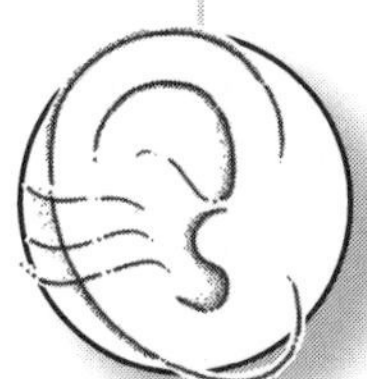

LISTENING (Musical, Intrapersonal)

Play traditional Irish folk music (bagpipes, jigs, etc.). Encourage the children to listen to the music. Ask how the music makes them feel.

MATH (Logical-Mathematical, Naturalist, Interpersonal)

Provide a box of shamrocks and four-leaf clovers. Encourage the children to sort the three- and four-leaf clovers.

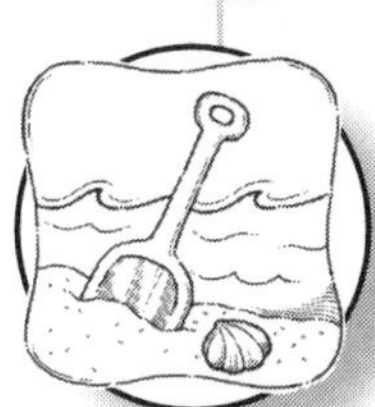

SAND AND WATER (Naturalist)

Spray medium-size pea gravel with gold paint. Hide it in the sand table. Provide strainers and encourage the children to sift the sand for the leprechaun's gold.

SNACK (Interpersonal)

Give the children green apple wedges and cream cheese that has been colored with green food coloring. Invite them to spread the cream cheese on the apple wedges to make Irish Treats.
(Check for allergies)

Closing Circle (Reflections on the Day)

Ask the children:

1. Did you see the leprechaun at any time today? Where?
2. What have you learned about St. Patrick's Day?

Mother's Day

Morning Circle

1. Encourage the children to bring a picture of their mother or a person who is special to them to school. Let children show their pictures and say something special about their mothers or special friends. Be sensitive to the fact that some children may not have a mother who plays an active role in their lives.
2. Read "Family Fun" (Appendix p. 316) to the children. Ask them what things they do with their mothers or special friends
3. Find out what the children know about Mother's Day.
4. Tell the children that Mother's Day is a special day for showing appreciation and affection for mothers or other people who are special to us. Many countries celebrate this day but not all on the same day. In Australia, mothers are honored at the same time we celebrate in this country. In England, however, the celebration is two weeks before Easter.
5. Talk about things mothers or special friends do for children. Brainstorm a list of special things the children can do on Mother's Day to show appreciation to their mothers or special friends.
6. Tell the children that today's activities will be about mothers and special friends.

Story Circle

The Day We Met You by Phoebe Koehler
How I Was Adopted: Samantha's Story by Joanna Cole
The Mother's Day Mice by Eve Bunting
Mother's Mother's Day by Lorna Balian

Music and Movement

Play "Mother, May I" (Appendix p. 364).

Act out "Five Little Ducks" (Appendix p. 286). Switch the role of the mother and the father in the song.

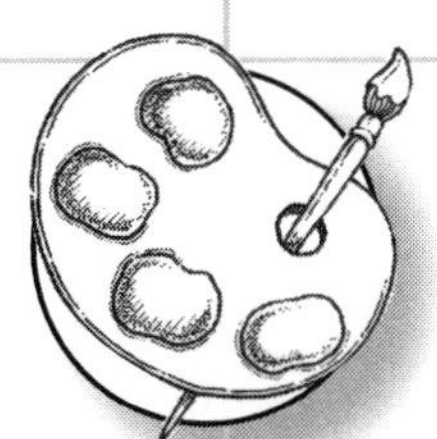

Art (Linguistic, Spatial, Intrapersonal, Interpersonal)

Provide paper, crayons, paints, lace, and glue. Invite the children to make a Mother's Day or Special Friend card. Provide a verse they can copy inside or help the children write individual messages inside.

Dramatic Play (Interpersonal, Intrapersonal)

Provide mommy dress-up clothes and invite the children to play dress-up. Be sure to offer some fancy hats and a big mirror.

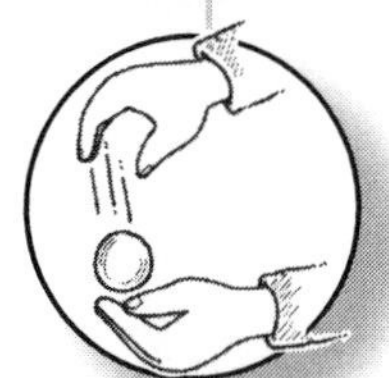

Fine Motor (Bodily-Kinesthetic)

Provide magazines, scissors, glue, and paper. Invite the children to look through the magazines for things mothers or special friends do and make a collage of the things they find.

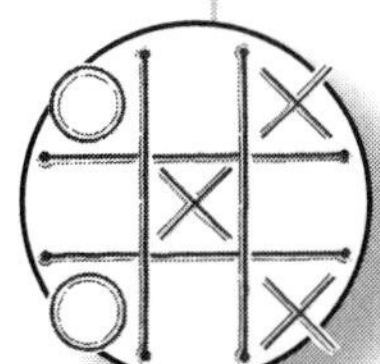

Games (Intrapersonal, Naturalist, Logical-Mathematical)

Invite the children to sort the pictures in "Things I Like to Do" Activity Cards (Appendix p. 539) into "Things I like to do with Mom or my special friend" and "Things I like to do alone."

Language (Linguistic, Musical, Intrapersonal, Interpersonal, Bodily-Kinesthetic)

Invite the children to use the Family Puppets Patterns (Appendix p. 469-470) to create a play about Mom or their special friend.

Writing (Linguistic, Interpersonal, Intrapersonal)

Invite the children to dictate and illustrate recipes of their favorite thing their mother or their special friend cooks. Collect the recipes and put them into a book. Give the books to mom or to a special friend for Mother's Day.

Closing Circle (Reflections on the Day)

Ask the children:

1. What is your favorite thing to do with your mother or with your special friend? Why?
2. What special thing will you do to celebrate Mother's Day?

Father's Day

Morning Circle

1. Encourage the children to bring a picture of their father or of a person who is special to them to school. Let the children show their pictures and say something special about their fathers or special friends. Be sensitive to the fact that some children may not have a father who plays an active role in their lives.
2. Read "Family Fun" (Appendix p. 316) to the children. Encourage the children to think of things they like to do with their fathers or with their special friends.
3. Find out what children know about Father's Day.
4. Tell children that Father's Day is a special day for showing appreciation and affection for fathers or special friends. Many countries celebrate this day but not all on the same day. In Australia, fathers are honored in August.
5. Talk about things fathers or special friends do for children. Brainstorm a list of special things the children can do on Father's Day to show appreciation to their fathers or special friends.
6. Tell the children that today's activities will be about fathers and special friends.

Story Circle

The Day We Met You by Phoebe Koehler
Happy Father's Day by Steven Kroll
Hooray for Father's Day by Marjorie Sharmat
How I Was Adopted: Samantha's Story by Joanna Cole
Owl Moon by Jane Yolen
A Perfect Father's Day by Eve Bunting

Music and Movement

Play "Father, May I?" as you would "Mother, May I?" (Appendix p. 364).

Act out "Five Little Ducks" (Appendix p. 286) .

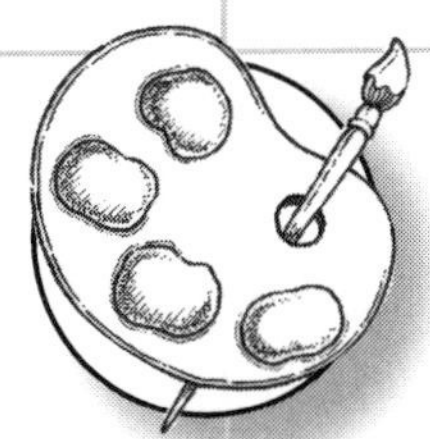

ART (Linguistic, Spatial, Intrapersonal, Interpersonal)

Provide paper, crayons, paints, lace, and glue. Invite the children to make a Father's Day or special friend card. Provide a verse they can copy inside or help the children write individual messages inside.

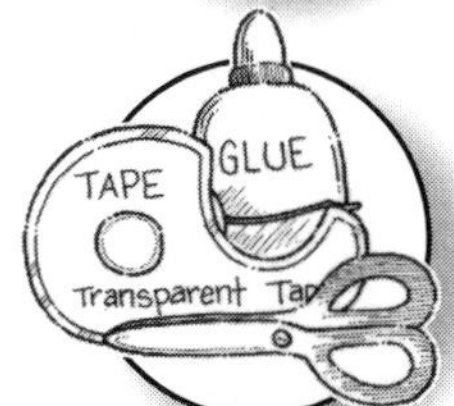

CONSTRUCTION (Bodily-Kinesthetic, Spatial)

Make a pencil holder for Dad or for a special friend. Give each child an empty orange juice can. Show them how to tear off 1" pieces of masking tape and place them in an overlapping fashion on the can. Use brown shoe polish to rub over the can when finished.

DRAMATIC PLAY (Interpersonal, Intrapersonal)

Provide daddy dress-up clothes and invite the children to play dress-up. Be sure to offer fancy ties, hats, and a big mirror.

FINE MOTOR (Bodily-Kinesthetic)

Provide magazines, scissors, glue, and paper. Invite the children to look through the magazines for things fathers do and make a collage of the things they find.

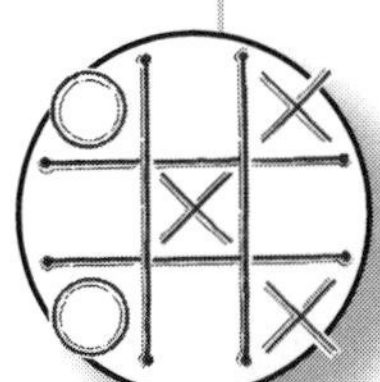

GAMES (Intrapersonal, Naturalist, Logical-Mathematical)

Invite the children to sort the pictures in "Things I Like to Do" Activity Cards (Appendix p. 539) into "Things I like to do with Dad or a special friend" and "Things I like to do alone."

LANGUAGE (Linguistic, Musical, Intrapersonal, Interpersonal, Bodily-Kinesthetic)

Invite the children to use the Family Puppets Patterns (Appendix p. 469-470) to create a play about Dad or special friends.

Closing Circle (Reflections on the Day)

Ask the children:

1. What is your favorite activity to do with Dad or with a special friend? Why?
2. What will you do to help celebrate Father's Day?

Fourth of July

Morning Circle

1. Invite the children to wear red, white, and blue today.
2. Sing "Yankee Doodle" (Appendix p. 307) with the children.
3. Find out what children know about July 4th. Encourage them to talk about their experiences.
4. Discuss July 4th.
   - July 4th is also known as Independence Day. It celebrates the United States' freedom from England. It was first celebrated in 1777 (more then 200 years ago).
   - The war between England and America lasted for five years.
   - Today's Independence Day activities are much the same as those of 1777. Festivities include red-white-and-blue parades, speeches, family picnics, and fireworks displays.
5. Tell the children that today's activities will be about July 4th customs and traditions.

Story Circle

Celebration by Jane Resh Thomas
The Fourth of July Story by Alice Dalgliesh
Happy Birthday, America by Marsha Wilson Chall
Hats Off for the fourth of July by Harriet Ziefert
Hurray for the Fourth of July by Wendy Watson
On the Day the Tall Ships Sailed by Betty Paraskevas

Music and Movement

Play marching music and have a parade.
Sing and move to "The Grand Old Duke of York" (Appendix p. 288).
Sing "Yankee Doodle" (Appendix p. 307).

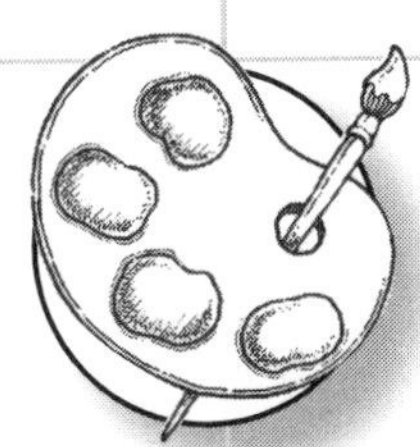

Art (Spatial)

Provide dark blue construction paper and brightly colored tempera paint. Show the children how to place a small amount of colorful paint on their paper and blow it through a straw to create a fireworks display.

Dramatic Play (Interpersonal, Intrapersonal)

Provide props for a picnic and invite the children to have a pretend picnic. Don't forget the Horse Shoe Game (Appendix p, 390).

Fine Motor (Bodily-Kinesthetic, Spatial)

Show the children how to fold a Parade Hat (Appendix p. 397). Provide tempera paint, feathers, markers, and collage materials for the children to use to decorate their hats.

Math (Logical-Mathematical)

Provide 1" strips of red, white, and blue construction paper. Invite the children to make patterns. After the children have experimented with making patterns, give them glue and challenge them to make paper chains using the strips.

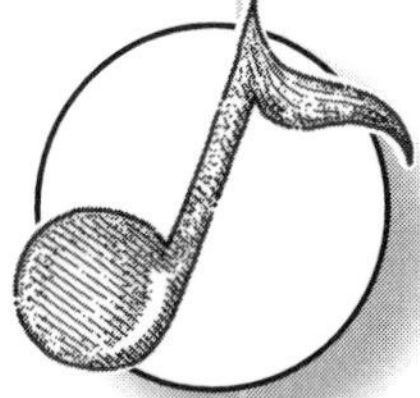

Music (Musical)

Provide materials and challenge the children to make Drums (Appendix p. 387). When they have finished constructing their drums, invite them to try them out while playing to march music.

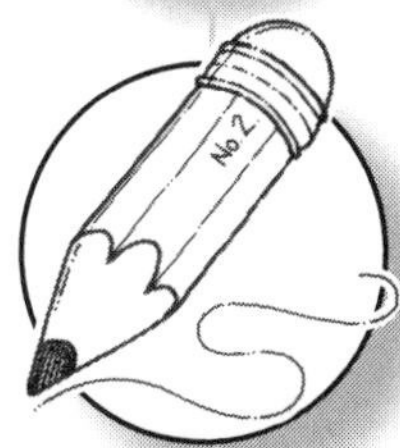

Writing (Linguistic)

Write the words "red," "white," and "blue" in red, white, and blue markers respectively on 4" x 6" index cards. Provide tracing paper and red, white, and blue crayons for the children to use to trace the color words.

Closing Circle (Reflections on the Day)

Ask the children:

1. What do you like best about the Fourth of July? Why?
2. How is the Fourth of July like New Year's Eve?

Halloween

Morning Circle

1. You may want to allow the children to dress in costume today.
2. Say "Five Little Pumpkins" (Appendix p. 310) with the children. For added fun, use Glove Puppets (Appendix p. 480) with the fingerplay.
3. Find out what the children know about Halloween. Let them talk about their experiences.
4. Discuss Halloween.
   - Halloween began as a religious holiday. It was originally celebrated on November 1, which is the day after the day we celebrate Halloween. This is because it has long been a custom for people to have a party before a religious holiday. Most people no longer observe the religious holiday but we have kept the party element of the celebration.
   - Our modern-day version of Halloween includes parties, costumes, trick or treat, and carnivals. It is a time to let your imagination run wild.
5. You may want to carve a pumpkin with the group or at least serve some Toasted Pumpkin Seeds (Appendix p. 374). You might also make and serve No-Bake Pumpkin Custard (Appendix p. 373).
6. Tell the children that today's activities will be about Halloween.

Story Circle

The Biggest Pumpkin Ever by Steven Kroll

Clifford's First Halloween by Norman Bridwell

The Hallo-Wiener by Dav Pilkey

It's Halloween by Jack Prelutsky

Pumpkin Moonshine by Tasha Tudor

"The Strange Visitor" prop story (Appendix p. 346)

Music and Movement

Sing "I Made a Pumpkin Yellow" (Appendix p. 290), "Jack-A-Lantern" (Appendix p. 291), "Halloween Is Coming" (Appendix p. 289), or "Five Little Pumpkins" (Appendix p. 310).

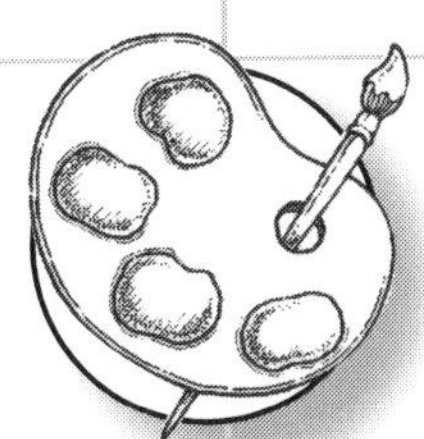

DISCOVERY (NATURALIST, MUSICAL)

Give the children dried pumpkin seeds, a funnel, an oatmeal box, a small coffee can, and a plastic bottle. Show the children how to use the funnel to put some seeds in each of the three containers. Invite them to shake each container and determine how the sounds of each are different.

DRAMATIC PLAY (INTERPERSONAL, SPATIAL)

Provide costumes for the children to dress in. Be sure to offer a mirror.

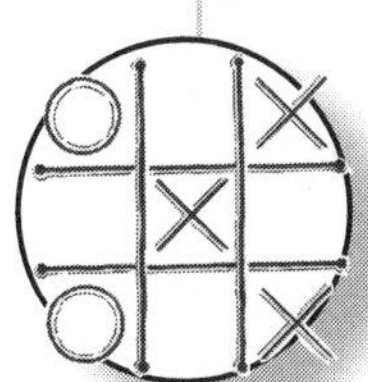

GAMES (INTERPERSONAL, LINGUISTIC)

Encourage the children to play Pumpkin Concentration using the patterns provided (Appendix p. 508).

GROSS MOTOR (BODILY-KINESTHETIC)

Draw a large jack-o'-lantern on bulletin board paper and place it on the floor. Provide beanbags and challenge the children to call out a feature on the jack-o'-lantern's face and then toss the beanbag on that feature.

LANGUAGE (LINGUISTIC, INTERPERSONAL, SPATIAL, INTRAPERSONAL)

Provide felt pumpkins and jack-o'-lantern facial features. Invite the children to create faces and names for their jack-o'-lanterns.

MATH (LOGICAL-MATHEMATICAL)

Give the children Corn Candy Puzzles (Appendix p. 386). Invite them to put the puzzles together. What is the pattern?

Closing Circle (Reflections on the Day)

Ask the children:

1. What colors are most often associated with Halloween?
2. What have you learned about Halloween today?
3. Why do you think Halloween is so much fun?

Thanksgiving

Morning Circle

1. Teach the children "Mighty Fine Turkey" (Appendix p. 323) and "Five Little Pilgrims" (Appendix p. 316). Use the Puppet Glove (Appendix p. 479) with the "Five Little Pilgrims" fingerplay.
2. Find out about what children know about Thanksgiving.
3. Discuss Thanksgiving.
   - Throughout time, people have held days of thanksgiving for harvest and other good fortune.
   - Thanksgiving, in this country, is the descendant of the harvest celebration of the Pilgrims at Plymouth Colony.
   - The first Thanksgiving was the celebration of a successful crop of corn that the Indians had taught the Pilgrims to plant. Without that crop, the pilgrims would not have had enough food to last through the winter. Many of them would have died.
   - The Indians who befriended the pilgrims were invited to attend the first Thanksgiving feast. They brought food with them, which is how the custom of sharing food on Thanksgiving originated. The celebration lasted three days. The pilgrims and the Indians ate, enjoyed each other's company, and played games.
   - Today we celebrate Thanksgiving in much the same way—by spending time with our families and sharing food (some of same foods the Pilgrims and Indians enjoyed).
4. Tell the children that today's activities will be about Thanksgiving customs and traditions.

Story Circle

Corn Is Maize: The Gift of the Indians by Aliki
Squanto and the First Thanksgiving by Teresa Celsi
Thanksgiving Day by Gail Gibbons
Thanksgiving Is by Louise Borden

Music and Movement

Sing and move to "Five Fat Turkeys Are We" (Appendix p. 316), "Our Turkey Is a Big Fat Bird" (Appendix p. 312), "Over the River and Through the Woods" (Appendix p. 299), or "She'll Be Comin' 'Round the Mountain" (Appendix p. 300).

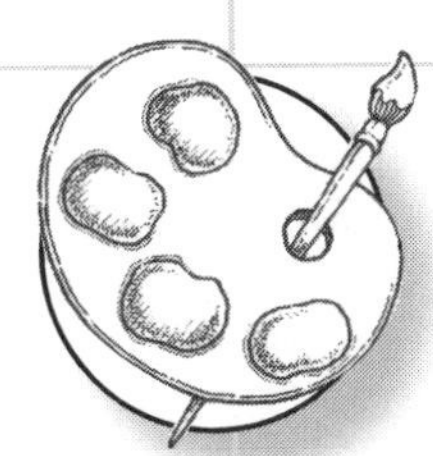

ART (Spatial)

Give the children some tempera paint and paper. Encourage them to make a handprint on their paper. Show them how to add an eye and a warble to the thumb and two legs and feet just under the palm to make a turkey.

DISCOVERY (Naturalist)

Provide corn for the children to shuck. Point out the corn silk, kernels, and cob.

DRAMATIC PLAY (Interpersonal, Intrapersonal)

Provide hats, collars, ears of corn, plastic fruits, and vegetables for the children to act out the first Thanksgiving, or props for a modern day Thanksgiving. Ask the children how the celebration makes them feel. How do they think the people at the first Thanksgiving may have felt?

LANGUAGE (Linguistic, Interpersonal)

Invite the children to draw a family portrait. Encourage them to label each member of the family.

MATH (Logical-Mathematical)

Give the children the Corny Counting Game (Appendix p. 386) and encourage them to use tweezers to place the correct number of corn kernels into each tub.

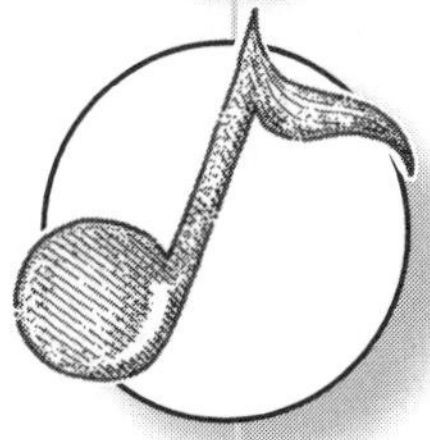

MUSIC (Interpersonal, Musical, Intrapersonal, Bodily-Kinesthetic)

Give the children the Five Fat Turkeys Puppets (Appendix p. 473-474) and invite them to act out "Five Fat Turkeys Are We." How did the turkeys feel before Thanksgiving Day? How do they feel when Thanksgiving is over?

Closing Circle (Reflections on the Day)

Ask the children:

1. Why do we celebrate Thanksgiving?
2. What is your favorite part of Thanksgiving? Why?

Hanukkah

Morning Circle

1. Sing "My Dreidel" (Appendix p. 296) with the children.
2. Find out what children know about Hanukkah. Encourage them to discuss their experiences.
3. Discuss Hanukkah.
   - Hanukkah commemorates the victory of the Jews over the Syrian tyrant Antiochus IV. According to the Jewish holy book, when Judas Maccabee prepared to rededicate the great Temple of Jerusalem, he found there was only one night's supply of holy oil with which to light the Temple lamp. By a miracle, the oil burned for eight days, enough time to prepare more holy oil.
   - Hanukkah is celebrated with parties and gifts. A favorite gift is Hanukkah gelt (pieces of chocolate shaped like coins and wrapped in gold foil).
   - During Hanukkah families perform the ceremonial lighting of the menorah. One candle is lit on the first night, two on the second, and so on for eight consecutive nights.
   - One of the favorite Hanukkah foods is latkes, a type of potato pancake.
   - A favorite game played during Hanukkah is played with a dreidel (a special top). Another favorite activity is a Torchlight Relay, which races through 35 Israeli towns.
4. Tell the children that today's activities will be about Hanukkah customs and traditions.

Story Circle

Hanukkah by Miriam Nerlove

Hanukkah: Eight Nights, Eight Lights by Malka Drucker

Latkes and Applesauce: A Hanukkah Story by Fran Manushkin

My First Chanukah by Tomie dePaola

Music and Movement

Do the Torchlight Relay (Appendix p. 368).

LEARNING CENTERS

CONSTRUCTION (Spatial, Bodily-Kinesthetic)

Invite the children to make a dreidel (Appendix p. 358).

COOKING (Logical-Mathematical, Linguistic, Interpersonal, Naturalist)

Invite the children to make latkes (Appendix p. 373)

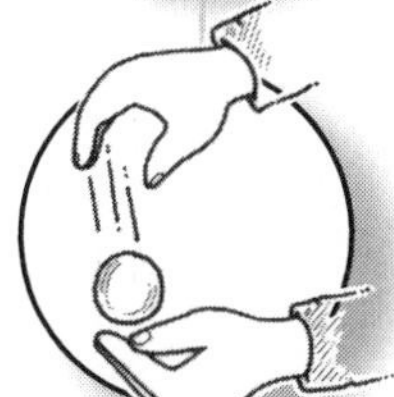

FINE MOTOR (Logical-Mathematical, Spatial)

Make a menorah, eight candles, and eight flames out of felt. Encourage the children to assemble a menorah on the flannel board.

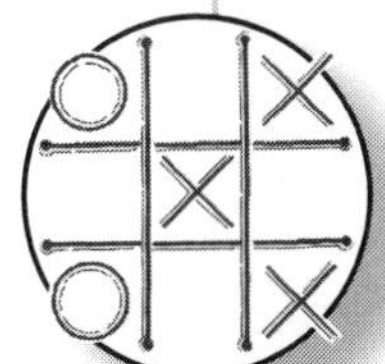

GAMES (Interpersonal, Linguistic, Bodily-Kinesthetic)

Teach the children how to play dreidel (Appendix p. 358).

LANGUAGE (Linguistic)

Make a double set of the Hebrew letters found on the dreidel. Challenge the children to play a game of Concentration with the letters.

MATH (Bodily-Kinesthetic, Logical-Mathematical)

Invite the children to make a Star of David by taking two triangles and inverting the second one over the first. Explain that this star is a Jewish symbol.

Closing Circle (Reflections on the Day)

Ask the children:

1. What did you learn about Hanukkah today?
2. What was your favorite activity today? Why?
3. How is Hanukkah like Christmas? How is it different?

Christmas

Morning Circle

1. Sing "We Wish You a Merry Christmas" (Appendix p. 306) with the children.
2. Find out what children know about Christmas. Encourage them to discuss their experiences.
3. Discuss Christmas.
   - Christmas is a Christian holiday. It commemorates the birth of Christ.
   - Christians believe that Christ was born to spread the word of Christianity.
   - Symbols of Christmas include Santa Claus (borrowed from Europe), Christmas trees, gifts, Christmas Carols, stars, nativity scenes, and sparkling lights.
4. Tell the children that today's activities will be about Christmas traditions.

Story Circle

The Cobweb Christmas by Shirley Climo
The Night After Christmas by James Stevenson
The Night Before Christmas by Clement Moore
The Twelve Days of Christmas by Jan Brett

Music and Movement

Play Musical Hide and Seek (Appendix p. 365).
Play the bells while singing "Jingle Bells" (Appendix p. 292).

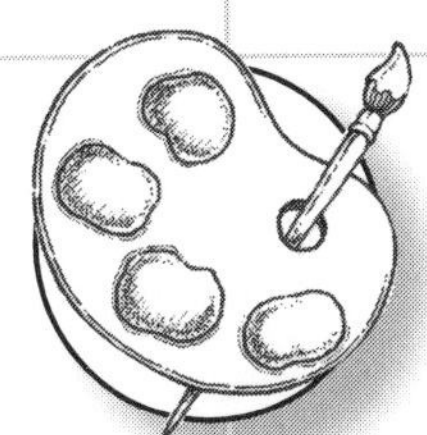

Art (Spatial)

Provide white Puff Paint (Appendix p. 377) and black paper. Invite the children to paint a snowy picture.

Cooking (Spatial, Interpersonal)

Bake sugar cookies using a pre-mixed cookie dough. Provide cookie cutters so that the children can cut out their favorite shape. Use a toaster oven so the cookies can cook in the classroom. Then children can watch their cookies bake and, at the same time, smell the wonderful aroma of baking cookies. Provide icing and decorations for the children to use to decorate their special cookie. (Supervise closely at all times!) (Check for allergies)

Discovery (Naturalist)

Provide ingredients (e.g., cinnamon sticks, nutmeg, pine cones, peppermint extract, etc.) for the children to make Christmas potpourri. Give them a zipper closure plastic bag and have them fill it with the items they want. Show them how to punch very small holes in the bag to release the aroma. (Check for allergies)

Dramatic Play (Interpersonal, Bodily-Kinesthetic)

Set up a "gift wrapping station" and invite the children to wrap gifts.

Math (Logical-Mathematical, Musical)

Give the children Jingle Bell Bags (Appendix p. 391) to arrange from lightest to heaviest, softest sound to loudest sound, or in numerical sequence.

Writing (Linguistic, Intrapersonal)

Encourage the children to dictate their letters to Santa to you. Prepare the letters to send to the North Pole. You may want to send copies to the local paper; sometimes they will publish them.

Closing Circle (Reflections on the Day)

Ask the children:

1. What is your favorite thing about Christmas? Why?
2. What have you learned about Christmas today?
3. How is Christmas like your birthday?

Everybody's Birthday

Morning Circle

1. Sing "Happy Birthday to Us" (Appendix p. 289), "Happy Special Day to You" (Appendix p. 290) or "Today Is a Birthday" (Appendix p. 306).
2. Talk about birthdays. Encourage the children to talk about birthdays they have experienced. Help the children understand that birthdays are special days set aside to celebrate the day you were born. Everybody has a birthday.
3. Tell the children that the day's activities will be about birthdays.

Story Circle

A Chair for My Mother by Ezra Jack Keats
Happy Birthday, Moon by Frank Asch
Happy Birthday to You by Dr. Seuss
It's My Birthday, Too! by Lynne Jonell
Not Yet, Yvette! by Helen Ketteman

Music and Movement

Play Cooperative Musical Chairs (Appendix p. 357).
Act out "Let's Pretend to Bake a Cake" action story (Appendix p. 337).

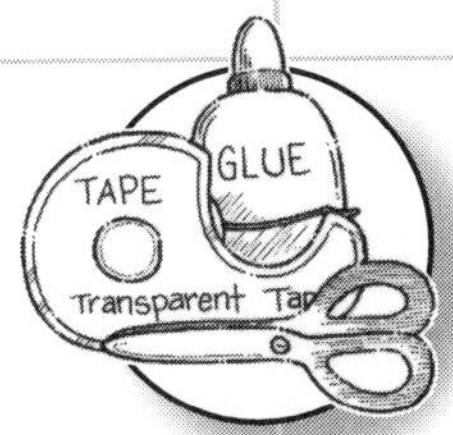

Construction (Bodily-Kinesthetic, Spatial, Linguistic)

Give the children some Icing Paint (Appendix p. 376) and some circles cut out of cardboard to represent cake tops. Provide tongue depressors and invite the children to ice their cakes. Challenge them to put their names on their cakes using alphabet cereal.

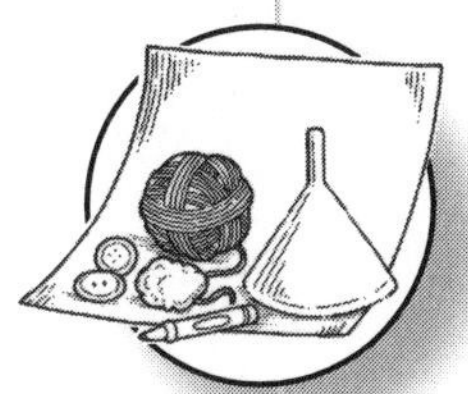

Discovery (Naturalist, Logical-Mathematical)

Wrap five presents of easy-to-determine different weights. Invite the children to arrange the gifts from the heaviest to the lightest.

Dramatic Play (Interpersonal)

Provide birthday hats, whistles, napkins, and plates. Encourage the children to have a pretend birthday party.

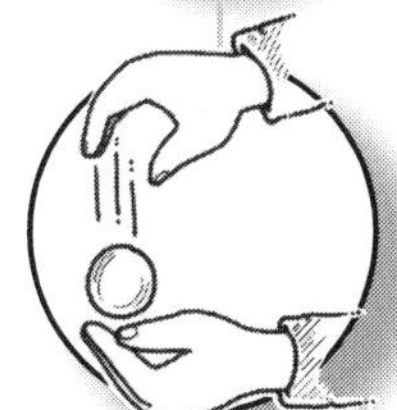

Fine Motor (Bodily-Kinesthetic, Interpersonal)

Provide small boxes, wrapping paper, ribbons, and tape. Invite the children to wrap presents. How does it feel to open birthday presents?

Math (Logical-Mathematical)

Give the children cakes and candles cut from felt. Invite them to put candles on the cakes.

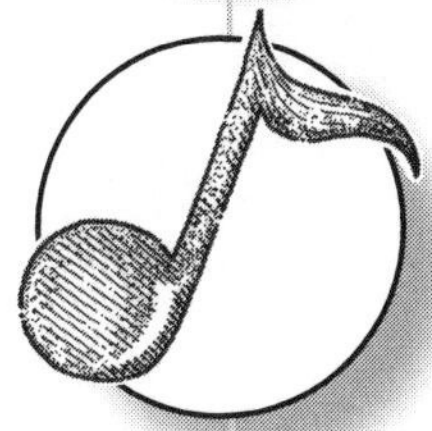

Music(Musical, Intrapersonal)

Create a birthday band. Give the children rhythm band instruments and invite them to create some music to go with the song, "Happy Birthday to You."

Closing Circle (Reflections on the Day)

Ask the children:

1. What was your favorite activity today? Why?
2. What will you do on your next birthday?
3. Should mommies and daddies have birthday parties?

Assessment for "Celebrations"

Intellectual Strength	Assessment
Linguistic	Have the children name some symbols for each holiday. Invite the children to make up a story about how the heart became part of Valentine's Day or the shamrock part of St. Patrick's Day.
Spatial	Challenge the children to use clay or playdough to shape some of the symbols from the holidays. For example, they may shape a shamrock for St. Patrick's Day, a heart for Valentine's Day, and/or a candle for birthdays.
Musical	Encourage the children to think of songs that go with each celebration. Ask them to find one song that would work for more than one holiday. For example, "Happy Birthday" could be sung at both Christmas time and for someone's birthday celebration.
Bodily-Kinesthetic	Have the children work together to think of ways to use their bodies to shape symbols for some of the holidays. For example, they may make a heart for Valentine's Day, a flag for July 4th, a menorah for Hanukah, or a tree for Christmas.
Logical-Mathematical Naturalist	Have the children group holidays by things they have in common. For example, which holidays involve gifts, which involve songs, which involve food, and so forth.
Intrapersonal Interpersonal	Ask the children to describe what people seem to enjoy most about each holiday.

Books Used in "Celebrations"

A Chair for My Mother by Ezra Jack Keats
A Leprechaun's St. Patrick's Day by Sarah Kirwan Blazek
A Perfect Father's Day by Eve Bunting
Bee My Valentine by Miriam Cohen
The Biggest Pumpkin Ever by Steven Kroll
Celebration by Jane Resh Thomas
Clifford's First Halloween by Norman Birdwell
The Cobweb Christmas by Shirley Climo
Corn Is Maize: The Gift of the Indians by Aliki
The Day We Met You by Phoebe Koehler
The Fourth of July Story by Alice Dalgliesh
Happy Birthday to You by Dr. Seuss
Happy Birthday, America by Marsha Wilson Chall
Happy Birthday, Moon by Frank Asch
Happy Father's Day by Steven Kroll
Hats Off for the Fourth of July by Harriet Ziefert
Hooray for Father's Day by Marjorie Sharmat
How I Was Adopted: Samantha's Story by Joanna Cole
Hurray for the Fourth of July by Wendy Watson
It's Halloween by Jack Prelutsky
The Hallo-Wiener by Dav Pilkey
It's My Birthday, Too! by Lynne Jonell
Leprechaun's Gold by Teresa Bateman
Little Mouse's Big Valentine by Thacher Hurd
Love and Kisses by Sarah Wilson
Love Is by Wendy Anderson Halperin
The Mother's Day Mice by Eve Bunting
Mother's Mother's Day by Lorna Balian
Not Yet, Yvette! by Helen Ketteman
On the Day the Tall Ships Sailed by Betty Paraskevas
One Zillion Valentines by Frank Modell
Owl Moon by Jane Yolen
Pumpkin Moonshine by Tasha Tudor
Squanto and the First Thanksgiving by Teresa Celsi
St. Patrick's Day by Gail Gibbons
St. Patrick's Day in the Morning by Eve Bunting

Books

Thanksgiving Day by Gail Gibbons
Thanksgiving Is by Louise Borden
The Night After Christmas by James Stevenson
The Night Before Christmas by Clement Moore
The Twelve Days of Christmas by Jan Brett
The Valentine Bears by Eve Bunting
Valentine Cats by Jean Marzollo
Valentine Mice! by Bethany Roberts

Other Books About Celebrations

Bunny Cakes by Rosemary Wells
Celebrations by Myra Cohn Livingston
Danny and the Easter Egg by Edith Kunhardt
The Easter Egg Artists by Adrienne Adams
Easter Bunny's Lost Egg by Sharon Gordon
Happy Holidaysaurus! by Benard Most
I'm in Charge of Celebrations by Byrd Baylor
Miss Spider's Wedding by David Kirk (Illustrator)
Over the River and Through the Woods by Lydia Child
The Story of Easter by Aileen Lucia Fisher
A Tale for Easter Tasha Tudor (Illustrator)
The Three Bears Holiday Rhyme Book by Jane Yolen

Appendix

Dear Family,

It is my intent to provide your child with the best opportunities to become a successful learner. To do so, I am planning classroom activities and experiences that will allow the children to express the many ways in which they are smart. This dynamic approach is based on the theory of Multiple Intelligences, developed by Dr. Howard Gardner, a psychologist at Harvard University.

Dr. Gardner has identified the following eight intelligences:

Linguistic (Word Smart)
Logical-Mathematical (Number Smart)
Spatial (Picture Smart)
Bodily-Kinesthetic (Body Smart)
Musical (Music Smart)
Naturalist (Nature Smart)
Interpersonal (People Smart)
Intrapersonal (Self Smart)

What this means is that in my classroom, your child will learn not only through reading, writing, and math but also through music, art, building, moving, engaging in outdoor learning experiences, interacting with other children, thinking, and reflecting. Since children exhibit these various ways of learning at different levels of ability, I will try to match learning experiences with their particular ways of "being smart."

To strengthen our school-home connection and to help your child expand upon his or her learning, the following are a few examples of things you can do at home:

- Read to your child and let your child read to you.
- Encourage your child to write stories, poems, and books.
- Play logic, card, and board games such as Crazy Eights, Old Maid, Go Fish, Dominoes, Bingo, and Concentration.
- Visit science museums, children's museums, hobby stores, electronic exhibits, and so on.
- Provide an area where your child can design and construct creations.
- Have a variety of art and craft materials available.
- Provide opportunities for physical activity both inside and outside the home.
- Provide old throwaway mechanical objects for your child to examine, take apart, or reassemble.
- Play a variety of music from the radio, records, tapes, and CDs.
- Encourage your child to make up songs, raps, and chants.
- Plant a garden with your child.
- Go on walks around the neighborhood and other fun places.
- Encourage your child to participate in group activities.
- Encourage your child to express his or her feelings.
- Encourage your child to write in a personal journal on a daily basis.
- Provide a quiet space in the home for your child to think and reflect.

Finally, because we are all intelligent in a variety of ways, I want to invite you to come to our classroom to share and express the ways in which you are smart. Do you play an instrument? Do you enjoy a hobby or craft? Do you play a sport? Do you dance or write poems or stories? Please come and share your talents or interests with the class; or just come and visit, ask questions, and learn more about what we are doing.

Sincerely,

Dear Family,

One of the goals of our curriculum is to meet all children where they are developmentally and to assist them in continuing to develop to their full potential. Children develop in a similar manner but on a timetable that is unique to each child. That means that at any given time in the classroom, the children are at a variety of ability levels developmentally.

One four-year-old may be reading while another is just starting to recognize the alphabet. The same child who is able to read may still be challenged when it comes to socially interacting with his or her classmates. The child who is just beginning to recognize the alphabet may be the most agile child when it comes to playing a game of catch and keep away.

Our curriculum strives to meet the individual needs and assist the development of all children in all developmental areas or domains: intellectual, social, emotional, and physical. We utilize what is called whole child instruction. This means that we support the concept that young children are developing in several areas or domains simultaneously and that each of these areas of development are equally important to the child. Not only are they equally important, they are also interwoven. It has been said that the social/emotional well-being of the child fuels the intellect. At the same time, without intellectual capabilities, the child's social/emotional development would suffer. The latest research indicates that these two developmental areas, intellectual and social/emotional, actually develop hand in hand.

Activities you can do at home to support each area of development for your child include:

Intellectual Domain—the development and refinement of rational thought.

- Ask questions. Encourage your child to reflect on things he or she has learned or experienced. For example, if your child plays a soccer game ask him how he feels about winning (or losing) the game. Ask him what he thinks he might want to practice in order to be a better player for the next game.
- Encourage your child to solve her own (child-size) problems. If a ball gets stuck in a tree, let your child brainstorm and try to retrieve the ball. If the sun gets in your child's eyes in the car, ask her to think of ways to block the sun.
- Teach your child a new vocabulary word each day. See how many times a day each of you can use the word in a sentence.

Social/Emotional Domain—the development of trust, impulse control, self-awareness, cooperation, tolerance, and negotiation

- Spend a few minutes of quiet time with your child each day-a special time that is just for the two of you and a special time your child can count on as his. Maybe you want to read to your child (or with your child) each evening. Spending quiet time together helps build a bond of trust and caring.
- Teach your child to control her impulses. Set boundaries. Children should be able to control their impulses by the age of four.
- Provide opportunities for your child to experience group activities. It is important for him to learn to play with children who are both older and younger than him.

Physical Domain—the development of coordination, balance, agility, speed, force, and strength.

- Challenge your child to a race. Fly a kite. Toss a Frisbee.
- Encourage your child to help you wrap gifts, shell peas, shuck corn, or fold towels. All of these things take physical coordination.
- Take your child to the park. Every piece of play equipment there supports physical development.

Have a good time. The journey through early childhood is a once-in-a-lifetime event.

Sincerely,

Materials Needed

Dear Parents,

We need the following materials that have a check mark. Please send them in with your child. Thank you!

- ☐ Aprons
- ☐ Beads
- ☐ Beanbags
- ☐ Berry baskets
- ☐ Binoculars
- ☐ Blocks
- ☐ Bowls
- ☐ Brushes
- ☐ Bubble soap
- ☐ Bubble wrap
- ☐ Butcher paper
- ☐ Cardboard boxes
- ☐ Circles
- ☐ Clay
- ☐ Coffee cans
- ☐ Coloring books
- ☐ Construction paper
- ☐ Cookie cutters
- ☐ Cookie sheet
- ☐ Crayons
- ☐ Crepe paper streamers
- ☐ Cups
- ☐ Dried pumpkin seeds
- ☐ Easel paper
- ☐ Empty paper towel tubes
- ☐ Epsom salt solution
- ☐ Eyedroppers
- ☐ Fabric
- ☐ Felt
- ☐ Funnel
- ☐ Glitter
- ☐ Glue
- ☐ Hand mixer
- ☐ Hats
- ☐ Ink pad
- ☐ Jingle bells
- ☐ Lace
- ☐ Large box
- ☐ Liter bottles
- ☐ Magazines
- ☐ Magnets
- ☐ Magnifying glasses
- ☐ Marbles
- ☐ Markers
- ☐ Masking tape
- ☐ Matchboxes
- ☐ Newspaper
- ☐ Oatmeal box
- ☐ Old socks
- ☐ Paint
- ☐ Paper
- ☐ Paper bags
- ☐ Plastic bottles
- ☐ Plastic eggs
- ☐ Plastic jars
- ☐ Paper bowls
- ☐ Paper plates
- ☐ Pelon
- ☐ Pencils
- ☐ Photo of children
- ☐ Ping-Pong balls
- ☐ Pint-size milk cartons
- ☐ Pipe cleaners
- ☐ Playdough
- ☐ Popsicle sticks
- ☐ Potato chip cans
- ☐ Prisms
- ☐ Puff paint
- ☐ Resealable plastic bags
- ☐ Ribbon
- ☐ Rolling pins
- ☐ Scissors
- ☐ Scoop
- ☐ Sequins
- ☐ Service bell
- ☐ Shamrock stencils
- ☐ Sheets
- ☐ Sponges
- ☐ Stencils
- ☐ Strainers
- ☐ Straws
- ☐ Sunglasses
- ☐ Tablecloths
- ☐ Tempera paint
- ☐ Tennis balls
- ☐ Tissue paper
- ☐ Tongue depressors
- ☐ Toothpicks
- ☐ Towels
- ☐ Tweezers
- ☐ Velcro
- ☐ Watercolors
- ☐ Wiggle eyes
- ☐ Yarn

Songs

Animal Fair

I went to the animal fair,
The birds and the beasts were there.
The big baboon by the light of the moon
Was combing his auburn hair.
You should have seen the monk;
He sat on the elephant's trunk.
The elephant sneezed and fell on her
knees.
And what became of the monk?
The monk, the monk, the monk?

Annie Mae

Annie Mae, where are you going?
Up the stairs to take a bath.
Annie Mae with legs like toothpicks
And a neck like a giraffe.
Annie Mae stepped in the bathtub.
Annie Mae pulled out the plug.
Oh my goodness!
Oh my soul!
There goes Annie Mae down that hole.
Annie Mae?
Annie Mae?
Gurgle, gurgle, glug.

The Ants Go Marching

The ants go marching one by one
Hurrah, hurrah.
The ants go marching one by one
Hurrah, hurrah.
The ants go marching one by one,
The little one stops to suck his thumb.
And they all go marching down
To the ground
To get out
Of the rain.
BOOM! BOOM! BOOM! BOOM!

Two. . . tie her shoe. . .
Three. . . climb a tree. . .
Four. . . shut the door. . .
Five. . . take a dive. . .

Apples and Bananas

I like to eat eat eat apples and bananas.
I like to eat eat eat apples and bananas.

I like to ate ate ate aypuls and baynaynays.
I like to ate ate ate aypuls and baynaynays.

I like eet eet eet eeples and beeneenees.
I like eet eet eet eeples and beeneenees.

I like to ote ote ote opples and bononos.
I like to ote ote ote opples and bononos.

I like to ute ute ute uupples and bununus.
I like to ute ute ute uupples and bununus.

Autumn Leaves

(Tune: London Bridge Is Falling Down)

Autumn leaves are falling down
Falling down, falling down *(wiggle finger in downward motion)*
Autumn leaves are falling down *(wiggle finger in downward motion)*
Gently to the ground. *(wiggle finger in downward motion until you touch the ground)*

Baby Bumblebee

I caught myself a baby bumblebee.
Won't my mommy be so proud of me?

I caught myself a baby bumblebee
Ouch! He stung me!
I'm talking to my baby bumblebee.
Won't my mommy be so proud of me?
I'm talking to my baby bumblebee.
"Oh," he said, "I'm sorry."
I'm letting go my baby bumblebee.
Won't my mommy be so proud of me?
I'm letting go my baby bumblebee,
Look! He's happy to be free!

Be Kind to Your Web-Footed Friends

(Tune: Stars and Stripes Forever)

Be kind to your web-footed friends,
For a duck may be somebody's mother.
Be kind to the birds in the swamp,
For the weather is very damp
Oh, you may think that this is the end,
Well, it is!

Bear Went Over the Mountain

(Tune: For He's a Jolly Good Fellow)

The bear went over the mountain,
The bear went over the mountain,
The bear went over the mountain
To see what he could see.

To see what he could see,
To see what he could see.
The bear went over the mountain,
The bear went over the mountain,
The bear went over the mountain
To see what he could see.

Bingo

There was a farmer had a dog
And Bingo was his name-o,
B-I-N-G-O *(clap letters of name)*
B-I-N-G-O
B-I-N-G-O
And Bingo was his name-o.

Continue song, dropping one letter and clapping in its place each time the song is sung.

Calliope Song

Sound 1: Oom-pa-pa
Sound 2: Oomp-tweedle-dee-dee
Sound 3: Oom-shh-shh

Divide children into four groups to make a human carousel. Group One says, "Oom-pah-pah," as they bend and then straighten their knees. Group Two says, "Oomp-tweedle-dee-dee," as they rise up on their tiptoes and back down. Group Three says, "Oom-shh-shh," as they rock back and forth. Group Four hums as they sway side to side.)

Cap, Mittens, Shoes, and Socks

(Tune: Head, Shoulders, Knees, and Toes)

Cap, mittens, shoes, and socks,
Shoes and socks.
Cap, mittens, shoes, and socks,
Shoes and socks.
And pants and belt, and shirt and tie
Go together wet or dry
Wet or dry!

Catalina Magnalina

She had a peculiar name but she wasn't to blame.
She got it from her mother, who's the same, same, same.

Chorus:
Catalina Magnalina, Hootensteiner Bogentwiner
Hogan Logan Bogan was her name.

She had two peculiar teeth in her mouth,
One pointed north and the other pointed south.

Chorus

She had two peculiar eyes in her head,
One was purple and the other was red.

Chew, Chew, Chew Your Food

by Pam Schiller (Tune: Row, Row, Row Your Boat)

Chew, chew, chew your food
A little at a time.
Chew it slow, chew it good,
Chew it to this rhyme.

Clean, Clean, Clean Your Teeth

(Tune: Row, Row, Row Your Boat)

Clean, clean, clean your teeth
Clean them twice a day.
Thoroughly, thoroughly, thoroughly, thoroughly,
That's the only way.

The Color Song

(Tune: I've Been Workin' on the Railroad)

Red is the color for an apple to eat.
Red is the color for cherries, too.
Red is the color for strawberries.
I like red, don't you?

Blue is the color for the big blue sky.
Blue is the color for baby things, too.
Blue is the color of my sister's eyes.
I like blue, don't you?

Yellow is the color for the great big sun.
Yellow is the color for lemonade, too.
Yellow is the color of a baby chick.
I like yellow, don't you?

Green is the color for the leaves on the trees.
Green is the color for green peas, too.
Green is the color of a watermelon.
I like green, don't you?

Orange is the color for oranges.
Orange is the color for carrots, too.
Orange is the color of a jack-o-lantern.
I like orange, don't you?

Purple is the color for a bunch of grapes.
Purple is the color for grape juice, too.
Purple is the color for a violet.
I like purple, don't you?

Crocodile Song

She sailed away on a bright and sunny day
On the back of a crocodile.
"You see," said she, "he's as tame as he can be;
I'll ride him down the Nile."
The croc winked his eye as she bade her mom good-bye,
Wearing a happy smile.
At the end of the ride the lady was inside
And the smile was on the crocodile!

Do Your Ears Hang Low?

(Tune: Turkey in the Straw)

Do your ears hang low? *(point to ears)*
Do they wobble to and fro? *(move hands side to side)*
Can you tie them in a knot? *(make tying motion)*

Can you tie them in a bow? *(pretend to tie a bow)*
Can you throw them over your shoulder *(toss hands over shoulder)*
Like a Continental soldier? *(salute)*
Do your ears hang low? *(point to ears)*

The Donut Song

(Tune: Turkey in the Straw)

Oh, I ran around the corner
And I ran around the block
I ran right in to the baker shop.
I grabbed me a donut
Right out of the grease
And I handed the lady
A five-cent piece.
She looked at the nickel
And she looked at me.
She said, "This nickel
Ain't no good to me.
There's a hole in the nickel
And it goes right through."
Said I, "There's a hole in your donut, too!
"Thanks for the donut. Good-bye!"

Down by the Bay

Down by the bay where the watermelons grow
Back to my home I dare not go
For if I do my mother will say,
"Did you ever see a pig dancing the jig?"
Down by the bay.

Additional verses:
...Did you ever see a whale with a polka dot tail?...
...Did you ever see a bear combing his hair?...
Make up your own additional verses.

Down by the Station

Down by the station
Early in the morning,
See the little puffer-bellies
All in a row.

See the engine driver
Pull the little throttle.
Puff, puff! Toot, toot!
Off we go.

Five Little Ducks

Five little ducks went out one day,
Over the hills and far away,
Papa duck called with a "Quack, quack, quack."
Four little ducks came swimming back.

Repeat, losing one more duck each time until you are left with one duck. Have momma duck call and end with "five little ducks came swimming back."

Five Little Speckled Frogs

Five little speckled frogs
Sitting on a speckled log
Eating some most delicious bugs – yum, yum!
One jumped into the pool
Where it was nice and cool
Now there are four little speckled frogs – croak, croak!

Four little speckled frogs...Now there are three little speckled frogs – croak, croak!
Three little speckled frogs... Now there are two little speckled frogs – croak, croak!
Two little speckled frogs... Now there is one little speckled frog – croak, croak!
One little speckled frog... Now there are no little speckled frogs – boo-hoo!

Found a Peanut

(Tune: Clementine)

Found a peanut, found a peanut,
Found a peanut just now,
Oh, I just now found a peanut,
Found a peanut just now.

Cracked it open, cracked it open,
Cracked it open just now,
Oh, I just now cracked it open,
Cracked it open just now.

It was rotten…
Ate it anyway…
Got a stomachache…
Called the doctor…
Felt better…
Found a peanut…

Frosty the Snowman

(Flannel Board Story/Song) (See patterns on p. 418-420)

Frosty the snowman was a jolly, happy soul,
With a corncob pipe and a button nose and two eyes made out of coal.
Frosty the snowman is a fairy tale they say.
He was made of snow but the children know how he came to life one day.
There must have been some magic in that old silk hat they found.
For when they placed it on his head, he began to dance around.
Oh, Frosty the snowman was alive as he could be,
And the children say he could laugh and play just the same as you and me.

Frosty the Snowman knew the sun was hot that day,
So he said, "Let's run and we'll have some fun now before I melt away."
Down to the village with a broomstick in his hand,
Running here and there all around the square, sayin', "Catch me if you can."
He led them down the streets of town right to the traffic cop.
And he only paused a moment when he heard him holler, "Stop!"
For Frosty the snowman had to hurry on his way.
So he waved goodbye, sayin', "Don't you cry; I'll be back again someday."

Thumpety, thump thump, thumpety thump thump,
Look at Frosty go;
Thumpety thump thump, thumpety thump thump,
Over the hill of snow.

Good Morning

(Tune: Where Is Thumbkin?)

Good morning, good morning,
How are you? How are you?
Very well, I thank you,
Very well, I thank you.
How about you? How about you?

Good afternoon, good afternoon,
How are you? How are you?
Very well, I thank you,
Very well, I thank you.
How about you? How about you?

Good evening, good evening,
How are you? How are you?
Very well, I thank you,
Very well, I thank you.
How about you? How about you?

Today is Monday, today is Monday.
How are you? How are you?

Songs

Very well, I thank you,
Very well, I thank you.
How about you? How about you?

Today is Tuesday...
Today is Wednesday...
Today is Thursday...
Today is Friday...
Today is Saturday...
Today is Sunday...

The Grand Old Duke of York

The grand old Duke of York *(salute)*
He had ten thousand men. *(hold up ten fingers)*
He marched them up to the top of the hill *(point up)*
And he marched them down again. *(point down)*
And when they're up, they're up. *(stand tall)*
And when they're down, they're down. *(squat)*
But when they're only half way up, *(stoop down)*
They're neither up nor down. *(open arms and shrug)*

Grasshopper

(Tune: Battle Hymn)

The first grasshopper jumped right over the second grasshopper's back,
Oh, the first grasshopper jumped right over the second grasshopper's back,
The first grasshopper jumped right over the second grasshopper's back,
Oh, the first grasshopper jumped right over the second grasshopper's back,
They were only playing leapfrog,
They were only playing leapfrog,
They were only playing leapfrog,
When the first grasshopper jumped over the second grasshopper's back.

Gray Squirrel

Gray squirrel, gray squirrel, *(stand with hands on bent knees)*
Swish your bushy tail. *(wiggle your behind)*
Gray squirrel, gray squirrel, *(stand with hands on bent knees)*
Swish your bushy tail. *(wiggle your behind)*
Wrinkle up your funny nose, *(wrinkle nose)*
Hold an acorn in your toes. *(pinch index and thumb fingers together)*
Gray squirrel, gray squirrel, *(stand with hands on bent knees)*
Swish your bushy tail. *(wiggle your behind)*

Great Green Gobs by Pam Schiller

(Tune: Row, Row, Row Your Boat)

Great green gobs of grass,
Great green gobs of peas,
Grass and peas, peas and grass,
All in great green gobs.

Great green gobs of frogs,
Great green gobs of leaves,
Frogs and leaves, leaves and frogs,
All in great green gobs.

Green Grass Grew All Around

In the park there was a hole,
Oh, the prettiest hole you ever did see.
A hole in the park,
A hole in the ground,
And the green grass grew all around, all around,
And the green grass grew all around.

And in that hole there was a sprout,
Oh, the prettiest sprout you ever did see.
Sprout in the hole,
Hole in the ground,
And the green grass grew all around, all around,
And the green grass grew all around.

And from that sprout there grew a tree,
Oh, the prettiest tree you ever did see.
Tree from a sprout,
Sprout in a hole,
Hole in the ground,
And the green grass grew all around, all around,
And the green grass grew all around.
And on that tree there was a branch,
Oh, the prettiest branch you ever did see.
Branch on a tree,
Tree from a sprout,
Sprout in a hole,
Hole in the ground,
And the green grass grew all around, all around,
And the green grass grew all around.

And on that branch there was a nest,
Oh, the prettiest nest you ever did see.
Nest on a branch,
Branch on a tree,
Tree from a sprout,
Sprout in a hole,
Hole in the ground,
And the green grass grew all around, all around,
And the green grass grew all around.

And in that nest there was an egg,
Oh, the prettiest egg you ever did see.
Egg in a nest,
Nest on a branch,
Branch on a tree,
Tree from a sprout,
Sprout in a hole,
Hole in the ground,
And the green grass grew all around, all around,
And the green grass grew all around.

And in that egg there was a bird,
Oh, the prettiest bird you ever did see.
Bird in an egg,
Egg in a nest,
Nest on a branch,
Branch on a tree,
Tree from a sprout,
Sprout in a hole,
Hole in the ground,
And the green grass grew all around, all around,
And the green grass grew all around.

Halloween Is Coming

Halloween is coming when we'll be
Dressed in funny clothes and then you'll see,
Pumpkins in the windows burning bright.
Oh, we'll have a good time on Halloween Night.

Bobbing for the apples, oh, what fun.
Then we'll come a-calling on the run
Children in their costumes such a sight
Yes, we'll have a good time on Halloween Night.

Happy Birthday to Us

Happy Birthday to us,
Happy Birthday to us,
Happy Birthday to everyone,
Happy Birthday to us.

Happy Special Day to You

Happy Special Day to you,
Happy Special Day to you,
Happy Special Day, you're wonderful,
Happy Special Day to you.

Head, Shoulders, Knees, and Toes

(Touch body parts as they are mentioned in the song)
Head, shoulders, knees and toes,
Knees and toes.
Head, shoulders, knees and toes,
Knees and toes.
And eyes and ears and mouth and nose.
Head, shoulders, knees and toes
Knees and toes!

Hickory Dickory Dock

Hickory dickory dock
The mouse ran up the clock.
The clock struck one,
The mouse ran down.
Hickory dickory dock.

How Much Is That Doggie in the Window?

How much is that doggie in the window?
The one with the waggily tail?
How much is that doggie in the window?
I do hope that doggie's for sale.

I Have Something in My Pocket

I have something in my pocket
It belongs across my face
I keep it very close at hand
In a most convenient place.
I bet you couldn't guess it
If you guessed a long, long while
So I'll take it out and put it on.
It's a great big happy SMILE!

I Made a Pumpkin Yellow

I made a pumpkin yellow. *(make a big circle with arms)*
I gave it two round eyes. *(point to eyes)*
I cut a circle for the nose *(point to nose)*
And a funny mouth that smiles. *(point to mouth)*
Then I hid behind the bush *(squat and pretend to hide)*
And waited there till dark.
When Daddy came along
Out I jumped. *(jump up)*
"Boo!" I shouted. *(place hands on each side of mouth)*
What a surprise! *(hold hands out to side with palm up)*

If You're Happy and You Know It

If you're happy and you know it, clap your hands. (*clap hands twice*)
If you're happy and you know it, clap your hands. (*repeat*)
If you're happy and you know it then your face will surely show it. (*point to face*)
If you're happy and you know it, clap your hands. (*clap hands twice*)

Additional verses:
...stomp your feet
...shout hooray!
...point to a circle
...point to the color red

I'm a Little Acorn Brown

I'm a little acorn brown,
Lying on the cold, cold ground.
Everyone walks over me,
That is why I'm cracked you see.
I'm a nut (click, click).
In a rut (click, click).
I'm a nut (click, click).
In a rut (click, click).

The Insect Song by Pam Schiller
(Tune: Head, Shoulders, Knees, and Toes)

Head, thorax, abdomen,
Abdomen
Head, thorax, abdomen,
Abdomen
Six legs, four wings, antennae two
Head, thorax, abdomen
Abdomen.

Itsy Bitsy Spider (Puppet Song)
(See patterns on p. 461-462)

The itsy bitsy spider
Went up the waterspout.
Down came the rain
And washed the spider out.
Up came the sun
And dried up all the rain.
And the itsy bitsy spider
Went up the spout again.

I've Got Sixpence

I've got sixpence, jolly, jolly, sixpence,
I've got sixpence to last me all my life.
I've got two pence to spend and two pence
to lend
And two pence to take home to my wife,
poor wife!

Chorus:
No cares have I to grieve me
No pretty little girls to deceive me
I'm as happy as a lark, believe me
As we go rolling, rolling home.
Rolling home (rolling home),
Rolling home (rolling home),
As we go rolling, rolling home.

I've got four pence, jolly, jolly, four pence,
I've got four pence to last me all my life.
I've got two pence to spend and two pence
to lend
And no pence to take home to my wife,
poor wife!

Chorus

I've got two pence, jolly, jolly, two pence,
I've got two pence to last me all my life.
I've got two pence to spend and no pence
to lend
And no pence to take home to my wife,
poor wife!

Chorus

I've got no pence, jolly, jolly, no pence,
I've got no pence to last me all my life.
I've got no pence to spend and no pence to
lend
And no pence to take home to my wife,
poor wife!

Chorus

Jack-a-Lantern
(Tune: Clementine)

Jack-a-lantern, Jack-a-lantern,
You are such a funny sight,
As you sit there in my window,
Looking out into the night.

You were once a yellow pumpkin,
Growing on a sturdy vine,
Now you are my Jack-a-lantern,
Let your candlelight shine.

Jingle Bells

Dashing through the snow
In a one-horse open sleigh
O'er the fields we go
Laughing all the way
Bells on bobtail ring
Making spirits bright
What fun it is to ride and sing
A sleighing song tonight!

Chorus:
Oh! Jingle bells, jingle bells,
Jingle all the way!
Oh, what fun it is to ride
In a one-horse open sleigh!
Hey!
Jingle bells, jingle bells
Jingle all the way!
Oh, what fun it is to ride
In a one-horse open sleigh!

A day or two ago
I thought I'd take a ride;
And soon Miss Fannie Bright
Was seated by my side.
The horse was lean and lank;
Misfortune seemed his lot;
He got into a drifted bank,
And we, we got upsot.

Chorus

Now the ground is white,
Go it while you're young;
Take the girls tonight,
And sing this sleighing song.
Just get a bobtailed bay,
Two-forty for his speed;
Then hitch him to an open sleigh,
And crack! You'll take the lead.

Chorus

Johnny Appleseed

Oh, the earth is good to me,
And so I thank the earth,
For giving me the things I need -
The sun, the rain, and the apple seed.
The earth is good to me.

Lavender Blue

Lavender blue, dilly dilly, lavender green,
If I were king, dilly dilly, I'd need a queen
Who told me so, dilly dilly, who told me so?
I told myself, dilly dilly, I told me so.
If your dilly dilly heart feels a dilly dilly way,
And if you answer yes,
In a pretty little church on a dilly dilly day,
You'll be wed in a dilly dilly dress of
Lavender blue, dilly dilly, lavender green.
Then I'll be king, dilly dilly, and you'll be my queen.

Little Bunny Foo-Foo

(Tune: Down by the Station)

Little Bunny Foo-Foo, hopping through the forest,
Scooping up the field mice and boppin' 'em on the head.
Down came the good fairy –and she said:
"Little Bunny Foo-Foo, I don't want to see you
Scooping up the field mice and boppin' 'em on the head.
I'll give you three chances, and if you don't behave,
I'll turn you into a goon!" The next day:

Sing again changing next to the last line to say, "I'll give you two more chances..."
Sing a third time changing the next to the last line to one more chance...
Sing a fourth time changing the next to the last line to say, "I gave you three chances and you didn't behave. Now you are a goon! POOF!"

Little Hunk of Tin

(Tune: I'm a Little Acorn Brown)

I'm a little hunk of tin.
Nobody knows what shape I'm in.
Got four wheels and a running board.
I'm a four-door.
I'm a Ford.

Chorus:
Honk, honk (*pull ear*)
Rattle, rattle. (*shake head*)
Crash, crash. (*push chin*)
Beep, beep. (*push nose*)

Repeat chorus twice.

Little Rabbit

In a cabin in the woods, *(draw a square in the air with index finger)*
Little man by his window stood. *(make glasses with index finger and thumb)*
Saw a rabbit hopping by *(hop index finger and middle finger)*
Knocking at his door. *(knocking motion)*
"Help me! Help me! Help me!" he cried! *(throw hands in air)*
"I'm so tired – can I come inside?" *(hold hands palm up and lift up and down)*
Little Rabbit come inside *(beckoning motion)*
Safely to abide. *(place one hand in lap and pet imaginary rabbit with the other)*

Little Red Caboose

Little red caboose, chug, chug, chug.
Little red caboose, chug, chug, chug.
Little red caboose, behind the train, train, train, train.
Smokestack on his back, back, back, back.
Chugging down the track, track, track, track.
Little red caboose behind the train.

Little Skunk's Hole

(Tune: Turkey in the Straw)

Oh, I stuck my head
In the little skunk's hole,
And the little skunk said,
"Well, bless my soul!
Take it out! Take it out!
Take it out! Remove it!"

Oh, I didn't take it out,
And the little skunk said,
"If you don't take it out
You'll wish you had.
Take it out! Take it out!"
Pheew! I removed it!

London Bridge Is Falling Down

London Bridge is falling down,
Falling down, falling down.
London Bridge is falling down, My fair lady.

Take the key and lock her up,
Lock her up, lock her up.
Take the key and lock her up,
My fair lady.

Repeat first verse

Two children stand facing each other, holding hands up over their heads to make an arch (bridge). The rest of the children form a line and go under the bridge and then around and back under the bridge again as the class sings the song, "London Bridge Is Falling Down." When the children sing the words, "my fair lady," the children who are making the bridge bring their arms down to catch the child who is passing under the bridge at that moment. As the children continue to sing the song, have the two bridge makers gently swing their arms back and forth to rock the captive. At the end of the song, the captive takes the place of one of the bridge makers and the game starts again.

MacNamara's Band

My name is MacNamara,
I'm the leader of the band,
And though we're small in number,
We're the best in all the land.
Of course, I'm the conductor
And I've often had to play
With all the fine musicians
That you read about today.

Chorus:
The drums they bang, the cymbals clang,
The horns they blaze away,
Macarthy puffs the ould bassoon,
Doyle and I the pipes do play.
Hennessey tuteily tootles the flute,
The music is something grand,

And a credit to ould Ireland's boys
Is MacNamara's Band.

Just now we are practicing
For a very grand affair,
It's an annual celebration,
All the gentry will be there.
The girls and boys will all turn out
With flags and colours grand,
And in front of the procession
Will be MacNamara's Band.

Chorus

Make New Friends

Make new friends, but keep the old.
One is silver, the other's gold.

Mary Had a Little Goat

(Tune: Mary Had a Little Lamb)

Mary had a little goat,
Little goat, little goat.
Mary had a little goat;
It's hair was white as snow.

Mary Had a Little Lamb

Mary had a little lamb,
Little lamb, little lamb.
Mary had a little lamb,
Whose fleece was white as snow.

Everywhere that Mary went
Mary went, Mary went.
Everywhere that Mary went
The lamb was sure to go.

It followed her to school one day,
School one day, school one day.
It followed her to school one day
Which was against the rules.
It made the children laugh and play,
Laugh and play, laugh and play.
It made the children laugh and play
To see a lamb at school.

Michael Finnegan

There was an old man named Michael
Finnegan.
He had whiskers on his chinnegan.
They fell out and then grew in again.
Poor old Michael Finnegan,
Begin again.

There was an old man named Michael
Finnegan.
He went fishing with a pin again.
Caught a fish and dropped it in again.
Poor old Michael Finnegan,
Begin again.

There was an old man named Michael
Finnegan.
He grew fat and then grew thin again.
Then he died and had to begin again.
Poor old Michael Finnegan,
Begin again.

Mister Moon

Oh, Mister Moon, Moon,
Bright and shiny Moon
Won't you please
Shine down on me?

Oh, Mister Moon, Moon,
Bright and shiny Moon,
Won't you please
Set me fancy free?

I'd like to linger
But I've got to run,
Mama's callin'
"Baby get your homework done!"

O Mister Moon, Moon,
Bright and shiny Moon,
Won't you please
Shine down on me?
Talk about your shine on,
Please shine down on me.

Mister Sun

Oh Mister Sun, Sun, Mister Golden Sun,
Won't you please shine down on me?
Oh Mister Sun, Sun, Mister Golden Sun,
Hiding behind a tree,
This little child is asking you
To please come out so I can play with you.
Oh Mister Sun, Sun, Mr. Golden Sun,
Please shine down on me!

The More We Get Together

The more we get together,
Together, together.
The more we get together,
The happier we'll be.
For your friends are my friends,
And my friends are your friends.
The more we get together,
The happier we'll be.

The Muffin Man

Oh, do you know the muffin man,
The muffin man, the muffin man?
Oh, do you know the muffin man
Who lives in Drury Lane?

The Mulberry Bush

(suit actions to words)
Here we go 'round the mulberry bush,
(hold hands and walk in circle)
The mulberry bush, the mulberry bush.
Here we go 'round the mulberry bush
So early in the morning.

This is the way we wash our clothes,
Wash our clothes, wash our clothes.
This is the way we wash our clothes
So early Monday morning.

This is the way we iron our clothes...
Tuesday morning.
This is the way we scrub the floors...
Wednesday morning.
This is the way we sew our clothes...
Thursday morning.
This is the way we sweep the house...
Friday morning.
This is the way we bake our bread...
Saturday morning.
This is the way we go to church...
Sunday morning.

My Dog Rags

I have a dog and his name is Rags, *(point to self)*
He eats so much that his tummy sags, *(put hands together in front of stomach)*
His ears flip flop and his tail wig wags, *(bend first left and then right hand at wrist)*
And when he walks he zig, zig, zags! *(make an imaginary "Z" with index finger)*

My Dreidel

I have a little dreidel,
I made it out of clay;
And when it's dry and ready,
Then dreidel I shall play.

Oh dreidel, dreidel, dreidel,
I made it out of clay;
Oh dreidel, dreidel, dreidel,
Now dreidel I shall play.

It has a lovely body,
With legs so short and thin;
And when it is all tired,
It drops and then I win.

My Hand on Myself

My hand on my head, *(place hand on head)*
What have I here? *(open arms palm up)*
This is my topnotcher, *(point to head)*
Mamma, my dear.
Topnotcher, topnotcher, *(point to head again)*
Dickie, dickie, doo. *(knock on head)*
That's what I learned in school. *(shake index finger)*
Boom! Boom!

My hand on my brow, *(place hand on brow)*
What have I here? *(open arms palm up)*
This is my sweat boxer, *(point to forehead)*
Mamma, my dear.
Sweat boxer, topnotcher, *(point to head and then forehead)*
Dickie, dickie, doo. *(knock on head)*
That's what I learned in school. *(shake index finger)*
Boom! Boom!

(continue adding body parts and suit hand motions to words)
Eye. . . eye blinker
Nose. . . nose blower
Mouth. . . food grinder
Chin. . . chin chopper
Heart...chest ticker
Stomach...bread basket
Knees...knee benders
Toes...pedal pushers

My Hat, It Has Three Corners

My hat it has three corners,
Three corners has my hat.
And if it hadn't three corners,
It wouldn't be my hat.

___ hat it has three corners,
Three corners has ___ hat.
And if it hadn't three corners,
It wouldn't be ___ hat.

___ ___ it has three corners,
Three corners has ___ ___.
And if it hadn't three corners,
It wouldn't be ___ ___.

___ ___ it has ___ corners,
___ corners has ___ ___.
And if it hadn't ___ corners,
It wouldn't be ___ ___.

___ ___ it has ___ ___,
___ corners has ___ ___.
And if it hadn't ___ ___,
It wouldn't be ___ ___.

Use gestures to replace missing words.
My *(point to self)*
Hat *(point to head)*
Three *(hold up three fingers)*
Corners (*use finger of both hands to make a triangle)*

My Little Red Wagon

(Tune: Ten Little Indians)

Bumping up and down in my little red wagon,
Bumping up and down in my little red wagon,
Bumping up and down in my little red wagon
Won't you be my darlin'?

Nobody Likes Me

Nobody likes me,
Everybody hates me,
Going outside to eat worms.
Long, thin, slimy ones
Short, fat, juicy ones
Itsy, bitsy, fuzzy, wuzzy worms.

Down goes the first one,
Down goes the second one,
Oh how they wiggle and squirm.

Up comes the first one,
Up comes the second one,
Oh how they wiggle and squirm.

Oats, Peas, Beans, and Barley Grow

Oats, peas, beans, and barley grow.
Oats, peas, beans, and barley grow.
Not you nor I or anyone knows,
How oats, peas, beans, and barley grow!

Old Gray Mare

The old gray mare, she
Ain't what she used to be,
Ain't what she used to be,
Ain't what she used to be.
The old gray mare, she
Ain't what she used to be,
Many long years ago.

Many long years ago,
Many long years ago.
The old gray mare, she
Ain't what she used to be,
Many long years ago.

Old MacDonald Had a Band (Variation)

Old MacDonald had a band, E-I-E-I-O
And in this band he had some drums, E-I-E-I-O
With a boom, boom here,
And a boom, boom there
Here a boom, there a boom
Everywhere a boom, boom
Old MacDonald had a band, E-I-E-I-O

Additional verses:
Triangle –ring, ring
Maracas – shake, shake
Sticks – tap, tap

Old MacDonald Had a Farm

Old MacDonald had a farm
E-I-E-I-O
And on this farm she had a cow
E-I-E-I-O
With a moo, moo here,
And a moo, moo there,
Here a moo, there a moo,
Everywhere a moo, moo.
Old MacDonald had a farm
E-I-E-I-O!

Additional verses:
Pig – oink, oink
Cat – meow, meow
Dog – bow-wow
Horse – neigh, neigh

Open Shut Them

(suit hand motions to words)
Open, shut them.
Open, shut them.
Give a little clap.
Open, shut them.
Open, shut them.
Put them in your lap.
Creep them, crawl them, *(walk fingers up chest to chin)*
Creep them, crawl them.
Way up to your chin.
Creep them, crawl them, *(walk fingers around face, but not into mouth)*
Creep them, crawl them,
Do not let them in.

Open, shut them.
Open, shut them.
Give a little clap.
Open, shut them.
Open, shut them.
Put them in your lap.

Over in the Meadow

Over in the meadow, in the sand, in the sun,
Lived an old mother frog and her little froggie one.
"Croak!" said the mother; "I croak!" said the one,
So they croaked and they croaked in the sand, in the sun.
Over in the meadow, in the stream so blue,
Lived an old mother fish and her little fishies two.
"Swim!" said the mother; "We swim!" said the two.
So they swam and they swam in the stream so blue.

Over in the meadow, on a branch of the tree,
Lived an old mother bird and her little birdies three.
"Sing!" said the mother; "We sing!" said the three,
And they sang and they sang on a branch of the tree.

Over the River and Through the Woods

Over the river and through the woods,
To grandfather's house we go;
The horse knows the way
To carry the sleigh,
Thru the white and drifted snow, oh!
Over the river and through the woods,
Oh, how the wind does blow!
It stings the toes,
And bites the nose,
As over the ground we go.

Over the river and through the woods,
To have a first-rate play;
Oh, hear the bell ring,
"Ting-a-ling-ling!"
Hurrah for Thanksgiving Day-ay!
Over the river and through the woods,
Trot fast my dapple gray!
Spring over the ground,
Like a hunting hound!
For this is Thanksgiving Day.

Peanut Butter

Chorus:
Peanut, peanut butter—jelly!
Peanut, peanut butter—jelly!

First you take the peanuts and *(pretend to dig peanuts)*
You dig 'em, you dig 'em.
Dig 'em, dig 'em, dig 'em.
Then you smash 'em, you smash 'em. *(pretend to smash peanuts)*
Smash 'em, smash 'em, smash 'em.
Then you spread 'em, you spread 'em. *(pretend to spread the peanuts)*
Spread 'em, spread 'em, spread 'em.

Chorus

Then you take the berries and *(pretend to pick berries)*
You pick 'em, you pick 'em.
Pick 'em, pick 'em, pick 'em.
Then you smash 'em, you smash 'em. *(pretend to smash berries)*
Smash 'em, smash 'em, smash 'em.
Then you spread 'em, you spread 'em. *(pretend to spread berries)*
Spread 'em, spread 'em, spread 'em.

Chorus

Then you take the sandwich and
You bite it, you bite it. *(pretend to bite a sandwich)*
Bite it, bite it, bite it.
Then you chew it, you chew it. *(pretend to chew a sandwich)*
Chew it, chew it, chew it.
Then you swallow it, you swallow it. *(pretend to swallow peanut butter sandwich)*
Swallow it, swallow it, swallow it.
Hum chorus.

Rain, Rain, Go Away by Pam Schiller

Rain, rain, go away.
Little children want to play.

Clouds, clouds, go away.
Little children want to play.

Thunder, thunder, go away.
Little children want to play

Rain, rain, come back soon.
Little flowers want to bloom.

SONGS

The Raindrop Song

If all of the raindrops *(wiggle fingers in the air)*
Were lemon drops and gum drops *(tap one index finger against palm of other hand)*
Oh, what a rain it would be. *(wiggle fingers in the air)*
I'd stand outside with my mouth open wide.
Ah-ah-ah-ah-ah-ah-ah-ah-ah-ah! *(stand, looking up with mouth open)*

If all of the snowflakes
Were candy bars and milk shakes,
Oh, what a snow it would be.
I'd stand outside with my mouth open wide.
Ah-ah-ah-ah-ah-ah-ah-ah.

Row, Row, Row Your Boat

Row, row, row your boat
Gently down the stream.
Merrily, merrily, merrily, merrily,
Life is but a dream.

A Sailor Went to Sea

A sailor went to sea, sea, sea.
To see what she could see, see, see.
But all that she could see, see, see.
Was the bottom of the deep blue sea, sea, sea.

Say, Say, My Playmate

Say, say, my playmate,
Come out and play with me.
And bring your dollies three.
Climb up my apple tree.
Look down my rain barrel.
Slide down my cellar door.
And we'll be jolly friends forever more.

She'll Be Comin' 'Round the Mountain

She'll be comin' 'round the mountain when she comes, *(circle hand around over head)*
She'll be comin' 'round the mountain when she comes,
She'll be comin' 'round the mountain,
She'll be comin' 'round the mountain,
She'll be comin' 'round the mountain when she comes.

She'll be drivin' six white horses when she comes, *(pretend to hold reins and drive horses)*
She'll be drivin' six white horses when she comes,
She'll be drivin' six white horses,
She'll be drivin' six white horses,
She'll be drivin' six white horses when she comes. Yee-Haw!

We'll all have chicken and dumplin's when she comes, *(pretend to eat)*
We'll all have chicken and dumplin's when she comes,
We'll all have chicken and dumplin's,
We'll all have chicken and dumplin's,
We'll all have chicken and dumplin's when she comes. Yum-Yum!

She Waded in the Water

(Tune: Battle Hymn of the Republic)

She waded in the water and she got her feet all wet
She waded in the water and she got her feet all wet
She waded in the water and she got her feet all wet
But she didn't get her (clap, clap) wet (clap) yet. (clap)

Chorus:
Glory, glory, hallelujah!
Glory, glory, hallelujah!
Glory, glory, hallelujah!
But she didn't get her (clap, clap) wet (clap) yet. (clap)

She waded in the water and she got her ankles wet (three times)
But she didn't get her (clap, clap) wet, (clap) yet. (clap)

(*Sing chorus after each verse*)

She waded in the water and she got her knees all wet…
She waded in the water and she got her thighs all wet…
She waded in the water and she finally got it wet…
She finally got her bathing suit wet!

Sing a Song of Opposites by Pam Schiller (Tune: Mary Had a Little Lamb)

This is big and this is small,
This is big; this is small,
This is big and this is small,
Sing along with me.

Other verse possibilities:
This is tall and this is short…
This is up and this is down…
This is in and this is out…
This is happy and this is sad…
This is soft and this is hard…
This is fast and this is slow…
This is here and this is there…

Six White Ducks

Six white ducks that I once knew,
Fat ducks, skinny ducks, they were, too,
But the one little duck with the feather on her back,
She ruled the others with a quack, quack, quack!

Down to the river they would go,
Wibble, wobble, wibble, wobble all in a row.
But the one little duck with the feather on her back,
She ruled the others with a quack, quack, quack!

Spring Is Here!

(Tune: The Mulberry Bush)

All the grass is turning green,
Turning green, turning green,
All the grass is turning green,
Spring is here!

Additional verses:
All the flowers are growing tall…
All the birds are building nests…
All the trees are budding now…

Summer Is Coming

(Tune: Are You Sleeping?")

Summer is coming,
Summer is coming,
Yes, it is!
Yes, it is!
Fun is in the air.
Sunshine here and there.
Summer's here.
Summer's here.

Take Me Out to the Ball Game

Take me out to the ball game
Take me out with the crowd.
Buy me some peanuts and crackerjacks,
I don't care if I ever get back.
So it's root, root, root for the home team,
If they don't win it's a shame,
For it's one, two, three strikes
You're out! At the old ball game.

Ten in the Bed

There were ten in the bed *(hold up ten fingers)*
And the little one said,
"Roll over! Roll over!" *(roll hand over hand)*
So they all rolled over
And one rolled out. *(hold up one finger)*

There were nine in the bed. . . *(repeat hand motions)*
Eight in the bed. . .
Seven n the bed. . .
Six in the bed. . .
Five in the bed. . .
Four in the bed. . .
Three in the bed. . .
Two in the bed. . .

There was one in the bed
And the little one said,
"Alone at last!" *(place head on hands as if sleeping)*

There Once Were Three Brown Bears

(Tune: Twinkle, Twinkle, Little Star)

There once were three brown bears,
Mother, Father, Baby Bear.
Mother's food was way too cold.
Father's food was way too hot.
Baby's food was all gone.
Someone ate it, so he cried.

There once were three brown bears,
Mother, Father, Baby Bear.
Mother's chair was way too low.
Father's chair was way too high.
Baby's chair was just so right,
But when she sat—she broke it.

There once were three brown bears,
Mother, Father, Baby Bear.
Mother's bed was way too soft.
Father's bed was way too hard.
Baby's bed was occupied.
Someone strange was sleeping there.

"Come here quickly," Baby cried.
"Someone's sleeping in my bed!"
"Who are you?" asked Baby Bear.
"Who are you?" asked Goldilocks.
"You better run," said Baby Bear.
"I will!" said Goldilocks.

There Was an Old Lady Who Swallowed a Fly

(Puppet Song) (See puppet patterns on p. 485-487)

I know an old lady who swallowed a fly.
I don't know why she swallowed a fly.
Perhaps she'll die.

I know an old lady who swallowed a spider
That wiggled and jiggled and tickled inside her.
She swallowed the spider to catch the fly,
But I don't know why she swallowed the fly.
Perhaps she'll die.

I know an old lady who swallowed a bird
How absurd! She swallowed a bird.
She swallowed the bird to catch the spider
That wiggled and jiggled and tickled inside her.

She swallowed the spider to catch the fly,
But I don't know why she swallowed the fly.
Perhaps she'll die.

I know an old lady who swallowed a cat
Think of that! She swallowed a cat.
She swallowed a cat to catch the bird.
She swallowed the bird to catch the spider,
That wiggled and jiggled and tickled inside her,
She swallowed the spider to catch the fly,
I don't know why she swallowed the fly.
Perhaps she'll die.

I know an old lady who swallowed a dog
What a hog! She swallowed a dog.
She swallowed the dog to catch the cat,
She swallowed the cat to catch the bird,
She swallowed the bird to catch the spider,
That wiggled and jiggled and tickled inside her,
She swallowed the spider to catch the fly,
But I don't know why she swallowed the fly.
Perhaps she'll die.

I know an old lady who swallowed a goat
It stuck in her throat! She swallowed a goat.
She swallowed the goat to catch the dog,
She swallowed the dog to catch the cat,
She swallowed the cat to catch the bird,
She swallowed the bird to catch the spider,
That wiggled and jiggled and tickled inside her,
She swallowed the spider to catch the fly,
But I don't know why she swallowed the fly.
Perhaps she'll die.

I know an old lady who swallowed a horse
She's dead, of course!

These Are Things I Like to Do

(Tune: Mulberry Bush)

These are things I like to do,
Like to do, like to do,
These are things I like to do
I know a trick or two.

Additional verses:
This is the way I read a book, *(suit actions to words)*
Read a book, read a book.
This is the way I read a book
So early in the morning.

This is the way I paint a picture. . . I know a trick or two.
This is the way I ride my bike. . . I know a trick or two.
This is the way I work a puzzle. . . I know a trick or two.
This is the way I throw the ball. . . I know a trick or two.
This is the way I help my dad. . . I know a trick or two.
This is the way I climb a tree. . . I know a trick or two.

This Is Tiffany

This is Tiffany over here.
She has on a bright blue dress.
This is Tiffany our new friend,
We're so glad she's here.

Substitute names and characteristics to children in your classroom.

This Is the Way We Clean Our Teeth

(Tune: The Mulberry Bush)

This is the way we clean our teeth,
Clean our teeth, clean our teeth.

This is the way we clean our teeth
Every night and morning.

Take your brush, go up and down
Up and down, up and down.
Take your brush, go up and down,
Every night and morning.

Don't forget both back and front,
Back and front, back and front,
Don't forget both back and front,
Every night and morning.

This Is the Way We Dress for Summer

(Tune: Mulberry Bush)

This is the way we dress for summer,
Dress for summer, dress for summer.
This is the way we dress for summer
When we go out to play.

Additional verses:
This is the way we put on our shorts…
When we go out to play.
This is the way we put on our sunscreen…
When we go out to play.
This is the way we put on our sandals…
When we go out to play.
This is the way we wear sunglasses…
When we go out to play.

This Is the Way We Rake the Leaves

(Tune: Mulberry Bush)

This is the way we rake the leaves
Rake the leaves, rake the leaves.
This is the way we rake the leaves
Day after day in the fall.

This is the way we bag the leaves
Bag the leaves, bag the leaves.
This is the way we bag the leaves
Day after day in the fall.

Additional verses:
This is the way we toss the leaves…Day after day in the fall.
This is the way we play in the leaves…Day after day in the fall.

This Old Man

This old man, he played one. *(hold up one finger)*
He played knick-knack on my thumb. *(knock on thumb)*

Chorus:
With a knick-knack paddy whack give a dog a bone, *(knock on head, clap twice, pretend to throw a bone over your shoulder)*
This old man came rolling home. *(roll hand over hand)*

This old man, he played two. *(hold up two fingers)*
He played knick-knack on my shoe. *(knock on shoe)*

Sing chorus after each verse.

This old man, he played three. *(hold up three fingers)*
He played knick-knack on my knee. *(knock on knee)*

This old man, he played four. *(hold up four fingers)*
He played knick-knack on the door. *(pretend to knock on door)*

This old man, he played five. *(hold up five fingers)*
He played knick-knack on a hive. *(pretend to knock on a hive)*

Additional verses:
Six…sticks *(continue hand motions)*
Seven…heaven
Eight…gate
Nine…line
Ten…over again!

This Old Man (Variation) by Tracy Moncure and Pam Schiller (Flannel Board Story/Song) (See patterns on p. 451-453)

This old man, he played drums
With his fingers and his thumbs.

Chorus:
With a knick-knack paddy whack give a dog a bone.
This old man is rockin' on.

This old man, he played flute,
Made it hum and made it toot.

Chorus

This old man, he played strings,
Twangs and twops and zips and zings.

Chorus
This old man, he played bass,
With a big grin on his face.

Chorus
This old man, he played gong
At the end of every song.

Chorus
This old man, he could dance.
He could strut and he could prance.

Chorus
This old man was a band,
Very best band in the land.

Chorus

Three Bears Rap

Shh, shh, shh, shh, shh, shh, shh, shh, shh, shh.
Out in the forest in a wee little cottage lived the three bears.
Shh, shh, shh, shh, shh, shh, shh, shh, shh, shh.
One was the Mama Bear, one was the Papa Bear, and one was the wee bear.
Shh, shh, shh, shh, shh, shh, shh, shh, shh, shh.

Out of the forest came a walking, stalking, pretty little Goldilocks
And upon the door she was a-knockin'.
Clack, clack, clack.
But no one was there, unh-unh, no one was there.
So she walked right in and had herself a bowl.
She didn't care, unh-unh, she didn't care.
Home, home, home came the three bears.

"Someone's been eating my porridge," said the Mama Bear.
"Someone's been eating my porridge," said the Papa Bear.
"Baa-baa Barebear," said the little Wee Bear.
"Someone's broken my chair."
Crash!

Just then Goldilocks woke up.
She broke up the party and she beat it out of there.

"Good-bye, good-bye, good-bye," said the Mama Bear.
"Good-bye, good-bye, good-bye," said the Papa Bear.
"Baa-baa Barebear," said the little Wee Bear.
That's the story of the three little bears—yeah!

Today Is a Birthday

Today is a birthday I wonder for whom?
We know it's somebody who's right in this room.
So look all around you for somebody who *(look around as if trying to find the person)*
Is laughing and smiling—my goodness it's you! *(point to the birthday person)*

Happy Birthday _____
From all of us to you.
Happy Birthday _____
From Mommy and Daddy too.
We congratulate you,
With all good wishes for you.
Happy Birthday _____
May all of your good dreams come true.

Twinkle, Twinkle, Little Star

(Flannel Board Song)

(See patterns on p. 454-455)

Twinkle, twinkle, little star,
How I wonder what you are!
Up above the world so high,
Like a diamond in the sky.

When the blazing sun is set,
And the grass with dew is wet,
Then you show your little light
Twinkle, twinkle, all the night.

Then the traveler in the dark
Thanks you for your tiny spark.
How could he see where to go
If you did not twinkle so?

In the dark-blue sky you keep,
And often through my curtains peep,
For you never shut an eye,
Till the sun is in the sky.

As your bright and tiny spark
Lights the traveler in the dark,
Though I know not what you are,
Twinkle, twinkle, little star.

We Wish You a Merry Christmas

We wish you a Merry Christmas,
We wish you a Merry Christmas,
We wish you a Merry Christmas,
And a Happy New Year.

Now bring us some figgy pudding,
Now bring us some figgy pudding,
Now bring us some figgy pudding,
And a cup of good cheer.

We won't go until we get some,
We won't go until we get some,
We won't go until we get some,
So bring it right now.

We wish you a Merry Christmas,
We wish you a Merry Christmas,
We wish you a Merry Christmas,
And a Happy New Year.

The Wheels on the Bus

The wheels on the bus go round and round. *(move hands in circular motion)*
Round and round, round and round.
The wheels on the bus go round and round,
All around the town. *(extend arms up and out)*

Additional verses:
The wipers on the bus go swish, swish, swish. *(sway hands back and forth)*
The baby on the bus goes, "Wah, wah, wah." *(rub eyes)*
People on the bus go up and down. *(stand up, sit down)*

The horn on the bus goes beep, beep, beep. *(pretend to beep horn)*
The money on the bus goes clink, clink, clink. *(drop change in)*
The driver on the bus says, "Move on back." *(hitchhiking movement)*

Where Is Thumbkin?

Where is Thumbkin? *(hands behind back)*
Where is Thumbkin?
Here I am. Here I am. *(bring out right thumb, then left)*
How are you today, sir? *(bend right thumb)*
Very well, I thank you. *(bend left thumb)*
Run away. Run away. *(put right thumb behind back, then left thumb behind back)*

Additional verses:
Where is Pointer?
Where is Middle One?
Where is Ring Finger?
Where is Pinky?
Where are all of them?

Where, Oh, Where Has My Little Dog Gone?

Where, oh, where has my little dog gone?
Oh where, oh where can he be?
With his ears cut short and his tail cut long,
Oh where, oh where can he be?

White Wings

White wings they never grow weary
They cheerily carry me over the sea.
Night falls, I long for thee deary,
I lift up my white wings and fly home to thee.

Winter Is Coming

(Tune: Muffin Man)

Can you feel the wind blow cold?
The wind blow cold?
The wind blow cold?
Can you feel the wind blow cold?
Winter's coming soon.

Additional verses:
Can you see the darker skies?
Can you hear the cold wind blow?
Can you see the trees all bare?

Yankee Doodle

Father and I went down to camp
Along with Captain Gooding,
And there we saw the men and boys
As thick as hasty puddin'.

Chorus:
Yankee Doodle keep it up,
Yankee Doodle dandy,
Mind the music and the step,
And with the girls be handy.

And there was Captain Washington
Upon a strappin' stallion,
And all the men and boys around
I guess there were a million.

Chorus

Yankee Doodle went to town
Ridin' on a pony,
Stuck a feather in his hat
And called it macaroni.

Chorus

The Yellow Rose of Texas

There's a Yellow Rose in Texas
That I am going to see.
No other fellow knows her.
No, not a one but me.
She cried so when I left her,
It like to broke my heart.
And if I ever find her,
We never more will part.

Chorus:
She's the sweetest rose in Texas
That this man ever knew.
Her eyes are bright as diamonds;
They sparkle like the dew.
You may talk about your dearest May,
And sing of Rosa Lee.
But the Yellow Rose of Texas
Beats the belles of Tennessee.

Fingerplays

April Clouds

Two little clouds one April day *(hold both hands in fist)*
Went sailing across the sky. *(move fist from left to right)*
They went so fast they bumped their heads *(bump fists together)*
And both began to cry. *(gently rub eyes)*

The big round sun came out and said, *(make a circle with arms)*
"Oh, never mind, my dears,
I'll send sunbeams down *(wiggle fingers downward like rain)*
To dry your fallen tears."

Caterpillar

"Who's that ticklin' my back?" said the wall, *(crawl fingers up arm)*
"Me," said a small caterpillar, "I'm learning to crawl."

Cloud

What's fluffy white and floats up high *(point skyward)*
Like a pile of cotton in the sky?
And when the wind blows hard and strong, *(wiggle fingers moving horizontally)*
What very gently floats along? *(wiggle fingers moving downward)*
What brings the rain?
What brings the snow
That showers down on us below?
When you look up in the high blue sky,
What is that thing you see float by? *(look up and answer…)*
(A cloud.)

Eye Winker

Eye winker, *(point to eye)*
Tom Tinker, *(touch ears)*
Nose smeller, *(touch nose)*
Mouth eater, *(touch mouth)*
Chin chopper, *(tap chin)*
Chin chopper, *(tap chin)*
Chin chopper chin. *(tap chin)*

Falling Leaves

Little leaves are falling down, *(wiggle finger downward)*
Red and yellow, orange and brown. *(count on fingers)*
Whirling, twirling round and round *(twirl fingers)*
Falling softly to the ground. *(wiggle finger downward to the ground)*

Five Apples

Five little apples waiting to be sold. *(hold up five fingers on right hand)*
Five little customers marching up so bold. *(march left hand fingers up to the right hand)*
Each picked a favorite and each paid a cent. *(match left fingers to right fingers starting with little fingers)*
Each made a bow and away they all went. *(separate fingers just enough to bend finger for bows)*

Five Huge Dinosaurs

Five huge dinosaurs dancing a jig. *(hold up five fingers and dance fingers)*
They rumble and grumble and stumble

Because they are so big. *(spread hands apart)*
Five huge dinosaurs floating on a barge. *(hold up five fingers and make a boat with hands)*
They jiggle and wiggle and juggle
Because they are so large. *(spread hands apart)*

Five huge dinosaurs singing a song. *(hold up five fingers and put hands beside mouth)*
They bellow and holler and ramble
Because they sing it wrong. *(shake head no)*

Five huge dinosaurs taking a bow. *(hold up five fingers and bow)*
They bobble and hobble and tumble
Because they don't know how. *(hold hands out to side)*

Five huge dinosaurs making me laugh. *(hold up five fingers and then tummy)*
They stumble when they dance. *(dance fingers on arm)*
They juggle when they float. *(make boat with hands)*
The ramble when they sing. *(place hands beside mouth)*
They hobble when they bow. *(bow)*
But they can make me laugh! *(hold tummy-shake head yes)*

Five Little Ladybugs by Pam Schiller

Five little ladybugs dancing on my door
One flew home leaving only four.

Four dainty ladybugs looking for the sea
One went back leaving only three.

Three tiny ladybugs drinking morning dew
One joined a friend leaving only two.

Two pretty ladybugs bathing in the sun
One left to eat leaving only one.

One friendly ladybug still in the sun
She came home with me now there are none.

Five Little Monkeys

Five little monkeys jumping on the bed.
One fell off and bumped her head.
Mamma called the doctor, and the doctor said,
"No more monkeys jumping on the bed!"

Repeat, subtracting a monkey each time.

Five Little Pumpkins

Five little pumpkins growing on a vine,
First one said, "It's time to shine!"
Second one said, "I love the fall"
Third one said, "I'm round as a ball."
Fourth one said, "I want to be a pie."
Fifth one said, "Let's say good-bye."
"Good-bye," said one!
"Adios," said two!
"Au revoir," said three!
"Ciao," said four!
"Aloha," said five!
And five little pumpkins were picked that day!

Five Little Snowmen

Five little snowmen happy and gay, *(hold up five fingers and move one for each snowman)*
The first one said, "What a nice day!"
The second one said, "We'll cry no tears."

The third one said, "We'll stay for years."
The fourth one said, "But what happens in May?"
The fifth one said, "Look, we're melting away!" *(hold hands out as if saying all gone)*

Five Lively Leprechauns by Pam Schiller

Five lively leprechauns looking for fun. *(look around)*
First one said, "Let's turn back the clocks." *(point index finger and make a counter-clockwise circle)*
Second one said, "Let's mismatch the socks." *(point to socks)*
Third one said, " Let's stir up the cat." *(wiggle fingers of both hands in front of you)*
Fourth one said, "Let's hide the hat." *(put hands behind back)*
Fifth one said, "Let's scat, scat, scat!" *(run fingers away)*

Five Pink Valentines by Pam Schiller

Use the names of children in your class.

Five pink valentines from the card store, *(count off the valentines on your fingers)*
I gave one to Sam, now there are four.

Four pink valentines, pretty ones to see.
I gave one to Maddie, now there are three.

Three pink valentines, pink through and through,
I gave one to Austin, now there are two.

Two pink valentines having lots of fun,
I gave one to Gabrielle, now there is one.

One pink valentine, my story is almost done,
I gave it to you, now there are none.

Five Special Valentines by Pam Schiller

Five special valentines from the card store, *(count off the valentines on your fingers)*
The red one went to Gabby, now there are four.

Four special valentines, pretty ones to see.
The pink one went to Austin, now there are three.

Three special valentines, pink, white, and blue.
Richele got the white one; now there are two.

Two special valentines having lots of fun,
I gave one to Steve, now there is one.

One purple valentine, my story is almost done.
I gave it to you, now there are none.

Here Are My Eyes by Pam Schiller

Here are my eyes, *(point to eyes)*
One and two.
I can wink. *(wink)*
So can you.

When my eyes are open, *(open eyes wide)*
I see the light.
When they are closed, *(close eyes)*
It's dark as night.

Here Is the Beehive

Here is the beehive, *(close fist)*
Where are all the bees?
Hiding away
Where nobody sees.
They're all coming out now.
Sakes alive!
One! Two! Three! Four! Five! *(stick up thumb, first finger, second, etc.)*

Jack-in-the-Box

Jack-in-the-box *(tuck thumb into fist)*
Oh, so still.
Won't you come out? *(raise hand slightly)*
Yes, I will. *(pop thumb out of fist)*

My Airplane

If I had an airplane, *(use hand as an airplane)*
Zum, zum, zum,
I'd fly to Mexico. *(fly hand through the air)*
Wave my hand and off I'd go. *(wave)*
If I had an airplane, *(use hand as an airplane)*
Zum, zum, zum.

Our Turkey Is a Big Fat Bird

Our turkey is a big fat bird. *(hold hands out to indicate large)*
He gobbles when he talks. *(move hand, thumb to fingers, like talking)*
Our turkey is a big fat bird. *(hold hands out wide)*
He waddles when he walks. *(wiggle hand side to side)*
Our turkey is a big fat bird. *(hold hands out wide)*
He spreads his tail this way. *(spread fingers on hand like a fan)*
On Thanksgiving Day our fat bird *(hold hands out to indicate large)*
Lifts his wings and flies away. *(flap arms to fly)*

There Once Was a Turtle

There was a little turtle. *(make a fist)*
He lived in a box. *(draw a square in the air)*
He swam in a puddle. *(pretend to swim)*
He climbed on the rocks. *(pretend to climb)*
He snapped at a mosquito. *(use your hand to make a snapping motion)*
He snapped at a flea. *(snapping motion)*
He snapped at a minnow. *(snapping motion)*
And he snapped at me. *(snapping motion)*
He caught the mosquito. *(clap hands)*
He caught the flea. *(clap hands)*
He caught the minnow. *(clap hands)*
But he didn't catch me. *(wave index finger as if saying no-no)*

This Little Piggy

This little piggy went to market, *(wiggle big toe)*
This little piggy stayed home, *(wiggle second toe)*
This little piggy had roast beef, *(wiggle middle toe)*
This little piggy had none, *(wiggle fourth toe)*
And this little piggy cried "Wee-wee-wee!" all the way home. *(wiggle little toe)*

Three Little Monkeys

Three little monkeys sitting in a tree *(hold up three finger and bounce them)*
Teasing Mr. Alligator,
"Can't catch me! Can't catch me! *(point and shake index finger)*

Along came Mr. Alligator,
Quiet as can be—snap! *(walk index and middle fingers up arm)*
Two little monkeys sitting in a tree. *(hold up two fingers and bounce them)*

Keep counting down until there are no little monkeys sitting in a tree teasing Mr. Alligator, "Can't catch me. Can't catch me!"

Two Little Blackbirds

Two little blackbirds *(hold up index finger of each hand)*
Sitting on a hill.
One named Jack. *(hold right hand/finger forward)*
One named Jill. *(hold left hand/finger forward)*
Fly away, Jack. *(wiggle right finger and place behind your back)*
Fly away, Jill. *(wiggle left finger and place behind your back)*
Come back, Jack. *(bring right hand back)*
Come back, Jill. *(bring left hand back)*

Chants and Rhymes

Autumn Leaves

Autumn leaves are falling, falling, falling.
(move from standing position to squatting)
Autumn leaves are spinning, spinning, spinning. *(stand and turn quickly)*
Autumn leaves are floating, floating, floating. *(sway side to side)*
Autumn leaves are turning, turning, turning.
(turn slowly)
Autumn leaves are dancing, dancing, dancing. *(stand on toes, sway forward and back)*
Autumn leaves are blowing, blowing, blowing. *(take several steps forward)*
Autumn leaves are falling, falling, falling.
(squat)
Autumn leaves are sleeping, sleeping, sleeping. *(place hands together on side of face)*

Big and Small

I can make myself real big *(stand up on toes)*
By standing up straight and tall.
But when I'm tired of being big
I can make myself get small. *(stoop down)*

Birdie, Birdie, Where Is Your Nest?

Birdie, birdie, where is your nest?
Birdie, birdie, where is your nest?
Birdie, birdie, where is your nest?
In the tree that I love best.

Bubble Gum Jump-Rope Rhyme

Bubble gum, bubble gum, chew and blow.
Bubble gum, bubble gum, scrape your toe.
Bubble gum, bubble gum, taste so sweet.
Get that bubble gum off your feet.

Cold Fact by Dick Emmons

By the time he's suited
And scarved and booted
And mittened and capped
And zipped and snapped
And tucked and belted,
The snow has melted.

Counting Rhyme

One, two, three, four, five,
I caught a fish alive.
Six, seven, eight, nine, ten,
But I let it go again.

Why did I let him go?
Because he bit my finger so.
Which finger did he bite?
The little one upon the right.

Crocodile

If you should meet a crocodile
Don't take a stick and poke him;
Ignore the welcome of his smile,
Be careful not to stroke him,
For as he sleeps upon the Nile
He gets thinner and thinner
And whene'er you meet a crocodile,
He's looking for his dinner.

The Elephant

The Elephant goes *(move on all fours, slowly swaying like an elephant)*
Like this, like that.
He's terribly big, *(stand up and reach arms up)*
He has no fingers, *(hold hands in fists)*
He has no toes, *(wiggle toes)*
But goodness gracious,
What a nose! *(put thumb to nose and wiggle fingers)*

Eye Rhymes by Pam Schiller

You see me,
I see you.
Your eyes are blue/green/brown,
Mine are, too.

Your eyes are big, and round, and brown.
They must be the prettiest eyes in town.

When I look at you, know what I see?
Eyes as green as green can be.

Blue eyes, green eyes,
Brown eyes, hey.
Your eyes are gray,
And I love them that way.

Fall

Fall is here
Frost is in the air.
Chill is on my cheeks,
Static in my hair.

Colorful leaves fall like rain.
Sun and clouds play hide and seek.
The wind blows across the grass.
Apples are ripe and at their peak.

I help at home to rake the leaves.
We put them in a sack.
We sweep the roof and clean the eaves.
Before we finish...the leaves are back.

Fall is in the air,
Static in my hair.
Leaves on the lawn,
And autumn frost at dawn.

Fall Leaves

Leaves are drifting softly down,
They make a carpet on the ground.
Then, swish! The wind comes whistling by
And sends them dancing in the sky!

Fall Leaves on the Ground

Down, down,
Yellow and brown,
Fall leaves
All over the ground.

Rake them up
In a pile so high,
They almost reach
Up to the sky.

Falling Leaves

I saw a leaf fall from a tree
And to the earth below.
It was a lovely sight to see
As it danced to and fro.
Up and down and up it went
And then came tumbling down.
Feeling tired, the dancing leaf
Fell to the waiting ground.

Family Fun

Mommy and me dance and sing.
Daddy and me laugh and play.
Mommy, Daddy, and me
Dance and sing
Laugh and play
Kiss and hug
A zillion times a day!

Fido

I have a little dog
And his name is Fido.
He is nothing but a pup.
He can stand up on his hind legs
If you hold his front legs up.

Five Fat Turkeys Are We

Five fat turkeys are we.
We spent the night in a tree.
When the cook came around
We couldn't be found
And that's why we're here you see – gobble, gobble!

Oh, five fat turkeys are we.
We spent the night in a tree.
It sure does pay
On Thanksgiving Day
To sleep in the tallest tree – gobble, gobble!

Five Little Monkeys

Five little monkeys jumping on the bed.
One fell off and bumped her head.
Mamma called the doctor, and the doctor said,
"No more monkeys jumping on the bed!"

Repeat, subtracting a monkey each time. You can say the rhyme using fingers or let children act it out.

Five Little Pilgrims

Five little pumpkins on Thanksgiving Day,
The first one said, "I'll have cake if I may,"
The second one said, "I'll have turkey roasted,"
The third one said, "I'll have chestnuts toasted."
The fourth one said, "I'll have pumpkin pie,"
The fifth one said, "Oh, cranberries I spy."
But before they had any turkey and dressing,
They all bowed their heads for a Thanksgiving blessing.

Five Waiting Pumpkins

(suit actions to words)

Five little pumpkins growing on a vine,
First one said, "It's time to shine!"
Second one said, "I love the fall."
Third one said, "I'm round as a ball."
Fourth one said, "I want to be a pie."
Fifth one said, "Let's say good-bye."
"Good-bye," said one!
"Adios," said two!
"Au revoir," said three!
"Ciao," said four!
"Aloha," said five!
And five little pumpkins were picked that day!

Fuzzy Caterpillar

A fuzzy caterpillar went out for a walk.
His back went up and down.
He crawled and he crawled
And he crawled and he crawled
'Til he crawled all over town.
He wasn't disappointed
Not a bit to be a worm.
Not a tear was in his eye.

Because he knew what he'd become
A very, very pretty butterfly.

Going on a Bear Hunt

We're going on a bear hunt. *(pat thighs in rhythmic walking pattern)*
Want to come along?
Well, come on then.
Let's go! *(continue patting thighs in walking rhythm)*

Look! There's a river.
Can't go over it.
Can't go under it.
Can't go around it.
We'll have to go through it. *(pretend to swim across the river and then resume patting thighs)*

Look! There's a tree.
Can't go under it.
Can't go through it.
We'll have to go over it. *(pretend to climb up and over tree; then resume patting thighs)*

Look! There's a wheat field.
Can't go over it.
Can't go under it.
Can't go around it.
We'll have to go through it. *(pretend to walk through field, make swishing sounds by brushing hands together and then continue patting thighs)*

Add verses to make the chant as long as you want.

Look! There's a cave. *(point)*
Let's go inside? *(continue patting thighs slowly)*
Ooh, it's dark in here. *(look around, squinting)*
I see two eyes.
Wonder what it is. *(reach hands to touch)*
It's soft and furry.
It's big.
It's a bear! Let's run! *(retrace steps, patting thighs in running rhythm, through wheat field, in place, over tree, in place, across river, in place, then stop)*
Home safe. Whew!

Going on a Whale Watch

We're going on a whale watch.
Want to come along?
Well, come on then.
Let's go! *(walk in place)*

Look! There's our boat.
Can't go over it.
Can't go under it.
Can't go around it.
We'll need to get on it. *(pretend to walk onto boat, and locate a good place to stand. Shade eyes as if watching for a whale and begin tapping fingers as if impatiently waiting)*

Look! There's a ship.
Can't go over it.
Can't go under it.
Can't go through it.
We'll have to go around it. *(pretend to steer around the ship and then resume tapping fingers and watching for a whale)*

Look! There's an iceberg.
Can't go over it.
Can't go under it.
Can't go through it.
We'll have to go around it. *(pretend to*

steer around the iceberg and then resume tapping fingers and looking for a whale.)

Add verses to make the story as long as you want.

Look! There's a spout of water.
Is it a whale?
Ooh, I think it might be. *(look straight ahead, squinting)*
I see a huge head.
Wonder what it is.

I see a tail
It's big.
It's a whale! We found a whale!

Look out, here comes a s-p-l-a-s-h!
Too late. We're soaked!

Grasshopper Three

Grasshopper three a-fiddling went,
Hey, ho, never be still,
They had no money to pay the rent
But all day long with their elbows bent
They fiddled a tune called "Riddleby-Riddleby,"
Fiddled a tune called, "Riddleby Rill."

Head, Shoulders, Baby

Head, shoulders, baby 1, 2, 3.
Head, shoulders, baby 1, 2, 3.
Head, shoulders, head, shoulders,
Head, shoulders, baby 1, 2, 3.

Shoulders, hip, baby, 1, 2, 3.
Shoulders, hip, baby, 1, 2, 3.
Shoulders, hip, shoulders, hip,
Shoulders, hip, baby, 1, 2, 3.

Additional verses:
Hip, knees…
Knees, ankle…
Ankle, toes…
Toes, ankle…
Ankle, knees…
Knees, hips…
Hip, shoulders…
Shoulders, head…

Here We Go

Here we go – up, up, up. *(stand up on toes)*
Here we go – down, down, down. *(crouch down)*
Here we go – moving forward. *(take a step forward)*
Here we go – moving backward. *(take a step backward)*
Here we go round and round and round. *(spin)*

Humpty Dumpty

Humpty Dumpty sat on a wall.
Humpty Dumpty had a great fall.
All the king's horses and all the king's men
Couldn't put Humpty Dumpty together again.

Humpty Dumpty (variation by Pam Schiller)

(Flannel board rhyme)
(See patterns on p. 429-431)

Humpty Dumpty sat on a hill,
Humpty Dumpty had a great spill.
That genius, Jack Horner, pulled out his glue
And Humpty Dumpty's as good as new!

Humpty Dumpty (variation by Pam Schiller)

Humpty Dumpty sat on a wall,
Humpty Dumpty had a great fall.
But the children knew just what to do
They fixed him up with paste and glue!

I Can Do It Myself

Hat on head, just like this,
Pull it down, you see.
I can put my hat on
All by myself, just me.

One arm in, two arms in,
Buttons, one, two, three.
I can put my coat on
All by myself, just me.

Toes in first, heels down next,
Pull and pull, then see -
I can put my boots on
All by myself, just me.

Fingers here, thumbs right here,
Hands warm as can be.
I can put my mittens on
All by myself, just me.

I Can, You Can!

(suit actions to words)
I can put my hands up high. Can you?
I can wink my eye. Can you?
I can stick out my tongue. Can you?
I can nod my head. Can you?
I can kiss my toe. Can you?
I can pull on my ear. Can you?
I can wrinkle my nose. Can you?
I can give myself a great big hug. Can you?
And if I give my hug to you, will you give
yours to me?

I Help My Family by Pam Schiller

(suit actions to words)
I help my family when I can.
I fold the clothes.
I feed the dog.
I turn on the hose.

I crack the eggs.
I ice the cake.
Then I help eat
The good things we make.

I Like Black by Pam Schiller

I like black
Not yellow, red, or blue.
I like black
I bet you like it, too.
Blackbirds, black flowers
Tall and shiny black towers.
Tiny black baby kittens,
Warm and woolly black mittens.
Blackberries, black cherries,
Black socks, black rocks.
I like black
Not yellow, red, or blue.
I like black
I really, really do!

I Like Blue by Pam Schiller

I like blue
I really, really do.
I like blue
Do you like it, too?

I like white clouds on blue skies,
I like large ships on blue oceans,
I like the blue color of my sister's eyes,
I like blue lotions and notions.

Blue balls, blue cars,
Blue blankets, blue stars,
Blue birds, blue hats,
Do they make blue cats?

Blueberries are yummy
They tickle my tummy.
Blue suckers are dandy,
My most favorite candy.

I like blue,
I really, really do.
I like blue
Do you like it too?

I Like Green by Pam Schiller

I like green.
I like it a lot.
I like green frogs,
Believe it or not.

I like green Jell-O.
I like green bugs.
I'm a green fellow
From blankets to rugs.

Green ribbons are keen.
Green clover is neat.
I really love green.
It can't be beat.

I like green fish.
Oh, can't you see?
Think what you wish.
Green's the color for me.

I Like Red by Pam Schiller

I like red.
I like it a bunch.
I like red jam. I like red punch.
I like red flowers.
I like red shoes.
Red is the color I always choose.

I like red.
Red's the best.
I like red socks. I like red vests.
I like red hair.
Oh, can't you see?
Red is the only color for me.

I Like Yellow by Pam Schiller

I like yellow, yellow is swell.
I like yellow—bet you can tell.

Yellow balloons, big yellow bows,
Yellow nail polish on my toes.

Yellow kittens, yellow beach balls
Yellow mittens, bright yellow walls.

Yellow cake icing on my cake.
Yellow inner tubes on the lake.

Yellow flowers, sweet yellow bees
Big yellow leaves in yellow trees.
Yellow, yellow, yellow, yellow,
I'm a happy yellow fellow!

I Love Pink Bubble Gum by Pam Schiller

I love bubble gum pink and sweet,
I love bubble gum more than meat.
I can chew, I can blow,
There aren't many tricks
That I don't know.

I Measure Myself

(suit actions to words)

I measure myself from my head to my toes,
I measure my arms, starting right by my
nose.
I measure my legs and I measure me all,
I measure to see if I'm growing tall.

I Never Saw a Purple Cow by Gelett Burgess

I never saw a purple cow,
I never hope to see one:
But I can tell you, anyhow
I'd rather see than be one.

Ice Cream

You scream
I scream
We all scream
For ice cream!

I'm a Family Helper by Pam Schiller

I set the table every night
I learned to do it right.
One place for mom, one for me,
And Daddy's place makes three.

I pick my toys up every day,
I put everything away.
My cars, my blocks, my books
All go into their nooks.

A family helper is what I am
You can be one, too.
Mommy say's I'm quite a ham
When it comes to jobs I do.

I'm a Frozen Icicle

I'm a frozen icicle
Hanging by your door.
When it's cold, I grow some more.
When it's warm, I'm on the floor!

Inside Out by Pam Schiller

(suit actions to words)

When I'm happy on the inside,
It shows on the outside.
It is quite impossible you see
To hide what's inside of me.

When I am happy I dance.
I lift my feet and prance,
I twirl and spin and glide.

Jack and Jill (Flannel Board Rhyme)

(See patterns on p. 431-434)

Jack and Jill went up the hill
To fetch a pail of water.
Jack fell down and broke his crown
And Jill came tumbling after.

Then up Jack got and off did trot,
As fast as he could caper,
To old Dame Dob, who patched his nob,
With vinegar and brown paper.

Jack Frost

Jack Frost bites your noses.
He chills your cheeks and freezes your
toes.
He comes every year when winter is here
And stays until spring is near.

Ladybird

Ladybird, ladybird, fly away home!
Your house is on fire, your children all gone,
All but one, and her name is Ann,
And she crept under the pudding pan.

Little Jack Horner

Little Jack Horner sat in the corner.
Eating his Christmas pie.
He stuck in his thumb,
And pulled out a plum.
Then said, "What a good boy am I!"

Little Miss Muffet (Flannel Board Rhyme)

(See patterns on p. 435-436)

Little Miss Muffet sat on her tuffet
Eating her curds and whey.
Along came a spider
And sat down beside her
And frightened Miss Muffet away.

(New verse by Tamera Bryant)
Little Miss Muffet went back to her tuffet,
Looked the thing square in the eye.
"See here, you big spider,
Miss Muffet's a fighter.
And you're the one saying bye-bye."

Little Miss Spider by Pam Schiller

Little Miss Spider sat on her web
Eating fly etouffe.
Along came Miss Muffet
In search of her tuffet
And frightened Miss Spider away.

Little Mouse

Walk little mouse, walk little mouse. *(tiptoe around)*
Hide little mouse, hide little mouse. *(cover eyes with hands)*
Here comes the cat! *(look around)*
Run little mouse, run little mouse!
(walk quickly to the circle area and sit down)

Little Red Apple

A little red apple grew high in a tree. *(point up)*
I looked up at it. *(shade eyes and look up)*
It looked down at me. *(shade eyes and look down)*
"Come down, please," I called. *(use hand to motion downward)*
And that little red apple fell right on my head. *(tap the top of your head)*

The March Wind

I come to work as well as play;
I'll tell you what I do;
I whistle all the live-long day,
"Whoo-oo-oo-oo! Whoo-oo!"

I toss the branches up and down
And shake them to and fro,
I whirl the leaves in flocks of brown,
And send them high and low.

I strew the twigs upon the ground,
The frozen earth I sweep;
I blow the children round and round
And wake the flowers from sleep.

Mary Middling Had a Pig

Mary Middling had a pig
Not very little, not very big,
Not very pink, not very green,
Not very dirty, not very clean,
Not very good, not very naughty,
Not very humble, not very haughty,
Not very thin, not very fat;
Now what would you give for a pig like that?

Metamorphosis

I'm an egg *(curl up in fetal position)*
I'm an egg
I'm an egg, egg, egg!

I'm a worm *(open up and wiggle on the ground)*
I'm a worm
I'm a wiggly, humpty worm!

I'm a cocoon *(curl up in a fetal position with hands over the face)*
I'm a cocoon
I'm a round and silky cocoon!

I'm a butterfly *(stand and fly around using arms for wings)*
I'm a butterfly
I'm a grand and glorious butterfly!

Mighty Fine Turkey

I'm a mighty fine turkey and I sing a fine song—gobble, gobble, gobble.
I strut around the barnyard all day long.
My head goes—bobble, bobble, bobble.
On Thanksgiving Day I run away with a—waddle, waddle, waddle.
So on the day after my head will still—bobble, bobble, bobble.

Miss Mary Mack

Miss Mary Mack, Mack, Mack
All dressed in black, black, black
With silver buttons, buttons, buttons
All down her back, back, back.
She asked her mother, mother, mother
For fifteen cents, cents, cents
To see the elephants, elephants, elephants
Jump the fence, fence, fence.
They jumped so high, high, high
They touched the sky, sky, sky
And they didn't come back, back, back
Till the fourth of July, ly, ly.

Monday's Child

Monday's child is fair of face,
Tuesday's child is full of grace,
Wednesday's child is full of woe,
Thursday's child has far to go,
Friday's child is loving and giving,
Saturday's child works hard for a living,
But the child who is born on Sunday—
Is fair and wise and good and gay.

My Ears by Pam Schiller

My ears are my ears, my beautiful ears. *(point to both ears, one at a time)*
They takes care of all the noises I hears. *(place hands behind ears)*
There's one on the left and one on the right. *(point to left ear and then to the right ear)*
They are always here with me day and night. *(make a sunshine and then rest head on hands)*
My ears can wiggle and wobble and loop,
They can hold my earrings both stud and hoop.

My Head

(suit actions to words)
This is the circle that is my head.
This is my mouth with which words are said.
These are my eyes with which I see.
This is my nose that is part of me.
This is the hair that grows on my head,
And this is my hat I wear on my head.

My Shadow by Robert Louis Stevenson

I have a little shadow that goes in and out with me,
And what can be the use of him is more than I can see.
He is very, very like me from his heels up to his head;
And I see him jump before me when I jump into my bed.

The funniest thing about him is the way he likes to grow—
Not at all like proper children, which is always very slow:
For he sometimes shoots up taller like an India-rubber ball,
And he sometimes gets so little that there's none of him at all.

He hasn't got a notion of how children ought to play,
And can only make a fool of me in every sort of way.
He stays so close behind me, he's a coward you can see;
I'd think shame to stick to nursie as that shadow sticks to me.

One morning, very early, before the sun was up,
I rose and found the shining dew on every buttercup;
But my lazy little shadow, like an errant sleepy head,
Had stayed at home behind me and was fast asleep in bed.

Old Gray Cat

The old gray cat is sleeping, sleeping, sleeping.
The old gray cat is sleeping in the house.
(one child is the cat and curls up, pretending to sleep)

The little mice are creeping, creeping, creeping.
The little mice are creeping through the house. *(other children are mice creeping around sleeping cat)*

The old gray cat is waking, waking, waking.
The old gray cat is waking through the house. *(cat slowly sits up and stretches)*

The old gray cat is chasing, chasing, chasing.
The old gray cat is chasing through the house. *(cat chases mice)*

All the mice are squealing, squealing, squealing.
All the mice are squealing through the house. *(mice squeal; when cat catches a mouse, that mouse becomes the cat)*

One, Two, Buckle My Shoe (Flannel Board Rhyme) (See patterns on p. 441-442)

One, two, buckle my shoe.
Three, four, shut the door.
Five, six, pick up sticks.
Seven, eight, lay them straight.
Nine, ten, a big fat hen.

One Potato, Two Potato

One potato, two potato,
Three potato, four.
Five potato, six potato,
Seven potato, more.
Eight potato, nine potato,
Ten potato then...
Count the potatoes over again.

See-Saw, Millie McGraw

(two children sit facing each other, join hands and rock back and forth)
See-saw, Millie McGraw.
Starting slow,
Up and down we go.
See-saw, Millie McGraw.

Sing a Song of Sixpence (Flannel Board Rhyme) (See patterns on p. 443-444)

Sing a song of sixpence,
A pocket full of rye;
Four-and-twenty blackbirds
Baked in a pie!

When the pie was opened
The birds began to sing;
Was not that a dainty dish
To set before the king?

The king was in his counting-house,
Counting out his money;
The queen was in the parlor,
Eating bread and honey.

The maid was in the garden,
Hanging out the clothes;
When down came a blackbird
And snapped off her nose.

Sometimes

Sometimes I am tall, *(stand tall)*
Sometimes I am small. *(crouch low)*
Sometimes I am very, very, tall. *(stand on tiptoes)*
Sometimes I am very, very small. *(crouch and lower head)*
Sometimes tall, *(stand tall)*
Sometimes small. *(crouch down)*
Sometimes neither tall or small. *(stand normally)*

The Spider and the Fly by Mary Horowitz

"Will you walk into my parlour?"
Said the spider to the fly;
"'Tis the prettiest little parlour
That ever you did spy.
The way into my parlour
Is up a winding stair,
And I have many curious things
To show you when you're there."
"Oh, no, no," said the little fly;
"To ask me is in vain;
For who goes up your winding stair
Can ne'er come down again."

A Square Is a Square by Pam Schiller

A square is a square. *(make a square using fingers from each hand)*
No matter which where. *(turn the square all around)*
Turn it here, turn it there,
It's still a square! *(hold hands out to side)*

This Little Monkey

(hold up one finger for each monkey)
This little monkey ate bananas.
This little monkey ate peas.
This little monkey did a somersault,
This little monkey slapped her knees,
And this little monkey went, "Ooh! Ooh! Ooh!"
Swinging through the trees.

Three Little Monkeys

Three little monkeys sitting in a tree
Teasing Mr. Alligator:
"Can't catch me!"
"Can't catch me!"
Along comes Mr. Alligator
Quiet as can be – snap!
Two little monkeys sitting in a tree.

Two little monkeys sitting in a tree
Teasing Mr. Alligator:
"Can't catch me!"
"Can't catch me!"
Along comes Mr. Alligator
Quiet as can be – snap!
One little monkey sitting in a tree.

One little monkey sitting in a tree
Teasing Mr. Alligator:
"Can't catch me!"
"Can't catch me!"
Along comes Mr. Alligator
Quiet as can be – snap!
No little monkeys sitting in a tree.

Thunderstorm

Boom, bang, boom, bang,
Rumpety, lumpety, bump!
Zoom, zam, zoom, zam,
Clippity, clappity, clump!
Rustles and bustles,
And swishes and zings!
What wonderful sounds
A thunderstorm brings!

Tiny Seeds

Tiny seed planted just right, *(children tuck themselves into a ball)*
Not a breath of air, not a ray of light.
Rain falls slowly to and fro,
And now the seed begins to grow. *(children begin to unfold)*
Slowly reaching for the light,
With all its energy, all its might.
The little seed's work is almost done,
To grow up tall and face the sun. *(children stand up tall with arms stretched out)*

Walk-On Nursery Rhyme

Goldilocks, Goldilocks, turn around. *(turn around)*
Goldilocks, Goldilocks, touch the ground. *(touch the ground)*
Goldilocks, Goldilocks, knock on the door. *(knock with hand)*
Goldilocks, Goldilocks, eat some porridge. *(pretend to eat porridge)*
Goldilocks, Goldilocks, have a seat. *(squat)*
Goldilocks, Goldilocks, go to sleep. *(put head on folded hands)*
Goldilocks, Goldilocks, run, run, run. *(run off paper and back to beginning)*

Act out this rhyme using the Walk-On Nursery Rhyme Mat (see Appendix page 404).

Whether the Weather

Whether the weather be fine
Or whether the weather be not,
Whether the weather be cold
Or whether the weather be hot,
We'll weather the weather
Whatever the weather,
Whether we like it or not.

Who Has Seen the Wind? by Christina Rossetti

Who has seen the wind?
Neither I nor you:
But when the leaves hang trembling,
The wind is passing through.

Who has seen the wind?
Neither you nor I:
But when the trees bow down their heads,
The wind is passing by.

The Wind

Swoosh, swirl, swoosh, swirl,
Watch the leaves tumble and twirl.

Window Watching

See the window I have here,
So big and wide and square. *(draw a square)*
I can stand in front of it,
And see the things out there. *(shade eyes as if looking at something in distance)*

Tongue Twisters

Peter Piper

Peter Piper picked a peck of pickled
  peppers.
Did Peter Piper pick a peck of pickled
  peppers?
If Peter Piper picked a peck of pickled
  peppers,
Where's the peck of pickled peppers Peter
  Piper picked?

Short version:
Peter Piper picked a peck of pickled
  peppers.
How many pecks of pickled peppers did
  Peter Piper pick?

She Sells Seashells

She sells seashells by the seashore,
By the seashore she sells seashells.

Stories

The Ant and the Grasshopper (Listening Story)

Once among the land of an old farmer there lived an ant and a grasshopper. A long, hard winter had just passed and the ant, not wanting such a difficult winter again, began meticulously planning for the next winter. Immediately in the spring the ant began storing up and building a stronger home. The grasshopper, however, wanted to enjoy his summer, and so he paid no attention to the coming winter and played all day.

"Why are you working so hard?" inquired the grasshopper one day. " It is a beautiful day and you are spending it all on work!"

"I am preparing for the winter," replied the ant. "And you should too, or you will be sorry when it comes."

But the grasshopper ignored the ant, and continued playing as the ant continued working throughout the summer.

Then came August, and the farmer's son kicked over the ant's hill and pounded it into the ground, destroying all the work that the ant had put into it the entire summer. The ant knew there was no way he could re-do the work in time for winter. And as winter approached, he began to despair.

"Well," the ant said to the grasshopper, as snow began to fall and they both began to shiver. "It looks like we both will die."

"True," said the grasshopper. "But at least I enjoyed the summer."

Candy Land Journey by Pam Schiller (Action Story)

Before beginning, cut five circles out of pink construction paper to use as peppermint disks.

Let's go on a trip. Who wants to go to Candy Land? *(raise hands).* OK! Let's go! *(sweep arm in forward motion)*

It's just a short trip from here. First, we walk *(walk in place about 10 steps).* Now we need to get on a plane and fly *(put arms out to fly for a few seconds).* Look! We're here! *(put arms down and take a few steps)*

Wow! Here is a sidewalk made of peppermint disks. Let's hop on them and see where they go *(jump from disk to disk about five times).* Be careful not to fall off.

What do we have here? It looks like a river made of caramel. Let's try to walk across *(walk as if stepping in something gooey).*

That was fun! Who likes caramel? *(raise hands).* Let's taste some *(stoop and scoop up some caramel and pretend to taste it).* Mmmm!

Hey, look at the lemon drop tree *(point)*. Let's pick some lemon drops *(pretend to pick lemon drops).* Let's taste one *(pretend to chew/crunch).*

Let's go over there into the forest *(take a few steps).* Here are some licorice laces. Let's play jump rope *(pretend to jump rope).*

It's time to go now. Let's head back to the plane. We have to cross the river of caramel again *(cross river)* and hop across the peppermint disk *(jump from disk to disk)*.

Oh! Look at those great suckers growing like flowers in a garden. Let's pick one to take home *(pick a sucker).*

OK. Let's fly *(fly).*

Now let's walk back to our classroom *(walk).*

We're home! Who had a good time? *(raise hands).* Me, too. I love Candy Land!

Caps for Sale (Flannel Board Story) (See patterns on p. 409-410)

Once upon a time, there was a cap peddler, but he was not an ordinary peddler. He didn't carry his wares on his back or in a cart. He carried them on top of his head.

First, he had on his own checked cap. On top of that he had gray caps and then brown caps, blue caps, and yellow caps. On the very top, he had red caps. He walked slowly, very slowly, up and down the street. He had to walk very straight so that he wouldn't upset his caps.

As he walked along, he called, "Caps! Caps for sale! Fifty cents a cap!"

But this morning no one wanted any caps. Not a gray one or a brown one or a blue one or a yellow one. Not even a red one. The peddler was not happy. So he decided to take a walk in the country. He walked slowly, very, very slowly so that he wouldn't upset his caps. After a long time, he came to a big tree. "This looks like a nice place to rest," he said.

He sat down slowly, very, very slowly. He leaned back against the tree slowly, very, very slowly. Then he put his hand up to check the caps. Were they all there? He touched his own checked cap. He touched the gray caps and then the brown caps, the blue caps, and the yellow caps. On the very top, he touched the red caps. They were all there. He could go to sleep.

He slept a long time. He woke up. He yawned. He stretched slowly, very, very slowly. He didn't want to upset his caps.

His caps? Something felt funny. He touched his own checked cap. Then he touched..."Where are my caps?" he cried.

He looked here. He looked there. No caps.

He looked left. He looked right. No caps.

He looked down. He looked up. And what did he see? A tree full of monkeys. And on each monkey there was a cap. Gray caps and brown caps. Blue caps and yellow caps. At the very top of the tree, he saw red caps.

The peddler looked at the monkeys. The monkeys looked at the peddler. What to do?

"Hey, you monkeys," he shouted, shaking his finger. "Give me my caps."

"Tsk, tsk, tsk," said the monkeys, shaking their fingers at the peddler.

The peddler got mad. "Hey, you monkeys," he shouted, stamping his foot. "Give me my caps."

"Tsk, tsk, tsk," said they monkeys, stamping their feet at the peddler.
The peddler got madder.

"Hey, you monkeys," he shouted, jumping up and down. "Give me my caps."

"Tsk, tsk, tsk," said the monkeys, jumping up and down.

"Give me my caps." The peddler got even madder.

"That's it," the peddler said. He got so mad that he took off his cap and threw it on the ground.

Then each monkey took off its cap and threw it down. Caps came floating to the ground, slowly, very, very slowly. Gray caps and brown caps. Blue caps and yellow caps. And from the very top of the tree came red caps.

The peddler smiled. He put on his caps. And slowly, very slowly he walked back to town. "Caps! Caps for sale! Fifty cents a cap!"

Dressed for Play (Action Story) by Pam Schiller

The children were excited. They jumped up and down with delight *(jump up and down)*. It was time to go outdoors.

They put on their coats *(pretend to put on a coat)*. They put on their mittens (*pretend to put on mittens*). And then they put on their hats (*pretend to put on a hat*).

They opened the door (*pretend to open door*) and out they ran.

The wind was strong. It blew hard against them *(pretend to walk against the wind)*. The children walked more slowly toward the swings and the slide. They swung awhile *(pretend to swing)*. The wind blew their swings crooked *(pretend to go crooked)*. They decided to try the slide. They climbed up the ladder *(pretend to climb)*. When they went down the slide, the wind pushed them faster *(pretend to slide—land on bottom).*

Next some of the children rode on the tricycles *(pretend to pedal)* while others played ball *(pretend to catch a ball).*

Soon the children noticed that the wind had died down. They began to feel warm *(fan yourself).* The children took off their mittens *(pretend to take off mittens).* Then they went to play in the sand *(pretend to hold sand in your hand)*.

The children were still hot *(fan)*. They took off their hats *(pretend to take off hat).* They took off their coats *(pretend to take off coat).* They went back to play on the swings *(pretend to swing)* and the slide *(pretend to slide).*

Just then they began to feel raindrops *(hold out hand as if feeling for rain).* The children picked up their mittens, their coats, and their hats and ran inside. They were just in time, because when they looked out the window *(shade eyes as if looking)* they saw a big black cloud and lots and lots of raindrops.

Fat Cat: A Danish Folktale (Flannel Board Story) (See patterns on p.411-417)

There was once an old woman who was cooking gruel. She was going to visit a neighbor so she asked the cat if he could look after the gruel while she was gone. "I'll be glad to," said the cat. But when the old woman had gone, the gruel looked so good that the cat ate it all.

And the pot, too.

When the old woman came back, she said to the cat, "Now what has happened to the gruel?"

"Oh," said the cat, "I ate the gruel and I ate the pot, too, and now I am going to also eat you." And he ate the old woman.

He went for a walk and on the way he met Skohottentot. And Skohottentot said to him, "What have you been eating, my little cat? You are so fat."

And the cat said, "I ate the gruel and the pot and the old woman, too. And now I am going to also eat you."

So he ate Skohottentot.

Afterwards he met Skolinkenlot. Skolinkenlot said, "What have you been eating, my little cat? You are so fat."

"I ate the gruel and the pot and the old woman, too, and Skohottentot," said the cat. "And now I am going to also eat you."

So he ate Skolinkenlot.

Next he met five birds in a flock. And they said to him, "What have you been eating, my little cat? You are so fat."

"I ate the gruel and the pot and the old woman, too, and Skohottentot and Skolinkenlot. And now I am going to also eat you."

And he ate the five birds in a flock.

Later he met three girls dancing. And they, too, said to him, "Gracious! What have you been eating, my little cat? You are so fat."

And the cat said, "I ate the gruel and the pot and the old woman, too, and Skohottentot and Skolinkenlot and five birds in a flock. And now I am going to also eat you."

And he ate the three girls dancing.

When he had gone a little farther, he met a lady with a pink parasol. And she, too, said to him, "Heavens! What have you been eating my little cat? You are so fat."

"I ate the gruel and the pot and the old woman, too, and Skohottentot and Skolinkenlot and five birds in a flock and three girls dancing. And now I am going to also eat you."

And he ate the lady with the pink parasol.

And a little later he met a parson with a crooked staff. "Dear me! What have you been eating, my little cat? You are so fat."

"Oh," said the cat, "I ate the gruel and the pot and the old woman, too, and Skohottentot and Skolinkenlot and five birds in a flock and three girls dancing and the lady with the pink parasol. And now I am going to also eat you."

And he ate the parson with the crooked staff.

Next he met a woodcutter with an axe. "My! What have you been eating, my little cat! You are so fat."

"I ate the gruel and the pot and the old woman, too, and Skohottentot and Skolinkenlot and five birds in a flock and three girls dancing and the lady with the pink parasol and the parson with the crooked staff. And now I am going to also eat you."

"No. You are wrong, my little cat," said the woodcutter. And he took his axe and cut the cat open. Out jumped the parson with the crooked staff and the lady with the pink parasol and the three girls dancing and the five birds in a flock and Skolinkenlot and Skohottentot. And the old woman took her pot and her gruel and went home with them.

As for the cat—the woodcutter stitched him up and placed a bandage on his tummy and made him promise to eat only cat food.

Goldilocks and the Three Bears (Flannel Board Story)

(see patterns on p. 421)

Once upon a time there were three bears—Mama Bear, Papa Bear, and Baby Bear. They all lived in the forest. One day they went out for a walk to visit a sick friend.

While they were gone, a little girl named Goldilocks was walking in the woods. Finding that she had lost her way, she walked until she came to a small cottage. Upon entering the house she saw three bowls of porridge sitting on a table. She was very hungry. She tasted the porridge in the large bowl. It was too hot. So she tried the porridge in the middle-sized bowl. It was too cold. She tried the porridge in the small bowl. It was just right. Goldilocks ate it all up.

After eating she went over to the three chairs sitting before a fireplace. The biggest chair was too hard! The middle-size chair was too soft! She sat in the third chair because it seemed just right! As she sat in the chair it wobbled, rattled, and it fell apart.

By now the little girl was very tired and so she went into the other room and found three beds. The first was very hard! The second bed was too soft! The third bed was just right! She fell asleep right away.

Meanwhile, the bears came home from their walk. Finding an empty bowl on the table made Mama Bear and Papa Bear scratch their heads. At the same time, Baby Bear found his chair in pieces on the floor. He was very upset and started crying.

The little girl, hearing the noise, came down to find out what was wrong. When she saw the bears she was very surprised and a little frightened! She explained that she was lost and that she was sorry she ate up the porridge and broke the chair. The bears were kind bears. They told Goldilocks she was forgiven. Mama Bear packed Goldilocks a basket of cookies and Papa Bear and Baby Bear helped her find her way to the path back home.

The Great Big Pumpkin (Flannel Board Story) by Pam Schiller

(See patterns on p. 426-427)

One day Little Bear was out looking for honey. She was very hungry. But she couldn't find a single thing to eat.

Just as she was about to give up, she spied a very funny something. It was big, very big, and round, very round, and orange, very orange. Little Bear had never seen anything quite like it. She went to get a closer look.

"I'm going to take you home to my Mama," she said. Little Bear tried to roll the big, round, orange something. It didn't move. She tried again. It didn't move.

Just then Skunk came along. "Hey, what's that?"
"I don't know," said Little Bear. "I want to take it home to my Mama, but I can't move it."
"Let me help," said Skunk. Little Bear and Skunk pushed and pushed. The big, round, orange thing didn't move.

Just then Squirrel came along. "Hey, what's that?"

"We don't know," said Little Bear. "I want to take it home to my Mama, but we can't move it."

"Let me help," said Squirrel. Little Bear and Skunk and Squirrel pushed and pushed and pushed. The big, round, orange thing didn't move.

Just then Mouse came along. "Hey, what's that?"

"I don't know," said Little Bear. "I want to take it home to my Mama, but we can't move it."

"Let me help," said Mouse. Little Bear and Skunk and Squirrel and Mouse pushed and pushed and pushed and pushed.

Slowly, the big, round, orange thing started to move. Then it started to roll. It rolled and rolled and rolled all the way to Little Bear's den. Little Bear's Mama came out to see what was going on. "Where did you find this lovely, big, round, orange pumpkin?" she asked.

The four friends looked at each other and said, "PUMPKIN?"

The Great Big Turnip (Flannel Board Story) (See patterns on p. 427-428)

One day Little Bear was out looking for honey. She was very hungry. But she couldn't find a single thing to eat.

Just as she was about to give up, she spied a very funny something. It was big, very big, and leafy, very leafy, and green, and just peeking out of the dirt it was purple. Little Bear had never seen anything quite like it. She went to get a closer look.

"I'm going to take you home to my Mama," she said. Little Bear tried to pull the big, leafy, purple something. It didn't move. She tried again. It didn't move.

Just then Skunk came along. "Hey, what's that?"

"I don't know," said Little Bear. "I want to take it home to my Mama, but I can't move it."

"Let me help," said Skunk. Little Bear and Skunk pushed and pushed. The big, leafy, purple thing didn't move.

Just then Squirrel came along. "Hey, what's that?"

"We don't know," said Little Bear. "I want to take it home to my Mama, but we can't move it."

"Let me help," said Squirrel. Little Bear and Skunk and Squirrel pulled and pulled and pulled. The big, leafy, purple thing didn't move.

Just then Mouse came along. "Hey, what's that?"

"I don't know," said Little Bear. "I want to take it home to my Mama, but we can't move it."
"Let me help," said Mouse. Little Bear and Skunk and Squirrel and Mouse pulled and pulled and pulled and pulled.

Slowly, the big, leafy, purple thing started to move. Then it came right out of the ground. The four friends started to roll the big something. They rolled it and rolled it and rolled it all the way to Little Bear's den. Little Bear's Mama came out to see what was going on. "Where did you find this lovely, big, leafy, purple turnip?" she asked.

The four friends looked at each other and said, "TURNIP!?!"
Little Bear's mama made a big pot of vegetable soup and used the big turnip right up. It was a tasty turnip soup! Yum!

Let's Pretend to Bake a Cake (Action Story) by Pam Schiller

Act out the story, encouraging the children to copy your actions.

Who wants to bake a cake? I need all the bakers to come sit by me. Let's see. We need a mixer, two bowls, measuring cups and spoons, and a cake pan. *(Pretend to take items out of shelves and drawers.)* Now I think we are ready.

First we put our butter and sugar in our bowl. *(Place both into bowl.)* Now we need the mixer. *(Run it over bowl as you make a humming noise.)* That looks nice and smooth. Let's add the eggs. *(Count and crack four eggs into bowl.)* Let's mix again. *(Run mixer and hum.)* This looks good.

Now we need to add the flour. *(Measure two cups full and dump into bowl.)* Just one more ingredient—a teaspoon of vanilla. *(Measure in a teaspoon of vanilla.)* A final mix *(mix),* and we are ready to pour our batter into our cake pan. *(Pour.)* Now it's time to put our cake in the oven. *(Open oven door as you make a squeaking sound, slide the cake in, and close the door.)*

Now our cake is baking. *(Tap fingers to act like you are waiting.)* I can't wait! Who can smell it cooking? *(Sniff.)* That smells good! OK! Let's take our cake out of the oven. *(Take the cake out and smell it.)* Who wants some cake?

The Lion and the Mouse (Listening Story)

A lion was awakened from sleep by a mouse running over his face. Rising up angrily, he caught the mouse by his tail and was about to kill him, when the mouse very pitifully said, "If you would only spare my life, I would surely repay your kindness someday."

The lion roared with laughter. "How could a small little creature like you ever repay a mighty lion?" The lion roared another laugh and let the mouse go. He settled back down to finish his nap. "Thank you mighty lion. You won't be sorry."

It happened shortly thereafter that the mighty lion was trapped by hunters. The hunters caught him in a net made of ropes. The lion roared in anguish. The little mouse was not far away. He recognized the lion's roar and he came quickly and gnawed the ropes away to free the lion. The lion was very grateful and quite surprised to see the mouse—more surprised that such a small creature was able to save his life.

The mouse said, "You ridiculed the idea that I might ever be able to help you or repay you. I hope you know now that it is possible for even a small mouse to help a mighty lion." The lion and the mouse were friends from that moment on.

THE LION'S HAIRCUT (PROP STORY) BY PAM SCHILLER
(SEE P.340 FOR DIRECTIONS FOR MAKING THE PROP)

Leo was a lively baby lion. He loved to frolic in the green and grazy grass. He loved to chase butterflies. He loved to splash in the water of the nearby pond. But most of all he loved to look at his reflection in the pond and see how big he was growing. Leo wanted to be just like his dad. He would look at his paws and then search for his dad's paw prints to compare to his foot. He would look at his nose and ears and try to remember how much bigger his dad's looked when they were wrestling in the grass. He would look for his mane and simply sigh in sadness as he could tell without any measuring or remembering that it was nothing like his dad's.

Leo would say to his mom, "When will my mane grow?"

His mom would give him a lick and simply say, "In its own good time."

All through the spring, Leo watched his mane. It didn't grow an inch.

All through the summer, Leo watched his mane. It grew only a little *(pull mane through plate a little).*

All through the fall, Leo watched his mane. It grew only a little more *(pull mane through plate a little).*

All through the winter, Leo watched his mane. It grew only a little more *(pull mane through plate a little).*

Then when spring came again something happened. Leo's mane began to grow *(pull mane).* And it grew and it grew and it grew until he had a full mane just like his dad's *(pull until the mane is very long)*. Leo was so happy he felt like a million dollars or in lion talk, a million butterflies.

Leo frolicked in the green and grazy grass. He chased butterflies. He splashed in the pond. He stopped to take a look at his lovely, long mane and when the water had calmed down and he could see himself, he shrieked. His mane was a tangled and matted mess.

He ran home to his mom in tears. His mom gave him a lick and simply said, "It's time for a haircut." She took out a pair of scissors and began to snip *(cut mane to approximately 2")*. When she was through the tangles were gone and Leo still had a beautiful mane. It was just the right size for a lively little lion.

***Directions for Making the Lion Mask**: Photocopy the Lion Face (Appendix p. X). Color, cut it out, and laminate (optional). Glue it to the center of a 10" Styrofoam plate. Punch small holes all around the edges of the plate. Cut several 8" pieces of yarn. Tie a knot in one end of each piece of yarn. Use a crochet hook to pull the other end of the yarn through the plate, leaving only an inch of yarn exposed on the face side of the puppet. (The knotted side of the yarn will be on the back of the paper plate.) Glue the lion face to a tongue depressor if desired. You will pull the yarn through the plate during the story. You will need to replace the yarn each time you use the puppet.*

The Little Red Hen (Flannel Board Story) (See patterns on p. 437)

Once upon a time there was a Little Red Hen who shared her tiny cottage with a goose, a cat, and a dog. The goose was a gossip. She chatted with the neighbors all day long. The cat was vain. She brushed her fur, straightened her whiskers, and polished her claws all day long. The dog was lazy. He napped on the front porch all day long.

The Little Red Hen did all the work. She cooked, she cleaned, and she took out the trash. She mowed, she raked, and she did all the shopping.

One day on her way to market, the Little Red Hen found a few grains of wheat. She put them in her pocket. When she got home she asked her friends, "Who will plant these grains of wheat?"

"Not I," said the goose.
"Not I," said the cat.
"Not I," said the dog.
"Then I will plant them myself," said the Little Red Hen. And she did.

All summer long she cared for the wheat. She made sure that it got enough water, and she dug the weeds out carefully between each row. And when the wheat was finally ready to harvest, the Little Red Hen asked her friends, "Who will help me thresh this wheat?"

"Not I," said the goose.
"Not I," said the cat.
"Not I," said the dog.
"Then I will cut and thresh it myself," said the Little Red Hen. And she did!

When the wheat had been cut and threshed, the Little Red Hen scooped the wheat into a wheelbarrow and said, "This wheat must be ground into flour. Who will help me take it to the mill?"

"Not I," said the goose.
"Not I," said the cat.
"Not I," said the dog.
"Then I will do it myself," said the Little Red Hen. And she did.

The miller ground the wheat into flour and put it into a bag for the Little Red Hen. Then all by herself, she pushed the bag home in the wheelbarrow.

One cool morning a few weeks later the Little Red Hen got up early and said, "Today is a perfect day to bake some bread. Who will help me bake it?"

"Not I," said the goose.
"Not I," said the cat.
"Not I," said the dog.
"Then I will bake the bread myself," said the Little Red Hen. And she did.

She mixed the flour with milk and eggs and butter and salt. She kneaded the dough. She shaped the dough into a nice plump loaf. Then she put the loaf in the oven and watched it as it baked. The smell of the bread soon filled the air.

The goose stopped chatting. The cat stopped brushing and the dog woke up. One by one they came into the kitchen.

When the Little Red Hen took the bread from the oven she said, "Who will help me eat this bread?"

"I will," said the goose.
"I will," said the cat.
"I will," said the dog.
"You will?" said the Little Red Hen. "Who planted the wheat and took care of it? Who cut the wheat and threshed it? Who took the wheat to the mill? Who baked the bread? I did it all by myself. Now I am going to eat it all by myself." And she did.

Mr. Wiggle and Mr. Waggle (Action Story)

This is Mr. Wiggle *(hold up right hand, make a fist but keep the thumb pointing up—wiggle thumb)* and this is Mr. Waggle *(hold up left hand, make a fist but keep the thumb pointing up—wiggle thumb).* Mr. Wiggle and Mr. Waggle live in houses on top of different hills and three hills apart *(put thumbs inside fists).*

STORIES

One day, Mr. Wiggle decided to visit Mr. Waggle. He opened his door *(open right fist),* pop, stepped outside *(raise thumb),* pop, and closed his door *(close fist),* pop. Then he went down the hill and up the hill, and down the hill and up the hill, and down the hill and up the hill *(move right hand up and down in a wave fashion to go with text).*

When he reached Mr. Waggle's house, he knocked on the door—knock, knock, knock *(tap right thumb against left fist).* No one answered. So Mr. Wiggle went down the hill and up the hill, and down the hill and up the hill, and down the hill and up the hill to his house *(use wave motion to follow text).*

When he reached his house, Mr. Wiggle opened the door *(open right fist),* pop, went inside *(place thumb in palm),* pop, and closed the door *(close fist),* pop.

The next day Mr. Waggle decided to visit Mr. Wiggle. He opened his door *(open left fist),* pop, stepped outside *(raise thumb),* pop, and closed his door *(close fist),* pop. Then he went down the hill and up the hill, and down the hill and up the hill, and down the hill and up the hill *(move left hand up and down in a wave fashion to go with text).*

When he reached Mr. Wiggle's house he knocked on the door—knock, knock, knock *(tap left thumb against right fist).* No one answered. So Mr. Waggle went down the hill and up the hill, and down the hill and up the hill, and down the hill and up the hill to his house *(use wave motion to follow text).* When he reached his house, Mr. Waggle opened the door *(open left fist),* pop, went inside *(place thumb in palm),* pop, and closed the door *(close fist),* pop.

The next day Mr. Wiggle (*shake right fist*) decided to visit Mr. Waggle, and Mr. Waggle (shake left fist) decided to visit Mr. Wiggle. So they opened their doors *(open both fists),* pop, stepped outside *(raise thumbs),* and closed their doors *(close fists),* pop. They each went down the hill and up the hill, and down the hill and up the hill *(wave motion to follow text),* and they met on top of the hill.

They talked and laughed and visited *(wiggle thumbs)* until the sun went down. Then they went down the hill and up the hill, and down the hill and up the hill, to their own homes *(wave motion with both hands to text).* They opened their doors *(open fists),* pop, went inside *(tuck thumbs inside),* pop, closed their doors *(close fists),* pop, and went to sleep *(place your head on your hands).*

Ms. Bumblebee Gathers Honey (Puppet Story) (see patterns on p. 468)

Ms. Bumblebee spends her day gathering honey. Every morning she gets out of bed, walks to the edge of the beehive, and looks out at the beautiful spring flowers.

Most days, she starts with the red flowers because red is her favorite color. She swoops down from the hive, circles around, and lands right on the biggest red flower she can find. *(Hold the bee puppet in one hand and a red flower in the other. Move the bee slowly toward the flower, moving her in small circles as she approaches the flower.)* She drinks nectar from the flower and then carries it back to the hive to make honey. *(Move bee back to hive.)*

(Continue to move bee as directed above.)
Next Ms. Bumblebee tries the nectar of the blue flowers. Again she swoops from the hive and dances toward the flower. She drinks the nectar and then returns to the hive.

She continues to the yellow flowers, which are the queen bee's favorite flowers. She drinks the nectar and returns to the hive. A bee's work is very hard, but Ms. Bumblebee thinks it is also a lot of fun...and very tasty.

The last flowers Ms. Bumblebee visits are the orange zinnias. She likes them because they have lots of petals that make a big place for her to land. She takes a minute to look over the field of flowers *(move puppet as if it is looking all around)* before drinking and returning to the hive.

Ms. Bumblebee is tired. She is glad this is the last nectar for the day. Wait! What's this? Oh, it's that bear again. He wants to take the honey from the hive. Ms. Bumblebee is buzzing mad. She flies out and stings the bear right on the nose. The bear cries out, grabs his nose, and runs away. Ms. Bumblebee puts away her last bit of nectar and falls fast asleep.

Smart Cookie's Best Friend, Greta Graham by Pam Schiller

(Flannel Board Story) (see patterns on p. 446)

Smart Cookie is a wonderful, round, perfect chocolate chip cookie. Greta Graham is a fine, square, graham cracker. Smart Cookie and Greta Graham are best friends. They can't wait to get to school each day so they can play together. Their favorite activity is building in the block center. They make roads and highways, barns and farms, tall skyscrapers and cozy cottages.

Smart Cookie always finds a square block that matches Greta's graham cracker shape body and says with a laugh, "Hey, this block is the same shape you are." Greta finds two half circle arches, puts them together, and says with a laugh, "Hey, these blocks are the same shape you are." Both cookies laugh.

Next to playing with the blocks the cookies both love story time. They like all the Dr. Seuss stories but, of course, *If You Give a Mouse a Cookie* is their favorite story. Do you know why?

The cookies like drawing and painting. They love to play outdoors. They enjoy playing games with the other children and they both sing loudly during Morning Circle. The cookies love everything about school but there is no doubt that their favorite thing about school is the opportunity to spend time together. They are best friends. Do you have a best friend?

A Special Surprise (Chalk and Prop Story)

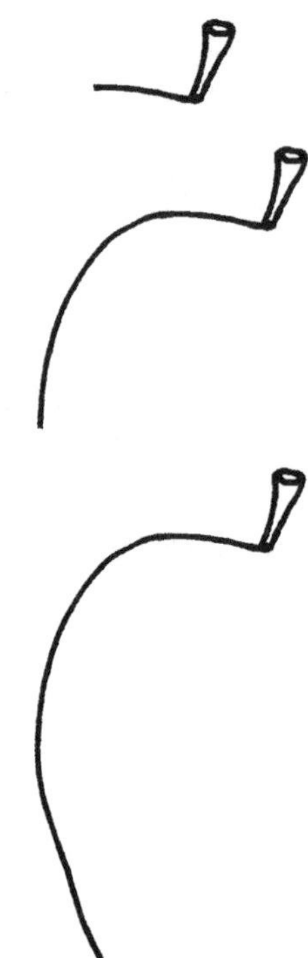

Once there was a little old lady named Annie, who lived in the mountains in a little house right here. *(Draw the stem and the top right part of the apple.)* One day Annie decided to go down the mountain to town, so she left her house and started down the road like this. *(Draw one half of the left side of an apple.)*

On the way she met Abraham, and he asked, "Where are you going on such a fine day?" "I'm going down to town," replied Annie.

"What are you going to get?" asked Abraham.

"You'll just have to wait and see," said Annie.

On she walked (draw more of the left side of the apple until she met Ashley and the other boys and girls. They all asked her, "Where are you going on such a fine day?"

"I'm going down to town," she replied.

"What are you going to get?" they asked.

"You'll just have to wait and see," Annie told them.

Annie finally reached town *(continue drawing the left side of the apple; stop at the center of the bottom of the apple).* She went in the store and she came out with a big bag. *(Hold up the paper bag.)*

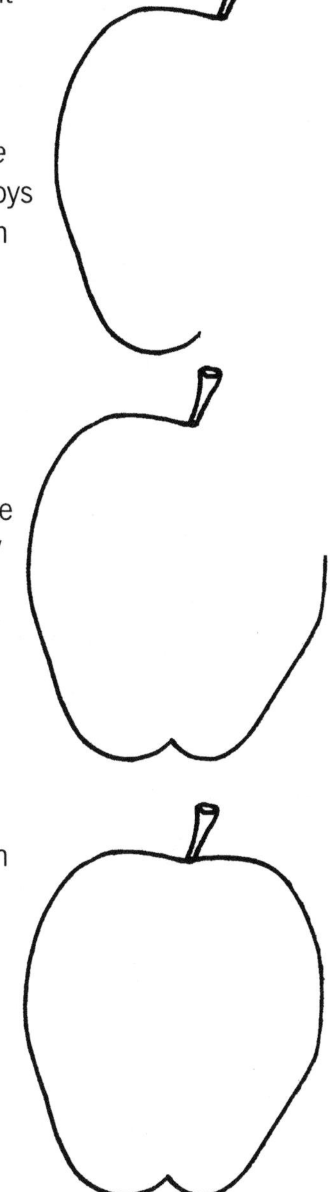

She started back up the mountain like this. *(Begin drawing the right side of apple from the bottom to the midpoint.)* All the boys and girls came running up to her. "What did you get? What's in your bag?" they all begged.

"I've got some stars," Annie answered.

"Walk home with me, and I'll give you each one."

So the little old lady and all the boys and girls continued up the mountain like this. *(Complete the drawing of the apple.).* They finally reached Annie's house.

Annie sat down and opened her bag. She pulled out an apple. *(Take an apple from the bag.)*

"But where are the stars?" asked the children.

Then Annie smiled and took out her knife. She cut the apple in half, and showed the children a beautiful star inside the apple. *(Cut apple in half horizontally and show the children the star.)* Then she cut all the apples in half and gave all the children a star of their very own.

***Props needed to tell the story**: You will need chalk and a chalkboard or a pen and a flip chart, a bag of apples, and a knife.*

The Strange Visitor (Prop Story)

Props needed to tell the story: Cut out two large shoes; two skinny, long legs; a pair of shorts; a shirt; two long, skinny arms; two large gloved hands; and a jack-o-lantern head out of construction paper. Place each piece in front of you on the floor as it enters the old woman's cottage.

A little old woman lived all alone in a little old house in the woods.
One Halloween she sat in the chimney corner, and as she sat, she spun.
Still she sat and
Still she spun and
Still she wished for company.

Then she saw her door open a little way, and in came
A pair of broad, broad feet, (*a pair of big shoes*)
And sat down by the fireside
"That is strange," thought the little old woman, but—
Still she sat and
Still she spun and
Still she wished for company.

Then, in came
A pair of long, long legs, *(a pair of long skinny legs)*
And sat down on the broad, broad feet;
"Now this is strange," thought the little old woman, but—
Still she sat and
Still she spun and
Still she wished for company.

Then, in came
A wee, wee waist, *(pair of shorts)*
And sat down on the long, long legs.
"Now this is strange," thought the little old woman, but—
Still she sat and
Still she spun and
Still she wished for company.

Then, in came
A pair of broad, broad shoulders, (*a shirt*)
And sat down on the wee, wee, waist.
"Now this is strange," thought the little old woman, but—
Still she sat and
Still she spun and
Still she wished for company.

Then, in came
A pair of long, long arms, *(a pair of long, skinny arms)*
And sat down on the broad, broad shoulders.

"Now that is strange," thought the little old woman, but—
Still she sat and
Still she spun and
Still she wished for company.

Then, in came
A pair of fat, fat hands, *(a pair of large gloved hands)*
And sat down on the long, long arms.
"Now this is strange," thought the little old woman, but—
Still she sat and
Still she spun and
Still she wished for company.

Then in came
A round, round head, *(big jack-o-lantern head)*
And sat down on top of all
That sat by the fireside.

The little old woman stopped her spinning and asked,
"Where did you get such big, big feet?"
"By much tramping, by much tramping," said Somebody.

"Where did you get such long, long legs?"
"By much running, by much running," said Somebody.

"Where did you get such a wee, wee waist?"
"Nobody knows, nobody knows," said Somebody.

"Where did you get such long, long arms?"
"Swinging the scythe, swinging the scythe," said Somebody.

"Where did you get such fat, fat hands?"
"From threshing, from threshing," said Somebody.

"How did you get such a huge, huge head?"
"Of a pumpkin I made it," said Somebody.

Then said the little old woman, "What did you come for?"
"YOU!" *

* If you are concerned that the end of the story might frighten young children, change it. Simply add, "to keep you company, to keep you company."

The Three Billy Goats Gruff (Flannel Board Story) (see patterns on p. 447-449)

Once upon a time there were three billy goats called Gruff. In the winter they lived in a barn in the valley. When spring came they longed to travel up to the mountains to eat the lush sweet grass.

On their way to the mountains, the three Billy Goats Gruff had to cross a rushing river. But there was only one bridge across it, made of wooden planks. And underneath the bridge there lived a terrible, ugly troll. Nobody was allowed to cross the bridge without the troll's permission—and nobody ever got permission. He always ate them up.

The smallest Billy Goat Gruff was first to reach the bridge. Trippity-trop, trippity-trop went his little hooves as he trotted over the wooden planks. Ting-tang, ting-tang went the little bell round his neck.

"Who's that trotting over my bridge?" growled the troll from under the planks.

"Billy Goat Gruff," squeaked the smallest goat in his little voice. "I'm only going up to the mountain to eat the sweet spring grass."

"Oh, no, you're not!" said the troll. "I'm going to eat you for breakfast!"

"Oh, no, please Mr. Troll," pleaded the goat. "I'm only the smallest Billy Goat Gruff. I'm much too tiny for you to eat, and I wouldn't taste very good. Why don't you wait for my brother, the second Billy Goat Gruff? He's much bigger than me and would be much more tasty."

The troll did not want to waste his time on a little goat if there was a bigger and better one to eat. "All right, you can cross my bridge," he grunted. "Go and get fatter on the mountain and I'll eat you on your way back!"

So the smallest Billy Goat Gruff skipped across to the other side.
The troll did not have to wait long for the second Billy Goat Gruff. Clip-clop, clip-clop went his hooves as he clattered over the wooden planks. Ding-dong, ding-dong went the bell around his neck.
"Who's that clattering across my bridge?" screamed the troll, suddenly appearing from under the planks.

"Billy Goat Gruff," said the second goat in his middle-sized voice. "I'm going up to the mountain to eat the lovely spring grass."

"Oh, no, you're not!" said the troll. "I'm going to eat you for breakfast."

"Oh, no, please," said the second goat. "I may be bigger than the first Billy Goat Gruff, but I'm much smaller than my brother, the third Billy Goat Gruff. Why don't you wait for him? He would be much more of a meal than me."

The troll was getting very hungry, but he did not want to waste his appetite on a middle-sized goat if there was an even bigger one to come. "All right, you can cross my bridge," he rumbled. "Go and get fatter on the mountain and I'll eat you on your way back!"

So the middle-sized Billy Goat Gruff scampered across to the other side.

The troll did not have to wait long for the third Billy Goat Gruff. Tromp-tramp, tromp-tramp went his hooves as he stomped across the wooden planks. Bong-bang, bong-bang went the big bell round his neck.

"Who's that stomping over my bridge?" roared the troll, resting his chin on his hands. "Billy Goat Gruff," said the third goat in a deep voice. "I'm going up to the mountain to eat the lush spring grass."

"Oh, no, you're not," said the troll as he clambered up on to the bridge. "I'm going to eat you for breakfast!"

"That's what you think," said the biggest Billy Goat Gruff. Then he lowered his horns, galloped along the bridge and butted the ugly troll. Up, up, up went the troll into the air... then down, down, down into the rushing river below. He disappeared below the swirling waters, and was gone.

"So much for his breakfast," thought the biggest Billy Goat Gruff. "Now what about mine!" And he walked in triumph over the bridge to join his two brothers on the mountain pastures. From then on anyone could cross the bridge whenever they liked—thanks to the three Billy Goats Gruff.

The Three Little Pigs (Flannel Board Story and Puppet Story) (see patterns on p. 450 or 488-489)

Once upon a time there were three little pigs, who left their mother and father to find their places in the world. All summer long, they roamed through the woods and over the plains, playing games and having fun. None were happier than the three little pigs, and they easily made friends with everyone. Wherever they went, they were given a warm welcome, but as summer drew to a close, they realized that folks were returning to their usual jobs, and preparing for winter.

Autumn came and it began to grow cold and rainy. The three little pigs decided they needed a real home. Sadly, they knew that the fun was over now and they must get to work like the others, or they'd be left in the cold and rain, with no roof over their heads.

They talked about what kind of home they would build. The first little pig said he'd build a house made from straw.

"It will only take a day," he said.

"It's too fragile," his brothers said. But the first pig didn't care. He was anxious to get back to playing.

Not quite so lazy, the second little pig went in search of planks of seasoned wood. "Clunk! Clunk! Clunk!" It took him two days to nail them together.

The third little pig did not like the wooden house.

"That's not the way to build a house!" he said. "It takes time, patience, and hard work to build a house that is strong enough to stand up to the wind and rain and snow, and most of all, protect us from the wolf!"

The days went by, and the wisest little pig's house took shape, brick by brick. From time to time, his brothers visited him, saying with a chuckle, "Why are you working so hard? Why don't you come and play?"

"No" said the last little pig. He diligently continued his work.

Soon his work was done, and just in time. One autumn day when no one expected it, along came the big bad wolf, scowling fiercely at the first pig's straw house.

"Little pig, little pig, let me in, let me in," ordered the wolf, his mouth watering.

"Not by the hair of my chinny, chin, chin!" replied the little pig in a tiny voice.

"Then I'll huff, and I'll puff, and I'll blow your house down!" growled the wolf angrily. The wolf puffed out his chest, and he huffed and he puffed and he blew the first little pig's house of straw right down.

Excited by his own cleverness, the wolf did not notice that the little pig had slithered out from underneath the heap of straw, and was dashing towards his brother's wooden house. When he realized that the little pig was escaping, the wolf grew wild with rage.

"Come back!" he roared, trying to catch the pig as he ran into the wooden house. The second little pig greeted his brother, shaking like a leaf.

"Open up! Open up! I only want to speak to you!" growled the hungry wolf.

"Go away," cried the two little pigs.

"Then I'll huff, and I'll puff, and I'll blow your house down!" growled the wolf angrily. So the angry wolf puffed out his chest and he huffed and he puffed and he huffed and he puffed and he blew the wooden house clean away.

Luckily, the wisest little pig had been watching the scene from the window of his own brick house, and he quickly opened the door to his fleeing brothers. And not a moment too soon, for the wolf was already hammering furiously on the door. This time, the wolf wasted no time talking. He puffed out his chest and he huffed and he puffed and he blew and blew and blew, but the little brick house wouldn't budge. The wolf tried again. He puffed out his chest and he huffed and he puffed and he huffed and he puffed, but still the little house stood strong.

The three little pigs watched him and their fear began to fade. Quite exhausted by his efforts, the wolf decided to try one of his tricks. He scrambled up a nearby ladder, on to the roof to have a look at the chimney. However, the now wiser little pigs knew exactly what the wolf was up to.

"Quick! Light the fire!" He is coming down the chimney."

The big bad wolf began to crawl down the chimney. It wasn't long before he felt something very hot on his tail. "Ouch!" he exclaimed. His tail was on fire. He jumped out of the chimney and tried to put the out the flames on his tail. Then he ran away as fast as he could.

The three happy little pigs, dancing round and round the yard, began to sing: "Tra-la-la! Tra-la-la! The big bad wolf will never come back...!" And he never did!

Tillie Triangle (Chalk Story)

Once there was a triangle called Tillie. *(Draw a triangle and add stick arms and legs and a round head.)*

Tillie was usually a very happy little triangle, but lately she had been feeling sad.

Tillie was unhappy with her shape. She didn't like just having three sides to her shape. She admired all the other shapes. The lovely square with four neat sides, the circle, all smooth and full.

Tillie decided to eat more food so she could grow another side. She ate and ate and ate. She ate candy and cookies and ice cream and wonderful cream puffs. Tillie ate for three days. On the fourth day when she woke up and looked in the mirror she had another side. She was a square. *(Erase triangle shaped body and draw a square)*

"Oh, boy," yelled Tillie. It worked.

But now Tillie thought, "If I keep on eating I will change again." So she kept right on eating all the sweet things she could find. Sure enough, after just two more days, Tillie woke up, looked in the mirror, and saw that she had become a circle. *(Erase square body and make a circle body.)* Tillie was so happy... at least for a while.

None of Tillie's friends recognized her. She had to tell them who she was. And worst of all Tillie couldn't stop eating. The more she ate the bigger she got. *(Erase circle body and make it bigger.)*

Tillie called the Doctor. He told her if she didn't stop eating she would pop. So Tillie made herself stop. She didn't eat anything.

In two days she was not so big. *(Erase circle and make it smaller.)* But Tillie was still lonesome for her old self.

In two more days, Tillie was a square again. *(Erase circle and make a square.)* Tillie was happy but she still wanted to be her old self again. After two more days it finally happened. Tillie woke up to find things back to normal. *(Erase square and draw triangle body.)* Tillie was so happy. She said, " I will never do such a silly thing again!"

Props needed to tell the story: You will need chalk and a chalkboard or a marking pen and chart paper.

Valencia Valentine (Flannel Board Story) by Pam Schiller (see patterns on p. 456-457)

It was almost Valentine's Day. Valencia couldn't wait. She had been looking forward to finally being old enough to be a store valentine. Her brothers, Victor and Vance, had left home last year, and now it was her turn.

She wanted to look vibrant. She put on her Victorian lace trim. She thought it was her very best outfit.

She found a good spot on the shelf at Valerie's Card Shop. She put on her best smile and waited. The first day came and went and no one bought Valencia. She was very sad. She didn't want to sound vain but she really thought she looked better than any other card. Valencia decided to put on her black hat with the lace veil. That should do it.

The next day was the same. People came and went and never even picked her up. When the school van came loaded with children and no one even noticed her, she was devastated.

That night Valencia gathered a honeysuckle vine and wrapped it around her middle. Then she picked a vacant spot on the shelf where she would be right in view of the door. Surely this will work, she thought.

But the next day was the same. When the store closed, Valencia started to cry. She was too sad to even think of another idea. Suddenly, she heard a voice beside her. It was Valentino, the Beanie Baby Bear. He said he knew a secret that would be just the right thing to make Valencia the most special Valentine on the shelf. He whispered it into her ear. Do you know what it was?

It was a special verse. Valencia wrote it right across her face with a violet crayon. It said:

"Roses are red,
Violets are blue,
Sugar is sweet

And so are you!"
And at last Valencia was victorious. She was the first valentine to be bought the next morning.

The Wind and the Sun (Listening Story) Aesop Fable

The Wind and the Sun were disputing which was stronger.

Suddenly they saw a traveler coming down the road, and the Sun said, "I see a way to decide our dispute. Whichever of us can cause that traveler to take off his cloak shall be regarded as the stronger. You begin."

So the Sun retired behind a cloud, and the Wind began to blow as hard as it could upon the traveler. But the harder he blew the more closely did the traveler wrap his cloak around him, until at last the Wind had to give up in despair.

Then the Sun came out and shone in all his glory upon the traveler, who soon found it too hot to walk with his cloak on.

Story Map

TITLE: ______________________

AUTHOR: ______________________

THEME: ______________________

PLOT

CHARACTERS

SETTING

CONFLICT

RESOLUTION

Games and Dances

Back-to-Back Lift

Children sit on the floor back to back and lean against each other to stand up. Locking arms may help.

Bunny Hop

Children stand in line with their hands on the waist of the child in front them. Everyone moves around the room to music, hopping in unison.

Cat and Mouse

This is a simple game of chase with you or one child being the Cat and the rest of the children being Mice. Cat chases Mice. The Mouse who is tagged becomes the next "Cat." You might also use the rhyme, "Old Gray Cat," (see Chants and Rhymes) to play a version of this game.

Circle 'Round the Zero

Circle 'round the zero.
Find your lovin' zero.
Back, back, zero.
Side, side, zero.
Front, front, zero.
Tap your lovin' zero.

Sing the song. "It" walks around the circle until the line, "Find your lovin' zero." Then It stops and stands back to back with the nearest child. Everyone sings the song again and It moves to the side and front as directed by the lyrics, and then taps the chosen child's shoulder. That child is the next "It."

Cooperative Musical Chairs

This game is a variation of Musical Chairs. Place chairs back to back in a line with one less chair than there are children playing the game. (This game proceeds best if there are eight or fewer children.) Play a piece of music. Encourage the children to walk around the chairs until the music stops. When the music stops everyone sits in a chair. Chairs can be shared so no one should be left out. The idea is to get everyone on a chair so everyone wins. Remove a chair and go again. The game becomes more amusing as more and more children try to fit into fewer and fewer chairs. Continue playing for as long as the children are interested.

Copycat

Two children stand face to face. One child creates actions and makes faces. The second child mimics the faces and actions.

Dog and Bone

Children sit in a circle. One child—"It"— walks around the outside of the circle, carrying a paper or plastic bone. Eventually It drops the bone behind a player. That player picks up the bone and chases It around the circle. If she taps It before they get around the circle, It goes to the "doghouse" (center of the circle). If she doesn't, It takes her place in the circle. The player with the bone becomes the new It, and the game continues.

Dreidel

Each player puts one token, such as nuts, raisins, marbles, toothpicks, pennies, and so on in the pot (bowl). One player spins the driedel. If the dreidel lands on "N," the player receives nothing. If it lands on "G," the player receives all the tokens in the pot. If it lands on "H," the player gets half. If it lands on "S," the player adds two tokens to the pot. The game continues until one player has won all the tokens.
Directions to make a dreidel: Collapse the top of a pint milk carton to make a square box. Cover the box with paper. Draw an "X" on the top and bottom of the box to create a center spot. Push a pencil through the center of the carton. Write the dreidel letters, "G," "H," "S," and "N" on each of the four sides of the box.

Drop the Handkerchief

Choose one child to be "It," while the other children sit in a circle facing the center. The child who is It skips or walks around the outside of the circle and casually drops the handkerchief behind one of the children sitting in the circle. This child picks up the handkerchief and chases It around the circle. It tries to run around the circle and sit in the second child's spot without being tagged. If It is not tagged, then she sits in her new spot in the circle and the child with the handkerchief is now It. If It is tagged, then she is It for another round.

Variations: Use a heart and play Drop the Heart, or a specific color of handkerchief for color recognition.

Duck, Duck, Goose

Children sit in a circle. One child—"It"—walks around the outside of the circle, tapping each player on the head and saying, "Duck." Eventually It taps a player and says, "Goose" instead. The tapped player gets up and chases It around the circle. If he taps It before they get around the circle, he gets to go back to his place. If he doesn't, he becomes the new It and the game continues.

Farmer in the Dell

Choose one child to be Farmer. Other children walk in a circle around the Farmer. Sing the song together:

The farmer in the dell, the farmer in the dell.
Heigh-ho the derry-o, the farmer in the dell.

The farmer takes a wife/husband/friend. *(farmer brings a second child into the circle)*
The farmer takes a wife/husband/friend.
Heigh-ho the derry-o, the farmer takes a wife/husband/friend.

The wife/husband/friend takes a child... *(wife chooses a third child to join in the circle)*
The child takes a dog...
The dog takes a cat...
The cat takes a rat...
The rat takes the cheese...

The cheese stands alone... (*everyone except cheese leaves the center of the circle)*

Feather Race

Make a masking tape start and finish line about 4" apart. Place two feathers on the start line. Provide straws, a paper towel tube, paper plates, and basters to use as pushers. Invite two children to each choose a "pusher" and then attempt to use their "pusher" to move the feather from the start to the finish line. They cannot touch the feather with their pusher. The first child to get the feather to the finish line is the winner and can then compete against another challenger.

Feed the Seal Game

Photocopy the pattern of the seal in the ocean animal patterns. Color it, cut it out, laminate it, and glue it to the top of a small stationery box. Cut a penny-size hole next to the seal's mouth. Provide tweezers and fish crackers. Invite the children to use the tweezers to pick up fish crackers and drop them in the hole next to the seal's mouth. When they are finished they can open the box and eat the fish crackers.

Follow the Leader

Select one child to be the leader. Other children line up behind the first child and copy his movements.

Fruit Basket Turnover

Divide the children into four groups and have them sit in the four corners of the room. Assign each group one of these fruits: bananas, apples, oranges, and grapes. Distribute a sheet of yellow construction paper to each member of the bananas group, red papers to the apples group, orange papers to the oranges group, and purple papers to the grapes group. Select a child to be "It," and instruct the rest of the children to sit down on their pieces of paper. Have "It" stand in the center, close his or her eyes, and call out, "Fruit salad!" The children stand up and find a seat on a different-colored sheet of paper to become a member of another fruit group. "It" tries to catch a child before he or she is able to sit down. That child other child then becomes the new "It."

Go In and Out the Windows

Go in and out the windows. *("It" walks around circle, weaving in and out between children)*
Go in and out the windows,
Go in and out the windows,
As we have done before.

Additional verses:
Stand and face your partner... *("It" chooses a partner)*
Now follow her/him to London... *("It" and partner weave through circle)*
Bow before you leave her/him... *("It" leaves partner [new "It"] and joins circle)*

Hide and Seek

One child is "It." All other players hide while It counts to a certain number. At the end of the count, It gives a warning ("Ready or not, here I come!") and then seeks out the hiders.

Hokey Pokey

(form a circle and act out the words)
You put your right hand in.
You take your right hand out.
You put your right hand in,
And you shake it all about.
You do the Hokey Pokey, (hold hands in the air and shake them)
And you turn yourself around.
That's what it's all about.

Repeat verses, using other body parts.

Hopscotch

Draw a Hopscotch grid on the sidewalk or floor with chalk. It is one square, one square, then two, then one, then two, then one, and finally two. Number the squares 1-10. Provide a chip or a rock. Children play this game one child at a time. The first child tosses the rock onto the first square of the grid, hops over that square, and then follow the pattern of the other squares, hopping on one foot and then jumping on two. At the end of the grid the child turns around and hops and jumps the patterns back to start (still jumping over the square with the rock.) The next child then takes a turn. When it is the first child's turn again, she tosses the rock or chip onto the square with the "two" written on it and goes through the grid again hopping and jumping but not touching square number two. The object of the game is to toss the chip onto each square during consecutive turns and execute the jumping and hopping pattern without putting a second foot down on single squares and without stepping in the square where the rock is.

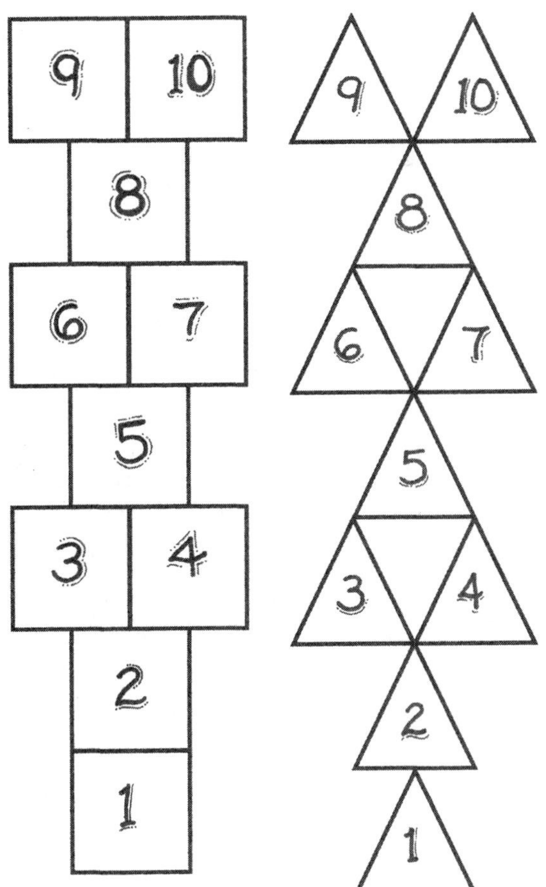

Variation: Make triangles instead of squares for your design.

Hot and Cold Hide and Seek

Hide an object in the classroom. As children look for it tell them if they are hot or cold. They are hot when they are close to the object and cold when they are not close to the object.

I Spy

Gather the children in a group and invite them to find items in the room. Choose easy-to-find things so the children can have a high level of success as they first learn to play. Increase the level of difficulty as children become more familiar with the game.

It's a Very Simple Dance to Do

Come on and do a dance with me.
It's just a little step or two.
I'll teach you how.
We'll start right now.
It's a very simple dance to do.

First you clap your hands. *(clap three times)*
Then stomp your feet. *(stomp three times)*
It's a very simple dance to do.

Wait I forgot to tell you.
There's another little step or two.
Turn around *(turn around)*
And touch your toes. *(touch your toes)*
It's a very simple dance to do.

Clap your hands. *(clap three times)*
Stomp your feet. *(stomp three times)*
Turn around *(turn around)*
And touch your toes. *(touch your toes)*
It's a very simple dance to do.

Wait I forgot to tell you.
There's another little step or two.
Pull your ears *(pull your ears)*
And flap your arms. *(flap your arms)*
It's a very simple dance to do.

Clap your hands. *(suit actions to words)*
Stomp your feet.
Turn around
And touch your toes.
Pull your ears
And flap your arms.
It's a very simple dance to do.

Wait I forgot to tell you.
There's another step and then we're through.
Stretch up high. *(stretch up high)*
All fall down. *(fall down)*
It's a very simple dance to do.

Clap your hands. *(suit actions to words)*
Stomp your feet.
Turn around
And touch your toes.
Pull your ears
And flap your arms.
Now stretch up high.
All fall down.
It's a very simple dance to do.

(Repeat last chorus)

Leap Frog

Select one child to be the "frog." Have the other children get on the floor on their hands and knees and crouch down. Invite the frog to leap over the children by placing her hands on the back of each child for support while she straddles her legs around their body and "leaps" over them.

London Bridge Is Falling Down

London Bridge is falling down,
Falling down, falling down.
London Bridge is falling down,
My fair lady.

Take the key and lock her up,
Lock her up, lock her up.
Take the key and lock her up,
My fair lady.

Repeat first verse

Two children stand facing each other, holding hands up over their heads to make an arch (bridge). The rest of the children form a line and go under the bridge and then around and back under the bridge again as the class sings the song, "London Bridge Is Falling Down." When the children sing the words, "my fair lady," the children who are making the bridge bring their arms down to catch the child who is passing under the bridge at that moment. As the children continue to sing the song, have the two bridge makers gently swing their arms back and forth to rock the captive. At the end of the song, the captive takes the place of one of the bridge makers and the game starts again.

Monkey See, Monkey Do

One child is selected as the Lead Monkey. The Lead Monkey creates an action and the rest of the "monkeys" copy it.

Mother, May I?

Play a teacher-directed game of Mother, May I? Call out to children one at a time, asking them to make animal movements such as puppy skips, cat jumps, horse gallops, and so on toward you. Encourage the children to make the sounds of the animals as they move. The children can't move until they ask, "Mother, May I?" The teacher responds, "Yes, you may."

The Mulberry Bush

Here we go 'round the mulberry bush, *(hold hands and walk in circle)*
The mulberry bush, the mulberry bush.
Here we go 'round the mulberry bush
So early in the morning.

This is the way we wash our clothes, *(suit actions to words)*
Wash our clothes, wash our clothes.
This is the way we wash our clothes
So early Monday morning.

Additional verses:
This is the way we iron our clothes. . . Tuesday morning.
This is the way we scrub the floors. . . Wednesday morning.
This is the way we sew our clothes. . .Thursday morning.
This is the way we sweep the house. . .Friday morning.
This is the way we bake our bread. . .Saturday morning.
This is the way we go to church. . . Sunday morning.

Musical Freeze

Invite the children to dance or move in a circle while a favorite song plays. When you stop the music, they stop moving and "freeze" in that position. When you start the music again, they start moving.

Musical Hide and Seek

Hide a musical toy just out of sight and see if children can find it.

One Elephant

One elephant went out to play,
Out on a spider's web one day.
He had such enormous fun,
He called for another elephant to come.

Children sit in a circle. One child places one arm out in front to make a "trunk," then walks around the circle while the group sings the song. When the group sings "called for another elephant to come," the first child chooses another to become an "elephant." The first child extends her free hand between her legs to make a "tail." The second child extends one arm to make a trunk and grabs hold of the first child's tail. The two walk trunk-to-tail as the song continues. Repeat the song and add more children to create a line of elephants.

Pease Porridge Hot

(Clap hands with a partner)
Pease porridge hot.
Pease porridge cold.
Pease porridge in the pot
Nine days old.

Some like it hot.
Some like it cold.
Some like it in the pot
Nine days old.

Pyramids

On a mat or the soft ground, show children how to make a pyramid. Have three children get on their hands and knees. Have two more children get on the backs of the first three children. Make sure the second group of children straddles their friends on the bottom with one arm and leg on one friend and the other arm and leg on a second child. Place a stuffed animal or doll on top of the second row of children. (Supervise closely at all times!)

Punchinello

Here Comes Punchinello, Punchinello.
Here comes Punchinello, funny you. *(children walk in a circle)*

What can you do Punchinello, Punchinello?
What can you do, Punchinello, funny you? *(child in the center of the circle initiates a movement)*
We can do it, too, Punchinello, Punchinello.
We can do it, too, Punchinello, funny you. *(children in the circle copy the movement)*

Who do you choose, Punchinello, Punchinello?
Who do you choose, Punchinello, funny you? *(child in the center chooses another child to take her place)*

Red Light! Green Light!

Choose one child to be the "stoplight." The other children line up side-by-side about 30 feet (9 meters) away from and facing the stoplight. When the child playing the stoplight turns his back to the other children he says, "Green light!" and the children may run toward him. When he turns back around and says, "Red Light!" all of the children must stop. If the child playing the stoplight sees any of the other children move after he has said "Red light!" then he says the child's name and that child must go back to the beginning. The first child to reach the stoplight is the stoplight in the next game of "Red Light! Green Light!"

Red Rover

Play a new version of Red Rover. Say "Red Rover, Red Rover, let (child's name) come over." As the child runs to the other side, say "Blue Thunder, Blue Thunder, let (child's name) go under." Let the child pass under the arms of the children in the line and then take a place at the end of that line.

Ring Around the Rosie

Ring around the rosie
Pocket full of posies,
Ashes, ashes,
All fall down.

Children hold hands and walk in a circle. Everyone falls down on the words "all fall down."

Roly Poly Relay Races

Divide the children into two teams. Use masking tape or yarn to create a start and a finish line, encourage one child from each team to roll from the start to the finish line in relay fashion. The team whose members finish the rolls first is the winning team.

Shadow Games

During outdoor playtime invite the children to look for shadows on the playground. Can they find shadows with a pattern? Can they use their own bodies to create shadows? Can they make up a shadow dance? Can they catch their shadow?

Shoo Fly

Shoo fly, don't bother me, *(walk in a circle to the left)*
Shoo fly, don't bother me, *(walk in a circle to the right)*
Shoo fly, don't bother me, *(walk in a circle to the left)*
For I don't want to play. *(place hands on hips and shake head no)*

Flies in the buttermilk *(walk around shooing flies)*
Shoo fly, shoo.
Flies in the buttermilk
Shoo fly, shoo.
Flies in the buttermilk
Shoo fly, shoo.
Please just go away. *(place hands on hips and shake head no)*

Shoo fly don't bother me, *(walk to the left in a circle)*
Shoo fly don't bother me. *(walk to the right in a circle)*
Shoo fly don't bother me, *(walk to the left in a circle)*
Come back another day. *(wave good-bye)*

Simon Says

Choose one child to be "Simon." All the other children stand side by side in a line facing Simon. The child playing Simon gives the other children orders that they have to carry out, but only when the orders follow the phrase "Simon says…" (for example, *"Simon says touch your nose."*). If a child follows an order that Simon did not say (for example, *"Touch your nose."),* then she is out and must sit down. The last child standing becomes the new Simon for the next game of "Simon Says."

Spider Walk

Four children stand back to back in a circle. They hook elbows for support then attempt to walk using eight legs.

Square Dance

Have the children choose a partner. Arrange them in a square. You may want to make a masking tape square on the floor for the children to use. Invite them to follow these simple steps:

Bow to your partner. *(bow)*
Swing your partner. *(lock arms and spin around twice)*
Do-si-do. *(fold arms across chest and "back" around your partner)*
Promenade. *(partners hold hands, right and left hands together and walk around the square)*

Torchlight Relay

Make two torches. Use paper towel tubes for the torches and orange construction paper for the flames. Divide the children into two relay teams. The idea is to run a lap and then pass the torch to the next team member. The first team to finish wins. This game is in honor of the torch that is run in Tel Aviv to begin the Hanukkah season.

Tug of Peace

Take Hula Hoops outdoors and encourage the children to play the Tug of Peace Game. It takes cooperative effort. Children sit around the Hula Hoop and grab hold with both hands. By pulling back on the hoop, can everyone stand up together?

Tummy Ticklers

Have the children lie on the floor on their backs with their heads on someone else's tummy. Do something silly to make the children start laughing, ask one child to say, "Ha" and the next child to say "Ha, ha," and the third to say, "Ha, ha, ha," and so on. What is making their heads jiggle? This activity should cause contagious laughter.

Waggle Dance

Bees do the Waggle Dance to communicate with each other. The direction they fly when they return to the hive lets the other bees know where pollen has been located. Bees also will circle around an area where food has been located. They wiggle their bottoms and circle the area. Explain to the children that this is similar to the Waggle Dance. Place a flower or a replica of a flower on the floor. Invite the children to spread their wings (arms) and circle the flower while wiggling their bottoms. After a few minutes change the location of the flower and invite the "bees" (children) to follow. Music adds to the fun.

Who Stole the Cookie from the Cookie Jar?

Who stole the cookie from the cookie jar?
(Name a child) took the cookies from the cookie jar.
Child says—Who me?
Class says—Yes, you.
Child says—*Couldn't be.*
Class says—Then who?

(Child who was named names another child) took the cookies from the cookie jar.
Who me?
Yes, you.
Couldn't be.
Then who?

The part of the chant that is in italics is said by the child who is being accused.

Pat your thighs and snap in a rhythmic motion as you say the chant. Continue until everyone has been accused. End by accusing the Cookie Monster.

Who's Got the Button?

Have children sit in a circle. Choose a child to be "It." Give It a button. Have the children close their eyes. Help It choose a friend to which he will give the button. Invite the children to open their eyes and try to guess who has the button. The child who guesses correctly becomes the next It.

Whose Dog Art Thou?

Bow, wow, wow. *(face a partner and stomp three times)*
Whose dog art thou? *(point index finger on left and right hand at partner)*
Little Tommy Tucker's dog. *(hold hands out to side)*
Bow, wow, wow. *(face partner and stomp three times)*

Recipes (Cooking)

Ants on a Log

peanut butter
celery
raisins
plastic knife

Invite the children to spread peanut butter on a strip of celery and then place raisins on top of the peanut butter to represent ants.

Apple Cider

32 oz. apple juice
1 teaspoon cinnamon
¼ cup lemon juice
2 tablespoons honey
measuring cups and spoons
large saucepan
mixing spoon
stove or hot plate

Mix, heat, and serve. Enjoy the wonderful aroma.

Baggie Ice Cream

One serving:
½ cup milk
1 tablespoon sugar
¼ teaspoon vanilla
small resealable plastic bag
large resealable plastic bag
3 tablespoons rock salt

Place the milk, sugar, and vanilla in the small bag and seal it. Place the small bag, the rock salt, and ice cubes in the large bag and seal. Shake.

Variation: For Peppermint Ice Cream, crush 3 pieces of peppermint candy (peppermint wheels work well) and add to the ingredients in the small plastic bag.

Bird Nest Candy

1 small package of butterscotch chips
1 small package of chocolate chips
1 large can of Chinese noodles
bowl or saucepan
wooden spoon
hot plate or microwave

Combine one small package of butterscotch chips and one small package of chocolate chips. Melt in a saucepan over low heat or in a microwave. Add Chinese noodles. When cool enough to touch, shape into bird nest. Let cool. Eat and enjoy!

Blender drinks

Banana Milk Shake

2 fully ripened bananas
1 cup chilled milk
1 tablespoon sugar
¼ teaspoon vanilla
blender

Peel and smash bananas. Put into blender. Slowly add milk and sugar and vanilla. Makes 4 small shakes.

Milkanilla

4 ounces milk
½ teaspoon sugar
⅛ teaspoon vanilla
1 drop food coloring
blender

Mix in blender and enjoy! Makes one individual shake.

Purple Cow Shakes

1 small scoop of vanilla ice cream
2 tablespoons of grape juice concentrate
2 tablespoons of milk

Place ingredients in a baby food jar. Close the lid and shake, shake, shake. Makes one individual shake. Enjoy!

Donuts

Invite the children to cut holes in refrigerator biscuits. Drop the biscuits in a deep fryer and fry them until they are golden brown and floating on the top of the grease. Remove from the oil and let drain. Invite the children to dust their donut with powdered sugar. (Supervise closely at all times!)

Frozen Yogurt

Place yogurt in a small container or keep in its original container. Put the container inside a coffee can. Fill the coffee can with ice and rock salt. Invite children to roll the can back and forth for about 15 minutes. When you take the yogurt out, it will be frozen.

Fruit Kabobs

Using plastic knives, help the children cut fruit into chunks. Invite them to thread fruit onto skewers.

Gelatin Jigglers

Mix flavored gelatin with half the amount of water suggested on the box. Let congeal. Cut into shapes or use a cookie cutter to cut.

Variations: Cut into Heart Shaped Gelatin Jigglers for Valentine's Day.

Homemade Applesauce

6 apples
½ cup water
1 teaspoon lemon juice
¼ cup sugar
pinch cinnamon
large saucepan
hot plate or stove
colander

Peel, core, and cut up six apples into a large saucepan. Add water, lemon juice, and sugar. Cook until tender. Add a pinch of cinnamon. Press through a colander and serve.

Homemade Butter

Allow a pint of whipping cream to reach room temperature. Pour a small amount of the cream in a baby food jar. Place the lid on the jar and shake, shake, shake. The butter will form a ball. There will be a residue of watery milk. Remove the ball of butter and serve on crackers or bread. Salt to taste.

Homemade Peanut Butter

1½ tablespoon vegetable oil
1 cup roasted peanuts
½ teaspoon salt
blender

Put ingredients into an electric blender. Blend to desired smoothness. Add a little more oil if needed.

Homemade Toothpaste

Mix one tablespoon of baking soda with two or three drops of peppermint extract. Stir in a small amount of water to make a paste.

Humpty Dumpty Eggs (Deviled Eggs)

Make Humpty Dumpty Eggs as you would deviled eggs. Boil eggs and invite the children to help peel the hard boiled eggs. Show them how to slice the eggs and how to remove the yolks and smash them. Add sweet relish and mayonnaise and let the children help stuff the Humpty Dumpty Eggs. Serve for snack.

Individual Puddings

Put one tablespoon of instant pudding mix in a small jar and add warm milk. Screw the lid on securely and let the children shake the jar. In a few minutes the pudding will set.

Latkes

1 grated onion
1 teaspoon salt
1 egg
6 medium potatoes (washed, pared and grated)
mixing bowl and spoon
3 tablespoons flour
½ teaspoon baking powder
cooking oil
frying pan
paper towels

Mix the onion, salt, and egg with the potatoes. Add flour and baking powder. Drop by spoonfuls into a hot oiled frying pan. Brown on both sides. Drain on paper towels. Serve with applesauce.

No-Bake Cookies

½ cup raisins
½ cup chopped dates
2 tablespoon honey
mixing bowl and spoon
graham crackers
resealable plastic bag
rolling pin

Pour raisins, dates, and honey into mixing bowl. Put several graham crackers in a resealable plastic bag and crush them with a rolling pin. Add crushed crackers to the other mixture until it's dry enough to roll into balls.

No-Bake Pumpkin Custard/Pudding

Mix two tablespoons of pumpkin pie filling, one tablespoon of marshmallow crème, and one tablespoon of whipped topping in a cup.

No-Cook Peanut Butter Balls

½ cup peanut butter
½ cup honey
1 cup nonfat powdered milk
mixing bowl and spoon

Mix ingredients well. Squeeze and pull until shiny and soft. Roll into balls and chill before eating.

Recipes

No-Cook Orange Ball Cookies

35 vanilla wafers
¼ cup orange juice
2 tablespoons sugar
powdered sugar
mixing bowl and spoon

Crush vanilla wafers. Add orange juice and sugar. Mix well. Roll into balls with moistened hands. Roll balls in powdered sugar.

Peanut Butter Playdough/Balls

½ cup peanut butter
½ cup honey
1 cup nonfat powdered milk
mixing bowl and spoon

Mix well. Squeeze and pull until shiny and soft.

Toasted Pumpkin Seeds

pumpkin seeds
frying pan
oil
cookie sheet
wooden spoon
garlic salt
oven

Wash the pumpkin seeds and dry them. Sauté the seeds in 1½ tablespoons of salad oil for two or three minutes. Place seeds on a cookie sheet and spread them with a wooden spoon. Sprinkle lightly with garlic salt. Bake at 250 degrees until brown (30-40 minutes). Cool and eat.

Recipes (Arts and Crafts)

Recipes

Bubble Soap

1 teaspoon glycerin
½ cup liquid detergent
½ cup water
container
spoon

Mix all ingredients gently. For best results, let the mixture sit overnight before blowing bubbles.

Colored Glue

Add tempera paint to glue to make various colors. Put in plastic squeeze bottles. Let the children squeeze their pictures instead of painting.

Colored Rock Salt

Dye rock salt by placing food coloring in alcohol and letting the salt sit in the food coloring-alcohol mixture for about 10 minutes. Drain on a paper towel. Use for art activities.

Epsom Salt Solution

Mix 1 cup of hot water with 4 tablespoons of Epsom salt. "Paint" over drawings or paintings. When dried, it creates a glazed appearance.

Face Paint

2 tablespoons cold cream
½ teaspoon glycerin
1 teaspoon cornstarch
1 teaspoon dry tempera
small mixing bowl and spoon

Stir ingredients together until well mixed.

Fingerpaint Recipe #1

Pour a tablespoon of liquid starch onto paper or directly onto tabletop. Sprinkle on a little powdered tempera. Let the children mix.

Fingerpaint Recipe #2

2 cups hot water
⅓ cup of cornstarch dissolved in ¾ cup of cold water
1 envelope Knox gelatin dissolved in ¼ cup of cold water
½ cup of Ivory Flakes (or Ivory Snow)
large saucepan
mixing spoon
hot plate or stove
containers
powdered tempera paint

Add 2 cups of hot water to cornstarch mixture and cook. Stir until the mixture is clear. Add gelatin mixture and stir to blend. Add Ivory Flakes or Ivory Snow. Divide into containers. Add desired color of powdered tempera to each container.

Fingerpaint Recipe #3

1½ cups of laundry starch
1 quart boiling water
1½ cups soap flakes
½ cup talcum
large saucepan
mixing spoon
hot plate or stove
containers
powdered tempera paint

Mix starch and cold water into a creamy paste. Add boiling water and cook until mixture becomes transparent or glossy-looking. Stir continually. Add talcum and allow mixture to cool. Add soap flakes and stir until they are evenly distributed. Pour into containers and add powdered tempera to color.

Gak

2 cups glue
1½ cups tap water
2 teaspoons Borax
1 cup hot water
food coloring
mixing bowls and spoons
shallow tray
resealable plastic bags

Combine glue, tap water, and food coloring in a bowl. In a larger bowl, dissolve Borax in hot water. Slowly add glue mixture to Borax. It will thicken quickly and be difficult to mix. Mix well and drain off excess water. Let stand for a few minutes, then pour into a shallow tray. Let dry for 10 minutes. Store in resealable plastic bags (will keep for 2–3 weeks).

Goop

2 cups salt
1 cup water
1 cup cornstarch
saucepan
mixing spoon
hot plate or stove
resealable plastic bag or covered container

Cook salt and ½ cup water 4-5 minutes. Remove from heat. Add cornstarch and ½ cup water. Return to heat. Stir until mixture thickens. Store in resealable plastic bag or covered container.

Icing Paint

1 cup powdered tempera paint
2 tablespoons wallpaper paste
¼ to ½ cup liquid starch
mixing bowl and spoon
Popsicle sticks

Mix until thick enough to spread like frosting. Use Popsicle sticks to spread on cardboard.

Paints

To one pint of tempera add the following ingredients to change paint consistency.

Slimy Paint: add 2 tablespoons Karo (corn syrup)
Gritty Paint: add ½ teaspoon sand
Slippery Paint: add 1 teaspoon glycerin
Lumpy Paint: add 1 tablespoon flour
Rough Paint: add 1 tablespoon sawdust
Shiny Paint: add ½ cup sugar
Sparkly Paint: add ½ cup salt (use immediately)
Creamy Paint: add ¼ cup liquid starch

Thick Paint: mix 3 parts powder to 1 part water

Helpful Hints:
Add liquid soap to any paint to make it easier to wash out of clothes.
Add 1 teaspoon alcohol to paint to keep it from souring.

Paste (that will keep)

2 tablespoons flour
½ teaspoon alum
oil of wintergreen (optional)
mixing bowl and spoon
double boiler
hot plate or stove

Mix flour with a small amount of water to form a paste. Pour 2 cups of boiling water into paste mixture. Boil for 3 minutes in a double boiler. Add alum. Add oil of wintergreen and food coloring if desired.

Playdough

3 cups flour
1½ cups salt
3 tablespoons oil
2 tablespoons cream of tartar
3 cups water
saucepan
mixing spoon
hot plate or stove

Combine all ingredients. Cook over very low heat until mixture is no longer sticky to the touch. Add food coloring to make colored playdough.

Puff Paint

2 tablespoons tempera paint
⅓ cup of white glue
2 cups shaving cream
Mix and use as finger paint.

Scented Playdough

Add 1 teaspoon scented extract (peppermint, vanilla, lemon, etc.) to basic playdough recipe. You can use massage oils in place of extract if desired.

Scratch and Sniff Paint

Mix flavored gelatin as directed using half the amount of water. Use the mixture as paint. When it dries children can scratch and sniff.

Soap Paint

1 cup Ivory Snow
water
mixing bowl and spoon
electric mixer
food coloring (optional)

Mix soap and enough water to form consistency of whipping cream. Beat with mixer until the mixture looks like shaving cream. Add food coloring if desired. Use like finger paint.

Soapsuds Clay

¾ cup soap powder
1 tablespoon warm water
mixing bowl
electric mixer

Mix soap powder and water in a bowl. Beat with electric mixer until it has the consistency of clay.

Tactile Fingerpaint

Mix 1 teaspoon salt into fingerpaint and let children enjoy a tactile fingerpainting experience.

Props and Concentration Games

Air Tent

Materials
clear plastic painter's drop cloth
duct tape
two fans
plastic garbage sacks (10-gallon size)

- Cut the corners off of the drop cloth to make a circle.
- Lay the circle flat on the floor. It will be about 10'-12' (3m-5m) in diameter.
- Pouch it up in the middle, creating a final size of about 6'-8' in diameter.
- Tape the perimeter of the circle to the floor using duct tape.
- Leave a 1½' section untaped in the perimeter to cut a slit for a door.
- Cut two 1' diameter circles into each side of the tent. Cut these about 18" up from the base. This is where you will attach the fans.
- Use the plastic garbage bags to make two 2½' long sleeves by cutting off the bottom of the bags. These sleeves will extend from the fans to the circles cut in the tent.
- Tape one end of the sleeve inside the circles cut in the tent and the other end to the face of the fan.
- Cut a 3' (approx. 1m) vertical slit in the space left for the door. Create an overlap so that air will not escape from the tent.
- Turn the fans on and watch the tent inflate.
- Use the tent for story time or any circle activities.
- Warn children not to touch the fans.

(Supervise closely at all times!)

(See illustrations on the next page.)

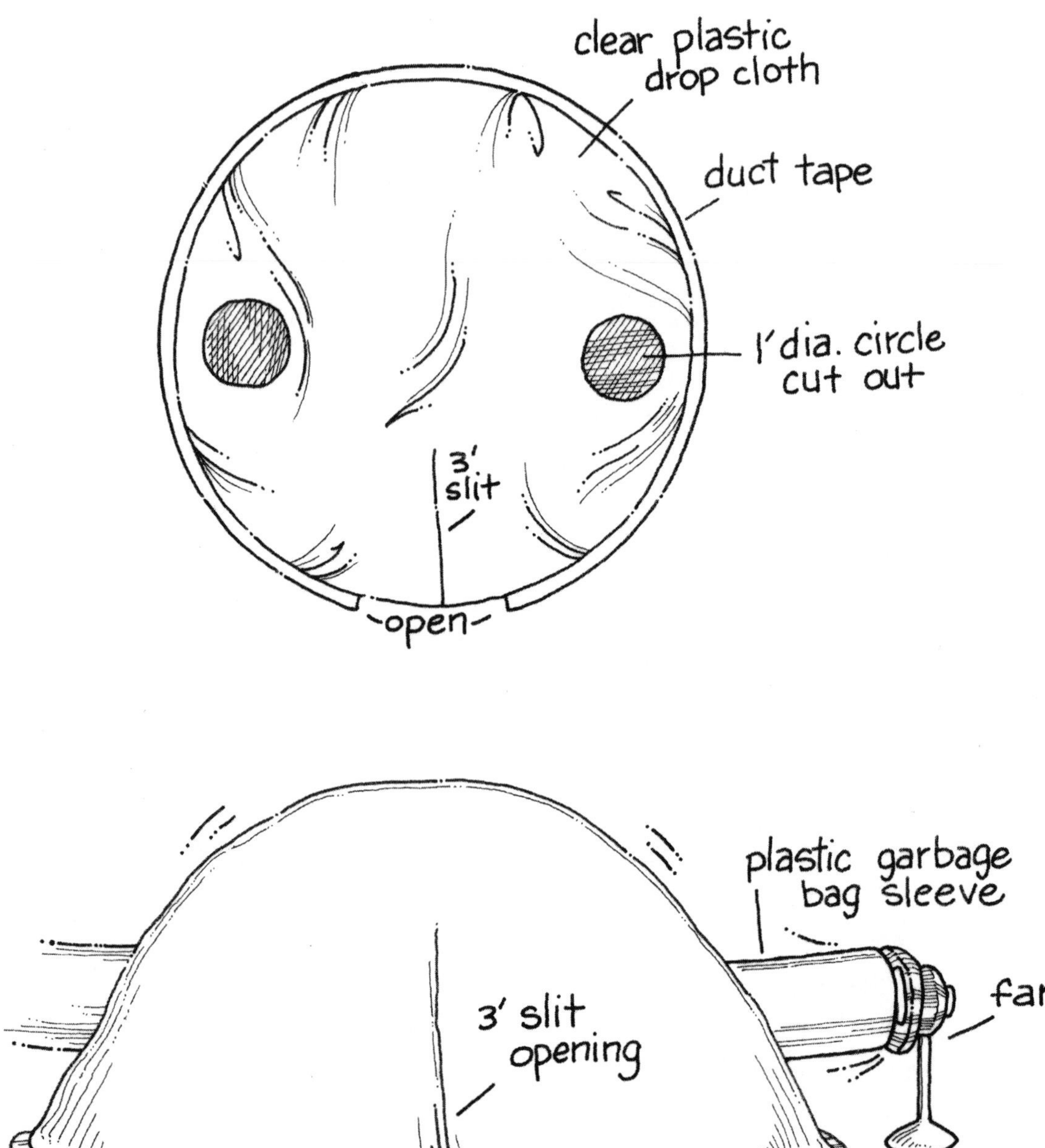
clear plastic
drop cloth
duct tape
1′ dia. circle
cut out
3′
slit
open
plastic garbage
bag sleeve
fan
3′ slit
opening

Animal Footprint Concentration Game

Make two photocopies of the Animal Footprint Patterns (Appendix p. 499). Color and laminate both copies. Cut one copy into individual footprint cards. Invite the children to match the cut-out cards to the pattern card or use the cards to play concentration.

Animal Masks

Photocopy the Animal Mask patterns (Appendix p. 511-517). Color them, cut them out, and laminate them. Glue the patterns to a paper plate and attach the plate to a tongue depressor. Cut out the eyes using a craft knife (adult only).

Animal Puppets

Use the animals in the Animal Patterns (Appendix p. 463-467). Photocopy the animals you want to use. Color, cut them out, laminate, and glue them to tongue depressors.

Animal Face Paper Bag Puppets

Paper Bag Puppets 1

Use lunch-size paper bags. Color, cut, and laminate the Animal Mask Patterns (Appendix p. 511-517). Glue the faces to the bottom of the paper bags.

Paper Bag Puppets 2

Provide lunch-size paper bags, construction paper, and crayons or markers. Invite the children to create their own animal faces.

Apple and Worm Match Game

Cut three apple shapes from red construction paper. Cut one hole in the first apple, two holes in the second apple, and three holes in the third apple. Cut six worms from green, yellow, or brown construction paper. Encourage children to match worms to holes.

Aroma Canisters

Soak cotton balls in scented oil. Put the cotton balls inside a margarine tub with holes poked in the lid. Make sure lids are taped or glued on securely. Scented oils are available at most candle and craft stores. Chamomile, orange, and lavender are soothing scents. For your own reference, write the name of the scent on each canister.

Bear Caves

Roll five brown lunch-size paper bags ¾ of the way down from the top of the bag to create a small bear caves. Number the caves 1-5. Encourage the children to count the appropriate number of bear counters into each cave.

Bird and Nest Matching Game

Make five photocopies of the Bird and Nest patterns (Appendix p. 500). Color, cut them out, and laminate. Make a matching game by either putting matching colored dots on the birds and the nests or by putting the numerals 1-5 on the birds and a corresponding set of dots on the nests.

Bound Books

The following are suggestions for making classroom books.

Baggie Books

Make baggie books by stapling five resealable plastic bags together across the bottom (the "unzippered" side). Cover the staples with duct tape. Let the children draw illustrations for the book on paper cut to fit inside the bags.

Cereal Box Books

Cut the front panel off cereal boxes. Punch two holes in the sides and attach book rings. Children can illustrate pages or dictate stories on paper cut to fit inside the books.

Felt Books

Sew together five felt squares on the left side to make a book. Cut felt scraps into geometric shapes and place them in a sandwich bag with a zipper top. Children can create objects, make sets, or reproduce patterns on the blank pages with the felt shapes.

Greeting Card Books

Cut the front off old greeting cards. Lay the cards on construction paper and trace around them. Cut them out for the backs of the books. Cut paper to fit in the books, then staple it between the card and construction paper. Let the children draw pictures or write stories in the books.

Photo Books

Make photocopies of photos you have collected. Cut them out and glue them onto 4" x 5" pieces of construction paper. Place photos in resealable plastic bags, two photos back to back in each bag. Staple all the bags together at their "unzippered" ends (so you can open them). Use colored tape to cover the staples.

Stapled Books

Fold two pieces of paper in half and staple. Have the children draw pictures, use stickers, or glue magazine pictures in the book.

Bowling Pins/Game

Collect several potato chip cans. Paint or cover them with colorful contact paper or construction paper. If you need to weight them, drop a few small stones in each one. Make sure the lids are glued and/or taped on securely.

Bug Eyes

Cut two connecting sections from a Styrofoam egg crate to form a pair of glasses. Cut small penny-size holes in the bottom of each crate. Hook pipe cleaners through the sides of the crates to form earpieces for the glasses. Decorate with paint or markers.

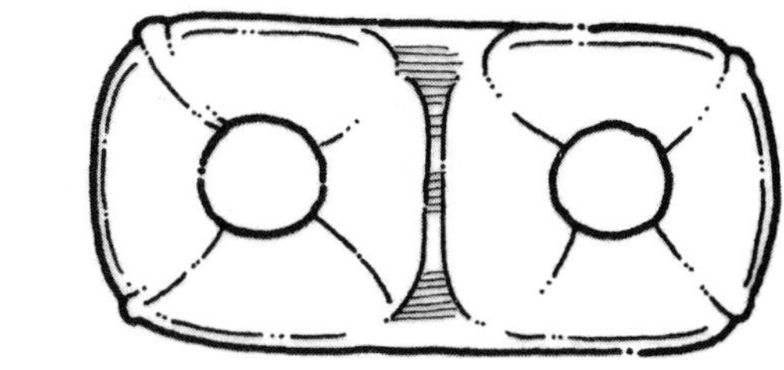

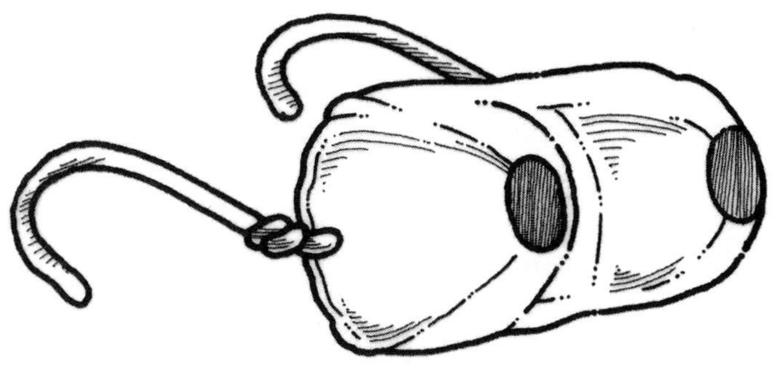

Butterfly Match Game

Make multiple photocopies of the butterfly in the Insect Concentration Game patterns (Appendix p. 506). Decorate and color each butterfly differently. Laminate the butterflies and cut them in half to make a matching game.

Calendar Number Match Game

Get two identical old calendars. Select one month to use from the calendars. Cut the squares that represent the days from one calendar and provide the matching page from the second calendar to use as a work mat. Invite the children to match the squares to the days on the mat.

Calendar Walk

Make 12 copies of the Calendar Page (Appendix p. 520). Photocopy and enlarge the Calendar Art (Appendix p. 518-519). Glue the appropriate symbol to the top of each calendar page. Laminate the pages.

January	Top Hat
February	Heart
March	Spring flowers or shamrock
April	Rain Cloud
May	Flowers
June	Sunshine
July	Flag
August	School House
September	Fall Leaf
October	Pumpkin or Jack-o-Lantern
November	Turkey
December	Snowman

Make additional copies of each symbol so that each child has a symbol for each month. Place the calendar pages on the floor in a path. Give each child a symbol for each month. Invite the children to walk beside the path of months, saying the month as they pass and putting the appropriate symbol for that month down on the calendar page.

Caterpillar/Butterfly Puppet

You will need one brown or black sock, four wiggle eyes, and two or three different colors of felt. Place a piece of cardboard inside the sock while you are working to prevent the glue from seeping through the sock. Cut a pair of wings from the felt (you can overlap colors of felt for a more colorful butterfly). Attach the wings with fabric glue or a hot melt glue gun at the heel of the sock. Glue 2 wiggle eyes onto the toe of the sock. When the glue is dry turn the sock inside out and glue 2 wiggle eyes onto the toe of the caterpillar side of the sock.

Circle Surprises

Cut several poster board circles 8" to 10" in diameter. Draw designs or color the circles on one side to look like something round, such as a happy face, a button, a baseball, a clock face, an orange, and so on. Cut the circles into four pie wedges. Stack the four wedges of each circle, colored side up. Punch a hole in the pointed end of the wedges and put a brad through the hole to hold the four pieces together. Invite the children to fan out the sections of Circle Surprises one at a time. As each section is revealed, encourage the children to guess what the circle is.

Clothespin Alligators

Paint wooden spring-type clothespins green to look like alligators. Glue two small wiggle eyes on the top of each clothespin. Paint the opening of the clothespin red for a mouth or add some red felt inside the clasp of the clothespin to make it look like a mouth.

Colorscopes

Cover one end of a toilet paper tube with colored cellophane or plastic wrap. Secure with glue and a rubber band or wide tape.

Corn Candy Puzzles

Cut a large triangle out of cardboard for a base. Using the cardboard as a pattern cut the three pieces of paper to make the corn candy. Cut a small white triangle for the top, a small yellow trapezoid to form the middle section, and a larger orange trapezoid for the bottom. Laminate the pieces and invite the children to put the candies together.

Corny Counting Game

Gather five margarine tubs. Cut a penny-size hole in the lid of each container. Label the containers 1-5. Provide corn kernels and a couple of pairs of tweezers. Invite the children to use the tweezers to place the correct number of corn kernels in each container.
(Supervise closely at all times!)

Dancing Spiders

Give each child four black pipe cleaners. Show them how to twist the pipe cleaners together in the middle to create eight legs. Attach an 18" piece of elastic thread to the middle of the spider.

Dog and Bone Match Game

Make five photocopies of the Dog and Bone patterns (Appendix p. 501-502). Color them, if desired, and cut them out. Put a numeral (1-5) on each dog's collar tag and make corresponding dots 1-5 on the bones. Laminate dogs and bones. Use a matte knife (adult only) to cut around the mouth of the dog so that the bone can be slipped into his mouth. Encourage children to match numerals on the dogs' collars to dots on the bones.

Drums

There are several easy ways to make a drum. One, of course, is to turn any empty container upside down and beat on the bottom. Coffee cans with plastic lids make good drums; so do oatmeal boxes. You might also stretch canvas or heavy-duty plastic over the open end of a box or other container. Stretch it tight to get the best sound and tape it securely.

Drumsticks

Wrap one end of a dowel rod with masking tape or duct tape. Place a large eraser on the end of a dowel rod. Use paintbrushes and pastry brushes.

Eye Graph

Color a pair of brown eyes, blue eyes, gray eyes, and green eyes. Cut out and glue onto a poster board or piece of butcher paper to make a graph. See page 29 for further instructions.

Fall Observation Bottles

Fill a clear, empty, half-liter bottle with fall leaf confetti and water. Glue the lid on securely. Fill a second bottle with fall leaves. Fill a third bottle with fall potpourri. Punch a few small holes with a tack (adult only) in the potpourri bottle so children will be able to smell the potpourri. Be sure all lids are glued securely.

Family Puppets

Photocopy the Family Patterns (Appendix p. 469-470). Color the family as desired. Laminate and glue to tongue depressors to make a set of Family Puppets.

Farm Puzzles

Make photocopies of the appropriate farm animal patterns (Appendix p. 526-527). Cut them out, color, glue onto construction paper (different color for each animal), and laminate. Cut them into puzzles pieces.

Farmyard Ground Cover

Cut an old white sheet into four sections to make four ground covers. Spray paint each section randomly with brown and green spray paint to create a ground effect. Having four ground covers allows different groups of children to each have a space to create a farm scene.

Feed the Chickens Game

Make five copies of the chicken from the Farm Animal Patterns (Appendix p. 526-527). Color and cut them out. Paste the chickens on the top of five plastic lids from small margarine tubs. Cut a penny-size hole beside the chicken's mouth and write the numerals 1-5 on the lids (one numeral on each lid). Provide corn kernels and tweezers. Encourage the children to pick up the corn with the tweezers and drop the correct number of kernels into the margarine containers.
(Supervise closely at all times!)

Feed the Elephant Game

Make five photocopies of the Elephants and Peanuts Patterns (Appendix p. 503-504). Color and cut out the elephants and peanuts. Write the numerals 1-5 on the saddles of the elephants. Laminate the elephants and the peanuts. Invite the children to count the number of peanuts according to the number on the elephant's saddle.

Finger Crochet

Tie a dime-size slipknot in one end of a piece of yarn. Make a second dime-size loop and pull it through the first loop. Continue pulling loops through each other until you have reached a desired length. Tie a knot or loop the final loop through the first loop again to make a circle to use as a bracelet, necklace, or belt.

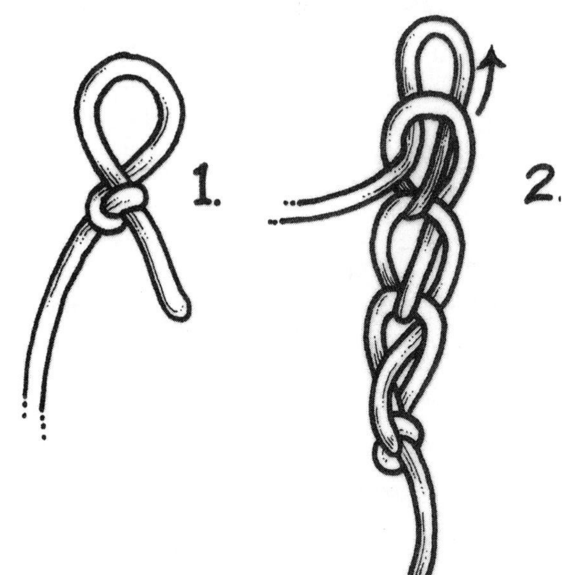

Fishing Game

Cut fat and thin fish out of construction paper. Place a paper clip on each fish's nose. Make a fishing pole from the cardboard tube from a coat hanger. Tape a piece of yarn at one end of the pole and tie a round magnet on the other end to serve as a "hook." Encourage children to "fish" to their hearts' content.

Flannel Board Stories

Trace patterns (Appendix p. 409-457) onto pelon with a black Sharpie pen. Color the patterns with crayons. Cut them out.

Flies on Pies Matching Game

Make 15 photocopies of the fly from the Insect Concentration Game patterns (Appendix p. 506). Cut construction paper circles to represent pies (decorate if you like). Write the numerals 1-5 and the corresponding number of dots on the pies. Encourage children to count out the number of flies on each pie.

Footprint Designs

Place a 12" piece of butcher paper on the floor. Prepare a shallow pan of tempera paint and place it at one end of the paper. Place a tub of sudsy water at the other end of the paper. Invite the children to take off their shoes, step in the paint, and walk the length of the paper. (This may be slippery, so support children as they walk.) Encourage them to stop along the path and make designs. When they get to the other end of the paper they can step in the sudsy water to clean their feet. Be sure to provide a towel.

Forest Animal Concentration

Make two photocopies of the Forest Animal patterns (Appendix p. 505). Color and laminate both copies. Cut one copy into individual animal cards. Invite the children to match the cut-out cards to the pattern card or use the cards to play concentration.

Frog Count Game

Cut five lily pads out of green construction paper. Write the numerals 1-5 on the lily pads. Make green frogs by cutting out small kidney-shaped pieces of green construction paper (about the size of a large lima bean) to look like a squatting frog. Add a pair of eyes on each frog with a paint pen or glue on a small pair of wiggle eyes. Have the children count the appropriate number of frogs onto each lily pad.

Garages

Collect several half-pint milk cartons. Wash them out and staple or tape the lids shut. Cut a garage opening in one side of each carton. Cover the cartons with contact paper or construction paper.

Glove Puppet

Glue Velcro to the fingers of an old work glove. Use the Glove Puppet Patterns (Appendix p. 476-483) with the glove to tell stories and lead fingerplays.

Goldilocks Puppets

Give children a 6" Styrofoam plate, a tongue depressor, markers, felt, yellow yarn or yellow paper ribbon, and glue. Invite the children to make a face using the felt or markers. Help them cut yarn hair or make curly hair by running the paper ribbons along the edge of their scissors to create curls for hair. Encourage the children to glue their faces onto a tongue depressor to make a Goldilocks puppet.

Grasshopper Hoppers

Spray paint three or four Ping-Pong balls green. Use a marker to make a pair of eyes on each ball. Tape on legs (optional). Challenge the children to get the Grasshopper Hoppers in a basket or box by bouncing them only once on the floor.

Grasshopper Puzzles

Use the grasshopper pattern from the Insect Patterns (Appendix p. 506) to make a grasshopper puzzle. Enlarge the pattern, color, laminate, and cut it into puzzle pieces.

Horse Shoe Game

Fill an empty half-liter soda bottle with pebbles to make a stake. Glue cap on securely. Cut the center from plastic coffee-can lids to make rings to serve as horseshoes. Children try to "ring" soda bottle with the coffee can lids.

Humpty Dumpty Puzzles

Make three or four enlarged photocopies of Humpty Dumpty from the "Humpty Dumpty" flannel board patterns (Appendix p. 429-431). Color, cut them out, and laminate. Cut each Humpty Dumpty into puzzles pieces. Make some of the puzzles more complex than others by cutting them into more pieces. Place matching colored dots on the back of the pieces of each puzzle so you can keep puzzle pieces from getting mixed up. Or, keep puzzle pieces easy to separate by mounting the eggs on different colors of construction paper before laminating and cutting them into puzzle pieces.

Ice Cream Cone Match Game

Use the Ice Cream Cone pattern from "The Very Hungry Caterpillar" (Appendix p. 543) to make five ice cream cones. Cut the cones from brown construction paper and the ice cream scoops from pink, lime green, orange, brown, and white construction paper. Place the numerals 1-5 on the cones. Encourage the children to put the number of scoops on each cone to correspond to the numeral on the cone.

Ice Painting

Provide ice cubes that have been frozen on Popsicle sticks. Invite the children to sprinkle dry tempera on construction paper and use the ice cubes as brushes.

Insect Concentration Game

Make two photocopies of the Insect Patterns (Appendix p. 506). Color and laminate both copies. Cut one copy into individual insect cards. Invite the children to match the cut-out cards to the pattern card or use the cards to play concentration.

Jingle Bell Bags

Cut two 3" squares of felt. Use a glue gun to glue the two pieces together on three sides, creating a pocket or bag. Attach a 1" piece of Velcro just inside the top of each pocket/bag. Place stick-on numbers from 1 to 5 on each bag.

Kazoos

Give each child a piece of paper (4" x 6") to color. When they are finished, help them glue the paper around the outside of an empty toilet paper tube. Secure a piece of wax paper over one end of the tube with a rubber band. Put tape over the rubber band to keep it in place. Show the children how to make music with their kazoos.

Kite

Give the children a paper bag. Invite them to color the bag, making any designs they choose. When they are finished, place masking tape around the opening of the bag to reinforce it. Then punch a hole through the tape in one side of the bag. Tie an 8' piece of yarn through the reinforced hole.

Ladybug Dot Match Game

Photocopy and enlarge four copies of the ladybug from the Insect Concentration Game patterns (Appendix p. 506). Color the ladybugs. Add dots to three of the bugs, two dots (one on each wing) at a time. You should end up with ladybugs that have two dots, four dots, six dots, and eight dots. Laminate the ladybugs and cut them in half. Invite the children to put the ladybugs back together by matching the dots on the wings.

Little Miss Muffet Lacing Card

Make several photocopies of Little Miss Muffet from the flannel board patterns for "Little Miss Muffet" (Appendix p. 435-436). Color the pattern, cut it out, and laminate it. Punch holes with a hole puncher about an inch apart all the way around the perimeter of the pattern. Provide shoelaces for lacing. Tape one end of the shoelace to the back of the card to secure it and leave the other end free for lacing.

Magnetic Maze

Draw a pathway in the bottom of a box (10" x 12"). Make a start spot and a finish spot. Provide a magnet and an object to move through the maze. (This might be an ant that is moving toward a cookie or a bee that is moving toward a hive.) Put one magnet on the back of the object that is navigating the maze. Use the second magnet under the box.

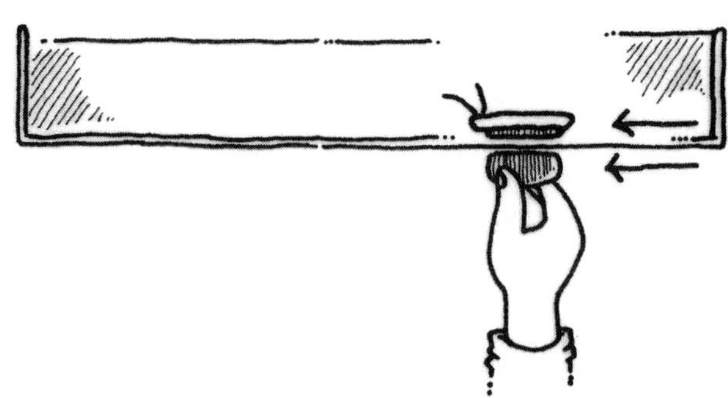

Milk Carton Shakers

Use empty pint-size milk cartons to make the shakers. Wash them thoroughly and let them dry. Put sound items such as jingle bells, paper clips, gravel, or marbles inside each carton. Close the tops of the cartons and staple shut. Cover the cartons with contact paper.

"Ms. Bumblebee Gathers Honey" Puppets

Photocopy the Bumblebee and Honey patterns (Appendix p. 468). Color, cut them out, and laminate. Glue the pieces to tongue depressors to make puppets.

Music Makers

For each music maker, you will need two 6" paper or Styrofoam plates and jingle bells. In the first music maker, put one jingle bell between the two plates, then staple the plates together. Music Maker number two will have two bells. Music Maker number three will have three bells, and so on.

Musical Balls

Cut four or five Ping-Pong balls in half or partially in half and put two or three jingle bells inside of each. Use masking tape or duct tape to put the Ping-Pong balls back together. If desired, place 1-5 bells in each Ping-Pong ball if you want to use the balls for seriation (by sound or by weight).

Nature Bracelets

Place a piece of masking tape around children's wrists (sticky side out). Invite the children to stick nature items such as flowers, clover, bark, pebbles, or leaves to the tape to create a nature bracelet.

Old Lady Floor Mat

Have someone lay on the floor on top of a piece of butcher paper. Trace around their body. Fill in the outline with details that make the tracing look like an old lady. Use as a playing surface for sequencing the items the old lady ate from "There Was an Old Lady Who Swallowed the Fly." Use the patterns on p. 485-487.

Pantyhose Wigs

Cut the feet off a pair of pantyhose. Slit each leg of the hose into three sections. Braid the three pieces to make pigtails. For a shorter wig, cut the length of the legs down. Show the children how to put the waistband of the pantyhose around their head to create a wig.

Paper Bag Blocks

Use small paper bags. Fill each bag about half-full with crumpled newspaper. Fold down the top and tape it closed. You can paint the bags red to make them look like bricks. You can also make bigger blocks by using large grocery bags.

Parade Hats

Fold one sheet of newspaper in half. Fold corners to meet in the middle about ¾ of the way to the bottom of the newspaper sheet. Fold each flap up toward top point of hat. Wear as is or decorate.

Pattern Combs

Cut several pieces of cardboard into 3" x 4" rectangles. Cut a pattern in one of the 4" sides. You can cut V's, scallops, teeth, and other designs. Pinking shears cut nice patterns.

Pendulum

Make a duct tape loop on the bottom of an empty mustard container. Fill the container with sand and close the spout. Tie your pulley rope to the loop to make a pendulum. Place a shower curtain liner or large piece of butcher paper on the floor under the pendulum. Open the spout of the container and invite the children to swing it and watch the tracks made by the sand. When the container is empty, sweep the sand up in a dustpan, pour it back into the container and try again.

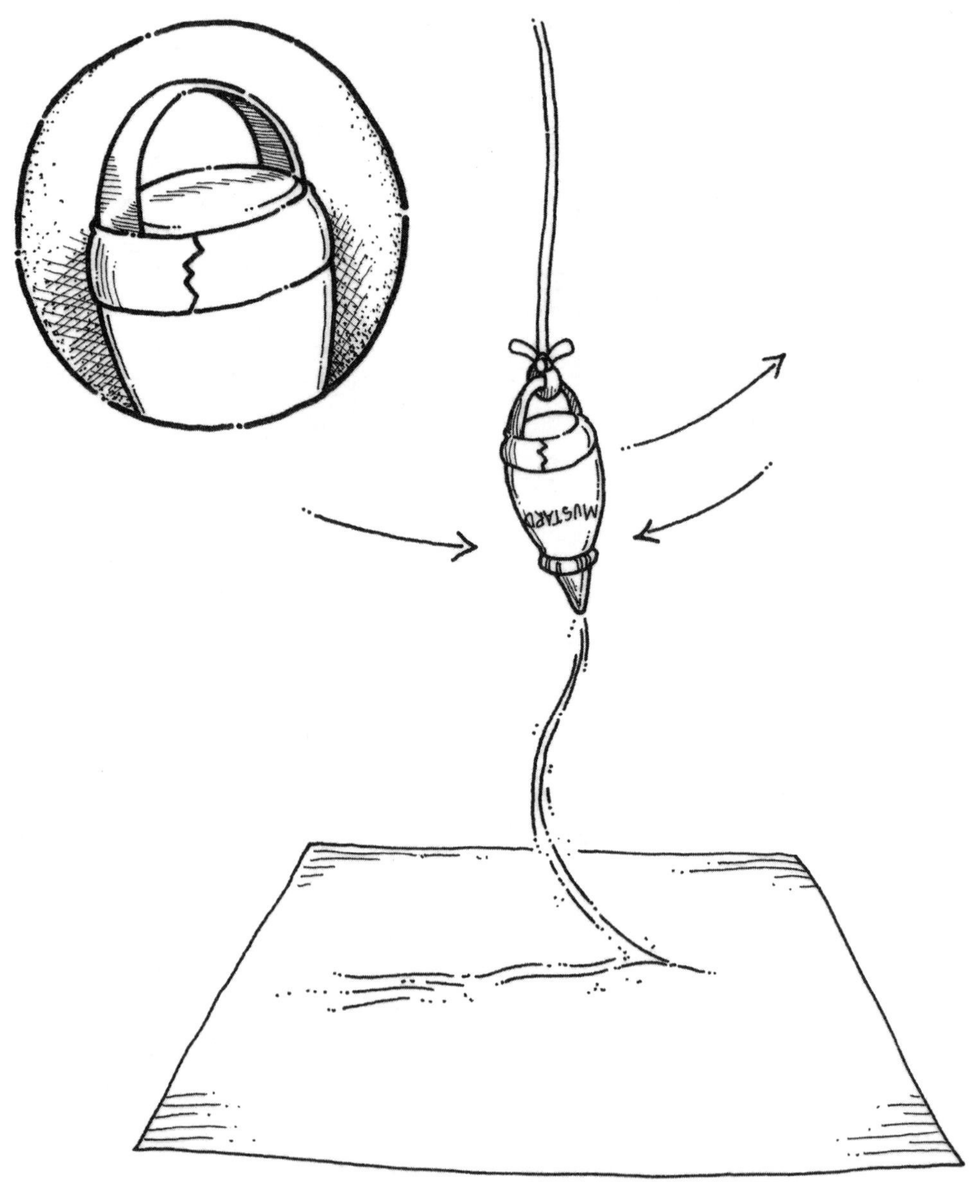

Pig and Wolf Stick Puppets

Make photocopies of the pigs and wolf from the "Three Little Pigs" patterns (Appendix p. 488-489). Color them, cut them out, and laminate them. Glue the characters to tongue depressors to create stick puppets.

Pumpkin Concentration

Make two photocopies of the pumpkins from "The Five Little Pumpkins" patterns (Appendix p. 508). Color both copies. Laminate one copy. Cut the other copy into individual pumpkins and glue each pumpkin onto 3" x 3" index cards. Laminate. Encourage the children to match the individual pumpkins to the whole card or to play concentration with the pieces.

Reptile Puzzles

Use the Reptile Concentration Game cards (Appendix p. 509). Photocopy and enlarge the cards. Color, laminate, and cut them into puzzle pieces.

Rubber Band Harp

Cut a piece of cardboard into a trapezoid. Make the top and bottom sides 15" long. Make the left side 8" high and the right side 16" high. Cut 1" slits, 2" apart across the top and parallel across the bottom of the trapezoid. Put rubber bands into the slits to make strings. You can also make this harp using a 15" x 15" rectangular piece of cardboard and cutting the slits across the top and bottom in a seriated fashion. Start with 1" slips and end with 3" slits.

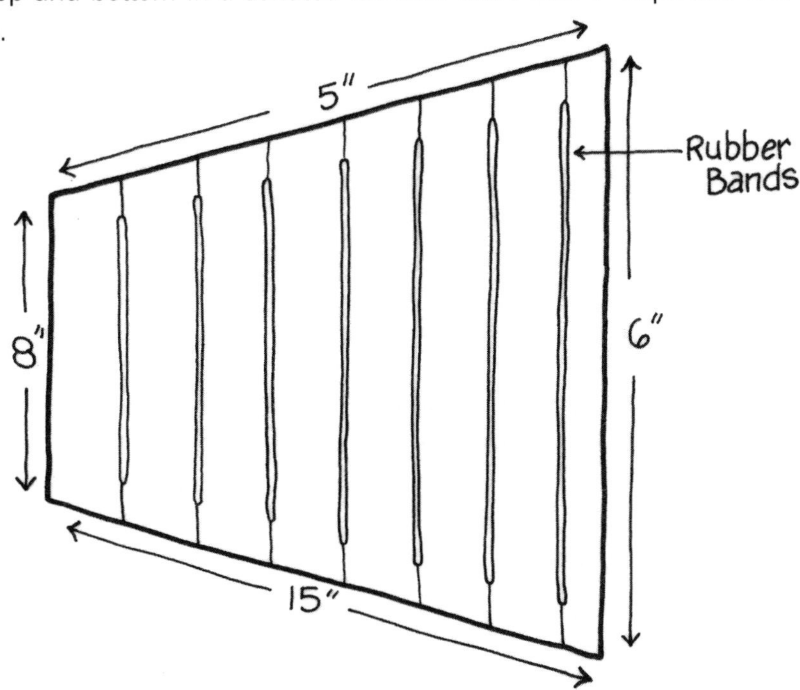

Sand Combs

Cut three or four pieces of poster board or cardboard into 4" x 8" strips. Cut teeth in an 8" side of each strip. Cut V-shaped (triangular) teeth in one and square teeth in another. Cutting scallops in another will give a circular look.

Season Mats

Copy the Season Mats (Appendix p. 533-536). Color them and laminate them. Or, use pages of an old calendar with pictures that are obviously from each of the four seasons.

Shoebox Guitars

Stretch rubber bands around empty shoeboxes. Use rubber bands of different widths and lengths to get a variety of tones and pitches.

Silo

Cover an oatmeal box with red construction paper. Cut an 8" diameter half circle and roll it into a cone for the roof.

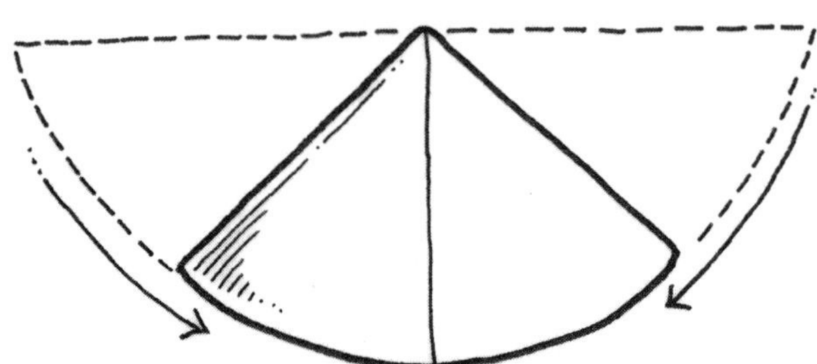

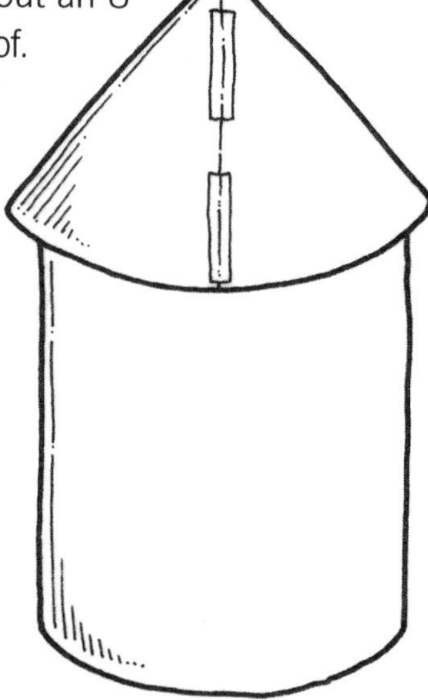

Snake Sock Puppet

Dye an old white sock green. Sew two button eyes on the top of the toe of the sock. Cut a tongue from red felt. Glue it under the toe.

Sound Maker Eggs

Place items that make sounds like jingle bells, gravel, or paper clips inside plastic eggs. Glue and/or tape securely. Make two eggs for each sound.

Spider Hats

Give each child a band of black construction paper to fit around her head. Give her eight strips of 1" x 8" black construction paper. Show her how to fold the strips back and forth like a fan to create spider legs. Attach all eight legs to the headband to create a Spider Hat.

Spiral Snakes

Cut a circle 6" in diameter out of construction paper. Draw a spiral 1" wide trail on one side of the circle to create a coiled snake. Make its head in the center of the spiral. Help the children cut along the line to create a spiral snake.

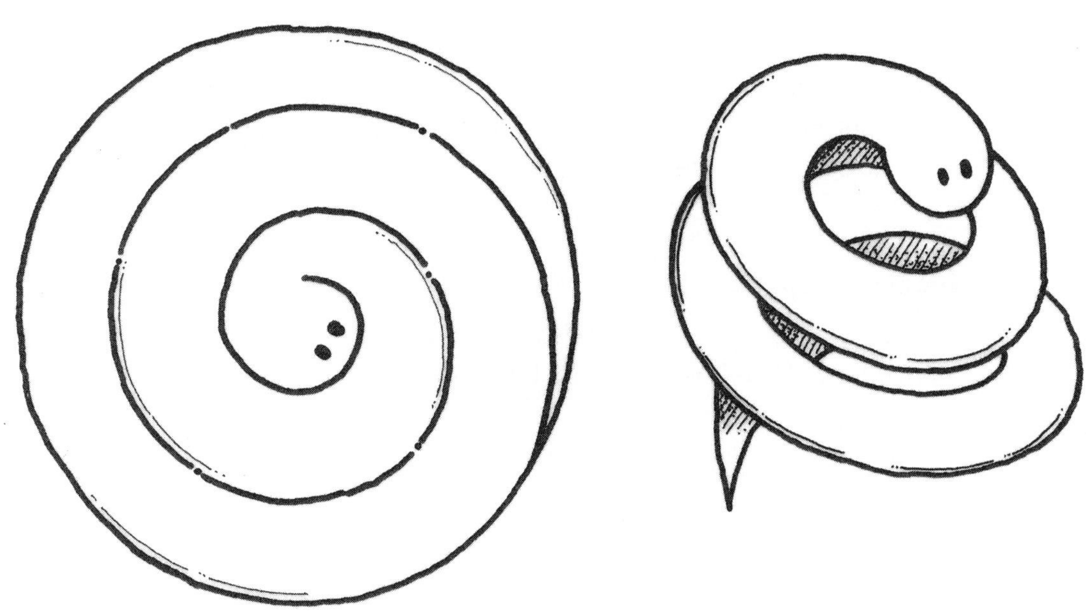

Sun Art

Give each child a sheet of dark blue or black construction paper. Provide objects such as leaves, puzzle pieces, cookie cutters, and so on. Invite the children to lay the objects on their paper in a design, and then place their paper outdoors in the sun. If the sun is bright enough, the paper around the designs should fade in two to three hours, leaving a design.

Three-D Glue Designs

Draw a design with Elmer's glue. Let it dry overnight. Invite children to place a piece of drawing paper over the dried design and make a crayon rubbing.

Things I Like to Do

Photocopy the "Things I Like to Do" Cards (Appendix p. 539). Color, cut them out, and laminate. Give them to children to sort into "things I like to do," "things I don't like to do," "things I like to do with Mom," and, "things I like to do with Dad."

Tornado in a Bottle

Fill a two-liter empty soda bottle with water and a few lightweight pebbles. Glue on the lid. Show the children how to make the water swirl around. What happens to the pebbles?

Tree and Flower Props

Photocopy and color the Tree and Flower patterns (Appendix p. 540-542). Glue them onto small lunch sacks that have been stuffed with newspaper (see Paper Bag Blocks, Appendix p. 396). Allow the children to position the sacks as scenery in the towns they build.

Turkey Puppets

Photocopy, color, cut, and laminate the turkey patterns from Five Fat Turkeys (Appendix p. 473-474). Glue the turkeys to tongue depressors.

Twirly Fish

Cut strips of copy paper into 1" x 12" sections. Hold the strips vertically and cut a ½" slit, one inch from the bottom of the strip on the right side and then a ½" slit, one inch from the top of the left side. Push the slits into each other to connect the strip and create a loop that resembles a fish. When the children hold the "fish" in the air and drop it, it will twirl to the floor.

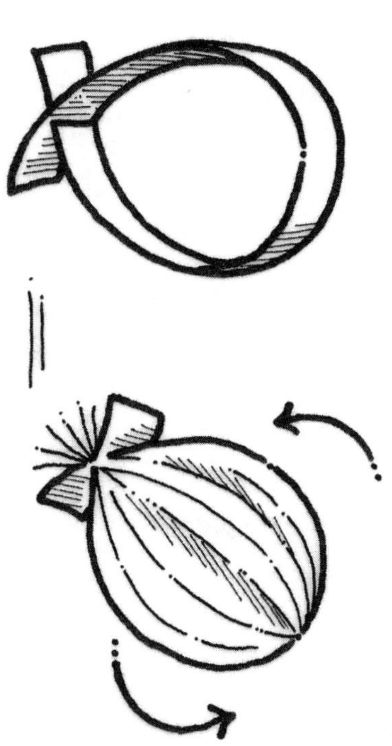

Twister

Cut a shower curtain liner in half. Use one-half to make the mat for a Twister Game. Put several large red, yellow, and blue stick-on dots randomly on the liner. Make a dice out of a ½ pint empty milk carton (folded into a square) or another square box of approximately the same size. Cover the box with contact paper. Cut out small red, yellow, and blue footprints and handprints. Glue a pair of hands and a pair of feet or hands in each color to each side of the box (dice).

Two-Sided Frog Puppet

Make a photocopy of two frogs (facing opposite directions) from the frog patterns (Appendix p. 475). Color them, cut them out, and laminate them. Position the frogs back to back and glue to a tongue depressor to create a Front Frog Fred and a Back Frog Jack.

Walk-On Nursery Rhyme Mat

Cut a piece of butcher paper 15' long. Draw the following items on the paper in this sequence: a pair of feet (trace shoes), a spiral arrow, a pair of walking feet, grass, a pair of walking feet, a door, a pair of walking feet, a bowl, a pair of walking feet, a chair, a pair of walking feet, a bed, a pair of walking feet, a pair of walking feet going off the end of the paper. Laminate. Use the mat with the Walk-On Nursery Rhyme (Appendix p. 326).

Walnut Shell Boats

Clean out half of a walnut shell. Place a small amount of playdough inside the shell. Cut a small triangular sail out of paper and tape it to a toothpick. Poke the sail in the playdough to hold it to the boat.

Watermelon Seed Transfer Game

Make copies of the Watermelon pattern that is part of The Very Hungry Caterpillar patterns (Appendix p. 543). Color the pattern (if desired), cut it out, and laminate it. Give the children tweezers and real watermelon seeds. Invite them to transfer the seeds from a dish to the watermelon, creating a one-to-one match with the seeds that are drawn on the watermelon. Supervise closely, especially if you have children who still put objects in their mouths.

Weather Wheel

Photocopy the Weather Wheel pattern (Appendix p. 547). Color, cut it out, and glue to a piece of poster board. Use a brad to hold the dial in place.

Weaving Looms

Meat Tray Loom

Cut ½" slits in the top and bottom of a meat tray. Tie a knot in one end of a piece of yarn and wrap it around the meat tray between the slits to create a loom.

(See illustration on next page)

Forked Branch Loom

Find a small (sling shot size) forked branch. Wrap a piece of yarn back and forth around the "V" part of the branch to create a loom.

(See illustration on next page)

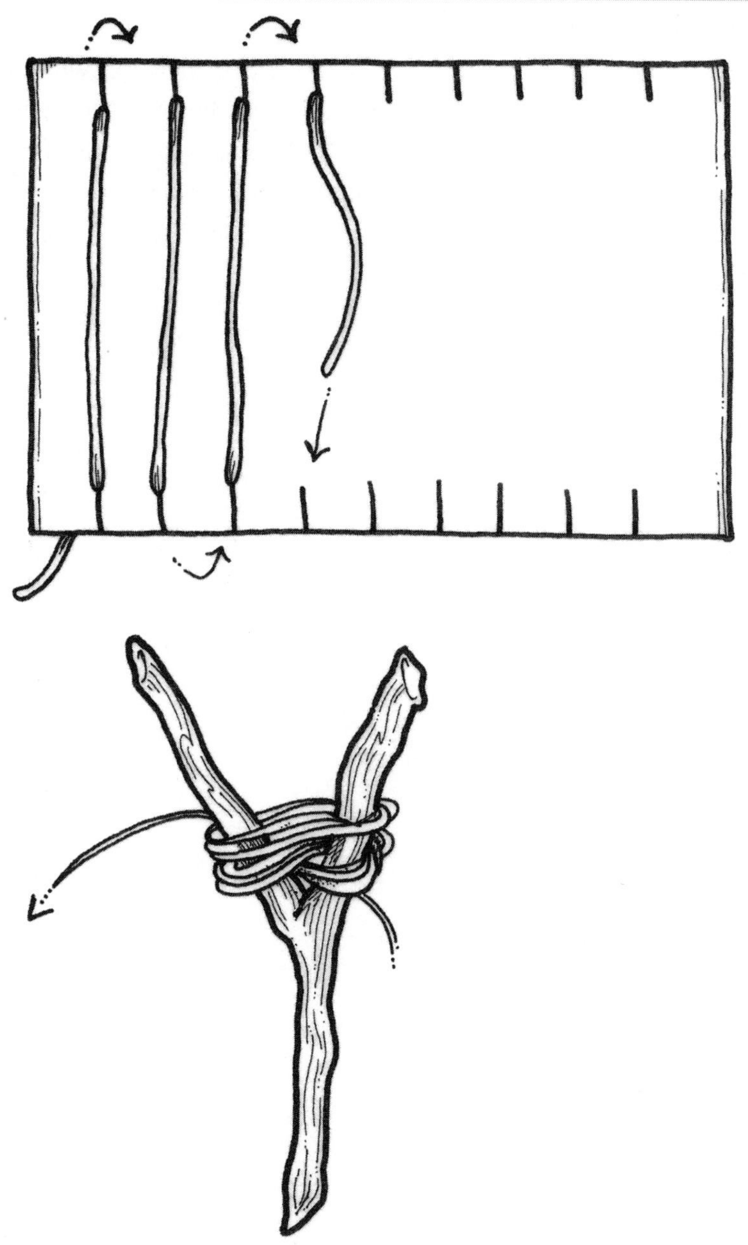

Wind Catcher

Cut a paper plate in half. Cut colorful crepe paper streamers in 12" strips. Help the children glue streamers on the curve of the half-plates.

Wind Chimes

Tie six or eight lightweight metal spoons to 12" pieces of yarn. Tie the other ends of the yarn to the bottom of a coat hanger. Hang the coat hanger outside and enjoy the chimes. You can also make a wind chime using seashells or small aluminum pie tins.

Winter Observation Bottles

Fill an empty, clear, half-liter soda bottle with water and white crayon shavings to create snow. Glue lid on securely. Fill a second soda bottle with winter items such as moss, holly berry, cones, acorns, and bark. Fill a third bottle with winter potpourri (pine needles and cinnamon sticks). Glue the lids on securely. Punch three or four holes in the potpourri bottle with a tack (adult only).

List of Patterns

Flannel Board Patterns

Caps for Sale
The Fat Cat
Frosty the Snowman
Goldilocks and the Three Bears
The Great Big Pumpkin
The Great Big Turnip
Humpty Dumpty
Jack and Jill
Little Miss Muffet
The Little Red Hen
Old MacDonald Had a Farm
One, Two, Buckle My Shoe
Sing a Song of Sixpence
Smart Cookie's Best Friend, Greta Graham
The Three Billy Goats Gruff
The Three Little Pigs
This Old Man
Twinkle, Twinkle Little Star
Valencia Valentine (Appendix page 353)

Story Card/Song Card Patterns

Brown Bear, Brown Bear Story Cards
Itsy Bitsy Spider Song Cards

Puppet Patterns

Animal Puppets
Bumblebee and Honey Puppets
Family Puppets
Five Little Ducks
Five Fat Turkeys Puppets
Frog Puppets
Glove Puppet Patterns
- Family Puppets
- Five Fat Turkeys
- Five Little Speckled Frogs
- Five Little Pilgrims
- Five Little Pumpkins
- Goldilocks and the Three Bears
- Three Billy Goats Gruff
- Three Little Pigs

Itsy Bitsy Spider Puppets
The Old Lady Who Swallowed the Fly
Three Little Pigs and Wolf Puppets

Rebus Patterns

Bird Nest Candy Recipe
Frozen Yogurt
Gak
Homemade Butter Recipe
Homemade Peanut Butter Recipe
Peanut Butter and Jelly Sandwich
Peppermint Baggie Ice Cream Recipe
Purple Cow Shakes
Vacation Packing List

Game Patterns

Animal Footprints
Bird and Nest
Dog and Bone
Elephant and Peanut
Forest Animal Concentration
Insect Concentration
Ocean Animal Concentration
Pumpkin Concentration
Reptile Concentration
Zoo Animal Concentration

MISCELLANEOUS PATTERNS

Animal Faces for Masks
Calendar Art
Calendar Page
Dancing Bear
Dress Me Dolls
Farm Animals
Finger Spelling
Fruit and Vegetable Patterns
Metamorphosis Sequence Cards
"My Favorite Things" Cards
Pyramid Template
Season Mats
Sign Language
Story Pyramid
"Things I Like to Do" Cards
Tree and Flower Patterns
Very Hungry Caterpillar Patterns
Weather Wheel

Caps for Sale (See story on p. 330)

Directions for Making the Flannel Board Pieces: Photocopy the following Caps for Sale patterns. Trace them onto Pelon. Color with crayons and cut them out.

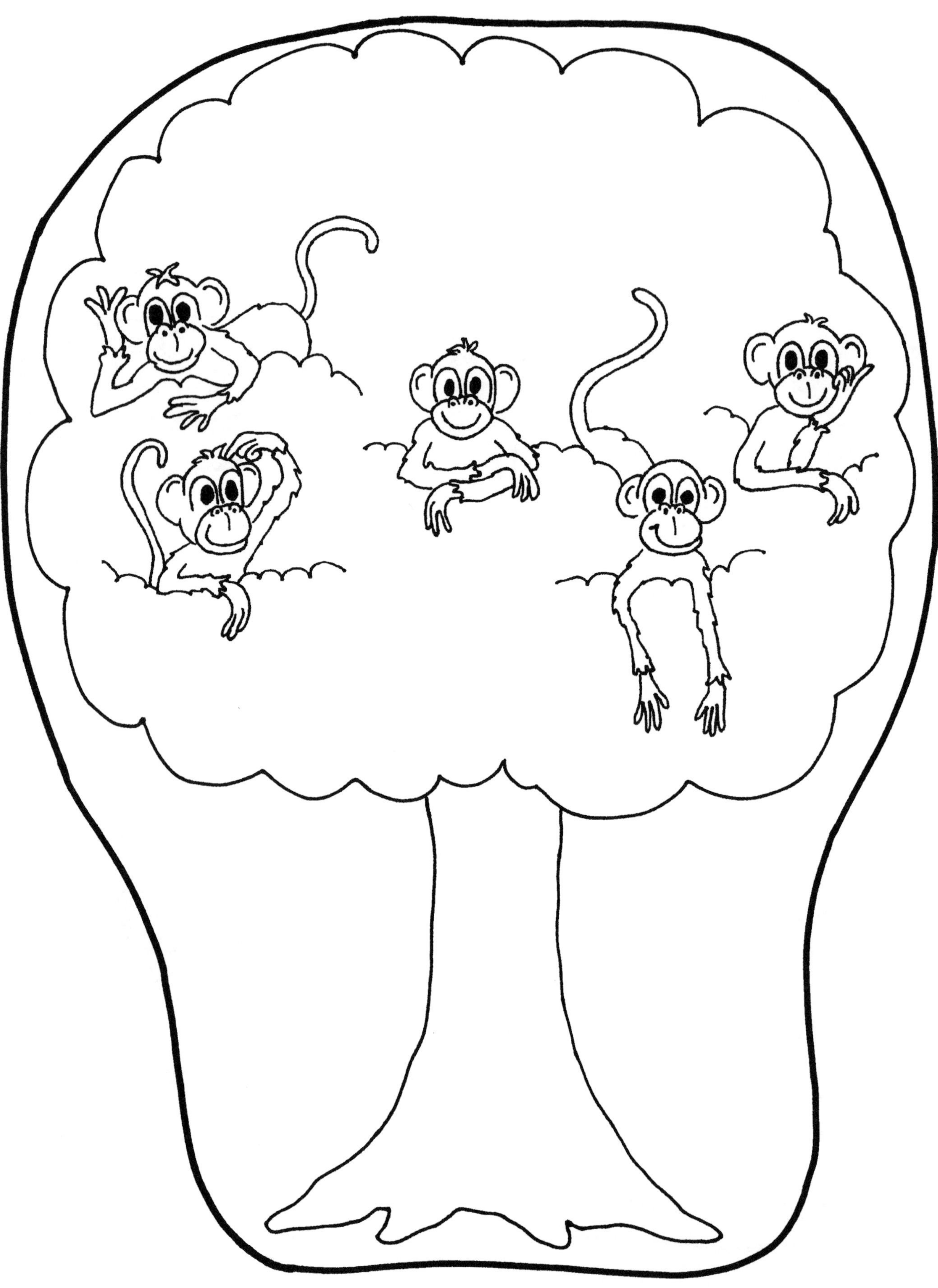

Fat Cat (See story on p. 333)

Directions for Making the Flannel Board Pieces: Photocopy the following patterns. Trace them onto Pelon. Color with crayons and cut them out.

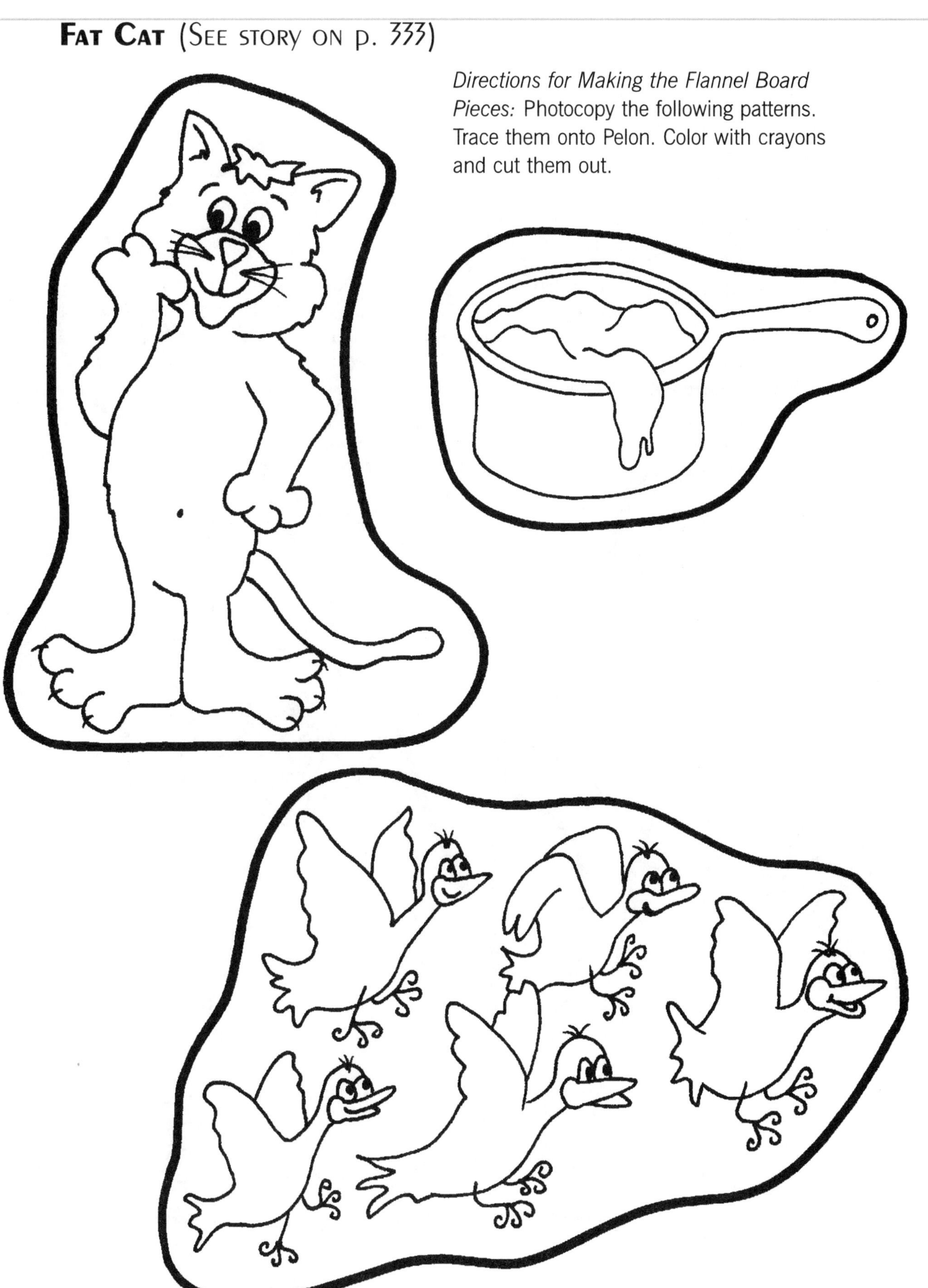

Fat Cat

Fat Cat

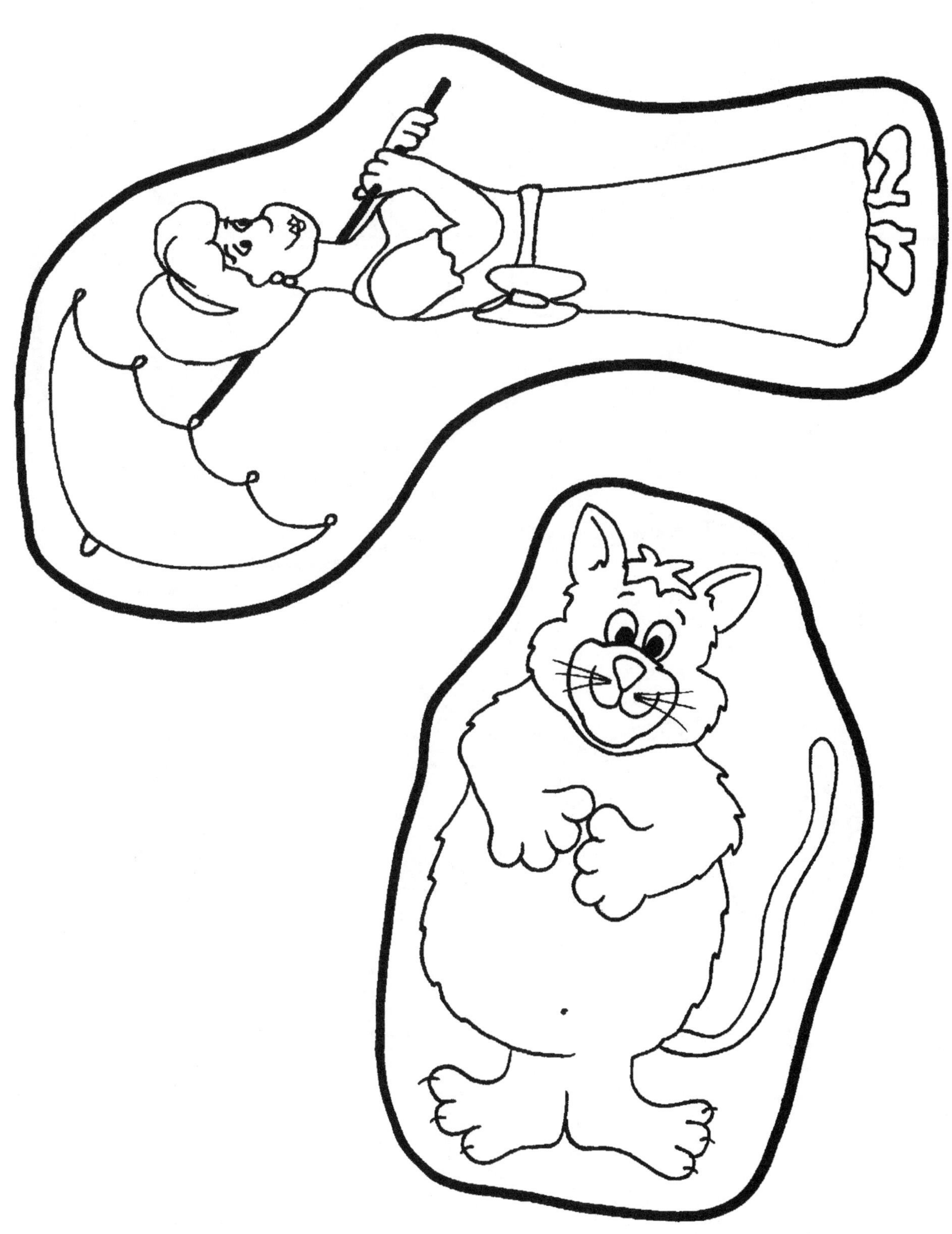

Fat Cat

Fat Cat

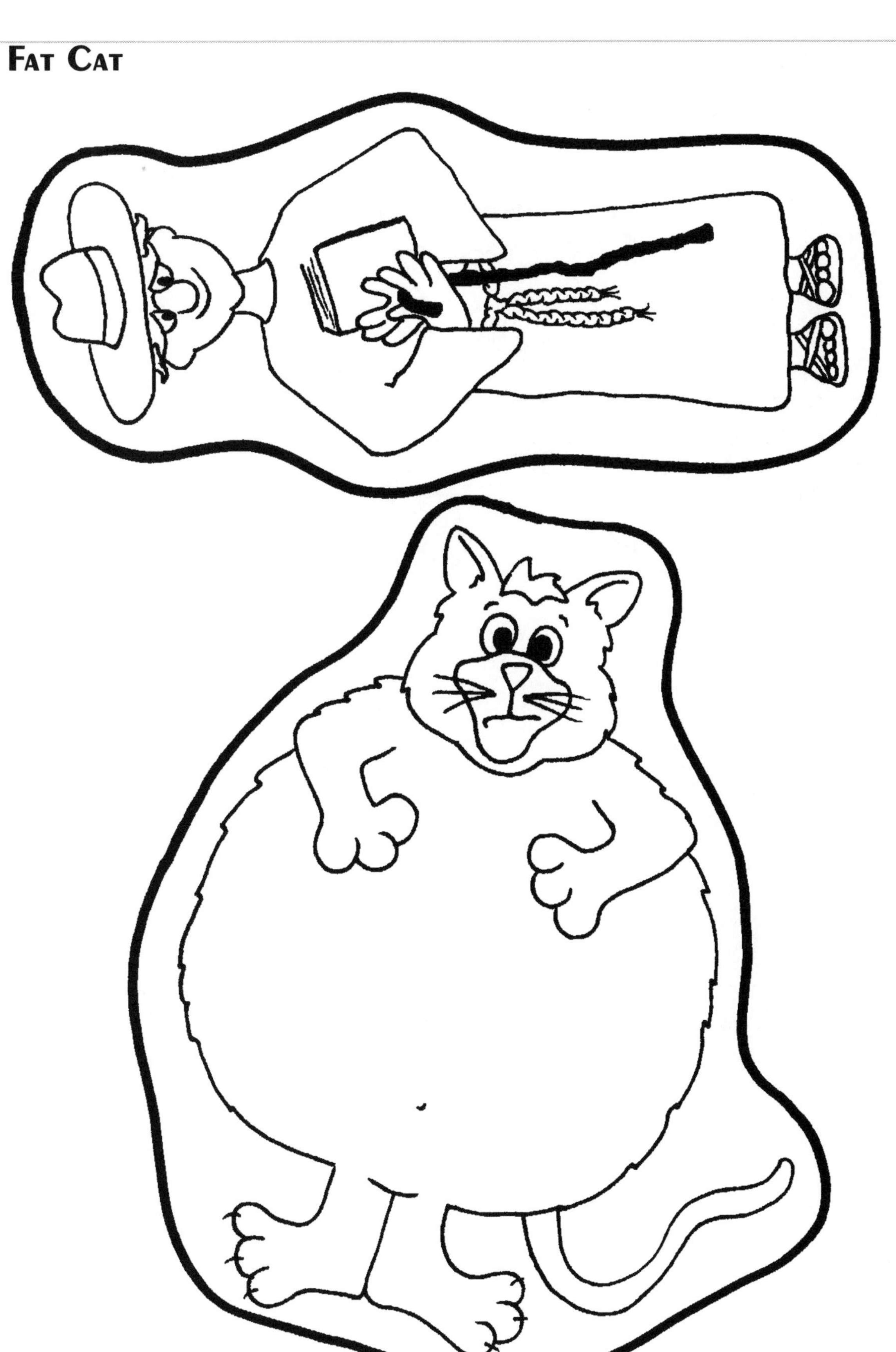

Fat Cat

Fat Cat

Frosty the Snowman (See song on p. 287)

Directions for Making the Flannel Board Pieces: Photocopy the Frosty the Snowman flannel board patterns. Trace them onto Pelon. Color them with crayons and cut them out.

Frosty the Snowman

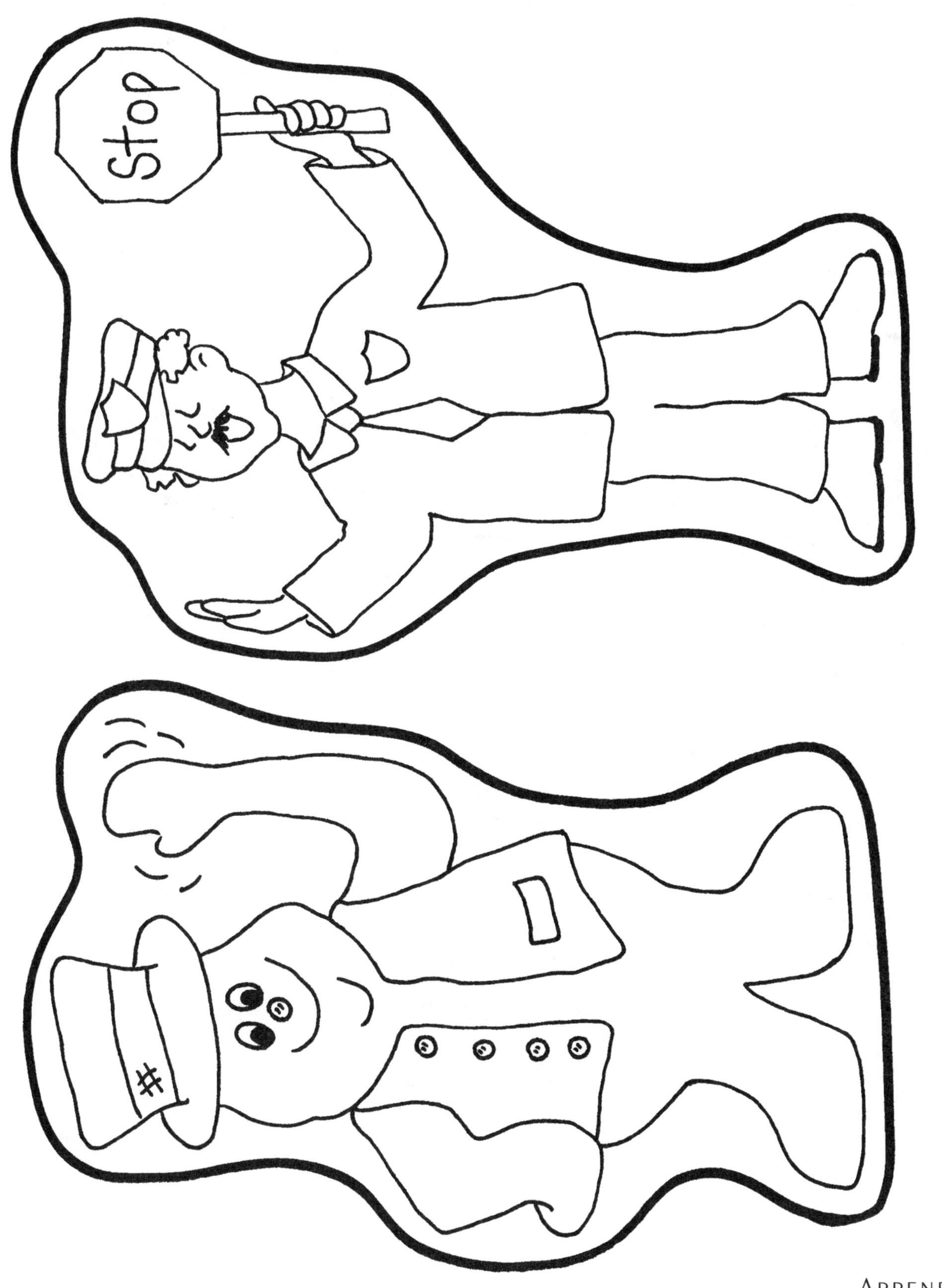

Frosty the Snowman

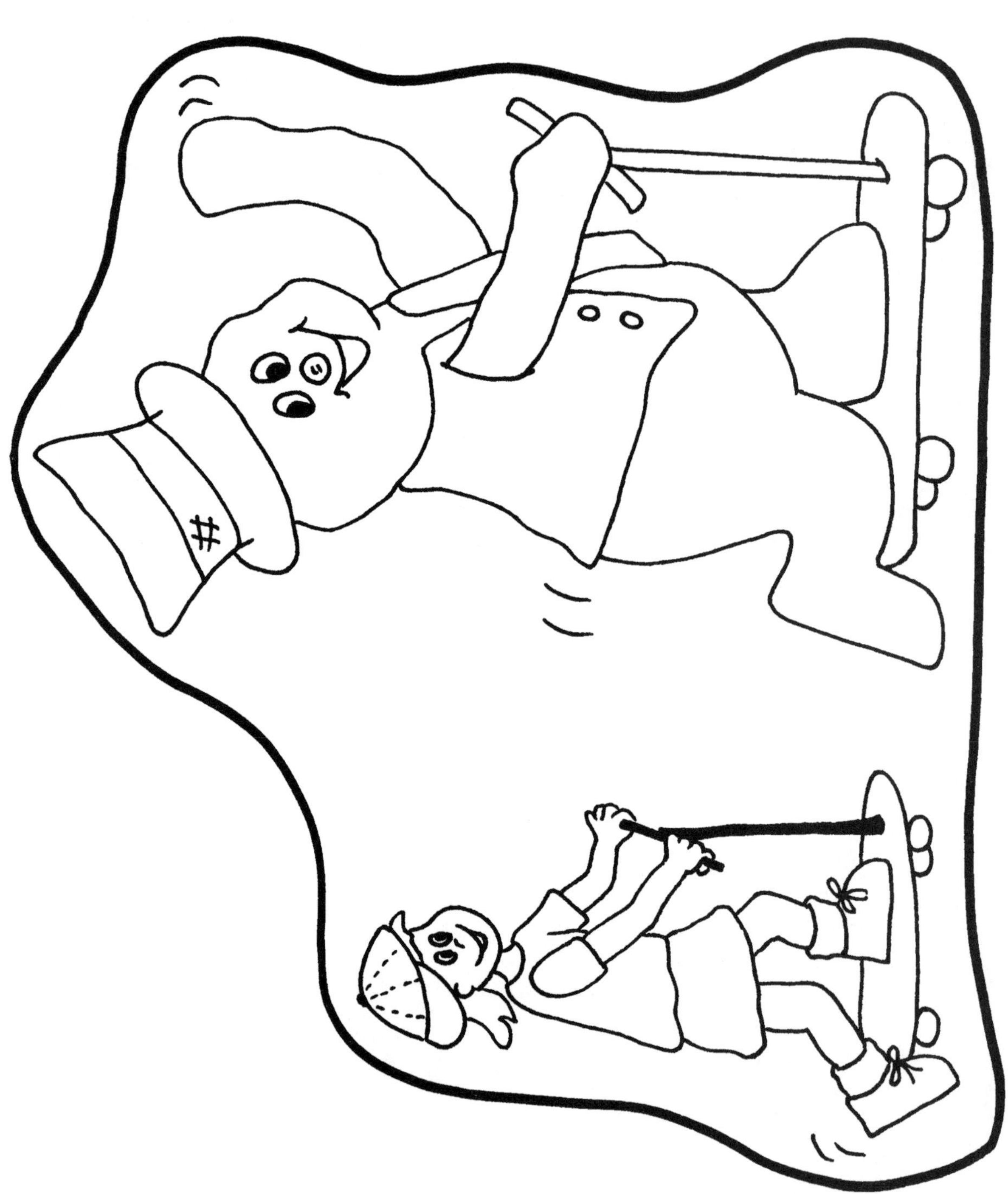

Goldilocks and the Three Bears (See story on p. 335)

Directions for Making the Flannel Board Pieces: Photocopy the following patterns. Trace them onto Pelon. Color with crayons and cut them out.

Goldilocks and the Three Bears

Goldilocks and the Three Bears

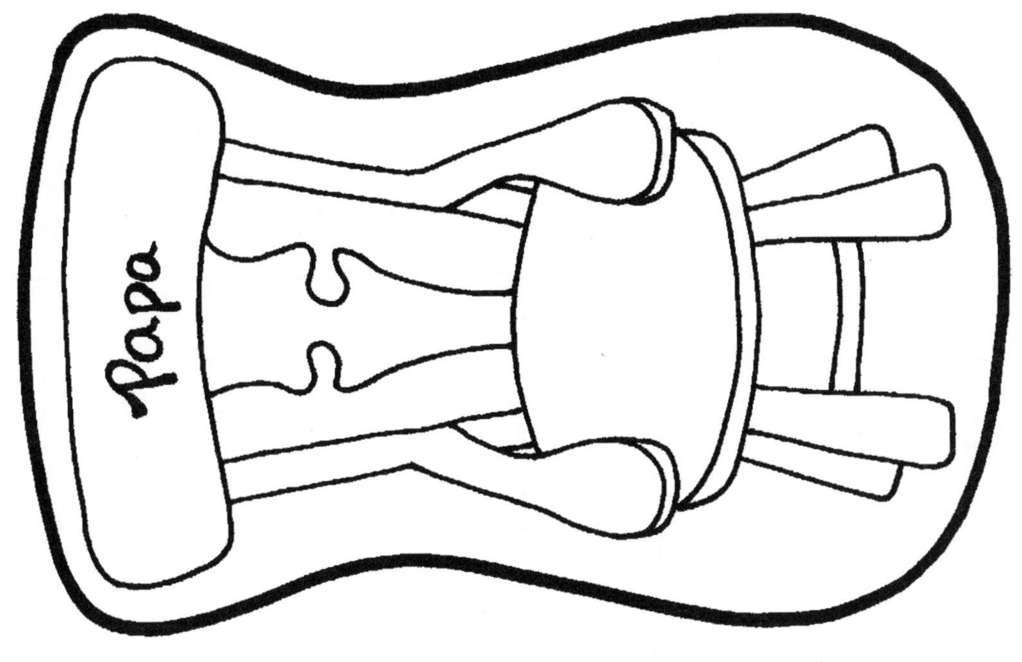

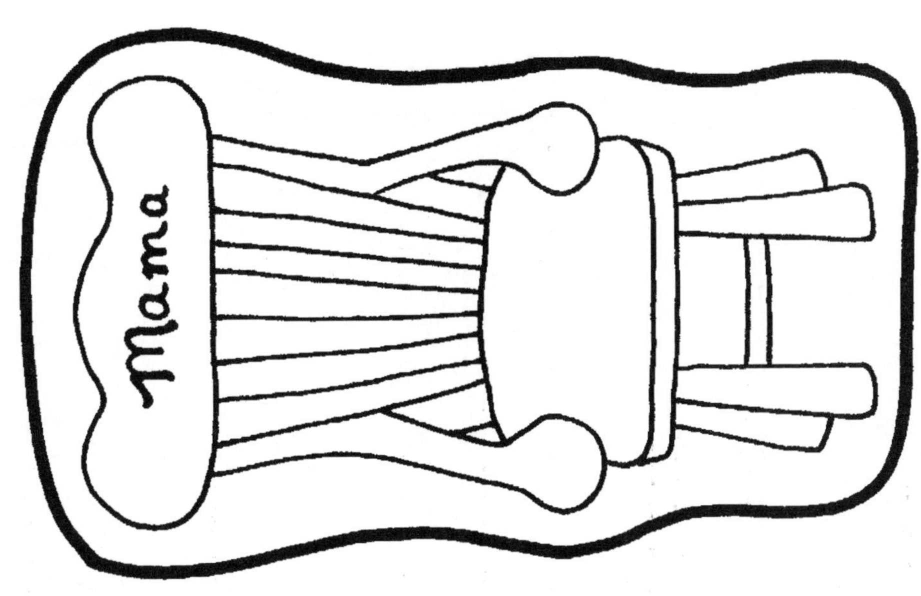

Goldilocks and the Three Bears

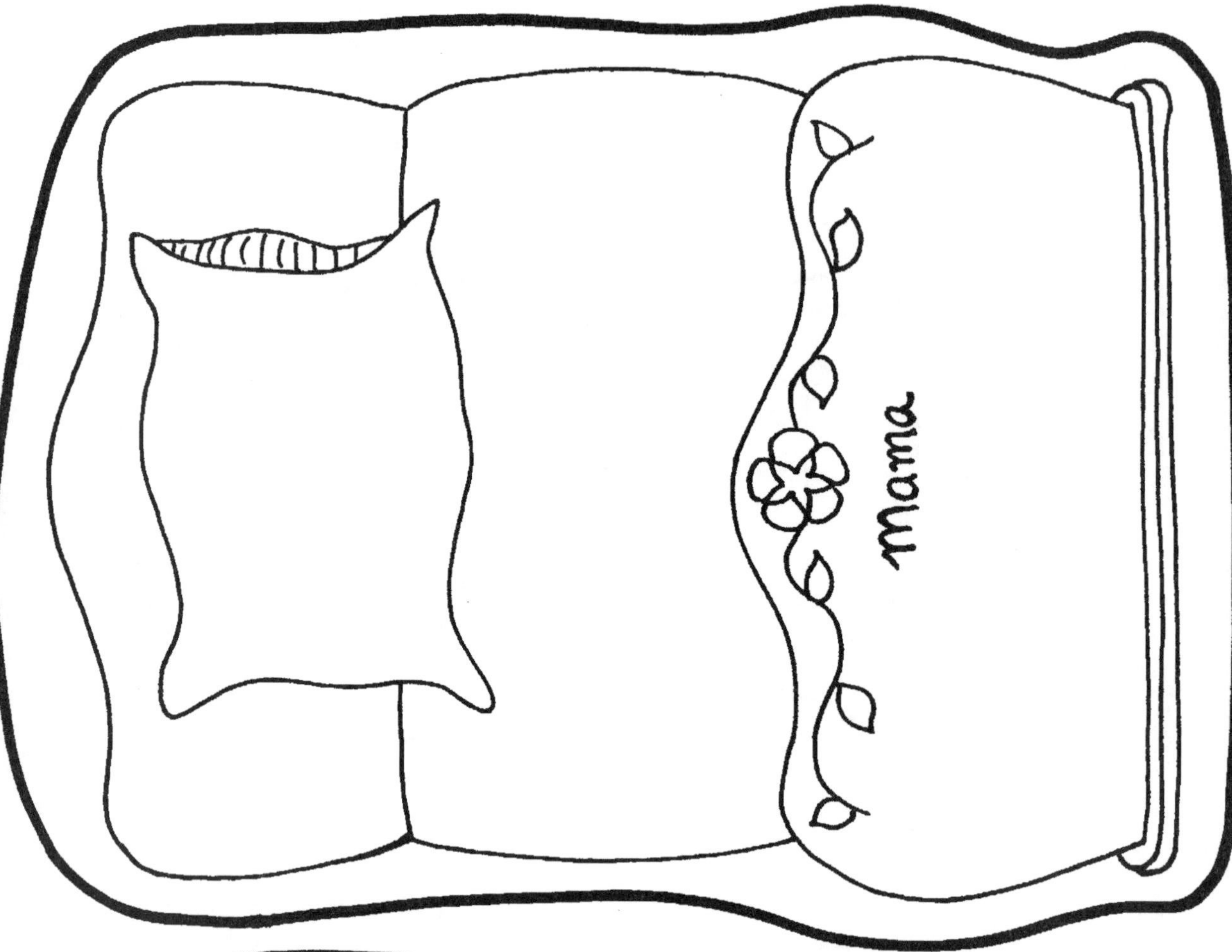

Mama

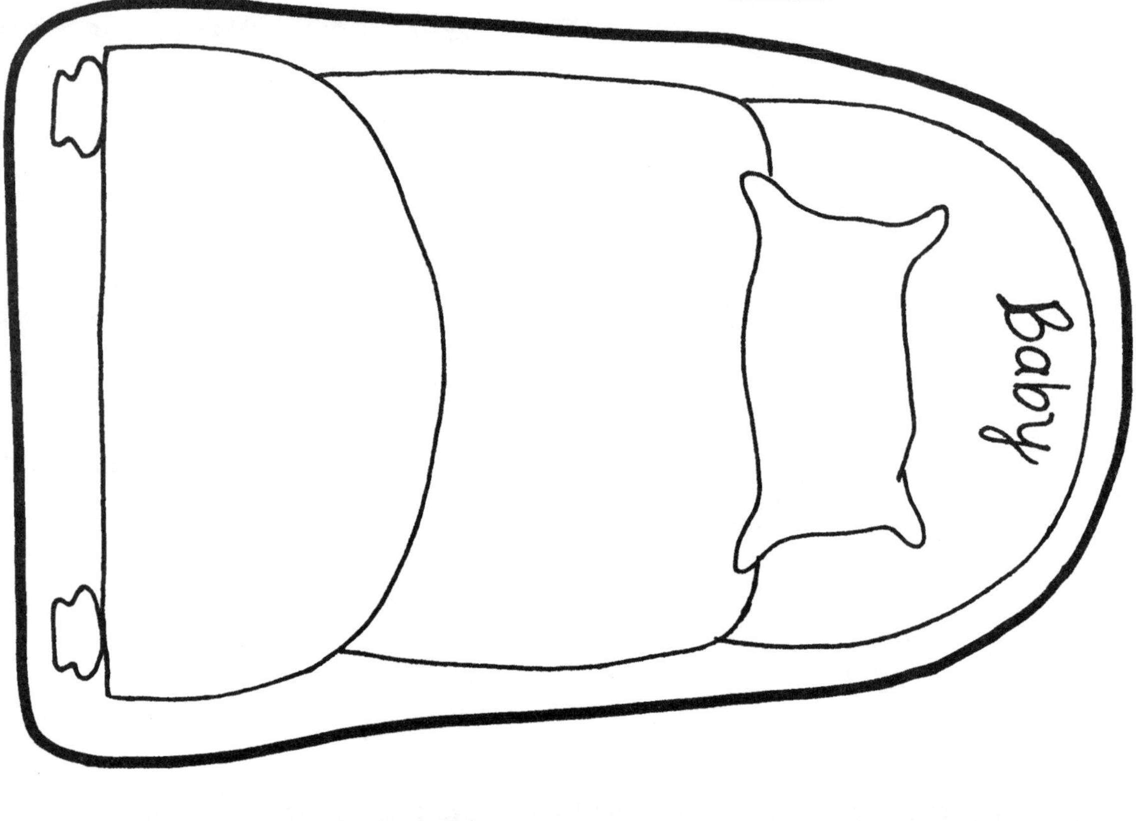

Baby

Goldilocks and the Three Bears

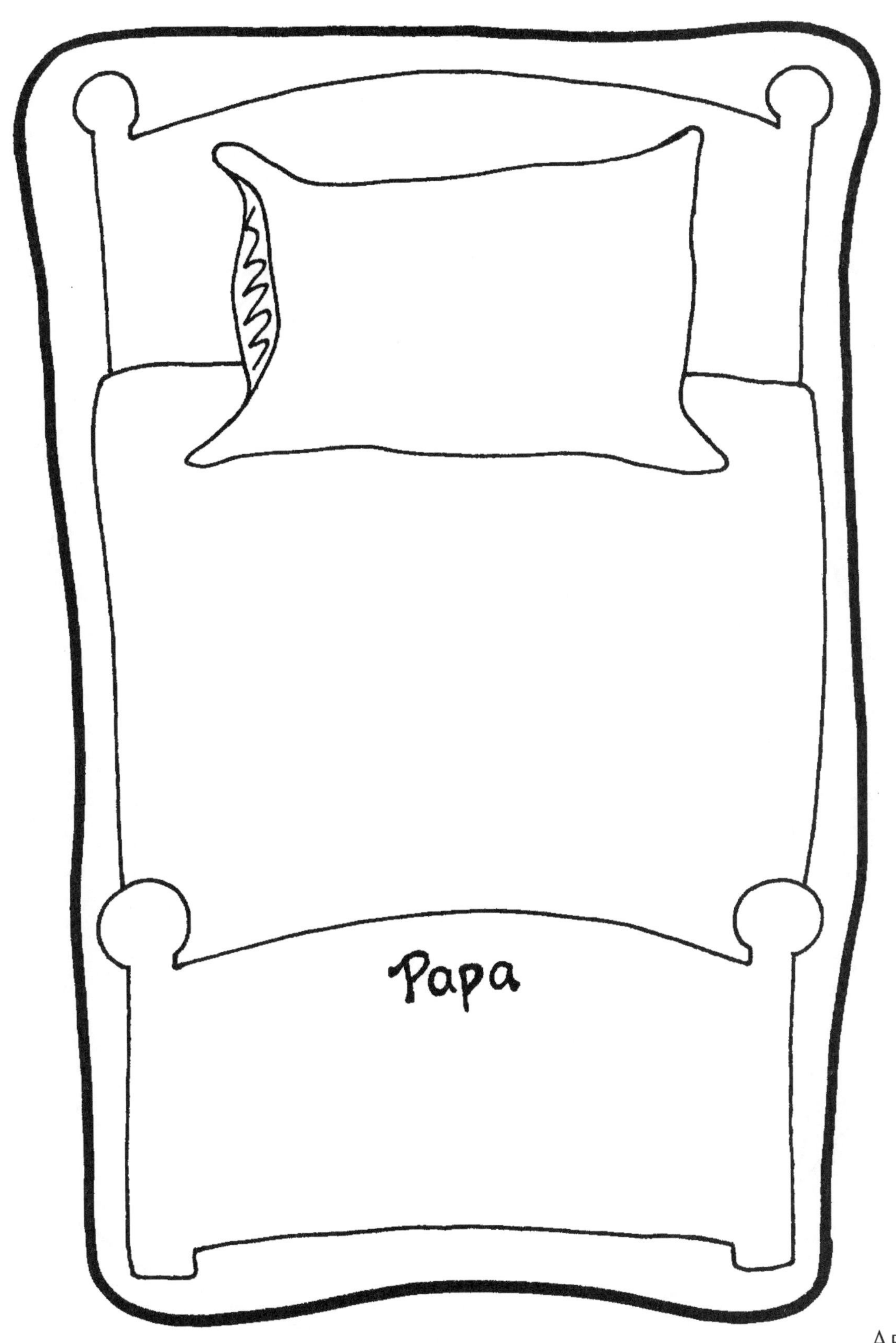

The Great Big Pumpkin (See story on p. 335)

Directions for Making the Flannel Board Pieces: Photocopy the story patterns. Trace them onto Pelon. Color with crayons and cut them out.

The Great Big Pumpkin

The Great Big Turnip (See story on p. 336)

Directions for Making the Flannel Board Pieces: Photocopy the following patterns. Use the same four animals as in The Great Big Pumpkin (on page 427). Trace them onto Pelon. Color with crayons and cut them out.

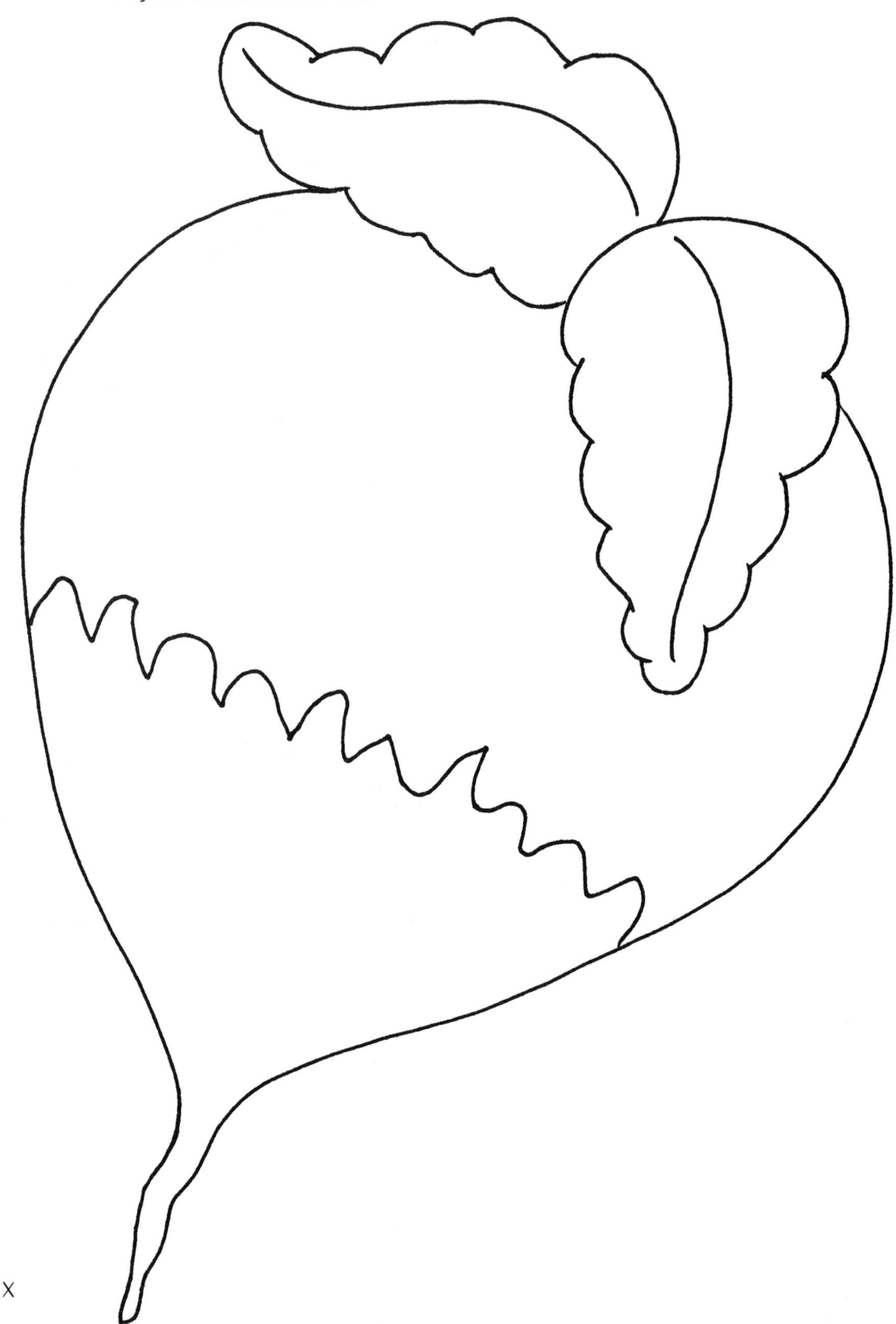

Humpty Dumpty (See rhyme on p. 318)

Directions for Making the Flannel Board Pieces: Photocopy the story patterns. Trace them onto Pelon. Color with crayons and cut them out.

Humpty Dumpty

Humpty Dumpty

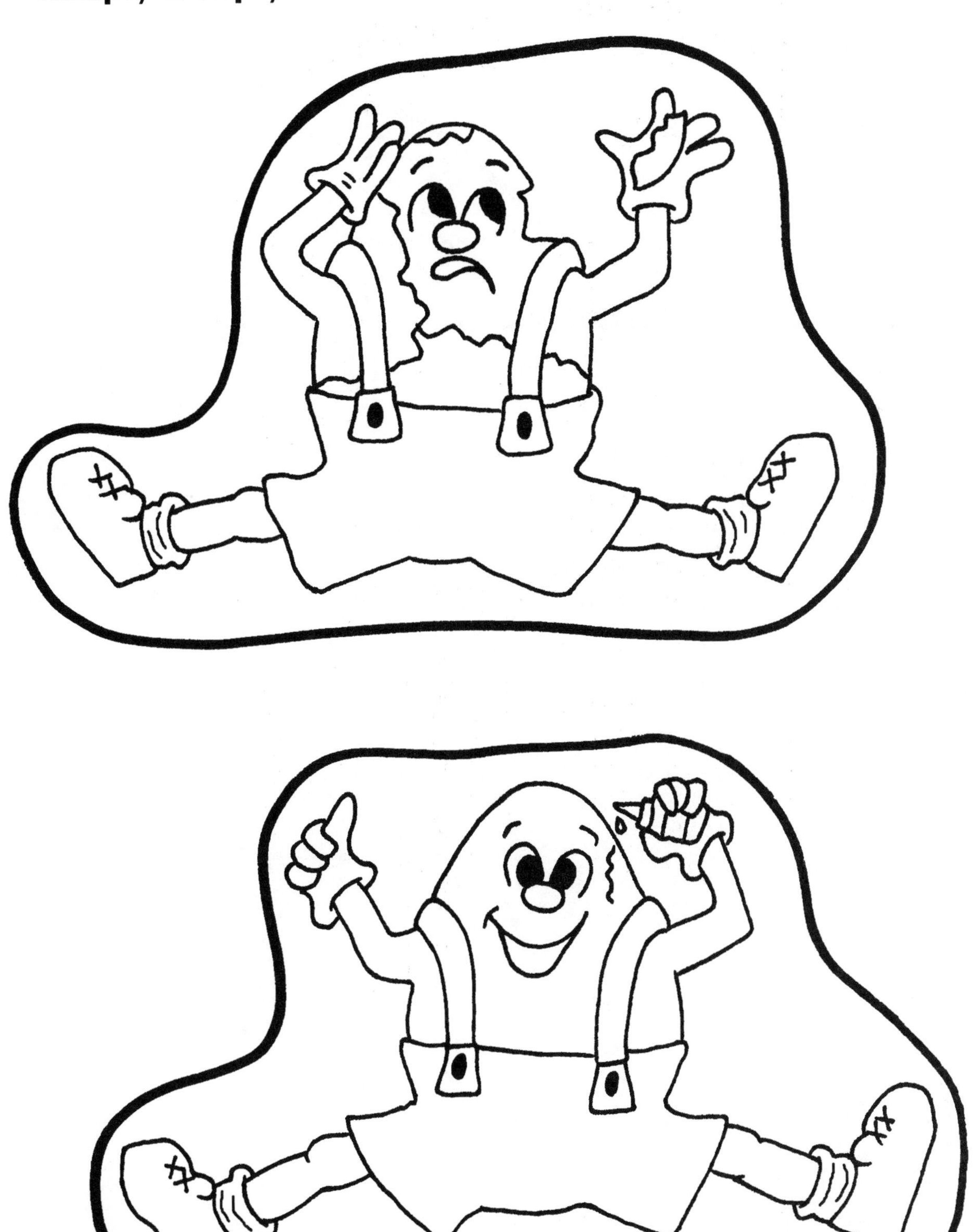

Jack and Jill (See rhyme on p. 321)

Directions for Making the Flannel Board Pieces: Photocopy the story patterns. Trace them onto Pelon. Color with crayons and cut them out.

Jack and Jill

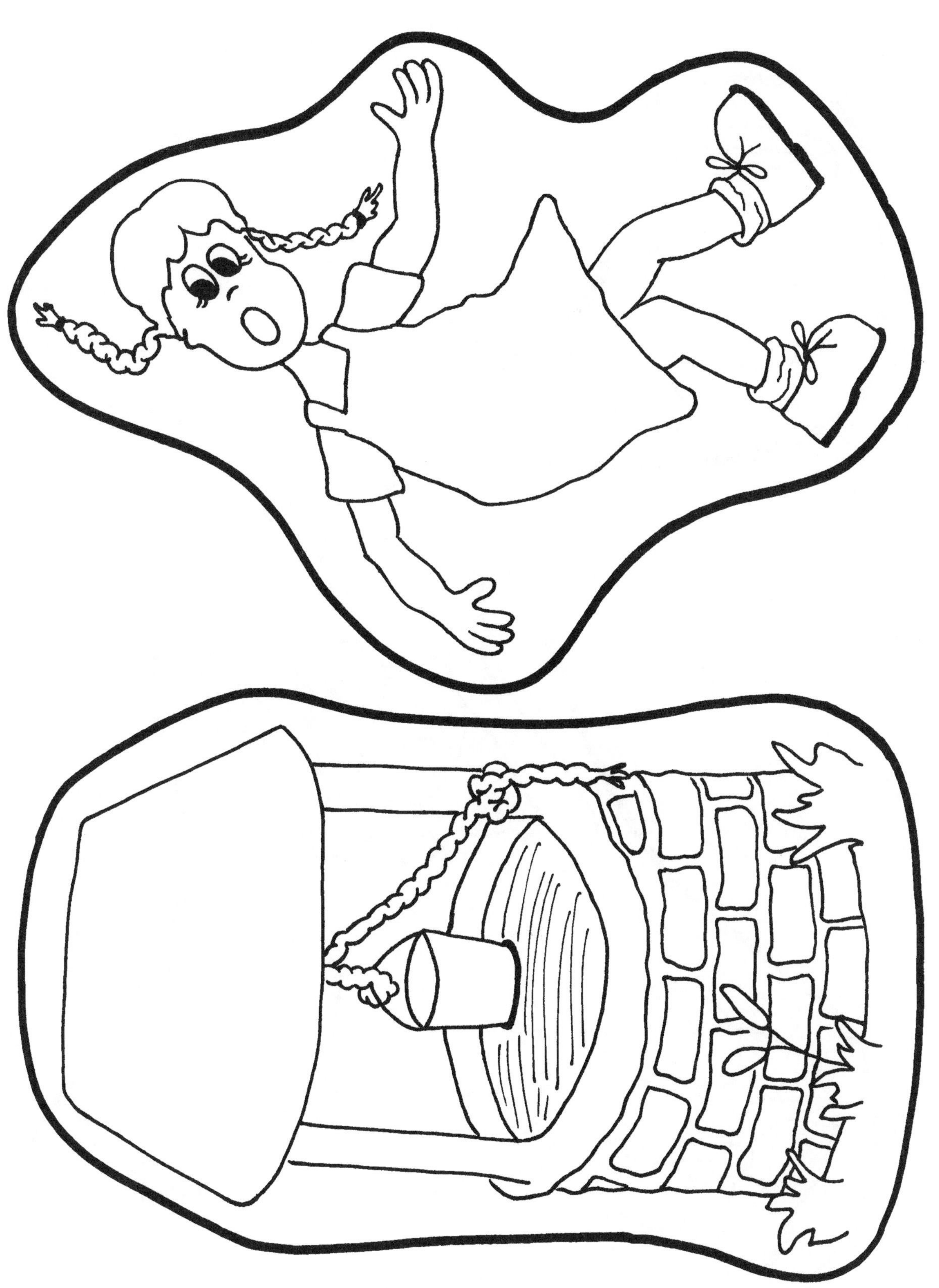

Jack and Jill

Little Miss Muffet (See rhyme on p. 322)

Directions for Making the Flannel Board Pieces: Photocopy the story patterns. Trace them onto Pelon. Color with crayons and cut them out.

Little Miss Muffet

The Little Red Hen (See rhyme on p. 340)

Directions for Making the Flannel Board Pieces: Photocopy the story patterns. Trace them onto Pelon. Color with crayons and cut them out.

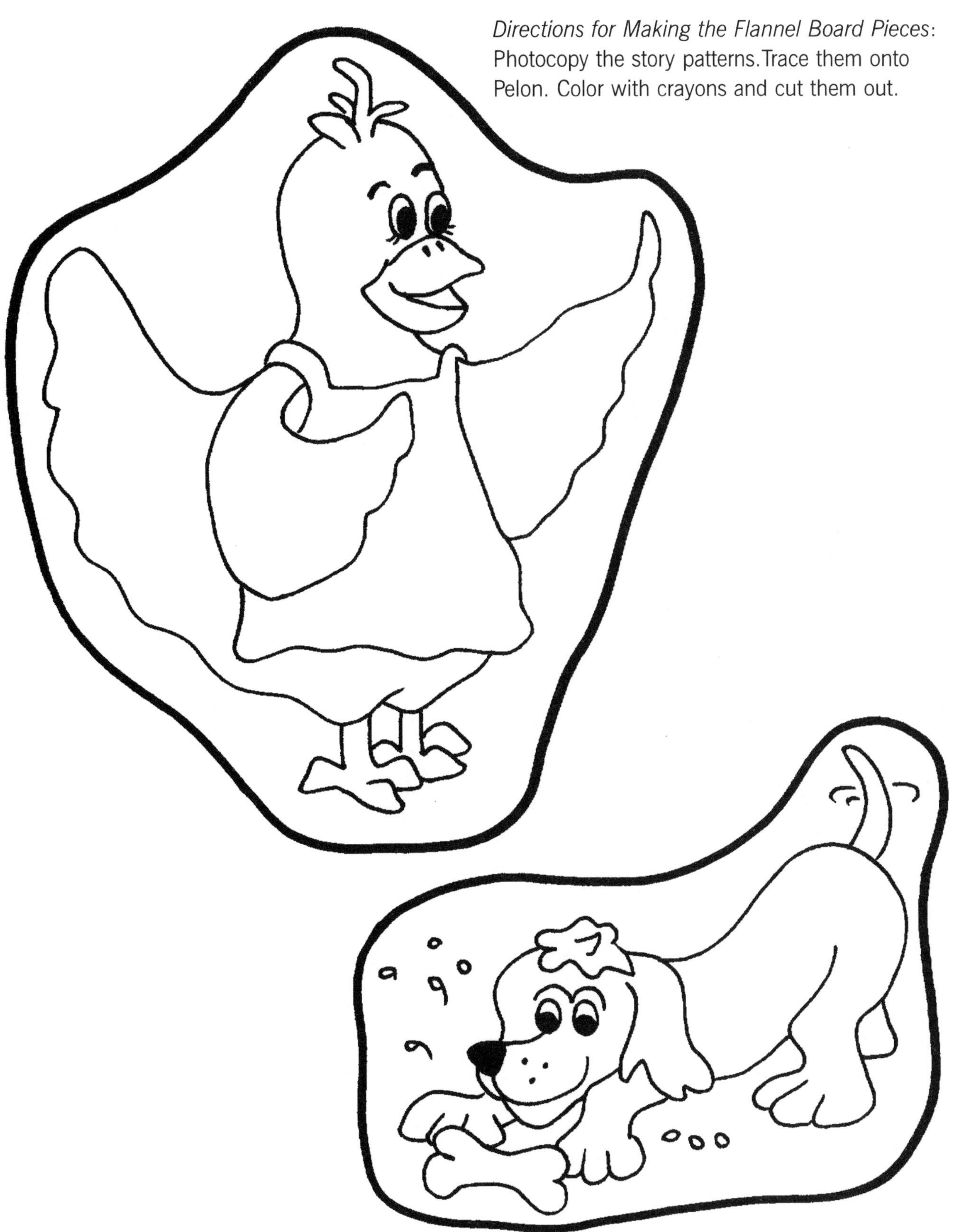

The Little Red Hen

Old MacDonald Had a Farm (See song on p. 298)

Directions for Making the Flannel Board Pieces: Photocopy the following patterns. Trace them onto Pelon. Color with crayons and cut them out.

Old MacDonald Had a Farm

One, Two, Buckle My Shoe (See rhyme on p. 324)

Directions for Making the Flannel Board Pieces: Photocopy the following patterns. Trace them onto Pelon. Color with crayons and cut them out.

One, Two, Buckle My Shoe

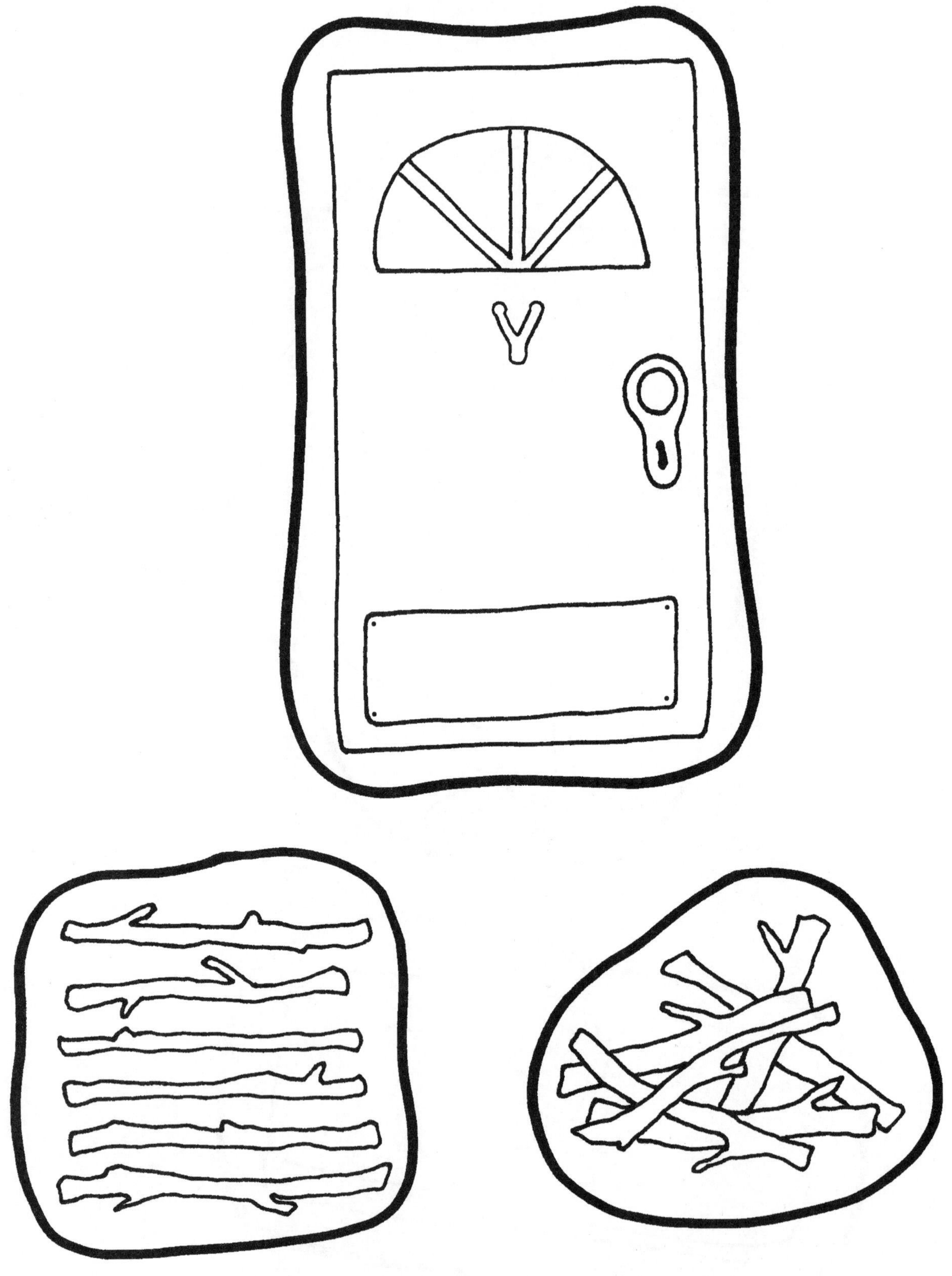

Sing a Song of Sixpence (See rhyme on p. 325)

Directions for Making the Flannel Board Pieces: Photocopy the following patterns. Trace them onto Pelon. Color with crayons and cut them out.

Sing a Song of Sixpence

Smart Cookie's Best Friend, Greta Graham

(See story on p. 343)

Directions for Making the Flannel Board Pieces: Photocopy the following patterns for Greta Graham. Trace them onto Pelon. Color with crayons and cut them out.

SMART COOKIE'S BEST FRIEND, GRETA GRAHAM

The Three Billy Goats Gruff (See story on p. 348)

Directions for Making the Flannel Board Pieces: Photocopy the following Three Billy Goats Gruff patterns. Trace them onto Pelon. Color with crayons and cut them out.

Flannel Board Patterns

The Three Billy Goats Gruff

The Three Billy Goats Gruff

The Three Little Pigs (See story on p. 350)

Directions for Making the Flannel Board Pieces: Photocopy the following patterns. Trace them onto Pelon. Color with crayons and cut them out.

This Old Man (See song on p. 305)

Directions for Making the Flannel Board Pieces: Photocopy the following patterns. Trace them onto Pelon. Color with crayons and cut them out.

This Old Man

This Old Man

Twinkle, Twinkle Little Star (See song on p. 306)

Directions for Making the Flannel Board Pieces: Photocopy the following patterns. Trace them onto Pelon. Color with crayons and cut them out.

Twinkle, Twinkle Little Star

Valencia Valentine (See story on p. 353)

Directions for Making the Flannel Board Pieces: Photocopy the following patterns. Trace them on pelon. Color with crayons and cut them out.

Valencia Valentine

Brown Bear, Brown Bear Story Cards

Brown Bear, Brown Bear Story Cards

Brown Bear, Brown Bear Story Cards

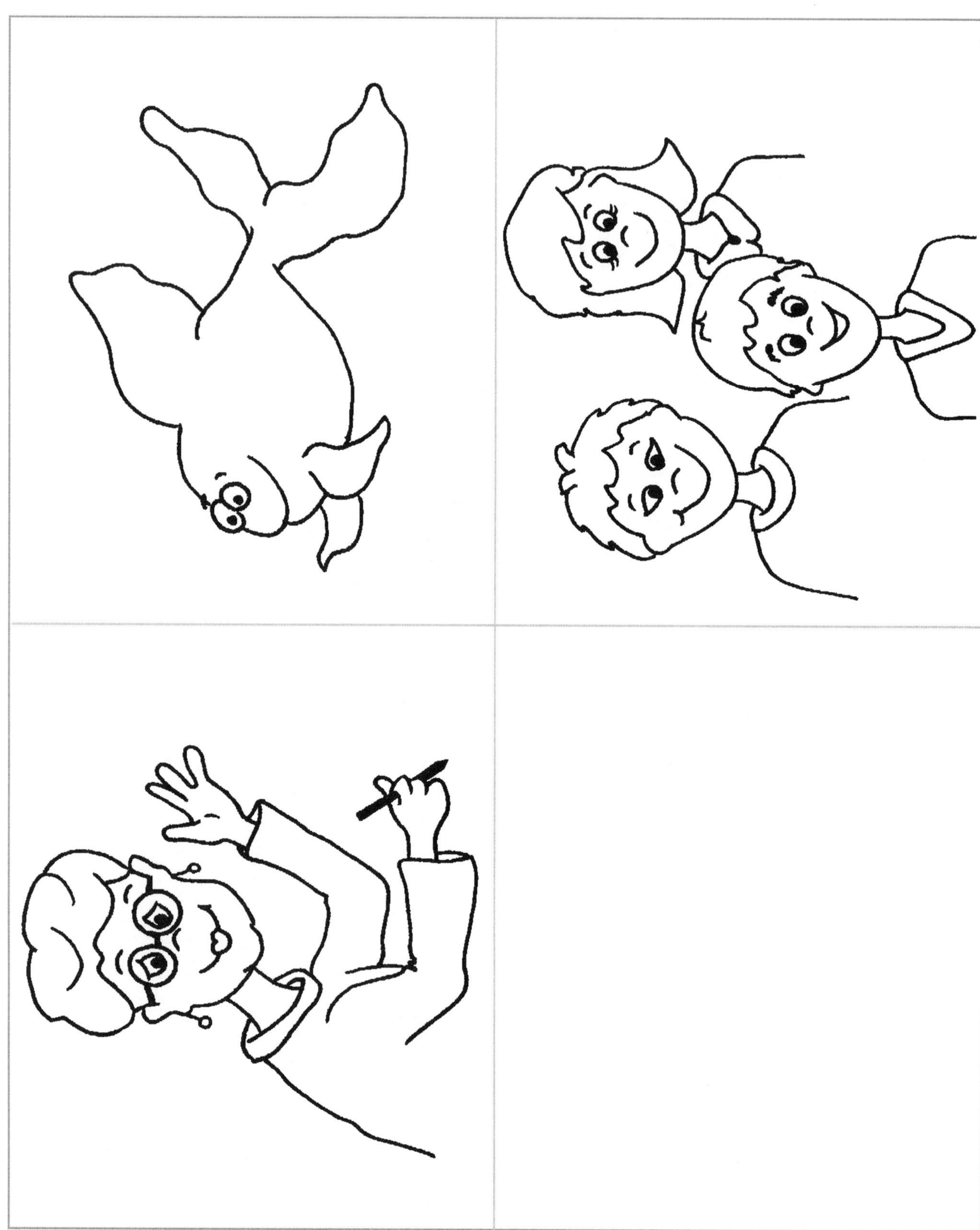

Itsy Bitsy Spider Song Cards

Itsy Bitsy Spider Song Cards

Animal Puppets

Directions for Making the Stick Puppets:
Photocopy the patterns. Color, cut them out, and laminate. Glue them onto tongue depressors.

Animal Puppets

Cat

Elephant

Animal Puppets

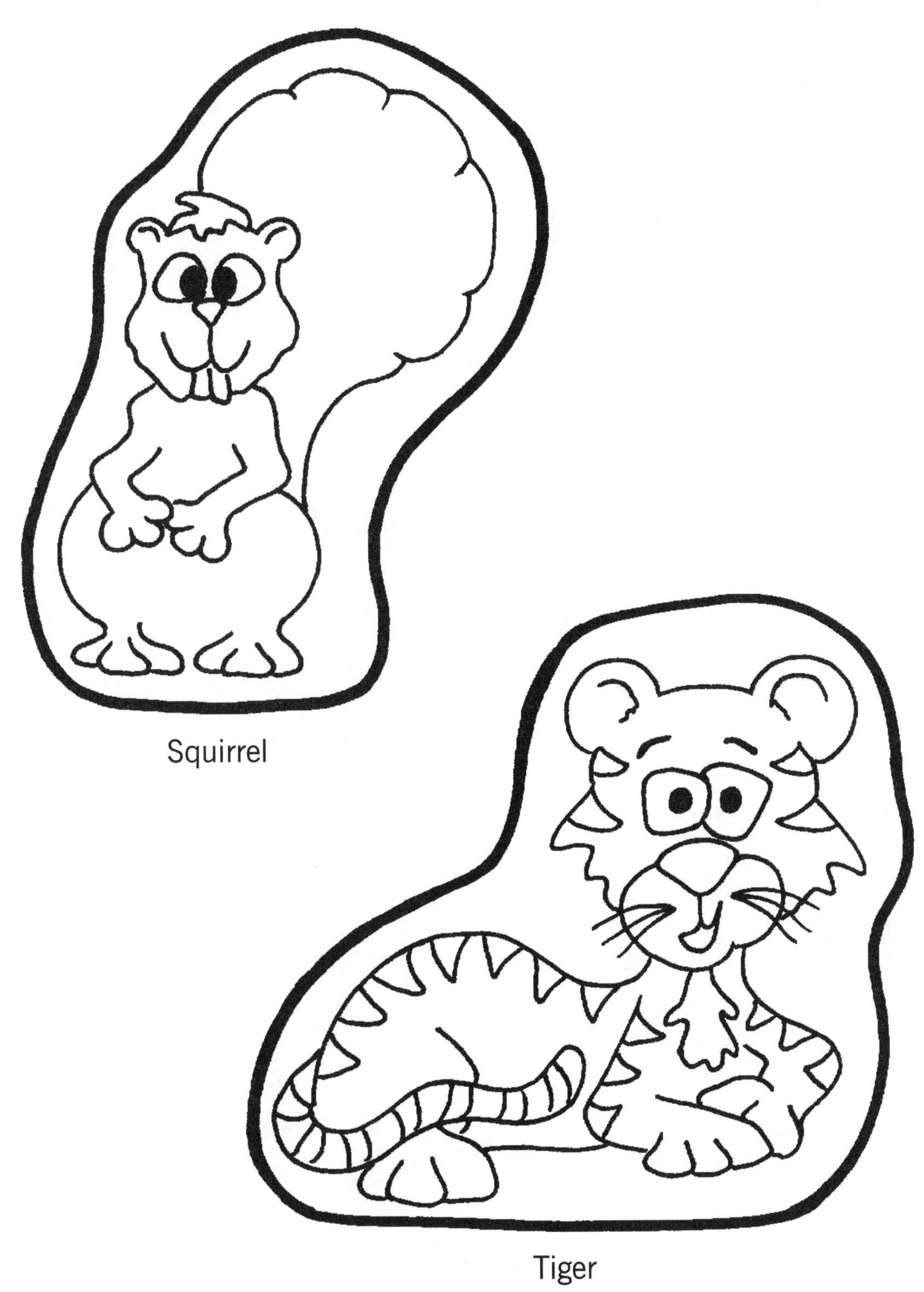

Squirrel

Tiger

Animal Puppets

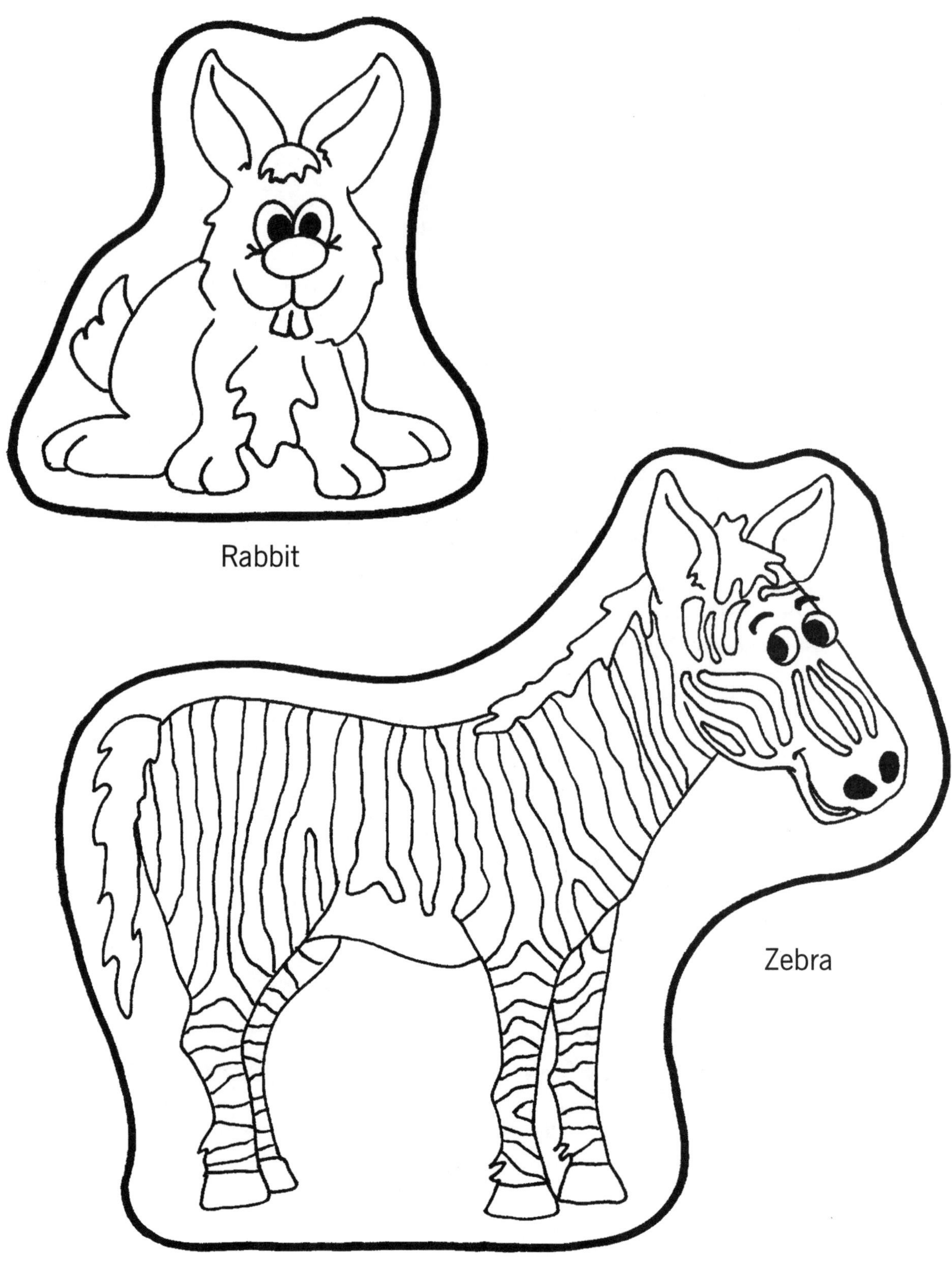

Rabbit

Zebra

Animal Puppets

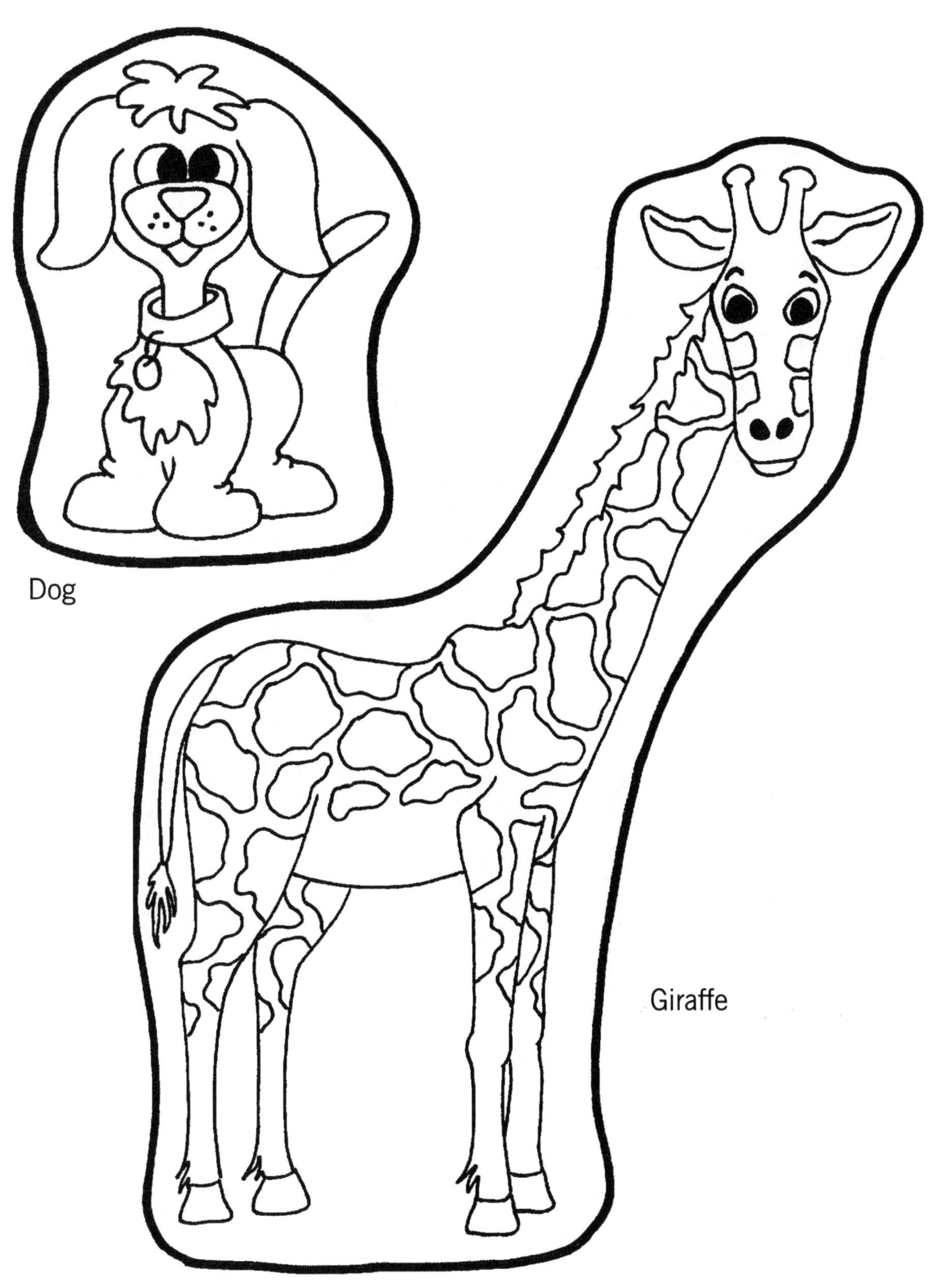

Dog

Giraffe

Bumblebee and Honey Puppets

Directions for Making the Stick Puppets: Photocopy the patterns. Color, cut them out, and laminate. Glue them onto tongue depressors.

Family Puppets

Directions for Making the Stick Puppets: Photocopy the patterns. Color, cut them out, and laminate. Glue them onto tongue depressors.

Family Puppets

Five Little Ducks

Directions for Making the Stick Puppets: Photocopy the patterns. Color, cut them out, and laminate. Glue them onto tongue depressors.

Five Little Ducks

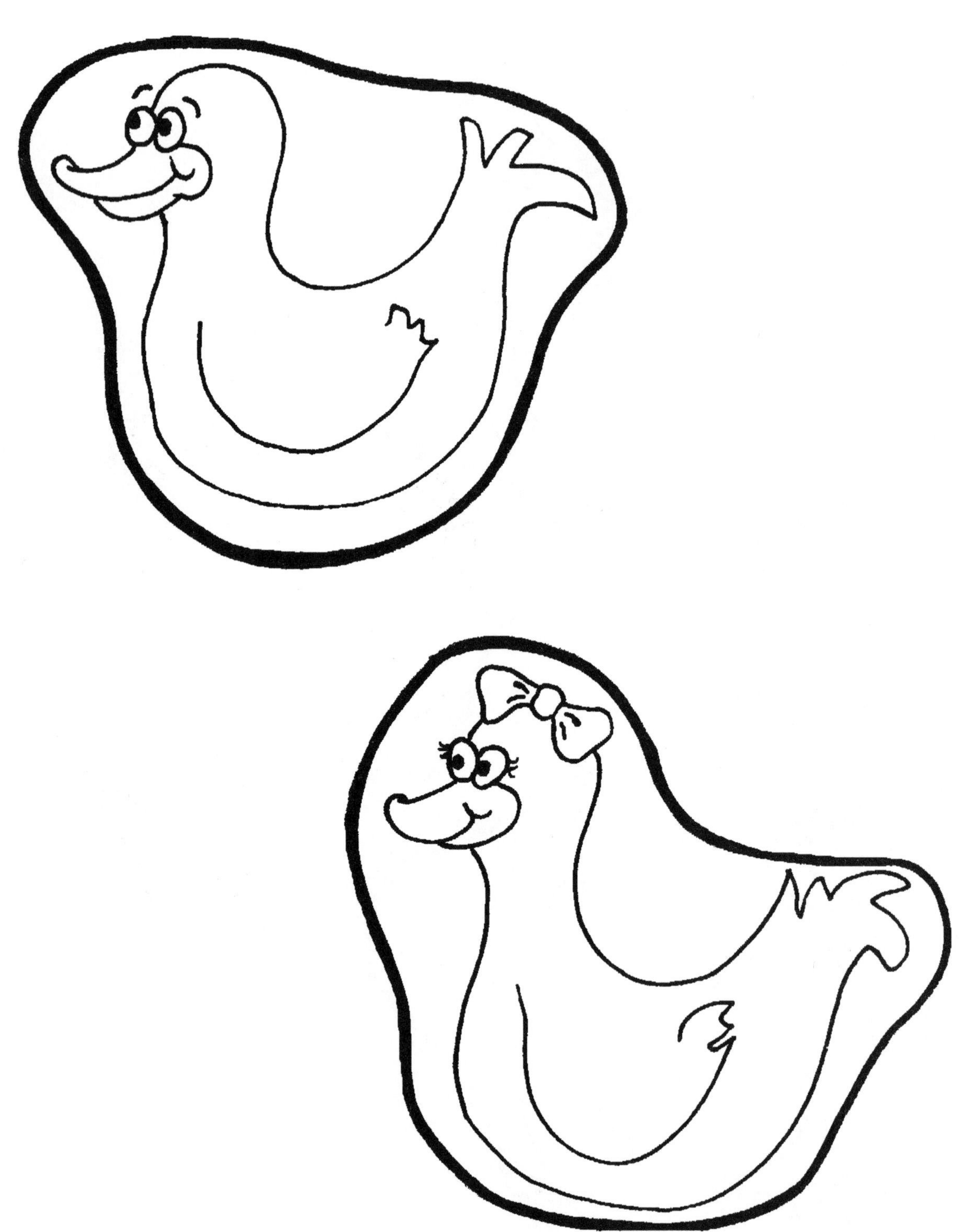

Five Fat Turkeys Puppets

Directions for Making the Stick Puppets: Photocopy the patterns. Color, cut them out, and laminate. Glue them onto tongue depressors.

Five Fat Turkeys Puppets

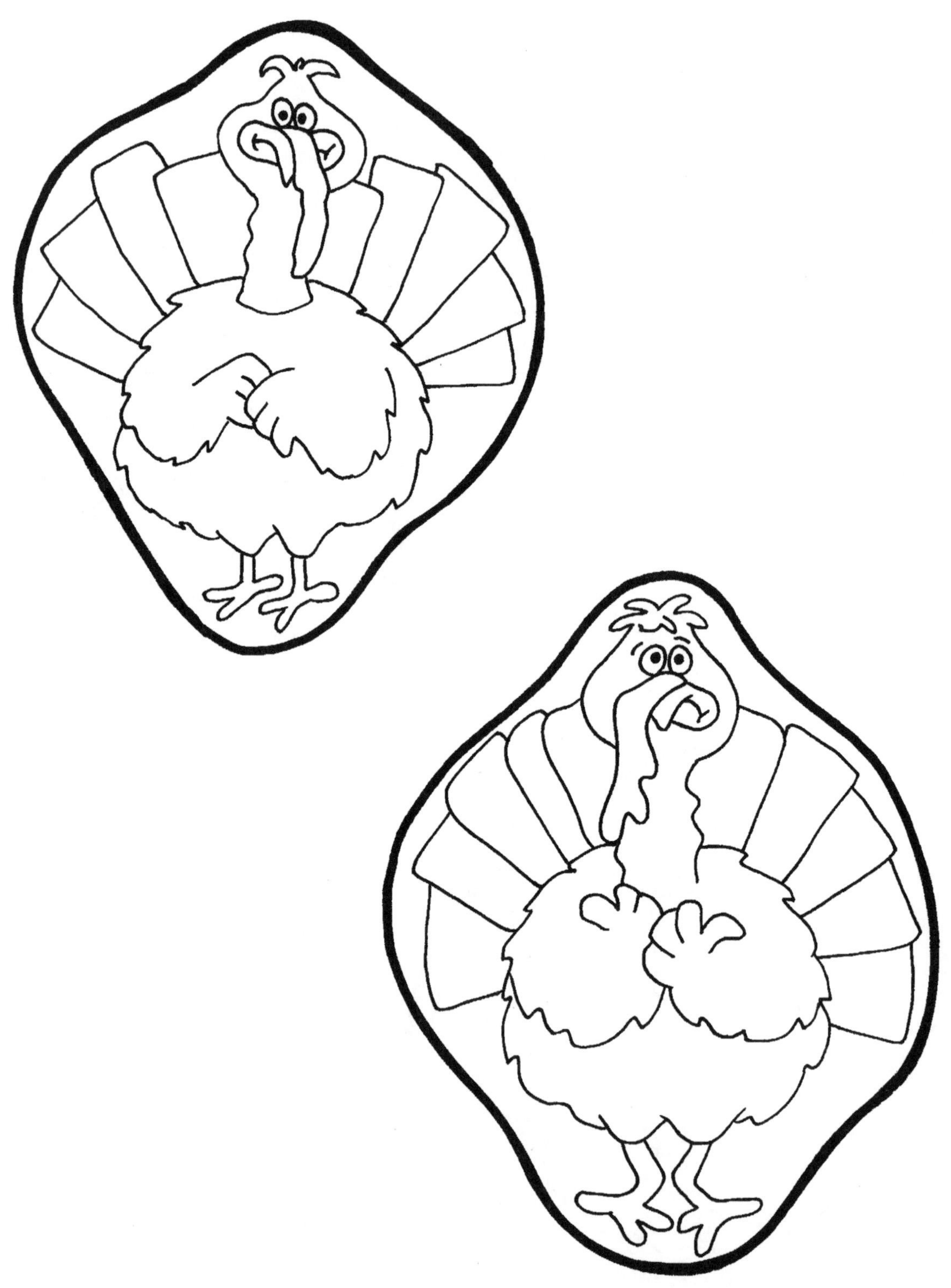

Frog Puppets

Make a photocopy of two frogs (facing opposite directions) from the frog patterns. Color them, cut them out, and laminate them. Position the frogs back to back and glue to a tongue depressor to create a Front Frog Fred and a Back Frog Jack.

Front-side Fred

Back-side Jack

Family Glove Puppets

Directions for Making the Glove Puppets: Photocopy the patterns. Color, cut them out, and laminate. Glue Velcro on the back of each puppet.

Five Fat Turkeys Glove Puppets

Directions for Making the Glove Puppets: Photocopy the patterns. Color, cut them out, and laminate. Glue Velcro on the back of each puppet.

Five Little Speckled Frogs Glove Puppets

Directions for Making the Glove Puppets: Photocopy the patterns. Color, cut them out, and laminate. Glue Velcro on the back of each puppet.

Five Little Pilgrims Glove Puppets

Directions for Making the Glove Puppets: Photocopy the patterns. Color, cut them out, and laminate. Glue Velcro on the back of each puppet.

Five Little Pumpkins Glove Puppets

Directions for Making the Glove Puppets: Photocopy the patterns. Color, cut them out, and laminate. Glue Velcro on the back of each puppet.

Goldilocks and the Three Bears

Directions for Making the Glove Puppets: Photocopy the patterns. Color, cut them out, and laminate. Glue Velcro on the back of each puppet.

Three Billy Goats Gruff Glove Puppets

Directions for Making the Glove Puppets: Photocopy the patterns. Color, cut them out, and laminate. Glue Velcro on the back of each puppet.

Three Little Pigs Glove Puppets

Directions for Making the Glove Puppets: Photocopy the patterns. Color, cut them out, and laminate. Glue Velcro on the back of each puppet.

Itsy Bitsy Spider Puppets

Directions for Making Stick Puppets: Photocopy the Itsy Bitsy Spider patterns. Color, cut them out, laminate, and glue them to straws or to tongue depressors. **For a Cup Puppet**, glue the patterns to straws. Make three small holes in the bottom of a Styrofoam cup. Push the straw through the holes so the pattern pieces can be pulled down into the cup. Move the pieces up and down with the words of the song.

There Was an Old Lady Who Swallowed a Fly

Directions for Making a Paper Bag Puppet: Photocopy the puppet patterns. Color, cut, and laminate the patterns for the things the old lady ate. Color, cut, and laminate the face of the old lady. Glue the old lady's face to the bottom of a paper sack.

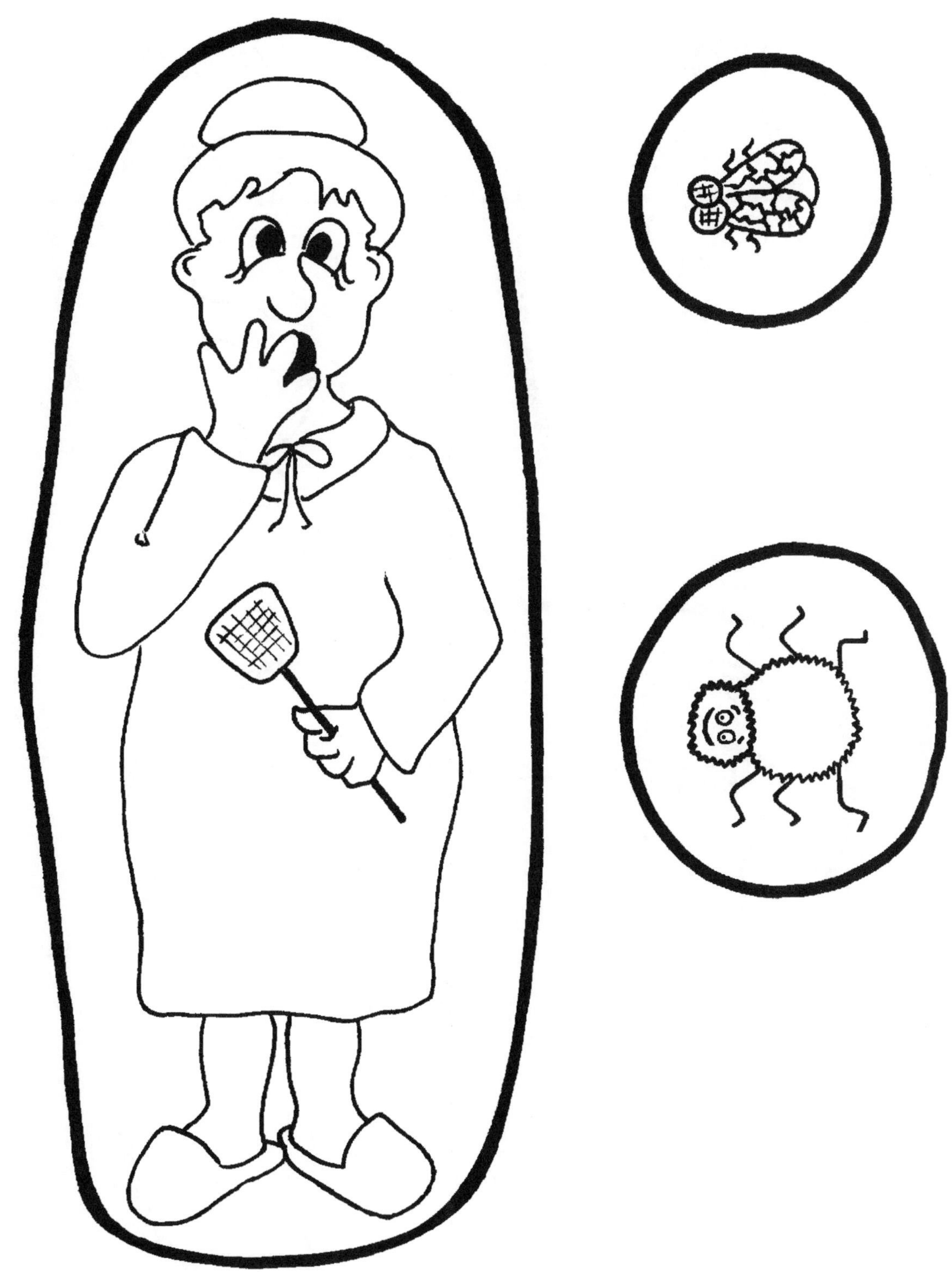

There Was an Old Lady Who Swallowed a Fly

There Was an Old Lady Who Swallowed a Fly

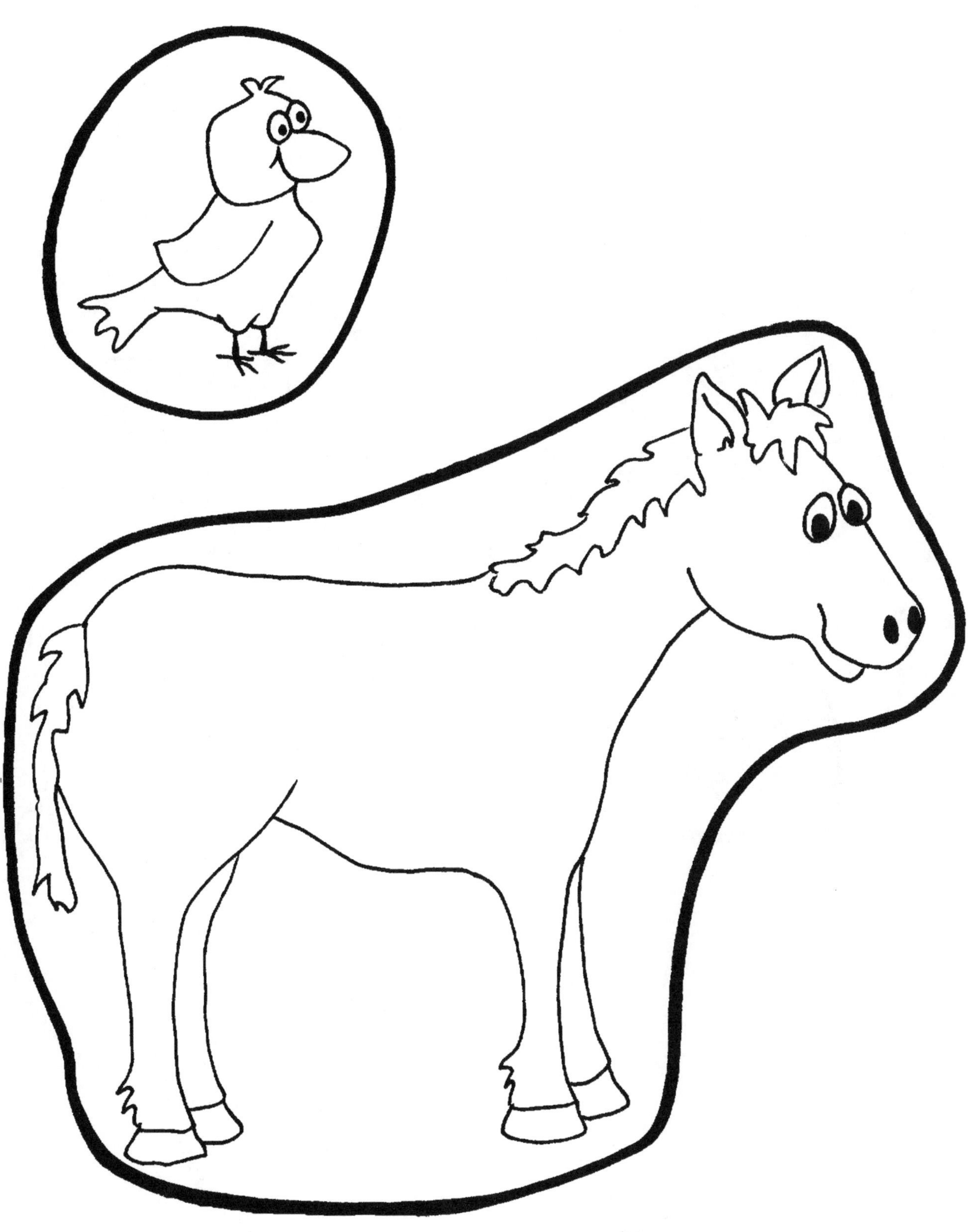

Three Little Pigs and Wolf Puppets

Directions for Making the Stick Puppets: Photocopy the patterns. Color, cut them out, and laminate. Glue them onto tongue depressors.

Three Little Pigs and Wolf Puppets

Bird Nest Candy Recipe

Bird Nest Candy

Frozen Yogurt
ROCK SALT
Fill coffee can with ice and rock salt.
1
Yogurt
Place yogurt container in coffee can.
Roll coffee can around for 15 minutes.
Eat.

Gak Rebus

Gak
2
Glue
1½
Water
2
RED
FOOD COLOR
Stir glue mixture.
1
HOT WATER
2 T.
BORAX
Stir Borax mixture.
Combine glue and Borax mixtures.
Play.

Homemade Butter

Pour whipping cream into baby food jar.

Shake.

Strain liquid from mixture.

Eat.

HOMEMADE PEANUT BUTTER RECIPE

Peanut Butter

1 1/2

Vegetable oil

1

1/2

Mix ingredients until smooth.

Spread on a cracker.

Eat.

Peanut Butter and Jelly Sandwich

Peppermint Baggie Ice Cream Recipe

Peppermint Baggie Icecream

1/2 Milk
1 T. Sugar
1/4 t. Vanilla
1

Crush peppermint with block.

Place all ingredients in plastic bag and seal.

Fill plastic baggie with ice and rock salt.

Put icecream bag inside big plastic bag and shake.

Eat.

Purple Cow Shake

Vacation Packing List

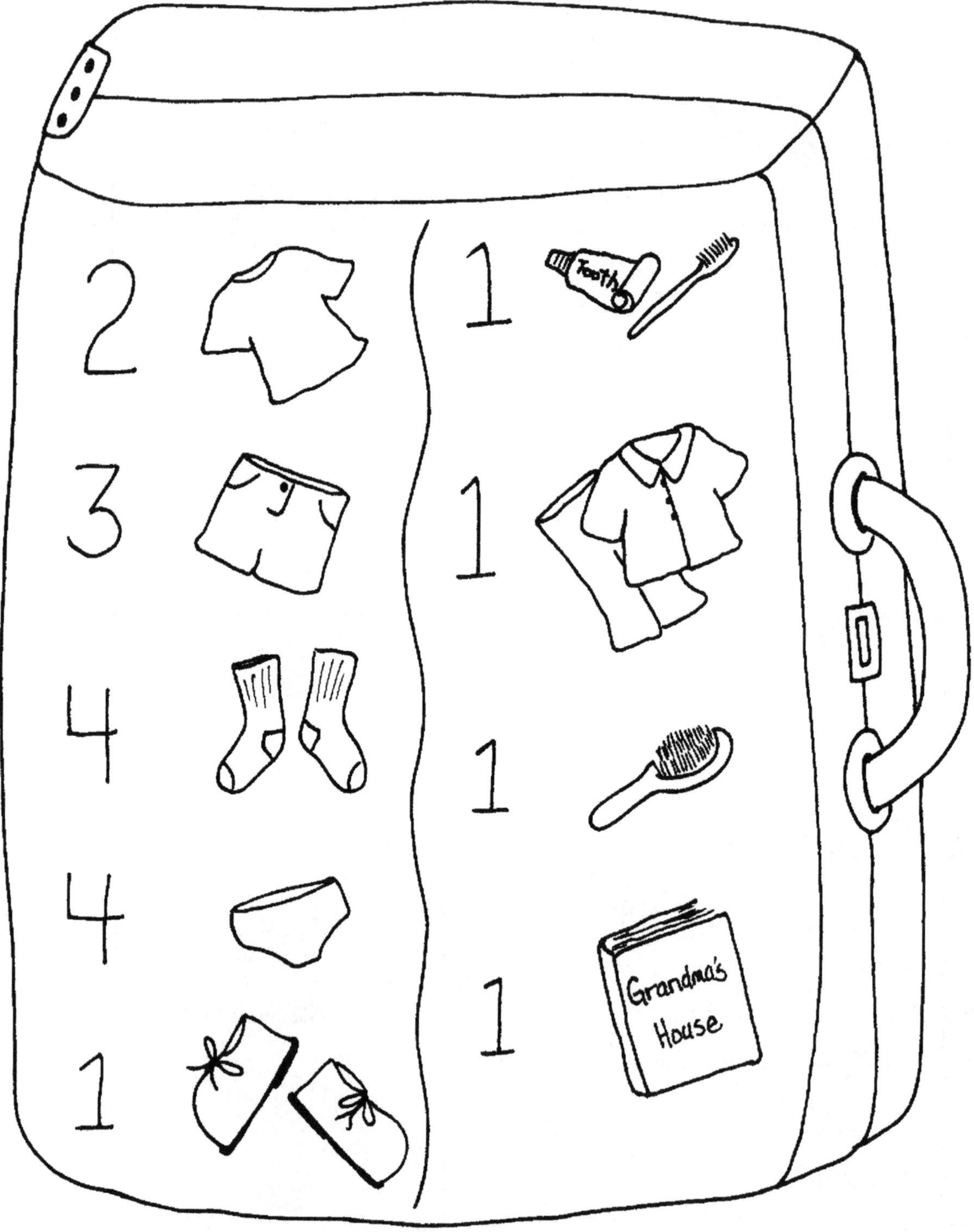

Animal Footprints

Make copies and cut out along grid lines.

Bird and Nest

Dog and Bone

DOG AND BONE

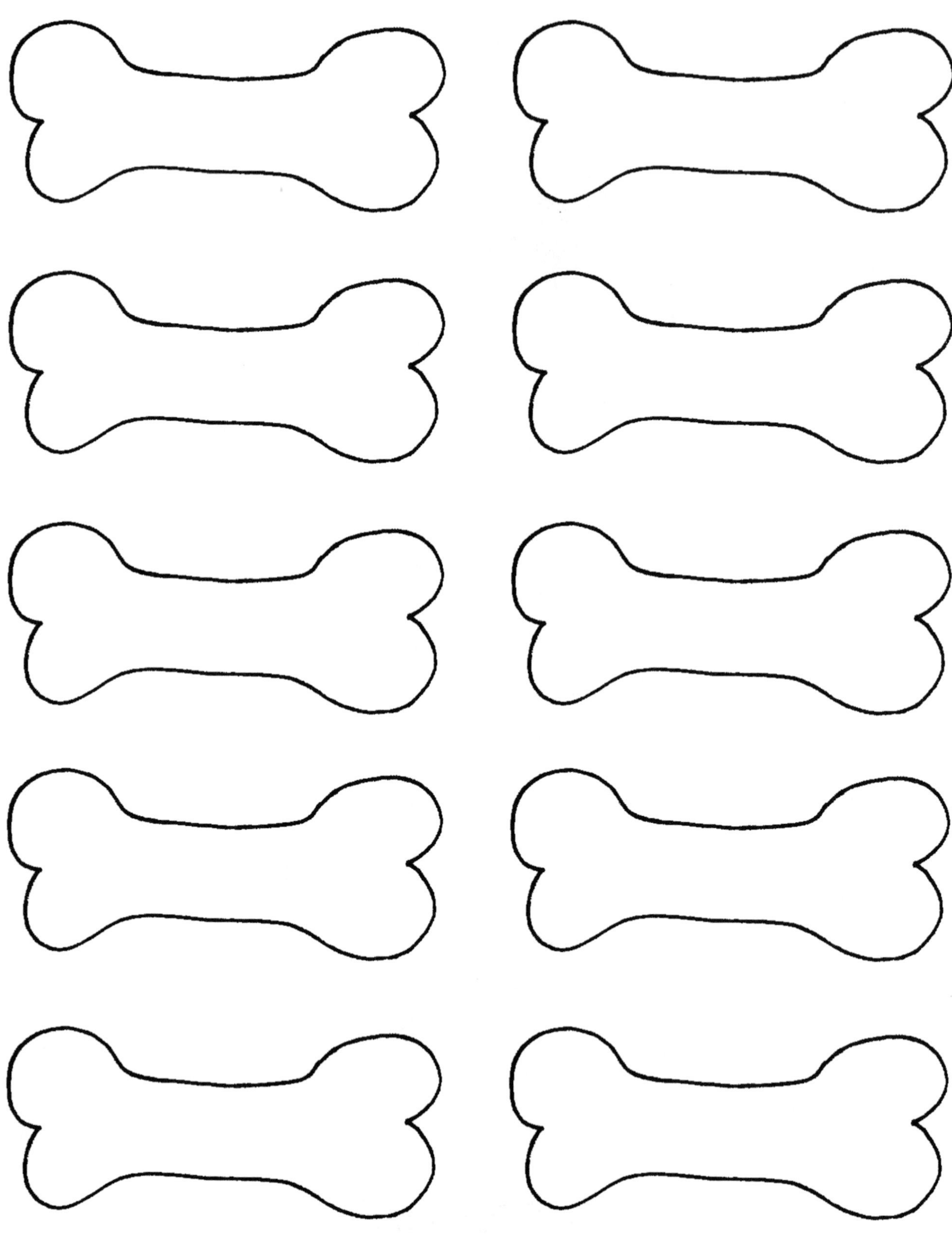

Elephant and Peanut

ELEPHANT AND PEANUT

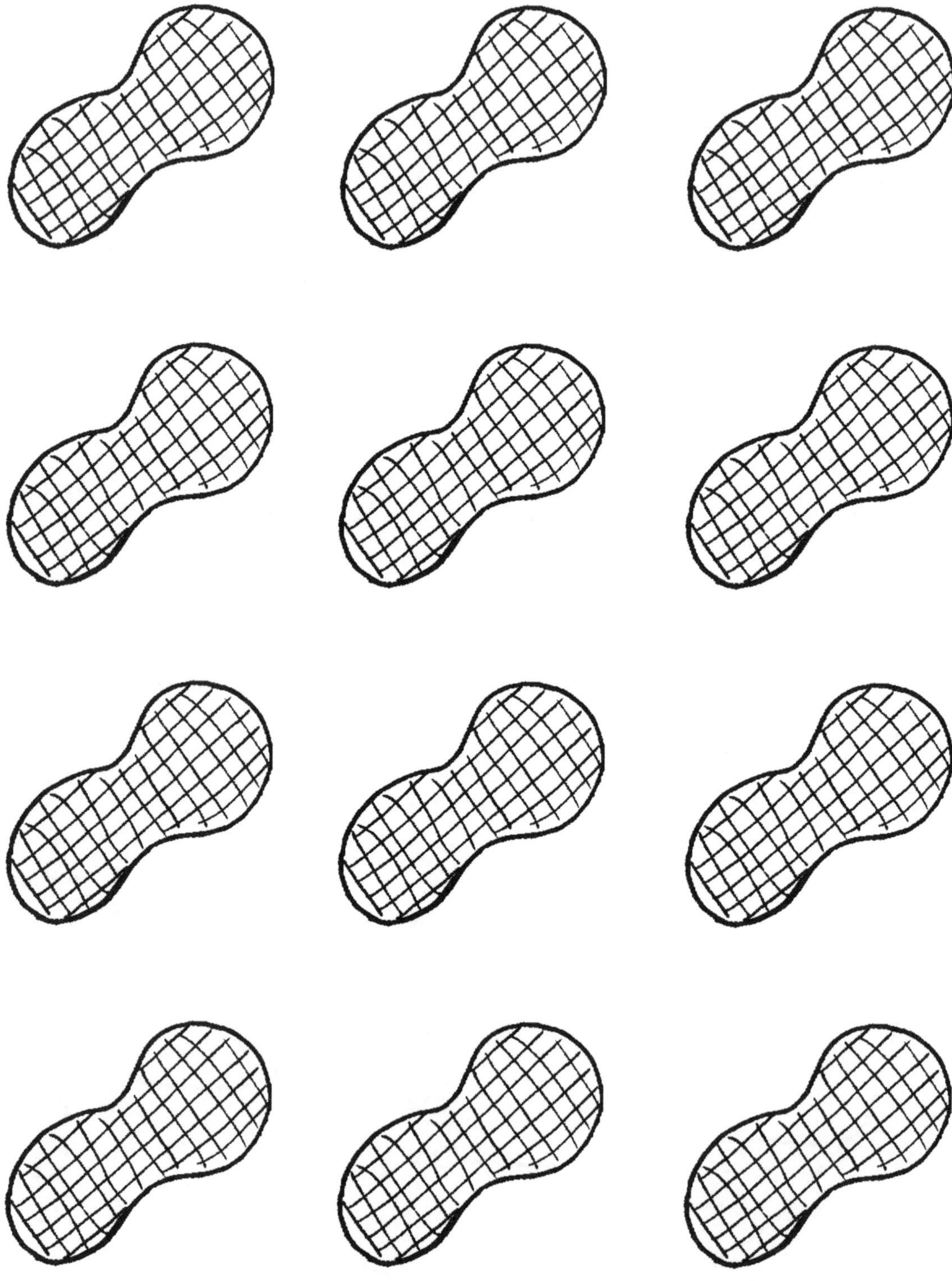

Forest Animal Concentration

Copy this page
twice for
concentration game.

INSECT CONCENTRATION

Ocean Animal Patterns

Pumpkin Concentration

Reptile Concentration

Zoo Animal Concentration

Lion

Animal Faces for Masks

Dog

Animal Faces for Masks

Pig

Animal Faces for Masks

Cat

Lamb

Animal Faces for Masks

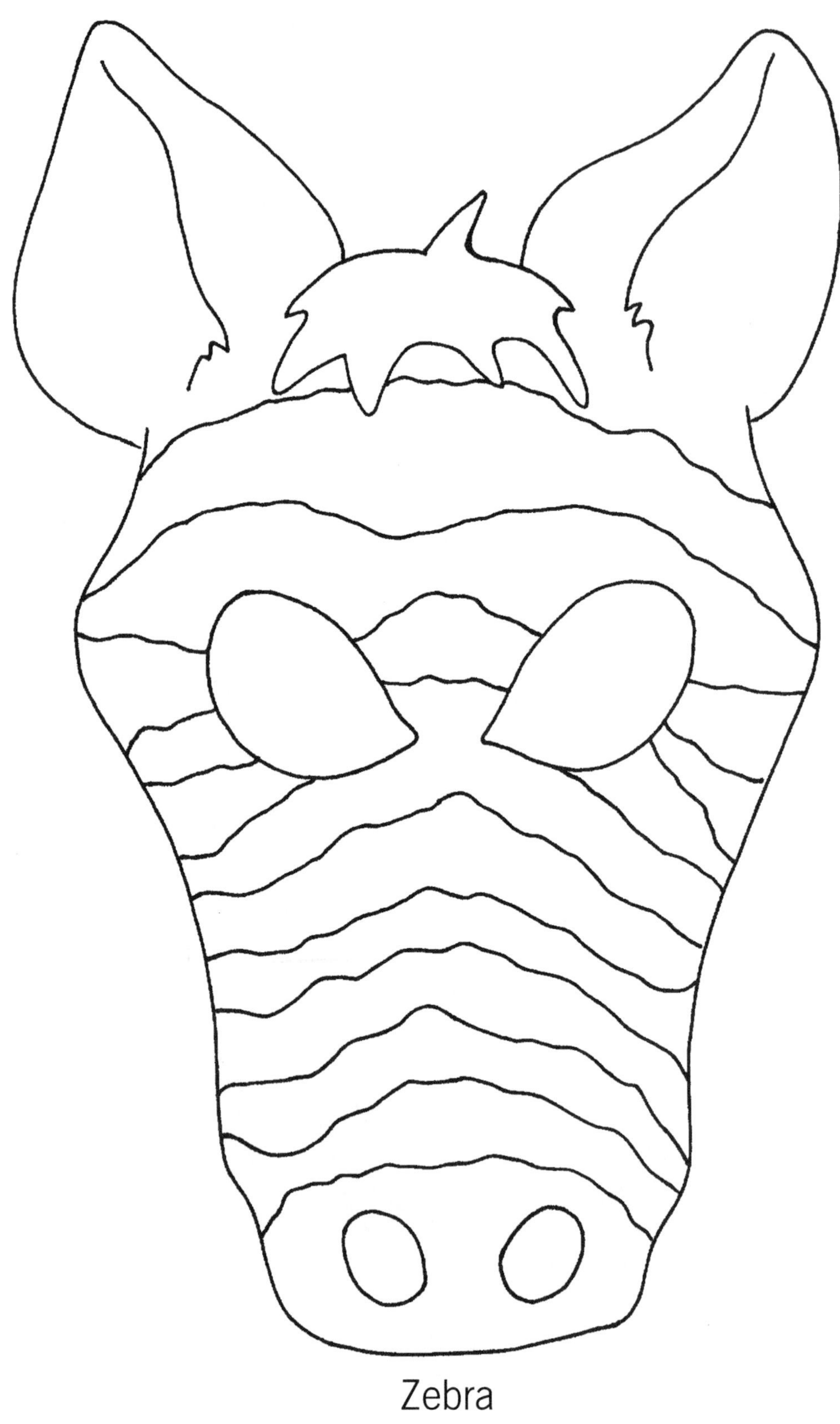

Zebra

Mouse

Calendar Art

Calendar Art

Calendar Page

Dancing Bear

Dress Me Dolls

Dress Me Dolls

Dress Me Dolls

Dress Me Dolls

Farm Animals

Farm Animals

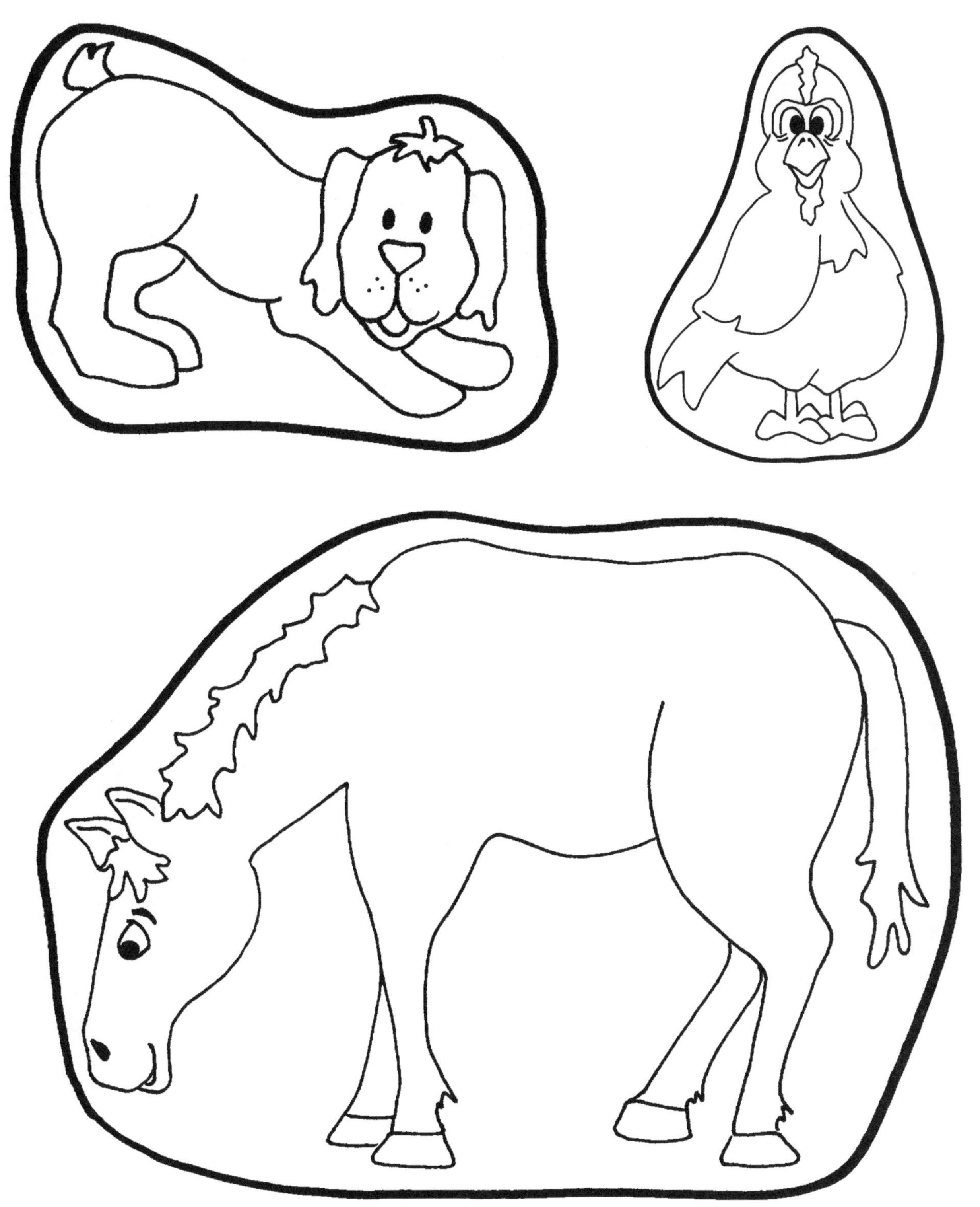

Finger Spelling

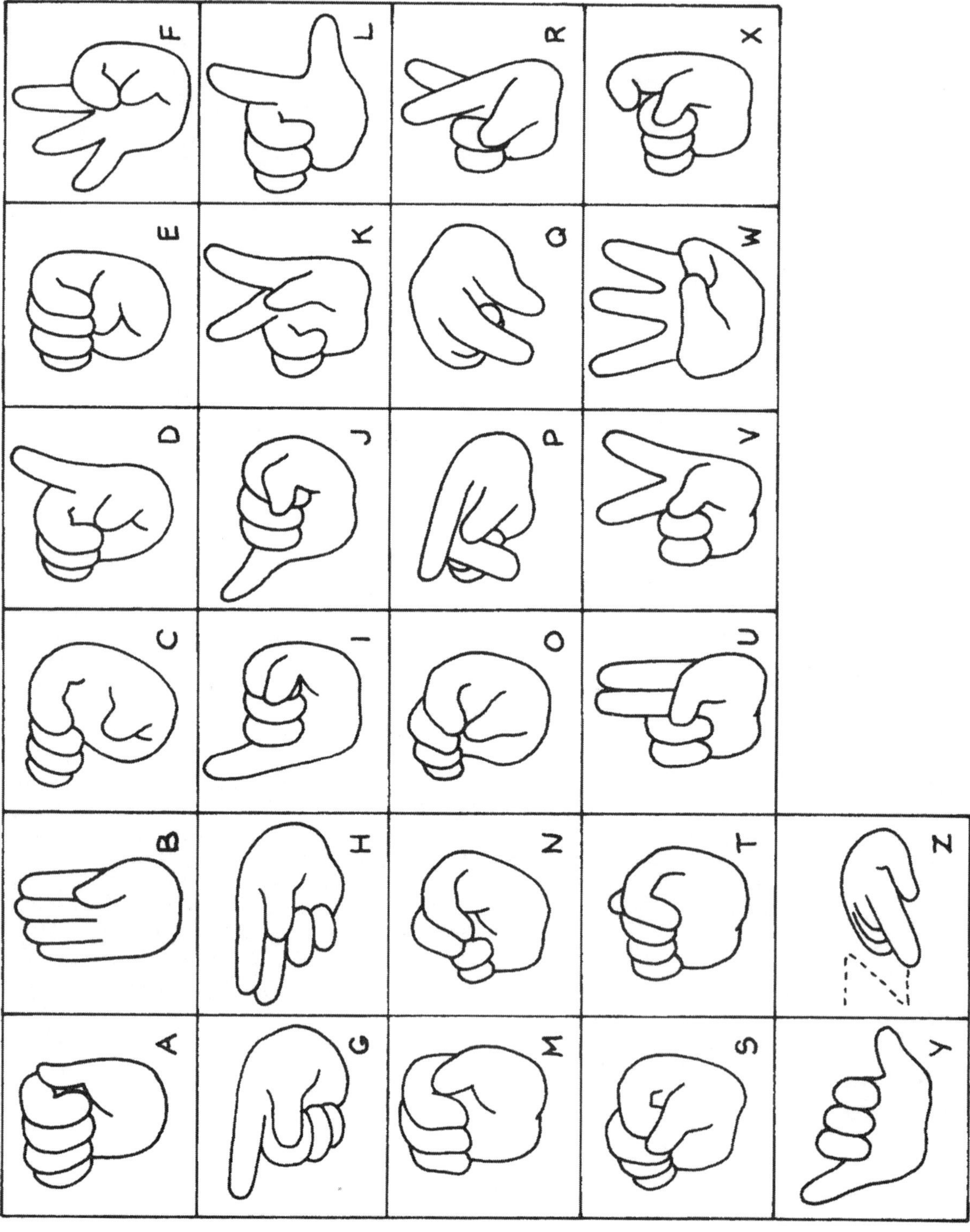

Fruit and Vegetable Patterns

Metamorphosis Sequence Cards

"My Favorite Things" Cards

Pyramid Template

Teacher Hint: Photocopy this page. Glue the page to one half of a manilla folder. Cut out the "Things I Like to Do" cards and "My Favorite Things" cards. Paperclip the cards to the file folder for easy access.

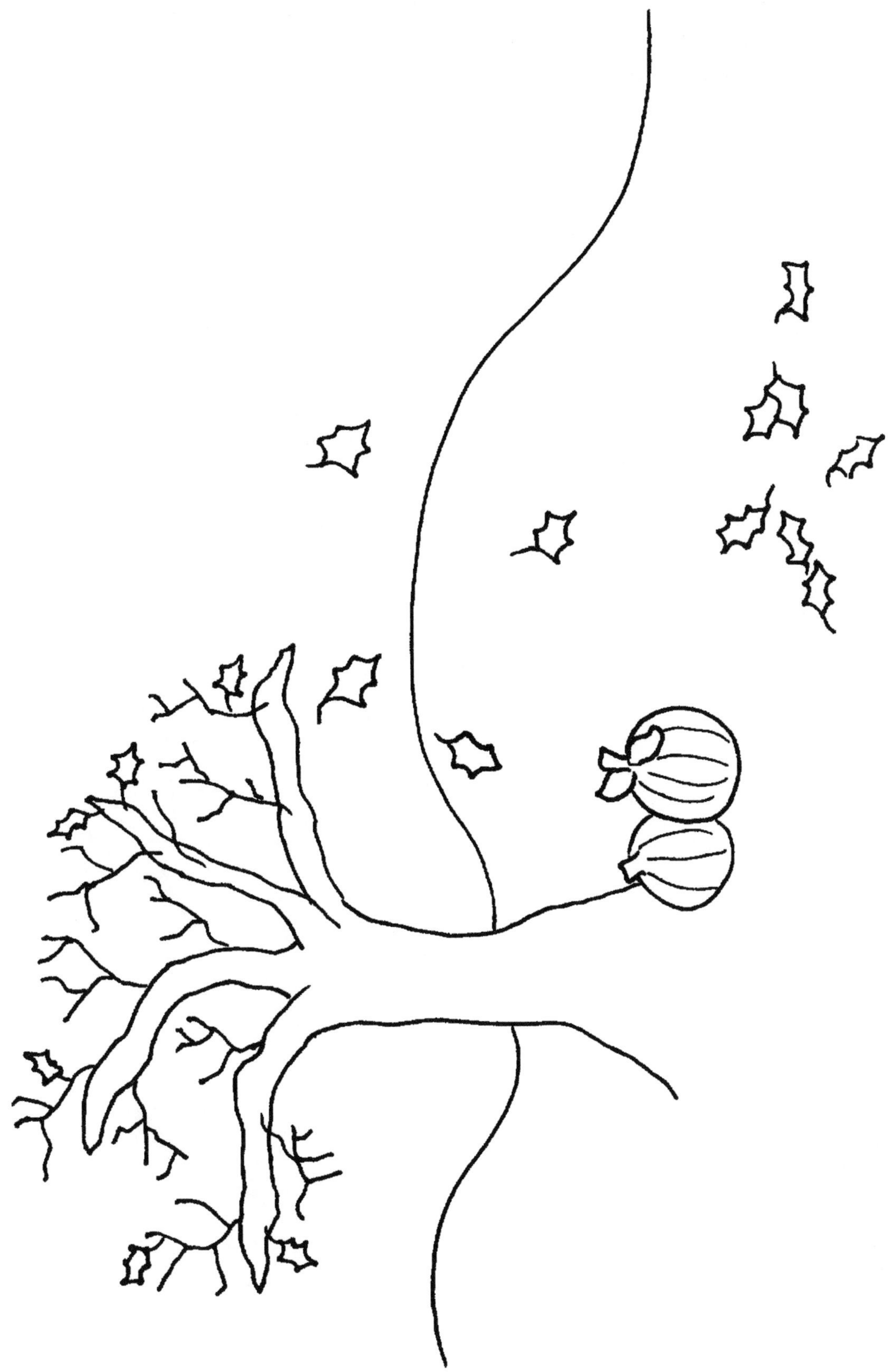

Season Mats

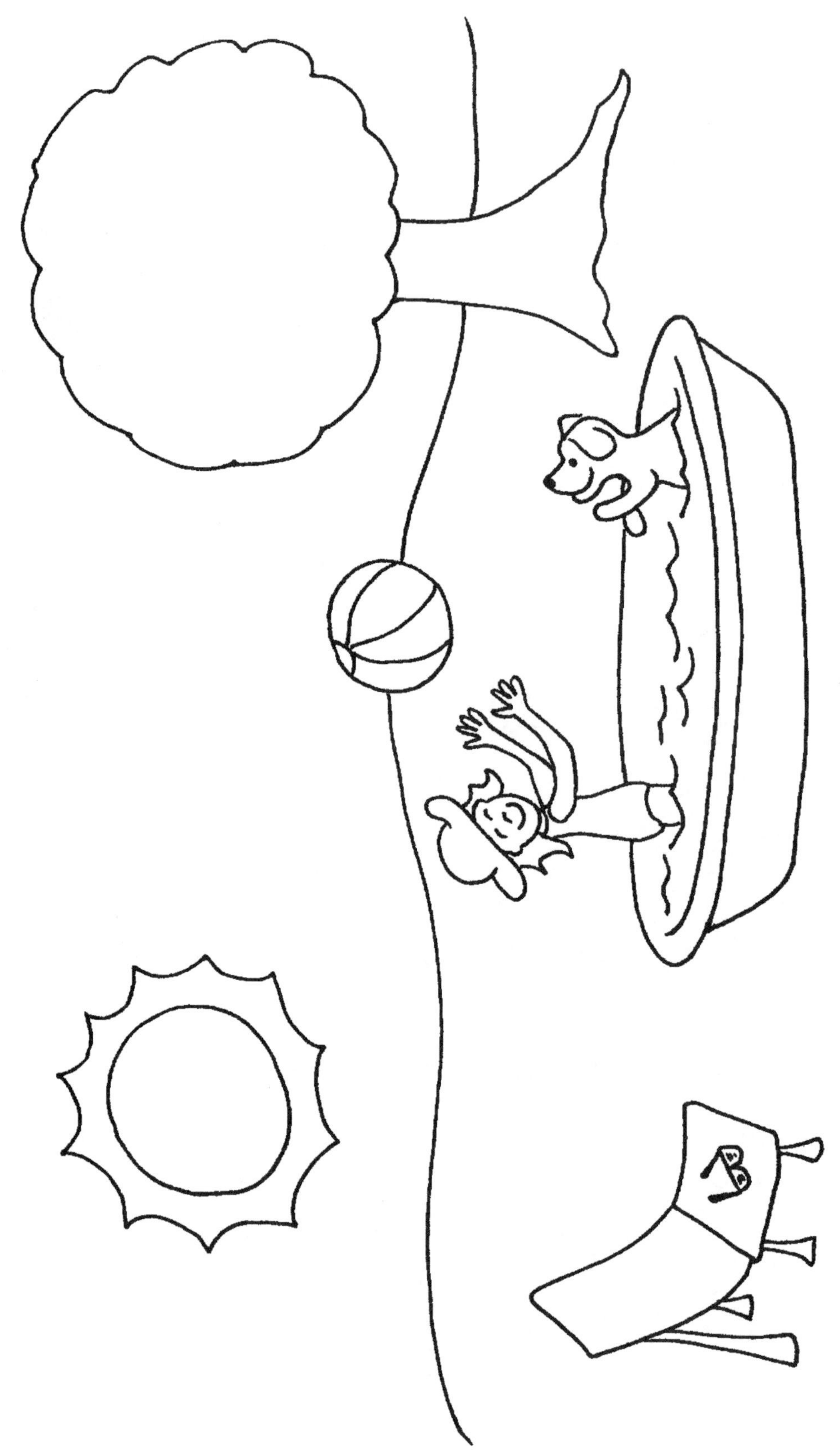

Season Mats

Season Mats

Sign Language

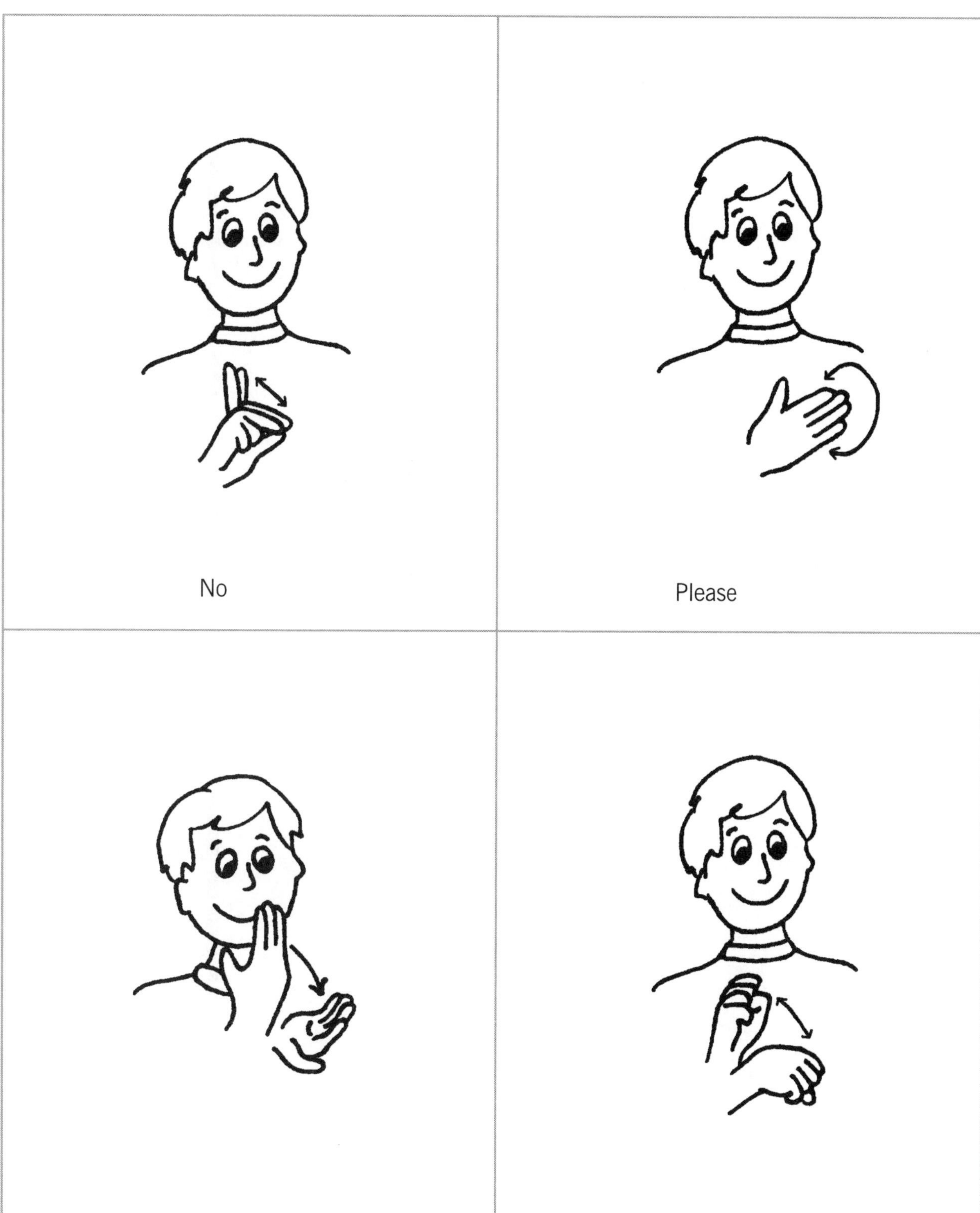

Story Pyramid

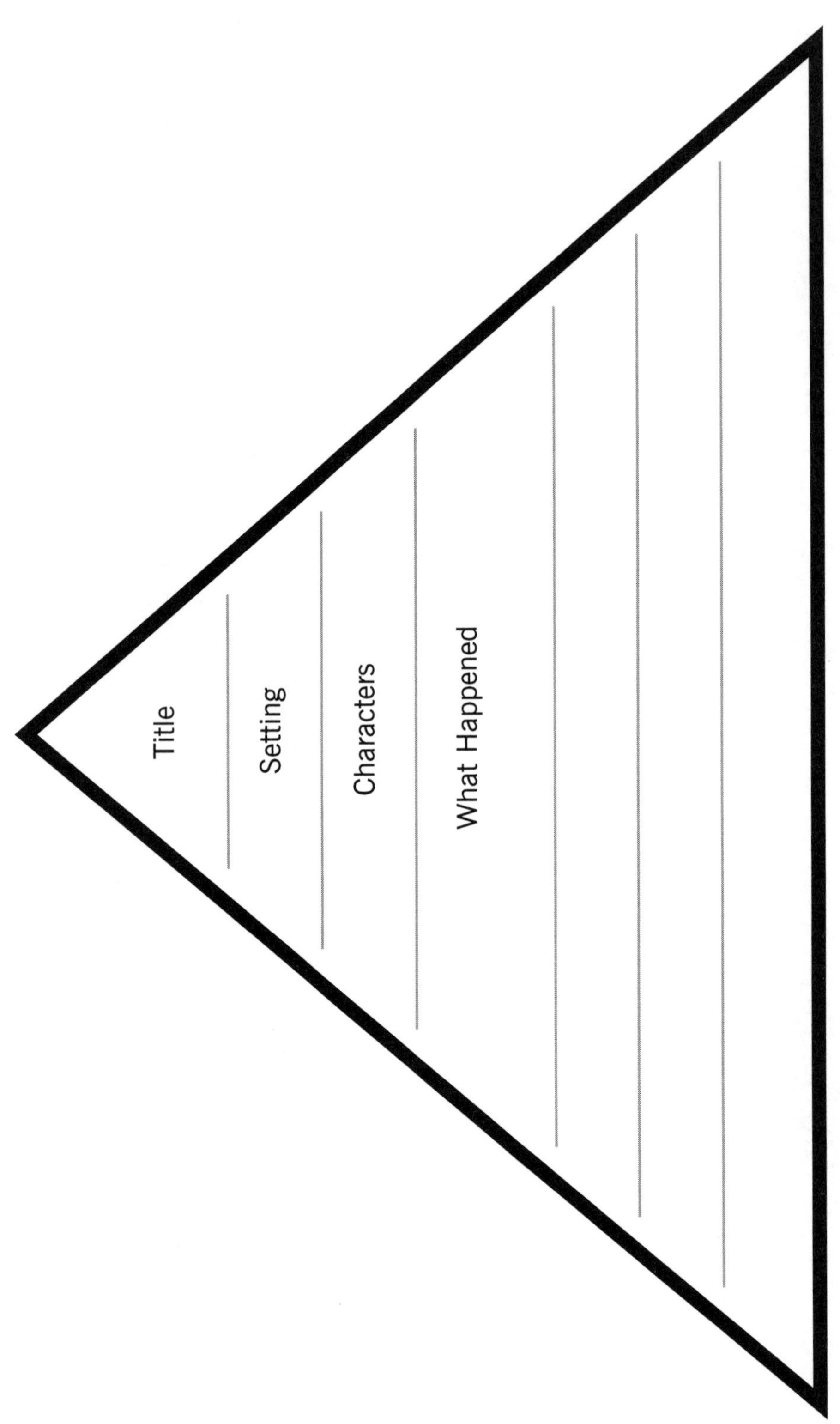

"Things I Like to Do" Cards

Tree and Flower Patterns

Tree and Flower Patterns

Tree and Flower Patterns

Very Hungry Caterpillar Patterns

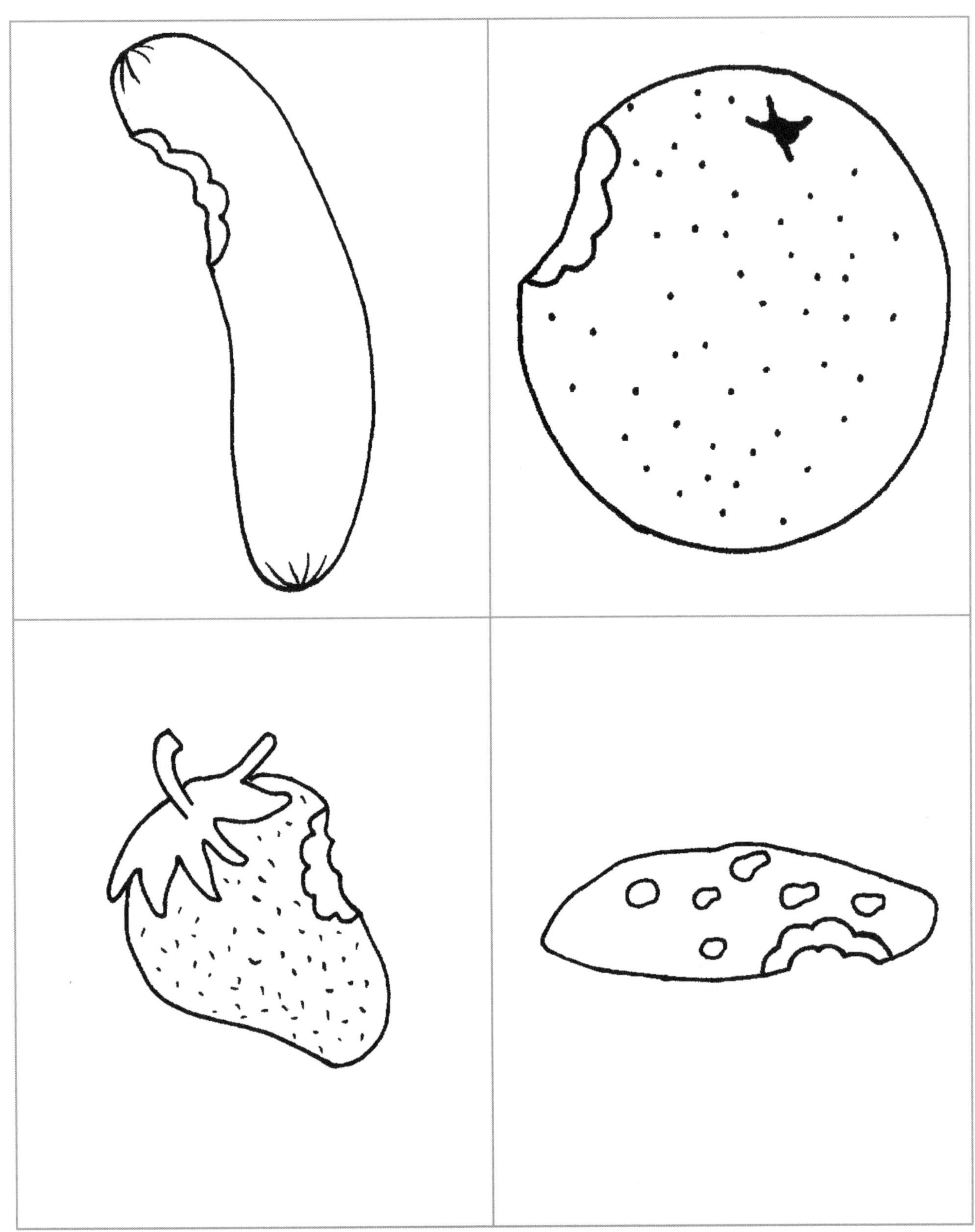

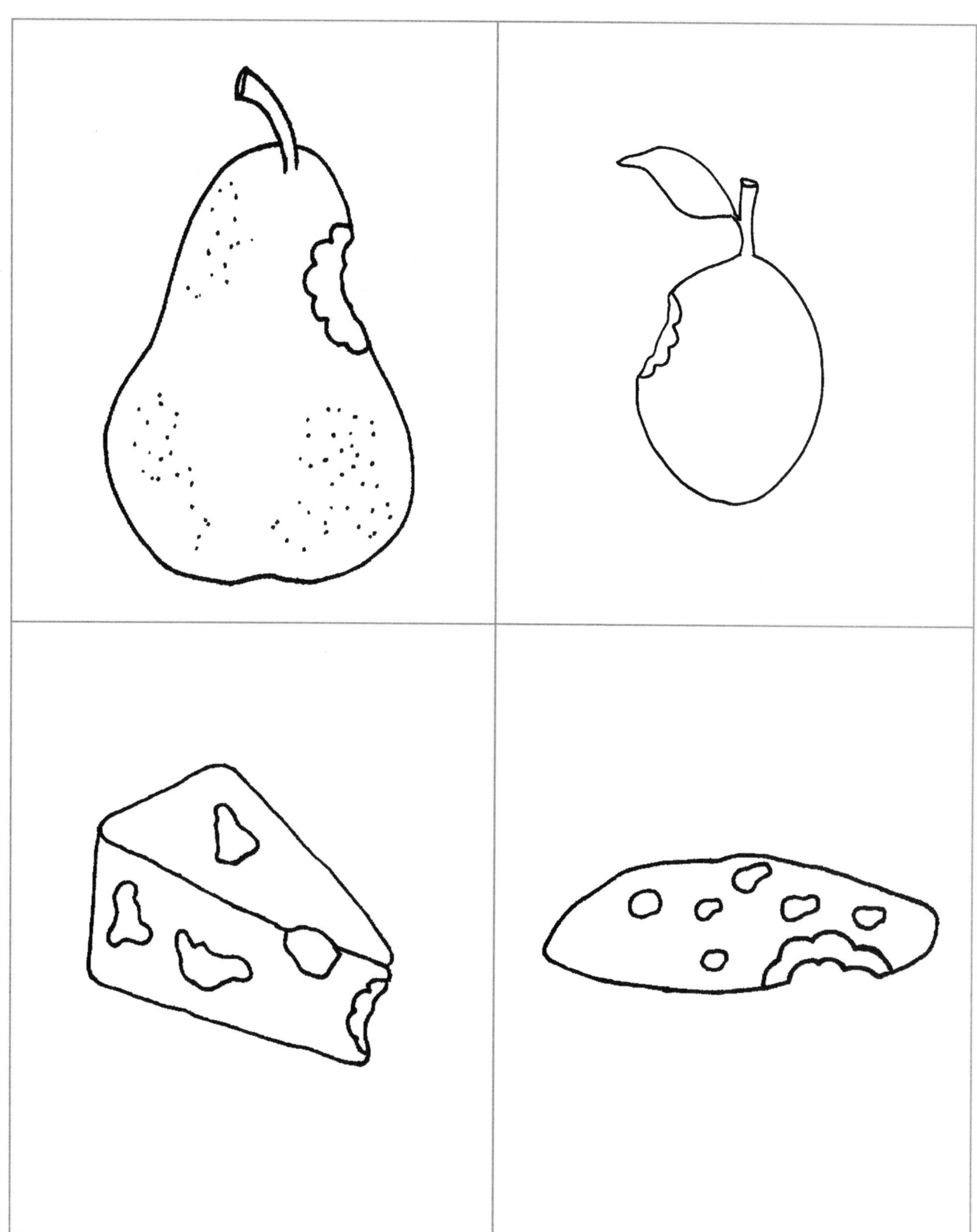

Very Hungry Caterpillar Patterns

Weather Wheel

Index

Themes and Materials

A

C

D

G

H

I

J

K

L

M

P

T

U

V

Children's Books Index

C

D

E

F

G

H

I

J

K

L

M

N

O

P

Q

R

S

T

U

V

W

Y

Stories, Rhymes, and Fingerplays Index

I

J

L

M

O

P

S

T

V

W

Songs Index

A

B

C

D

F

G

H

I

J

L

M

N

O

P

R

S

Games and Dances Index

F

G

H

I

L

M

O

Multiple Intelligences Index (by theme)

All About Me

Colors All Around

Index

The Shape of Things

Sing a Song of Opposites

World of Animals

It's Chow Time!

Mother Goose on the Loose (Nursery Rhymes)

Spatial (Picture Smart)

Tell Me a Tale (Favorite Stories)

Bodily-Kinesthetic (Body Smart)

Interpersonal (People Smart)

Intrapersonal (Self Smart)

Linguistic (Word Smart)

Logical-Mathematical (Number Smart)

Musical (Music Smart)

Naturalist (Nature Smart)

Spatial (Picture Smart)

Whether the Weather

Bodily-Kinesthetic (Body Smart)

Interpersonal (People Smart)

Intrapersonal (Self Smart)

Linguistic (Word Smart)

Logical-Mathematical (Number Smart)

Musical (Music Smart)

Naturalist (Nature Smart)

Spatial (Picture Smart)

'Tis The Season

Bodily-Kinesthetic (Body Smart)

Interpersonal (People Smart)

Intrapersonal (Self Smart)

Linguistic (Word Smart)

Logical-Mathematical (Number Smart)

Musical (Music Smart)

Naturalist (Nature Smart)

Spatial (Picture Smart)

Celebrations (Holidays)

Bodily-Kinesthetic (Body Smart)

Interpersonal (People Smart)

The Complete Resource Book

An Early Childhood Curriculum

Pam Schiller and Kay Hastings

The Complete Resource Book is an absolute must-have book for every teacher. Offering a complete plan for every day of every week of the year, this is an excellent reference book for responding to children's specific interests. Each daily plan contains:

- circle time activities
- music and movement activities
- suggested books
- six learning center ideas

The appendix, jam-packed with songs, recipes, and games, is almost a book in itself. *The Complete Resource Book* is like a master teacher working at your side, offering you guidance and inspiration all year long. 463 pages. 1998.

ISBN 0-87659-195-0 / Gryphon House / 15327 / PB

Creating Readers

Over 1000 Games, Activities, Tongue Twisters, Fingerplays, Songs, and Stories to Get Children Excited About Reading

Pam Schiller

Simple games and activities to help children learn the sound of every letter in the alphabet.

Learn the basic building blocks of reading with *Creating Readers*, the comprehensive resource that develops a strong foundation for pre-readers. *Creating Readers* gives teachers and parents the tools to teach pre-reading skills with over 1000 activities, games, fingerplays, songs, tongue twisters, poems, and stories for the letters of the alphabet. This invaluable resource develops the child's desire to read as well as the skills needed to begin reading. *Creating Readers* starts children ages 3 to 8 towards a future rich with books and reading. 448 pages. 2001.

ISBN 0-87659-258-2 / Gryphon House / 16375 / PB

- Early Childhood News Directors Award

Available at your favorite bookstore, school supply store, or order from Gryphon House at 800.638.0928 or www.gryphonhouse.com.

The Complete Book of Rhymes, Songs, Poems, Fingerplays, and Chants

Over 700 Selections

Jackie Silberg and Pam Schiller

Build a strong foundation in skills such as listening, imagination, coordination, and spatial and body awareness with over 700 favorite rhymes, songs, poems, fingerplays, and chants. In this giant book of rhythm and rhyme, you may even find a few of your own childhood favorites! 500 pages.

ISBN 0-87659-267-1 / Gryphon House / 18264 / PB

Count on Math

Activities for Small Hands and Lively Minds

Pam Schiller and Lynne Peterson

The activities in this book reflect children's real-world math experiences–counting candles on a birthday cake, sorting and classifying toys, making sure there is a one-to-one correspondence between children and cookies. Children learn spatial relationships, patterning, shapes, numeration, and many other math concepts from these simple activities. 272 pages. 1997.

ISBN 0-87659-188-8 / Gryphon House / 18251 / PB

The Values Book

Teaching 16 Basic Values to Young Children

Pam Schiller and Tamera Bryant

Young children learn best by doing, and that includes learning values. *The Values Book* addresses 16 different values and is packed with easy activities, projects, and ideas to help children learn values and build character. The perfect book to introduce and strengthen the teaching of values in any early childhood classroom or home. 168 pages. 1998.

ISBN 0-87659-189-6 / Gryphon House / 15279 / PB

- Benjamin Franklin Award
- Early Childhood News Directors Award

Where Is Thumbkin?

500 Activities to Use with Songs You Already Know

Pam Schiller and Thomas Moore

Sing over 200 familiar songs and learn new words set to familiar tunes. Organized by month, with a special section just for toddlers, this book provides easy song-related activities that span the curriculum in areas such as math, art, and language. 256 pages. 1993.

ISBN 0-87659-164-0 / Gryphon House / 13156 / PB

The Instant Curriculum

500 Developmentally Appropriate Learning Activities for Busy Teachers of Young Children

Pam Schiller and Joan Rossano

Children immerse themselves in 500 instantaneous, hands-on activities that encompass music, math, social studies, science, art, language, and dramatic play. These fun and easy activities promote self-esteem, imagination, thinking, problem-solving, and fine and gross motor skills. 390 pages. 1990.

ISBN 0-87659-124-1 / Gryphon House / 10014 / PB

It's Great to be Three

The Encyclopedia of Activities for Three-Year-Olds

Edited by Kathy Charner

Looking for tried and true ways to capture the attention of your three-year-olds? This comprehensive collection of over 600 teacher-created activities provides hours of fun and interesting activities perfectly tailored for three-year-olds. Comprised of the best activities selected from a nationwide contest, *It's Great to be Three* will invigorate your curriculum. Discover new ways to use everyday items to create fresh, exciting art projects, learn new classroom management techniques from other teachers, find helpful tips for working with three-year-olds. Can't think of a thing to do? Just open this book to any page and you'll be inspired! 576 pages.

ISBN 0-87659-226-4 / Gryphon House / 14935 / PB

It's Great to be Four

The Encyclopedia of Activities for Four-Year-Olds

Edited by Kathy Charner

The first book in this series from Gryphon House is a comprehensive collection of over 600 teacher-created, classroom-tested activities just for four-year-olds. *It's Great to Be Four* has everything from songs and books to activities in art, circle time, transitions, science, math, language, music and movement, and more! This complete resource of the best selections from a year-long contest is sure to become a classroom favorite. 624 pages. 2001.

ISBN 0-87659-261-2 / Gryphon House / 18649 / PB

- Early Childhood News Directors Award

The Giant Encyclopedia of Theme Activities for Children 2 to 5

Over 600 Favorite Activities Created by Teachers for Teachers

Edited by Kathy Charner

This popular potpourri of over 600 classroom-tested activities actively engages children's imaginations and provides many months of learning fun. Organized into 48 popular themes, from Dinosaurs to Circuses to Outer Space, these favorites are the result of a nationwide competition. 511 pages. 1993.

ISBN 0-87659-166-7 / Gryphon House / 19216 / PB

The Giant Encyclopedia of Circle Time and Group Activities for Children 3 to 6

Over 600 Favorite Circle Time Activities Created by Teachers for Teachers

Edited by Kathy Charner

Open to any page in this book and you will find an activity for circle or group time written by an experienced teacher. Filled with over 600 activities covering 48 themes, this book is jam-packed with ideas that were tested by teachers in the classroom. 510 pages. 1996.

ISBN 0-87659-181-0 / Gryphon House / 16413 / PB

The GIANT Encyclopedia of Art & Craft Activities for Children 3 to 6

More Than 500 Art & Craft Activities Written by Teachers for Teachers

Edited by Kathy Charner

A comprehensive collection of the best art and craft activities for young children. Teacher-created, classroom-tested art activities to actively engage children's imaginations! The result of a nationwide competition, these art and craft activities are the best of the best. Just the thing to add pizzazz to your day! 568 pages. 2000.

ISBN 0-87659-209-4 / Gryphon House / 16854 / PB

The GIANT Encyclopedia of Science Activities for Children 3 to 6

More Than 600 Science Activities Written by Teachers for Teachers

Edited by Kathy Charner

Leave your fears of science behind as our GIANT Encyclopedia authors have done. Respond to children's natural curiosity with over 600 teacher-created, classroom-tested activities guaranteed to teach your children about science while they are having fun. 575 pages. 1998.

ISBN 0-87659-193-4 / Gryphon House / 18325 / PB